Hard Living in
America's Heartland

ALSO BY PAULA vW. DÁIL

Women and Poverty in 21st Century America
(McFarland, 2012)

Hard Living in America's Heartland

Rural Poverty in the 21st Century Midwest

Paula vW. Dáil

McFarland & Company, Inc., Publishers
Jefferson, North Carolina

LIBRARY OF CONGRESS CATALOGUING-IN-PUBLICATION DATA

Dáil, Paula vW.
Hard living in America's heartland : rural poverty in the 21st century Midwest / Paula vW. Dáil.
 p.   cm.
Includes bibliographical references and index.

ISBN 978-0-7864-7481-3 (softcover : acid free paper) ∞
ISBN 978-1-4766-1838-8 (ebook)

1. Middle West—Economic conditions.   2. Middle West—Rural conditions.   3. Poverty—Middle West.   4. Middle West—Social life and customs.   5. Farm life—Middle West—History—21st century.   I. Title.

HC107.A14D35 2015   330.977—dc23   2014048465

BRITISH LIBRARY CATALOGUING DATA ARE AVAILABLE

© 2015 Paula vW. Dáil. All rights reserved

No part of this book may be reproduced or transmitted in any form or by any means, electronic or mechanical, including photocopying or recording, or by any information storage and retrieval system, without permission in writing from the publisher.

Printed in the United States of America

McFarland & Company, Inc., Publishers
Box 611, Jefferson, North Carolina 28640
www.mcfarlandpub.com

This book is dedicated to my dad, Paul Dáil,
who taught me to love the land and to never forget
that those who are born luckier than most
owe something to those who weren't.
This book is one more payment on that debt.

Table of Contents

Acknowledgments	xi
Preface	1
Introduction: Poverty in the Rural Midwest—If You Can Find It	11
Maps of Poverty Regions in Midwestern States	29
1. We Ain't Got Much, But We Got Plenty: Understanding Rural Poverty When the Usual Criteria Don't Apply	43
2. Living off the Land: A Brief History of Rural Midwestern America	58
3. America's Heartland: Life in the Midwestern Farm States	86
4. Feeding Candy to the Cows: The Rural Midwestern Farm Economy	104
5. Get Big or Get Out: Rural America Moves into the 21st Century	135
6. Throwing Cow Chips for Entertainment: The Pluses and Minuses of Rural Community Life	154
7. Poverty Makes You Sick: The Rural Health Care Problem	166
8. One-Cop Towns: Rural Crime and Punishment	193
9. Go to School or Go to Work? Is Formal Education the Answer?	205
10. Conclusion: The Invisible Poor	228
Appendix One: Methodology and Interview Schedules	235
Appendix Two: Agricultural Traits of Midwestern Farm States	239
Appendix Three: Medicaid Eligibility Groups and Services	245
Chapter Notes	251
Bibliography	261
Index	236

Acknowledgments

It goes without saying that this book would not have been possible without the rural poor who talked with me, answered my questions, and allowed me glimpses of their lives. I am especially grateful to those who had to be convinced that what they had to say was important because, by kindly sharing their stories with me, they gave me the heart of this book. To my assistants and colleagues Deb Culhane, Devin Dilts, Annette Kuhlmann and Alice Thieman; to Ken Holz, who checked my math and so willingly labored through my early drafts, I can't thank all of you enough.

And always, always, gratitude far beyond words to my husband Bill Ladewig – a patient listener when I need to thrash out ideas; my harshest, most trusted and most valuable critic; my best proof-reader, no matter how many drafts he has to suffer through; and number one go-to guy when something just doesn't make sense. An award-winning writer himself, when it comes to writing, he truly gets it. Never last nor least, our faithful dog Tennessee Ernie Beagle can always be counted on to come through just when he's needed most.

Preface

... but it's our land. We measured it and broke it up. We were born on it, and we got killed on it, died on it. Even if it's no good, it's still ours. That's what makes it ours—being born on it, working it, dying on it. That makes ownership, not a paper with numbers on it.—Tom Joad

In 1939 John Steinbeck gave us a riveting, intimate portrait of the suffering that befell the Joad family when they were forced off their land, leaving everything that mattered to them behind.[1] "How can we live without our lives? How will we know it's us without our past?" they asked each other. "How will it be not to know what land's outside the door? How, if you wake up in the middle of the night and know—and *know* the willow tree's not there? Can you live without the willow tree? Well, no, you can't. The willow tree is you."[2]

I understand some things about what Tom Joad was saying about the meaning of life and land because I come from a pioneer family that homesteaded on the eastern plains of Colorado—until the Dust Bowl era robbed them of everything they had worked for all of their lives. The story of that time in my own family's history has endured across the generations.

"Your grandfather held on as long as he could, which was a hell of a lot longer than most, but in the end we had to leave the ranch and move into town—and he died not long after," my dad, who was less than ten years old at the time this occurred, told me.

"Your grandmother believed that leaving the ranch is what killed him, and that we should've stayed. 'If he was going to die, we should've let him die on his own land,' she kept saying. That's what they both wanted—to die and be buried on their own land, and neither one got their wish," my father wistfully explained as I was helping him sort through family memorabilia left behind after his oldest sister had died a few weeks earlier. We had come across the original homestead certificates issued to my grandfather. He had proven up four 160-acre adjacent parcels of land northeast of Pueblo, Colorado, where he ran cattle and planted the crops that fed them—until the dust storms came.

"It was a hard life in the best of times," my father recalled. "But as long as a man has a good horse and a little land of his own nothing else really matters ... and when Dad lost all that, he didn't want to live anymore."

Eventually most of the family migrated west to California, where I was born and grew up. My dad wasn't interested in ranching as a livelihood, but nevertheless, we owned a small ranch on the upper end of California's Central Valley that was shared among family members. The ranch was no one's primary source of income; instead, it served another, far more important purpose—it provided us with land of our own— land we could walk on, ride a horse across, graze cattle on, live on when we wanted to, and plant. These acres belonged to us, and we loved them as much as we loved each other. This was the land that taught me, as I was growing up, about why land is more than just an economic asset. Being responsible for, and to, the land is a powerful, and profoundly grounding, life force.

Later on, I began to understand why, for those who do it despite the hardships, living off the land is the only life worth living. When a life is rooted deep in soil you call your own, not having any is life-ending. Not having land, when land is what you want around you, creates a poverty I also understand, because the poorest I ever felt was while living in an elegant condominium in an affluent, upper middle class suburb of a large city. I had no land under my feet to walk on or plant anything in, no place to go where I wasn't surrounded by people, tall buildings, traffic and noise so loud I never heard the birds sing. Coping with ordinary, day-by-day city life sucked my soul dry and robbed me of my spirit. I became angry, then depressed, and finally, to save my own life, I quit my job, packed up my car and my dog, and left—all in one day.

Deep in my heart I know that no matter the season or outside temperature, land is hope, optimism, life-giving and life sustaining. This is what the early homesteaders believed; this is what they passed on to their children, their children's children, and all the generations that followed, and this is what farmers believe today.

The land is a farmer's life and also his[3] religion, and walking out across his field, kicking up dirt clods, spitting a little tobacco, watching the sun rise and set, feeling a storm coming, and sinking his hands deep into the soil are all profoundly spiritual experiences that set his life's compass on true north. The farmer may not believe in God, but his faith in the life-giving force arising from the land never, ever waivers. Land that has been in a family for generations is that family's place of worship. It is the holy, sacred ground upon which they live, die, celebrate and mourn, thrive, triumph and languish ... it provides a sense of place and belonging that is home in the finest, deepest sense of home.

"I came back to the home farm because I wanted to raise my sons there, on that same land my grandpa plowed with a horse. I'd finally decided it's not how much money I make, it's how I make it is all that matters to me," a Wisconsin farmer told me during the course of writing this book. "You can't put a price tag on bein' able to get up every morning, walkin' out the back door and settin' foot on good, solid ground. Goin' out to the barn sets your head straight for the day," he stressed, with deep conviction. "All us farmers start every day the exact same way ... and if we earn some money doin' it, fine, but most of us would do it even if we didn't earn a dime ... and a lotta the time we don't!" he chuckled.

While farming is not the only occupation in the rural Midwest, agriculture is the backbone of the rural Midwestern economy. Most rural small businesses flow from, and depend upon, an agricultural base that requires land to operate, and regardless of the dollar amount of earned income from his farm operation, a farmer considers himself rich if he has access to land. Having cash flow problems is an unwelcome inconvenience that frequently accompanies farming as an occupation, but in the farmer's mind this doesn't rise to the level of poverty because if he has land, he knows, in his heart, he can figure out some way to survive.

This represents an entirely different world view than is commonly found in competitive business, in a materialistic, consumer-oriented environment, in city life, and in the corporate suburbs. It also represents an entirely different view of poverty.

Rural poverty in the 21st century clearly is not the poverty Steinbeck so poetically wrote about. For most farmers today, poor is what their grandfather went through during the Dust Bowl, or what happened to their dad during the '80's farm crisis, and they tend to believe that if they have held on to land through good and bad years, they still have a livelihood, so they aren't "really poor." Sometimes this means a farmer leases land from others. Other times it means planting both his own small acreage and leasing land someone else owns. Either way, farmers understand land as a functional income source. They also know that having a lot of money tied up in land and farm implements makes them asset-rich on paper, and frequently cash-poor and financially strapped in daily life. They can't sell off land or equipment to pay bills because to do so strips them of their livelihood. And while the bank might be the real owner of his land and equipment, the farmer is still working the land, so he doesn't consider himself poor.

"I'll never make any money farming, but it's what I want to do" is a comment I heard often while I was a professor and still in contact with students trying to decide whether to finish college at all, or what to do with a degree if they did graduate. The remark was usually followed by a litany of reasons why living in a city and holding down "a regular job," meaning one with a reliable paycheck, just wasn't an acceptable life choice. "Too many people; too much traffic; houses too close together; no personal space or time alone; too much emphasis on being like everybody else; too lonely in a big city…" and on it went. These young people were not driven by the desire to make huge amounts of money; they were driven by the much stronger need to be their own person. They'd rather work for themselves than for any corporation, and if they fail, at least they fail on their own terms and not on someone else's. But to a person, no one believed they would fail. "My dad'll teach me what I need to know—he made it and I can too," was a comment I heard again and again.

But the harsh reality is that farmers do fail. During the 1980s a catastrophic farm crisis swept across the Great Plains. Farms that had been in families for generations went under when the U.S., in a badly miscalculated act of political defiance, implemented a grain embargo policy against Russia, causing the bottom to fall out of the world grain markets. American farmers were left with extraordinary debts. Banks called in loans, and those who couldn't pay up, and many couldn't, lost their farms. "It was one of the saddest things I ever saw," said Alice Thieman, an Iowa State University Extension Family Development Specialist in rural Iowa during that time. "There were farm liquidation auctions most weekends, and many farmers committed suicide when faced with losing their farms. It was particularly wrenching for farmers who had inherited farms from parents and grandparents." As a result of one nearly fatal political misstep, rural life and rural agriculture experienced a sea change that has endured through all the years that followed.

Because life and land are so tightly interwoven in rural areas, and because many people who are "poor on paper" own substantial amounts of land worth considerable amounts of money, any discussion of rural poverty raises some very challenging questions: Who determines whether a person is poor—the person him or herself, or the government formula established in the 1960s that sets an income level below which the Federal government says one is classified as poor and above which, one is not poor? Is a farmer, with a wife and two kids, who owns a couple hundred acres of useable land and whose annual farm operations budget is several hundred thousand dollars, but whose net income in a good year, after all the bills are paid, is $20,000, actually poor? According to the current federal income guidelines for a family of four, he is definitely poor. However, the farmer and his family may see it differently.

Things become even more complicated when attempting to define the term "rural poverty," giving rise to another set of relevant questions: Do the usual definitions and concepts of poverty apply to a population that is self-sufficient, independent, and able to manage without government welfare even when their income falls below the poverty line? Is poverty in rural areas best measured by something other than income, and how would measuring poverty another way change the definition of who is poor and who is not? What role does a materialistic, consumer-oriented culture play in defining poverty? Is poverty just about income or do other things enter into the equation?

Another complicating factor is that a poverty-level income stretches considerably further in a rural than in an urban area, thereby rendering the needs that go unmet due solely to a lack of money fewer. Because land is a financial asset that figures into eligibility for poverty assistance programs, most farm families can't take advantage of this assistance, so they find other ways to get by. Sometimes this kind of "getting by" includes having fewer, and simpler, needs than urbanites.

Does this mean the commonly accepted measures of poverty really don't apply in rural areas? Maybe. At the very least using the usual, arbitrary definitions of poverty makes everything much more difficult for anyone wanting to carefully examine any notion of rural poverty.

Confounding matters further is that, in an urban area, not having enough money is usually obvious to the casual observer because poor people tend to cluster in fairly well-defined places and neighborhoods. And in the city, if you are poor it's nearly impossible to stay afloat, so you'll be seen in the line at the welfare office, the food bank, the free medical clinic, the Salvation Army store and the local soup kitchen.

This visual tip off isn't as obvious in rural areas where the tendency is for everyone to dress the same, to shop together at the same local Walmart and Farm 'n' Fleet, and to look out for one another in hundreds of informal ways that go unnoticed to the casual observer. And because most rural people, regardless of income, know how to fix things when they break, they prefer that option over buying a new one. They also barter and exchange goods for services. "I have several clients who pay me in home grown produce, alfalfa for my horses, and beef from the cow they slaughter every year—and in return I keep their backs straightened out!" a rural chiropractor told me.

These are people who tend not to want what they can't pay for. In other words, an old car is fine as long as it still runs, and most rural men (and many rural women) know how to keep a car running. Not only that, they are proud of it! And if they can't get the car running themselves, their neighbor is happy to help them figure it out. This neighborly dynamic occurs whether or not you are officially poor, and regardless of whether or not you can afford to replace your old junker with 200,000 miles on it.

The reality is that rural people define life on their own terms. Their values and aspirations are self-determined and less driven by media hype, competition among friends or the need to prove something either to themselves or to others. This isn't to say these things don't exist—but buying things to keep up with the neighbors, just for the sake of doing it, is more often viewed as pretentious and bad money management skills.

Referring to the misery he endured on his wife's "dream vacation" which was a three-week Caribbean cruise she'd saved up for ten years to go on, and involved his first airplane ride, a rural small businessman and farmer told me "hell would freeze over twice" before he'd ever spend that kind of money or be gone off his land that long again. "I didn't last three days before I was tired of fancy food and talking to people I didn't know, had nothing in common with, and would never see again.... I would've jumped off that boat and swam to shore if it would've got me back in time for the Thursday night pulled pork barbeque and a few hands of cards at Bob's," he declared. "First thing I did when I got home, before I even unpacked, was get on my dozer and push some dirt around ... and my wife's still mad at me about it ... she thinks I should've enjoyed myself more. 'More than bein' here?' I asked her."

Unlike my previous book *Women and Poverty in 21st Century America*, this book is not driven by the current feminist research agenda, feminist theory or a long career focused entirely on rural poverty, although I have learned some things about it over the years. Instead, my interest in writing this book is motivated by the belief that an often under-reported and rarely discussed social problem we all know exists deserves a hearing in the wider world of social issues. Other motivations include the following:

Most of the existing literature on rural poverty consists of small case studies of narrowly defined regions of this country or focuses on the rural areas of the developing world and other economically underdeveloped regions in countries very much less prosperous than the United States. This doesn't mean rural poverty isn't widespread in America—it just means it is a particularly difficult problem for the social sciences to address in a broader context. Rural Midwestern poverty is a kind of netherworld, and Midwesterners are proud people, so getting them to talk about hard times while they are living them is very difficult. As a result, hard data are hard to come by, so writing this book had to wait until I had the time to do the necessary digging.

My own fire-breathing feminism opened my eyes to observe that, in most rural areas of the American Midwest, women and men are, more often than not, equal partners both in marriage and farming. This creates a unique set of stresses for farm families, but in a feminist's mind, it's also "the way things ought to be" in a marriage and family life. Because, historically, women's labor force participation was critical to the advancing western frontier, and remains crucial in American agriculture today, women have enjoyed a level of social and family power in rural society that their urban sisters don't always achieve. Farmers and ranchers need capable wives who can work alongside them, and this means women who can drive a tractor, bail hay, milk cows, mend fences and run a manure spreader, in addition to keeping the farm books, canning food from the home garden and raising the kids. Added to all this is that both rural men and women frequently supplement the farm income with off-farm employment, without which the farm and the family would go under. When men and women work hard together, most often the result is a true partnership between them. "I don't need me some toned up, high-maintenance looker like you see on TV," a bachelor farmer friend of mine told me. "I need a smart wife who can make decisions and isn't afraid of a little dirt under her fingernails—and is damned proud of bein' able to slop the pigs or plow a field all on her own. In my mind, that's a real woman!"

Gender politics may play out in subtle ways in rural communities, but in the things that count, women speak their minds, and the men in their lives tend to listen to them because they know rural women are extraordinarily hard working, capable bearers of abundant common sense. When rural women express themselves they know what they are talking about—which rural men appreciate. This changes the entire dynamic of rural community life in some very important ways which, I believe are worth serious reflection as one reads this book.

I also strongly believe that most, if not all, of the social inequalities observed in today's American society, both urban and rural, are a direct result of our capitalist, profit-motive, free-enterprise economic system. The economic and social oppression of the poor is not a consequence of individual action so much as a consequence of the political, economic, and social structures endemic to capitalism. Years of poverty research have convinced me that Americans, both rural and urban, will be liberated from lives of poverty only when the wide divisions among classes are abolished and wealth is no longer the sole purview of the few, earned at the expense of the majority. In a more just and equal society the income gap narrows sufficiently enough so that while some people may have more than others, everyone has enough.

This is the prairie populism of old, which we don't see much of anymore, and is best described by Senator Tom Harkin of Iowa.[4] "Populism isn't a bashing of the wealthy or a bashing of those that have made it. It's a sense that together we can use the powers of government to make sure that the economy works for all," Harkin says. Conservative politics, he explains, emphasizes "Do it on your own. Pull yourself up by your bootstraps. Well, what if you don't have boots? That's where we split [from the conservatives]. Government needs to be used to ensure that people have their boots."

I firmly believe the bones of the farm economy, including the underlying national politics, deserve a more thorough consideration than most books on rural poverty provide. In the 1970s when Secretary of Agriculture Earl Butz famously told farmers to "Get big or get out," not only did the remark catch on and stick, it led to policies that became the landslide economic catastrophe that took out many Midwestern farmers during the 1980s and beyond. Butz encouraged agribusinesses and corporate farming to explode into the epitome of profit-motive capitalism at its finest. Meanwhile the family farmers who, heretofore, have been the backbone of American agriculture, and able to make a living at it, continue to struggle year after year, often with big holes in their boots.

It hasn't helped that Washington's prevailing political philosophy increasingly has been that it's too bad if the poor get poorer, but the rich deserve to get richer anyway—a belief that reaches deep into the heart of Midwestern rural America where the nation's food supply originates. Washington doesn't seem to care about how poor the family farmer gets, even though he is performing a vital service to humankind that even Washington can't live without.

Saying this, politics at the local level, where most land use decisions are made, tend to work much better. One reason is that the people who are affected by a political decision are not faceless strangers—they are the neighbors of the elected officials making the decisions. Over the years they have helped each other out and most likely see each other every day at the local café, grain elevator, or hardware store. Second, candidates for local office are personally known to the voters and the successful candidate knows he or she will be held accountable by people they have grown up with, their kids go to school with, and who have known them all their lives. Third, rural people don't just gripe about policies they don't like—they show up at public hearings, town councils and county board meetings to speak their mind about issues that matter to them. They are active participants in local government, and in the rural political environment where less than ten votes can decide an election, officials listen to the people who elect them very carefully.

I once heard a newly elected rural county board chair declare that "as long as I chair this board, every single issue before us will be decided based upon whether or not we are being good neighbors, because before anything else, that's who we are supposed to be, and by God, that's how we are supposed to act." People might not have always agreed with him, but they respected him because they knew he was true to his word and trusted that his decisions were always made with what he believed were the best interests of the county.

Do deals ever get cut over a beer in the local tavern or across the back fence? Of course they do. I once watched a rural county board systematically stand down several city lawyers to turn back a large corporate hog operation the local residents didn't want. The decision was based upon an obscure road maintenance policy no one had ever heard of, and unsubstantiated, most likely fabricated concerns that trucks hauling hog waste would be too heavy for the existing road, thereby creating a need for more frequent road maintenance, which would cost local taxpayers money. Technically (and legally) the county board couldn't deny the permit application based upon an unfounded, perceived threat of excessive road stress, but they did it anyway. All it took was the locals letting it be known they didn't want a big corporate pig farm stinking everything up, including the local hog market. The board chair's commitment to good neighbor public policy resulted in a unanimous refusal to cut any deals with corporate America.

As a result of this action the county board risked a lawsuit and turned down a lucrative opportunity to collect a large pot of tax revenue, which some people believed was foolish. "We didn't need the money that bad," the board chair told me later, "and we knew if we made it hard enough eventually the corporate guys would give up and go someplace else." When I asked who hatched the plan to turn down the application based on potential road stress, he smiled and told me I ought to hang out down at Lucky's Friday night fish fry more often.

Farmers and small business people in rural America find their life, difficult though it may be, profoundly satisfying. The ability to live on their own terms, in good and bad times, is so rewarding, in so many big and little ways, that it not only keeps rural people doing what they do, they can't imagine doing anything else. They are working for themselves, not for the government, a large corporation that sucks huge profits from their labor, at their expense, or for anyone else. Nevertheless, this costs them in ways that should not be so expensive and, in my view, Earl Butz was dead wrong when he told farmers to "get big or get out." He sold farmers a large load of hog manure, gave them a government barge to put it on, and then floated them straight down the free-enterprise capitalist river to the marketplace of new agricultural economics.

Butz pushed small farmers up against a powerful current of corporate interests in agriculture as a profitable business venture and set them up for an enduring economic struggle. His mistake was forgetting about the farmer's deep bonds with the land, their ability to effectively govern themselves, and their good neighbor personal and political philosophy, and he badly misjudged farmers' inherent optimism. Almost to a person, most farmers would rather remain engaged in this struggle than become tangled up in the expectations of corporate America where they work for someone else and then get ripped off the other way.

For this book, I decided to confine my interest in rural poverty primarily to the Midwestern states for several reasons: First, because the rural Midwest is not as dirt poor as some other rural areas of the country, Midwestern poverty has not been explored nearly as much as poverty in the rural south or southwestern United States; thus less is known about the poverty that does exist in the farm states. Second, most of the nation's food comes from the Midwest, and what happens there is of widespread general concern. Third, it's where I've lived for most of my adult life, and I "know" a few things about how life works here, albeit not nearly as much as third- or fourth-generation locals know. Fourth, rural poverty everywhere has several commonalities—lack of access to needed social and financial resources, isolation, and a dependence on some form of agriculture or natural resources, so what happens in one area is fairly easily generalizable to other areas, with two exceptions: Native American poverty and rural black poverty. These are distinctly different from each other and from poverty in any other populations in the country because both have unique cultures and suffer unresolved racial discrimination and historical trauma that set them apart from rural white poverty.

Every researcher, myself included, has biases. Traditionally the tendency has been toward viewing poverty as a catastrophic human condition which, I believe, is the direct result of unrestrained profit-motive economics gone wild. I do not believe poverty is the fault of the individual so much as a failure of public policy and political will to insure that those who cannot compete in the capitalist marketplace can still have a decent standard of living, and that competition is fair for those who do enter the marketplace. Rural people face dramatic economic injustice because they work hard and are not rewarded commensurate with their efforts.

Over the years, I have been deeply impressed by how the rural poor manage their lives despite the inconveniences of poverty. As a result, another bias of mine is that I have evolved in my thinking to a point where I no longer view rural poverty in quite the same way I see urban poverty. Rural poor tend not to suffer the same learned helplessness produced by a lifetime spent living off government programs that plague the urban poor, who express higher levels of despair. In contrast, most rural poor possess and retain a certain level of human dignity that serves them well as an effective coping strategy when economic troubles come and keeps them optimistic year after year after year.

Failing to consider the uniqueness of rural life, where very many people live with sparse economic circumstances but don't consider themselves poor, and weaving this information into the discussion would be, in my view, a big mistake. This is not to say rural poverty is less devastating for those who suffer it, but it is less black and white and is characteristically different from urban poverty in some very fundamental ways. And while it goes without saying that not everyone is capable of effectively meeting the challenges of rural poverty, many rural poor find themselves victims of a perfect storm that includes poor educational opportunities, lack of health care access, and scarce employment opportunities.

The first chapters of this book focus on background information that includes a brief history of rural America, a discussion of the poverty definition and measurement conundrum as applied to rural areas, profiles of the 12 Midwestern farm states, the

Midwestern farm economy, and 21st-century Midwestern agriculture and the public policy behind it. These chapters familiarize the reader with how rural life and the rural economy works—information the average urbanite is not likely to be familiar with.

Later chapters explore the ugly underbelly of rural poverty, including the realities of contemporary farm and rural community life, health care and mental health issues, farm health and safety issues, rural crime, the challenges of rural education, and the impact of corporate farming on local economies. These chapters reveal the realities of life for the rural poor who don't have many options and explain how they survive anyway.

My hope is that this book provides a glimpse into the realities of life for America's rural poor. It is not my intention to cover every nuanced detail of the economic conspiracy that keeps profits in the hands of corporate agriculture while holding the American family farmer hostage. One book cannot thoroughly explain why the average small farmer is caught in the middle of a free market enterprise that costs them in two directions and keeps them on the economic fringes of what is a vital and a very profitable industry, because the economic rules change faster than the corn grows in July, and what works one year can just as easily fail the next. Nevertheless, I hope my observations add to a general understanding about rural life and clarify some notions about rural poverty, bearing three points in mind:

First, poverty is both subjective and objective and is often defined by policy makers and others who are not poor, and probably have never been poor. They, like everyone, measure most things about the human experience against their own frame of reference and consider those whose economic life doesn't push them above the poverty line "poor." I am not convinced this is a fair assumption when considering the issue of rural poverty because it seems to be a much more complex social problem than the simple numbers behind the poverty line criteria suggest. The numbers are an arbitrary measure of poverty that places no value on the profound rewards of living a chosen lifestyle, even if one doesn't earn a lot of money doing it, and ignore the human dignity factor, which is a great equalizer when considering the concept of who is poor and who is not.

Second, I hope the reader will be moved to think much harder about what America "gains" by maintaining a poor class to do the needed labor that enables the rich to become richer, leaving the poor to struggle in the dust. It costs the nation over five hundred billion dollars per year to maintain this poverty class.[5] Wouldn't it be better if, instead, the rich were willing to give up enough to ensure everyone has access to adequate health care so they would be healthy enough to work, create educational systems that train an efficient and knowledgeable workforce, and establish a fair marketplace for the goods rural areas produce? Doesn't this make more sense than maintaining the current system, which divides the social classes and conquers the struggling impoverished, sentencing them to a lifetime in the poorhouse, at public expense? Why does America lack the political will to conquer this problem?

Third, farm and agriculture policies matter, and the politics surrounding these are intense. My intention is for the reader to gain a greater understanding of why this is so. The Farm Bill is vitally important to the Midwest, and it is significant that the 2012 Farm Bill stalled out in Congress until 2014. However, when considering that the Midwest has thousands of miles of low-population density rural areas, their representation in Congress, which is determined by population, is easily overshadowed by more populous urban interests, where greater numbers of voters live. It matters that only 20 percent of the House of Representatives (90 members) represent the 12 Midwestern states and that both North and South Dakota have only one representative each, Nebraska has three, and Iowa, Kansas and Missouri each has four.[6] Worse, in the 2010 reapportionment, five Midwestern states lost seats in the House of Representatives.

As with poverty everywhere, rural poverty is a human condition created by miles and miles of political missteps that happen because rural areas are not large voting blocks. Rural Midwestern America does not have, by the numbers, strong representation in Congress where the all-important Farm Bill is legislated. And because most politicians outside the Grain Belt don't think much about who grows their food or what it takes to keep the smaller farmers' businesses viable, they don't worry much about issues facing rural America. Rural areas have too few electoral college votes to sway a national election, thus are not quite important enough politically to bend over backwards for.

Ultimately, I hope readers of this book will be moved to think deeply about the strength and tenacity of rural people. Farmers work in an extremely unpredictable environment over which they exert little control, yet somehow they are able to make their lives work, even though Mother Nature is their business partner and she doesn't always play fair. When trouble comes, rural people don't go down easy—they work hard all the time. They know they can't depend on anybody, including the government or corporations who employ them, to save them, so they "figure stuff out" and save themselves. This problem-solving attitude toward life truly matters.

Look at it this way: would you rather march into battle next to a Harvard-trained lawyer who billed a million dollars during his first year of law practice but never had to fix so much as a toaster, or alongside a Kansas farm kid who didn't finish high school but knows how to keep a tractor running?

Introduction

Poverty in the Rural Midwest—If You Can Find It

> *There's plenty of poverty around here, but nobody ever admits they're poor, and the fact is, on the face of things it's often impossible to know who's poor and who's not, because everybody hangs together.* —J. Patrick Reilly, *The Dodgeville Chronicle*

As the youngest, and best-looking of the four Bender boys, Jack was the son who'd stayed back to help his dad farm. He'd never liked school and kept at it only because his mother wanted him to graduate from high school. "That boy'd rather slop pigs than open a book," his mother lamented, watching her lanky teenager head toward the barn to do chores every morning before school, wearing a John Deere cap she swore he slept in. "I haven't seen Jack without the hat in five years," she told his dad. "I don't even remember what color his hair is."

Joe Bender was grateful for Jack's help and didn't spend much time worrying about how his son was doing in school. He had other things on his mind as the farm struggled under a pile of debt they never seemed to quite get ahead of. Joe was haunted by the ghosts of his father and grandfather. Though long dead, those two men had managed to keep the farm going through the Great Depression and the farm crisis of the 80s, and the possibility of disappointing them by losing the farm they had entrusted to him caused Joe's heart to race so fast he broke out in a sweat.

Every spring, when he went to the bank for that year's operating loan, Joe feared he'd be turned down—a thought so dark he dared not mention it, even to his wife. She kept the books and knew how precarious their finances were and that bringing the subject up would send Joe into a drunken rage. The last couple years they'd not quite cleared the books. As a result, they received a smaller farm loan than they asked for, and at a slightly higher interest rate, because they were carrying prior-year debt. "I'd like to do better by you," the banker told them, "but if I loan more money than I can cover, I'm in trouble, and it's in nobody's interest for the bank to go under ... you understand what I'm saying?" Joe understood all too well what the loan officer was saying, but all the understanding in the world wouldn't put his crops in the ground or control the corn *futures that would determine his profit margin ... and he felt the bank could cut him a little more slack, since his family had been farming this land for three generations.*

Jack was just twenty when he suddenly found himself running the farm. Joe had suffered a heart attack a few months previously, which Jack's mother believed was brought on by years of trying to keep things afloat, and he died in his sleep. Almost immediately Jack phased out the beef cattle, increased the hog inventory, and planted feed crops in addition to the corn he sold to the ethanol plant. Eventually "Handsome Jack" became known as a pretty good farmer despite the old timers' opinion that he "doesn't know near as much as his old man did when he was half that age." Some locals thought Jack was a little full of himself but let it go because, at his age, they'd been that same way. They knew he always paid something on his bills, although never the entire amount, and he didn't use farming methods that raped the land. These were traits they respected in a man.

Most years Jack came within a few bucks of breaking even, but he never quite made it over the top. The last two years his total family income had nearly topped the poverty line because the hog markets had been fairly steady and corn prices were breaking even. But he couldn't raise enough feed to see his hogs through the winter. Still, he figured that, if he's lucky, pretty soon he'll have accumulated enough good years to pay down his farm debt to a near-manageable level. "Not quite there yet, but almost," he'd tell his wife, Sally.

Meanwhile, to help make ends meet, Sally, three years younger and his high school sweetheart, worked part-time as a nurse's aide at the county hospital 37 miles away. They'd married when Sally got pregnant the summer after her senior year of high school. "I don't want a baby, I want to go to teacher's college," Sally wailed to Jack when she broke the news of his impending fatherhood. "And I don't want to be a farmer's wife.... I saw what it did to my mother, and I don't have it in me to work that hard." Jack said it seemed to him neither one of them had much choice now.

Jack and Sally got married Labor Day weekend and Sally moved into the drafty old farmhouse Jack still lived in with his mother. "The pigs have it better than I do," Sally complained. "The barn's always in better shape than the farmhouse," Jack's mother growled. "Hasta be, because that's where the money comes from ... the rest we make do by planting a big garden, and shopping second hand."

Twelve years later, two weeks before Thanksgiving, while walking corn down the inside of a nearly full grain bin, Jack lost his footing and was quickly sucked into the vortex of loose, dry corn. It took six men nearly five hours to extract his lifeless body from the dusty tomb.

Jack was 32 years old when he died, had no life insurance, and owed just about as much on the farm as it was worth. Left to mourn him was a wife without enough cash on hand to bury him and four young sons. He was laid out in the only suit he ever owned, which he picked up at the Goodwill in Sioux Falls to wear to his high school prom. Sally hadn't gotten around to patching the hole where he put his knee through his pants, so she used duct tape to seal the rip from the wrong side before delivering the suit to the funeral home.

Between the day he died and the day he was buried the neighboring farmers finished up Jack's harvest. Local church women filled the Benders' cupboards with canned vegetables from their gardens. Bob Hoffman's teenaged sons started coming every night after school to help Sally with chores. The Hoffmans' land butts up against the Bender farm on two sides, and three years ago Jack agreed to share the cost of putting in a tiling system along the line between the two properties, allowing both their fields to drain better—a favor Bob never forgot.

Most everybody in town turned out for Jack's funeral. It was harvest season so some of the local farmers, pressed for time, drove their tractors directly from the field to the church parking lot. The minister grieved openly and the funeral director sat off to the side, his head in his hands, sobbing quietly. The three had grown up on neighboring farms, hunted, fished, triple dated, and regularly gotten drunk together since long before they were old enough to legally drink. Most Saturday nights all three could be found shooting pool at the local tavern. At the funeral lunch the minister passed the hat to help Sally pay the burial expenses.

Two months later, on a January Saturday night, it's 20 degrees below zero, with a 30-mile-per-hour wind out of the north whirling dry snow across the highway into town. Pick-up trucks are parked on both sides of the street outside the VFW hall, overflowing into the empty space along the north side, which doubles as the post office parking lot. The hand-painted sign on the door says "Benefit for Jack Bender's family—7 p.m. to midnight. Everybody welcome."

Inside the cavernous old building, someone has set a fire in the wood stoves, hoping to generate a little heat. Somebody else has plugged in the jukebox while waiting for the three-piece band to show up. A few teenagers are shooting pool in the corner. Because nobody dares show up at something like this empty handed, the north and south wall tables are set up with more homemade meat and noodle casseroles, apple pies, rolls, and jello salads than will possibly be eaten. The overhead lights are dim, and in the middle of the room a few people are dancing.

In the corner near the door the local tavern owner has tapped a keg; the other three he donated are behind the bar, where several men have congregated, musing about what will happen to the Bender farm. "Too much debt to hold onto it," one says. "It'll get foreclosed and auctioned off." Someone else speculates that the older Bender boys will come back and take it over. Another offers the opinion that the brothers won't want the debt that comes with the existing farm operation, but maybe Sally will try to hold out until land prices go up a little and she can break even. "My guess is Bob Hoffman's already had a conversation with Sally about exactly that and wants to be the first to know when she's ready to make a decision," the tavern owner offers.

At the end of the bar sits a five-gallon glass pickle jar with hand-printed instructions to "place donations here" taped to the front. People can drop money in the jar either coming in or going out. A few 20s and a hundred dollar bill are visible, but mostly it's ones, fives and tens. While an older couple waits their turn in the beer line, the man reaches into his coveralls pocket, pulls out three twenties and drops them into the jar.

"Why'd you do that, Homer?" his wife asks. "You never liked Jack, and we ain't got that much to spare."

"Don't matter whether I liked him, or how much extra we got," Homer replies. "Trouble's come to that family, and we gotta help out."

Rural people may have deep differences, but when trouble comes, the differences evaporate and everybody shows up to help out. "When my boy got hurt, the neighbors did chores and milked my cows twice a day for ten days, while the wife and I were at the hospital waiting to see if they could save Robbie. When they took him off life support, we found the hospital waiting room jammed with folks who came to sit with us ... some we didn't even recognize. When we finally got back home, the refrigerator was full and the milk receipts were on the kitchen table.... I never found out everyone who helped us through ... they just showed up and did it," Wisconsin dairy farmer Bob Symons told me not long after his 17-year-old son was crushed to death in a tractor accident.

Besides showing up to help out, everybody in rural areas looks and acts much the same, making it difficult to discern their economic circumstances or identify what sets them apart from each other. Rural life is a great equalizer in that way. Nobody really wants to be too different from everybody else because, in small towns, people notice differences and talk about them—and nobody wants to be the subject of a conversation that doesn't include them. Rural people try hard to fit in, and most are quite successful at doing it. This makes the rural Midwest a complicated, perplexing social enigma, because the people who live there are exceptionally skilled at hiding the things that distinguish them from one another and equally clever in their ability to cling to their similarities. They possess a deep, unspoken trust of one another that, rather than allowing them to be content to remain separate, draws them in close and binds them together.

The rural Midwest is also dominated by a rhythm and cadence born of the seasons and repetitive cycles of life. The people live by the demands of the land to be planted, cultivated, harvested, and quietly put to rest until the spring, when the cycle begins again. A lot of what happens year after year is out of anyone's control. Mother Nature has the last word on nearly everything, life is hard, and sometimes ends too soon. Rural people don't brood over these things. Instead they keep going, because no matter what happened today, chores still need doing tonight. They don't have time to wonder about the meaning of life because it is either already obvious to them or too time consuming to think about it. "If I ever started wondering about that I'd never get a damned thing done, and Lord knows I got plenty to do.... I can guarantee you none of it waits until I happen to get around to it," a feisty Missouri farm woman told me, promptly dismissing the question in a way that made me sorry I ever asked it.

Geography 101—The Midwest Is Very Flat

> *Iowa's so flat thousands of people ride bicycles west to east across the state every summer, through corn humidity so thick you can't breathe and actually think it's really fun ... but we don't have a lot of what other people call fun around here.*—Bernie Jacobs

Most of the Midwest[1] is encompassed by thousands of flat miles stretched smooth between the eastern slope of the Rocky Mountains and the western slope of the Appalachian range, occasionally interrupted by a water tower or grain elevator, the two tallest structures in most rural towns. Geographically the region is known as the Great Plains, and the Mississippi River flows south through its middle.[2] In some places, it is so level the distant horizon is just as evident as it is when looking out across the ocean. Flatlanders claim they can see into the distance, in any direction, all the way to where the earth curves, and when a storm crosses the Rocky Mountains from west to east, there's nothing stopping it until it hits the Appalachian Mountains in West Virginia.

And there's the matter of the scenery. Rural Midwesterners find awe in empty, wide open spaces, in cattle grazing in the pastures, and in miles of cornfields. "You gotta have a certain kind of eye to see the beauty in life around here," an 86-year-old farm woman living on the Iowa flatlands told me on a hot, late summer day while she was canning beans in her farm kitchen. "Maybe you gotta be born to it … maybe that's what makes it beautiful … it's home." she said.

Rural Midwestern towns aspire to functionality over attractiveness. Most consist of one or two blocks of Main Street that is a straight line of mostly vacant storefronts with cheap apartments above them, a few side streets, a stop sign or two, a gas station with an attached convenience store, and at least as many bars as churches. In towns with a population upwards of 1,000, there might be a few small businesses, including a hardware store and a grocery store. There's probably a café that serves a good enough breakfast to draw the men in after chores are done to talk about the weather—something rural Midwesterners do constantly.

Rural towns are boring. There might be a bowling alley not too far away, or a few pin ball machines in the local tavern, which doubles as the social hub of every small town; otherwise, there are high school sports and church socials. Occasionally there's a movie theatre but it probably can't afford a digital projector so it doesn't show first-run movies and is expensive to heat in winter, so is only open one weekend a month, for a 7 p.m. show everybody comes to, whether they want to see it or not. It's a cheap night out and a chance to visit with the neighbors. If the town has a school it probably has a one-room public library that might be connected to a state-wide library consortium that brings in special requests once a week. Glancing up and down Main Street, one is hard put to find anything resembling affluence anywhere. And the wind never stops blowing—ever.

Most rural farm houses are old, drafty and peeling paint, because maintaining the house is always a distant second to keeping the barn up. Occasionally, just ahead of the old one falling down, a farmer will build a newer, smaller house, but that doesn't happen until there's no other choice. Life revolves around the kitchen table, Sunday visitors always come in through the back door, the stink of manure is everywhere and most people view retirement as a dirty word, preferring instead to work until they drop dead, hopefully on their own land.

Everybody in a small town knows everybody else, and everybody else's business, just like in a family. Good news and bad news travels at about the same speed and a stranger moving to town remains a stranger for at least the next three generations, maybe longer. Most rural residents don't like it that everybody in town knows their deeper secrets, gossips about them, and often judges them harshly, but they live with it, because that's what you have to do to get along, and rural people need to get along, because when trouble comes, all they have is each other. For rural folks, the most interesting thing going on at any given time is often occurring in their friends' and neighbors' lives, and however dull those lives may be they are still the greatest source of entertainment and hottest topics in town.

People from big cities don't understand rural life at all and how could they? You have to rid yourself of all pretense, shed everything you think you need to stay afloat in big city life and get down to the core of what it really takes to survive before you can grasp rural life. This demands a tremendous amount of psychological effort, emotional courage and physical energy. Leaving the city for the country requires learning a new way of being in the world, and most people aren't willing to forgo the activities of urban life to do that. Rural folks believe city dwellers miss out on a lot and will never know how little it takes to live a happy, satisfying life. Only rural people know this, and they're proud to know it.

Rural Poverty and Clashing Values

> *Our vision of a just food system is to create rural economies based on self respect, respect for the land, food sovereignty and fair trade.* —Wisconsin dairy farmer

Sometimes rural poverty arises from a clash of values around how to farm and decisions about whether to use conventional/traditional, corporate/industrial, or alternative "designer" farming methods. The choices a farmer makes about how to farm directly impact the economic result and are driven by many factors: inherited family pressure to farm a particular way; beliefs around humans' relationship to the land, to nature, and to each other; the desire to build wealth versus the commitment to sustainability; and social, cultural, political or religious beliefs.

A farmer who raises seed corn to sell to corporate seed enterprises is essentially a company man. He must farm according to a plan set forth by corporate agriculture and produce a product according to criteria determined by someone else. This farmer's decisions are made for him, while a farmer trying to sustain a family farm will make farming decisions a different way, using criteria in accordance with his personal values and what he believes is "the right way to farm."

Unquestionably the smaller-enterprise family farmer will earn less money than his corporate counterpart, but he enjoys the personal satisfaction of farming for "the right reasons," which include being a good steward of the land, raising good food, and being a good neighbor. Corporate agricultural enterprises reflect none of these values, and most small, independent farmers view large corporate agricultural enterprises as the evil enemy.

Another important difference in values is that, unlike in cities and suburbs, rural business people don't necessarily aspire to make a lot of money. They want to make enough to meet their needs, which tend to be much simpler than their urban counterparts, but their business and personal relationships are too important to be sacrificed to chase after the almighty dollar at any cost. The hardware store owner enjoys visiting with his customers and would rather spend time "chewing the fat" than hurrying them along in the interests of better time management. The store owner is one of the most important people in town and loves helping customers figure something out, no matter how long it takes, and even when it entails stopping by their place later to personally examine the problem. He appreciates that everyone understands he is just trying to make a living like everybody else and want to support his business, even though his prices are higher than the nearest big-box store.

Local businesses are one-of-a-kind, only-show-in-town, enterprises, and they are vital to the life of the community. "We don't want to lose our grocery store, and God-forbid we'd ever lose the hardware store, so we support them however we can, and pay a little more to do it. It's kind of like paying an insurance premium to guarantee the town will survive," a local banker told me.

A third value difference unique to rural areas is a prevailing economy seriously lacking in diversity and opportunity. Poverty or prosperity rises and falls on an economic system that is different from all others in its unpredictability and vulnerability to market forces far afield of the reach of any local farmer or small businessman. And Mother Nature is a fickle business partner, so things can go bad fast. All it takes is a tornado, too little or too much rain, an early or late frost, and everything is lost—and everyone suffers accordingly.

Most rural communities are "one-job towns" when it comes to reliable, sustained employment. If someone is relying upon a job at the local manufacturing plant when an economic downturn forces the plant to close and that plant is in a town between 50 and 150 miles from a city large enough to have a diversified economic base, options for other employment in the area are severely curtailed. The rural reality is that the chances for pulling out of poverty are grim when the nearest job possibilities are more than 50 miles away, don't pay much more than minimum wage,[3] gas is $4 a gallon and your car already has 200,000 miles on it. This is one major reason there are proportionately greater numbers of poor people in rural areas than in urban population centers. Besides, rural people like living in rural areas among their kin and don't want to leave just to get a job that pays more money, so they work hard at figuring out some other way to stay afloat.

The cultural values the rural Midwestern poor, who comprise 25 percent of American poverty, subscribe to are not those generally found in urban areas. Those who are faring better economically are willing to step up and help the poor, because this is what good neighbors do, and what distinguishes the wealthy independent farmers from others is that they have a bigger buffer to fall back on when hard times come, market prices drop, or Mother Nature pulls a dirty trick.

While every rural community is unique, in the rural Midwest, most communities are more alike than different, and their values always include taking neighborliness very seriously. Most people manage to get by but do not aspire to achieving a lot more than that, because doing so would set them apart and they tend to believe there's something fundamentally un-neighborly about that. And notably, at no time while I was writing this book did I ever hear a poor farmer or any other poor person I spoke with bemoan his or her life. Each may have wished things were easier, but don't spend a lot of time worrying about it, and certainly don't expect government welfare programs to help them out. A 43-year-old single father of two living on an income just under 125 percent of the poverty line, and whose job is as a gas station and convenience store manager, explained it this way: "We definitely live paycheck to paycheck, but I'm lucky because I've had steady work for 15 years, and most of the time can pay the bills."

It's All About Funding Local Government

> *It's not that we don't want to help the folks down on their luck, because we do, but the money we have is the money we have—if there ain't any there, there ain't any there...*—Carroll Hayes, Iowa county board member

Poverty is a human condition that, sooner or later, always runs up against public policy and money for social welfare assistance. This is never more true than in rural areas, which must find some way to fund whatever social services are made available to the rural poor. This challenge frustrates local government officials like Iowa rural county board member Carroll Hayes who had great sympathy for the plight of the poor and needy, but would never agree to spending money the county doesn't have.

Local funding works this way: Rural communities operate off an agricultural and local business economy and depend upon various tax assessments to function.[4] Justice and public safety, health and protection of vulnerable populations (aging, children, developmentally disabled, mentally ill, economically disadvantaged), transportation (highways, airport, multimodal transportation), conservation, economic development, recreation, arts and education all depend upon funds from local units of government. Small rural communities don't have a vibrant and thriving tax base to draw from to support local services, no matter how badly needed the services are, so they must heavily depend upon state and county funding streams. When states and counties cut community funding programs, small communities go wanting and are forced into modes of informal assistance for the poor.

As an example of where the money comes from, in 2012 a typical three-person household in rural Sauk County, Wisconsin,[5] had an average property valuation of approximately $300,000. Of the total county property tax bill, $1,397.97 went to support county services; and $672.79 supported the sheriff's department, of which $392.01 was spent on the jail (if the jail were its own department it would be the county's largest department based on tax levy dollars used to support it). The remaining dollars are divided among the Human Services Department ($369.20), the Highway Department ($191.19), and the county nursing home ($77.13). The remaining $87.66 is divided among the 30 remaining county departments that provide services.[6] This is not a high per-household assessment to fund needed community support services for local residents.

Local elected officials assess local taxes, and in rural areas, regardless of the need, there is great reluctance to raise taxes on your neighbor, whom you know personally. Consequently, taxes tend to be lower than in urban areas, and the opportunity to tax multi-million-dollar homes or other enterprises rarely arises. Options for raising significant additional funds are sparse because those who can afford to make substantial donations to the cause, whatever it might be, are few. As a result, the rural poor don't have much of a government-funded social safety net to fall back on during hard times.

Who Are These People?
Grasping at Typical Midwestern Poverty

> *Is it easier being poor in the sticks than in the city? No. It's just easier to be forgotten.* —Lee Smith, CNN reporter

While each rural area of the twelve Midwestern states has unique economic concerns, most of the major issues facing the rural Midwest are universal to all rural areas. Typical characteristics of the rural poor include fewer single mothers and the presence of a father in the family, residing in a small town with a single industry as the source of off-farm employment, disproportionately high numbers of female elderly in the community, and considerable skepticism of social welfare programs. There is widespread denial of poverty, a fierce hold on independence and rugged individualism as cherished personal values, distant or nonexistent locally based social services, intolerance of differences, predominance of kin relationships as a chief source of social support, lack of anonymity, and less mobility.[7] The stigma of being poor that prevails in urban areas is not as clear-cut in rural areas, because most rural people understand, in their bones, that everybody has bad years, sometimes a whole string of them, and there's no shame in that as long as you keep trying.

The rural poor live in a time cycle dictated by ongoing daily needs (i.e., feeding the animals or milking the cows) and by the seasonal cycles of nature (spring planting and fall harvesting) that do not govern city life. They have space around them and are not forced to live in densely populated neighborhoods or deal with the psychological stress and irritants that accompany overcrowding in poor urban areas.

Rural areas have their own dangers, but these do not include the crime and violence that accompany city life. Rural children can freely wander about in their communities without fear of getting caught in the crossfire of gun violence or robbery, whereas urban poor children are never safe outside their homes or in their neighborhoods. Rural residents can take advantage of the low-cost/cost-free recreation nature affords, whereas urban residents do not have easy access to the peacefulness that comes with life lived in natural surroundings.

Sorry, We Don't Talk about Being Poor

> *Lots of people around here don't have much money, but I wouldn't call them poor exactly ... they seem to manage OK.* —Judy Prescott

After giving her several examples of how I was defining the term "poverty," rural Wisconsin village president Judy Prescott, who presides over a small (615 population), relatively isolated community located 14 miles off a main highway, nervously admitted to me that "maybe half" the residents of her community live in poverty. However, even a cursory look around the town, where most houses are old and small, yards are littered with junker cars and broken children's play equipment and equipment constructed from old tires sprouting weeds, would lead the average observer to conclude that the town residents are, uniformly, very poor.

Prescott said most of the poor she is aware of are elderly, but otherwise she doesn't know much about them. I found this hard to believe, because, as a native of the town and an elected community leader for more than 12 years, it is her business to know about the people she serves. "I'm not sure what poverty is, really," she finally said, looking down at the table while twisting her handkerchief, "so I guess I don't know how to answer your questions."

Prescott further indicated that those village residents who are employed mostly hold part-time jobs in communities ranging from 26 to 70 miles away. With the price of gas at $4 per gallon, it would not pay someone to drive between 52 and 140 miles, rount trip, to work part time, probably at a low-wage job. Nevertheless, Prescott claims this is exactly what local residents do.

The village lacks local child care for working mothers, and there is no senior center. "We participate in mutual aid services with other communities in the township, so someone delivers the meals to the shut-ins," she said, adding that the county has a bus that comes once a week and picks up anyone who wants to go shopping in the town 26 miles away. Other informal welfare arises out of the local church communities, and Prescott believes nearly everyone in town attends a church.

Although Prescott maintains there are no drug, alcohol or crime issues in the area, the village employs a full-time police officer. Small communities generally combine resources to support a full-time law enforcement position, which means one eight-hour-per-day shift seven days per week divided up among the supporting communities according to the proportion of the individual's salary a particular town provides. It is unusual for a community this small to have a full-time law enforcement officer, particularly if there is, as Prescott claims, no crime. "It's what the people wanted, and they were willing to add to their tax bill to pay for it," she said, explaining that otherwise they'd have to rely on the county sheriff, who is based 28 miles away and can't respond quickly. This is a somewhat fallacious perception of the level of protection a single police officer can provide because any law enforcement situation that is perceived as dangerous necessitates the officer calling the sheriff for back-up, and then waiting until he arrives.

Probing further, Prescott finally told me the officer spends his time "on patrol and doing paperwork—and an occasional domestic call, safety checks on the elderly, investigating ordinance violations, a barking dog problem or catching a speeder once in a while … and in the summer he spends a lot of time monitoring the park and beach."

While rural life can appear quietly idyllic, it really isn't. Stress among struggling rural families, particularly the rural poor, is acute. Retired Catholic priest John Herzog, who spent his active ministry in rural Iowa, says most of the farming families he knew were "dirt poor" and did not earn enough money from farming to make it, so one or both parents worked full-time off-farm, in towns 50 or 75 miles away, and were still just barely making it. "That's the definition of stress in my mind—two adults trying to do four full-time jobs and raise three or four kids," Herzog explains. "Not many ever talked to me about how hard their lives were, and I only heard about it, usually indirectly, when desperation set in and there was a lot of alcohol abuse and family violence going on…"

Playing into this scenario is the reality that small family farms have been in sharp decline for a long time. "Farms that have been in a particular family for generations now involve four or five thousand acres because they bought up smaller farmers in the vicinity who went bankrupt. All that reached a peak in the early 80s when prices dropped and only really big corporate producers could persevere. A lot of people hurt deep down inside when that happened," he says, recalling a horrific incident in Lone Tree, Iowa, when local farmer Dale Burr became distraught over his growing debt.

"He shot his wife in their farmhouse then went to the next town over to cash a check, and when they refused him, got his shotgun and killed the bank president. Next was his neighbor who had recently won a court settlement against his [Burr's] son. When the sheriff finally pulled the guy over, he put the gun in his mouth and shot himself," Herzog grimaced, adding that "the town's still not over it."

Diversifying in order to keep the farm operation alive hasn't been a good answer either, Herzog claims, particularly when it involves efficiencies that run up against humane agricultural practices. "In the late 90s I visited an old parishioner who had expanded into egg production. That involved six buildings on his farm, each containing 100,000 hens, all in small cages and without feathers. This bothered me so much I've been buying free range eggs ever since, even though they're twice as expensive."

Herzog holds a pessimistic view of the future and notes a "huge demographic challenge" in rural farm states as farms get bigger, becoming so self-sufficient they decimate local small-town businesses. "Small towns will disappear and small parishes will disappear.… In today's world any parish of less than 500 households is not going to be able to survive financially and there just aren't 500 Catholic households in a town of 1,200–1,300, or even two or three towns that size … and the same is true for other denominations. The social connections parish membership provides, and the informal safety net church communities give the elderly and poor in the area, will disappear and the elderly and handicapped won't be able to cope," Herzog says, pointing out that a parallel is already occurring as more and more smaller school districts are being consolidated to accommodate the shrinking rural population. "I just don't see any light at the end of the tunnel," he says.

And Then the Bottom Fell Out—The New Rural Poor

Yesterday's givers have become today's takers...—Rural food pantry volunteer

The economic meltdown of 2008 created a population of newly poor—those who have always been economically solvent and had never before been classified as poor. In rural areas these include both farmers and local business owners. "Farmers and small businesses have no real economic buffers, and what's really sad is they know what it's like when customers don't pay their bills, and then suddenly they've become one of those people," explained rural attorney Stephen Chiquoine. "The bottom can drop out of the ag [agricultural] markets really fast and then farmers are left with a lot of debt and no means to repay it. When total desperation sets in, they come to me asking what they can do."

Chiquoine says local banks try "very, very hard" to work with people, but he points out they have no power to forgive debt entirely and if their own debt-to-asset ratio gets too high they risk failing. As a result, for the first time in their lives long-time local residents in rural communities are finding themselves using food pantries and are forced to seek other social services they never thought they would need—and for many it's deeply humiliating. "There's no anonymity for them. Everybody in town knows how bad off they are," Chiquoine says, "and then they come up against not being able to afford school costs for their kids' extracurricular activities. It's not like other people in their community don't want to help them, but sometimes they just can't, because they don't have much spare cash either."

However, both Chiquoine and Ellen Clark, who administers a rural housing assistance program, believe the newly poor in particular don't handle their diminished circumstances appropriately. "They're still all caught up in the rampant consumer culture they were used to and spend money like they actually have it," Clark says, adding that "these families don't put together a reasonable game plan to deal with their situation ... and some are pretty unrealistic—they want a management position because they ran a business and won't lower themselves to work at the McDonald's over in the next town, even if the job will help pay the bills."

Chiquoine, who does collection work, says the work is very frustrating. "People who don't know how to manage hard times don't change their behavior when things get tight. They'll still buy a 64-inch TV on time, for $29 per week, never considering that the interest rate they're paying makes it cost three times that much ... and they still think each kid needs a Smartphone, which costs them a couple hundred a month, but they won't pay their propane bill and when the tank runs out in the middle of winter, they heat the house by leaving the oven door open because they know the utility company can't shut them off during the winter months. They're running up a huge natural gas bill they'll never get ahead of."

Clark concurs. "We try to teach our clients money management, and help them lay out a clear path toward a better financial future, but often they won't follow it. I understand that rural people have deep roots and don't want to leave family and friends to move to where jobs are, but I don't understand letting their mortgage get months in arrears so they have the money for things they don't need, but want anyway."

Then there are those who pay cash as they go. Clark says it's not terribly unusual to have clients, for the services her agency provides, who have no credit history because they pay cash for everything. "We're not sure where this cash comes from," she says, "but their credit records are clean." These are the poor who "know how to be poor" in that they shop in thrift stores and buy furniture and other household items second-hand. Nevertheless, it takes considerable cash to purchase a car or washing machine, and most are vague about how they manage to do this.

Clark describes the case of a mother of four, who divorced her husband after the economy forced his business into decline and he embezzled a large amount of money from investors and was sent to prison. "She moved closer to family and managed her severely downsized life pretty well for a couple years, then she met some guy, and immediately stopped paying her bills so she could save up for a tummy tuck and some face work ... and she'll probably lose her house as a result ... it's crazy—and my experience is most poor people don't act that way."

Rural Poverty in Other Places

> *No one, anywhere, who works for a living should live in poverty.*—Senator Edward Kennedy

The question of whether the rural poor in the Midwest differ significantly from the poor in other regions of the country begs a question that is beyond the purview of this book; nevertheless, in very general terms, the answer is both yes and no. In any rural area almost everyone struggling to survive works at some combination of jobs that brings in money, and most work very hard. What sets the Midwestern rural poor apart from the rural poor somewhere else is the economic basis of the region. The rural Midwest survives on a primarily agricultural and manufacturing economy while Appalachia's rural economy is driven by logging and coal mining. The rural Southern economy is agricultural, but overall farming costs are less, due to the milder climate, and major crops are different from the Midwest. The growing season for food crops is much longer in the Southern states, making it possible to grow more, and to produce food crops the Midwest can't produce because of the shorter growing season. The rural Southwest economy is based upon food crops and cattle, but the climate is arid and it is usually necessary to irrigate. Water is liquid gold in the Southwest and can be very expensive to purchase, which drives agricultural costs up.

While the rural poor in Appalachia and in the Midwest are overwhelmingly white, the poor in the rural South are mostly black sharecroppers, and the percentage of Southern black farmers owning land is much smaller compared to the number of Midwestern farmers. There is a saying in sociology that the most vulnerable person in America is a black female born into poverty in the rural south, where her birth becomes her destiny because race, gender and geographic location all conspire to keep her from ever overcoming her impoverished circumstances.

Many of the rural poor in the Southwest are Hispanic, American Indian, or both. Most are migrant farm workers, meaning that they travel around a particular area harvesting crops. Hispanic migrant farm workers also support the rural agricultural economy of California.

All rural states, regardless of location, suffer from a severe shortage of medical personnel and facilities, but most of the Appalachian states and many of the Southern states are, overall, much poorer than the Midwestern states, thus are unable to provide the same level of needed social services that rural Midwesterners can access. Poorer states are unable to adequately fund public education or provide the special educational services the poor often require, and there is no question that important cultural differences and operating social value systems among each of these regions impact rural poverty. For example, in a very conservative rural southern community, where the prevailing family value is that a woman's place is in the home and being the family breadwinner is a man's responsibility, if his earning capacity becomes significantly less than his wife's, or so low her income is necessary, this value may conspire to keep women out of the workforce.

The Midwest, on the other hand, still operates out of a frontier mentality where, historically, women's labor force participation has been a vital necessity. This is an important distinction because gender role flexibility is a strong predictor of family stability, and family stability is a strong predictor of economic security. Families with less flexible, more rigid gender role expectations tend to have more tension and frequent power struggles between spouses, which lead to general unhappiness with the marriage, a greater likelihood of divorce, and a downward slide on the economic ladder.

Third and Fourth World rural poverty, on the other hand, presents an entirely different set of circumstances simply because it exists in places where social problems abound. However, there have been some very successful programs to remedy rural poverty in these regions using the micro-loan program developed by Nobel Laureate Mohammad Yunus. Yunus convinced the Grameen Bank to facilitate micro-credit, micro-finance loans to individuals, most often women, too poor to receive conventional loans, and the concept has been quite successful in assisting the rural poor in some Third and Fourth World nations.

Regardless of the differences among them and the individualized coping strategies employed by the poor in a particular place anywhere in the world, the bottom line remains the same: people are poor because they don't have enough money. This is true no matter where one lives and is one very important thing all poor have in common. Poor people everywhere work, yet remain poor because of a lack of decent jobs that pay a living wage, unfair market competition for goods produced, and, of course, their government's lack of political will to correct the problem.

Research Methodology

> *If there is a rule about this form of research it might be reduced to something as simple as "pay attention."*—Steven Taylor and Robert Bogdan, *Introduction to Qualitative Research Methods*

Examining the entirety of rural Midwestern poverty in detail, in one book, is not possible; however, taking a careful look at rural poverty in one, fairly typical rural area within the Midwest is a suitable approach to further understanding the nuances of the problem and is one many others have undertaken. Accordingly for purposes of this book, all data suggest Wisconsin was a good choice to provide a more in-depth snapshot of the real-life struggles of the rural poor, for the following reasons:

First, depending upon which data set one examines, for the past several years Wisconsin either did okay economically or did very poorly; no data indicated the state made a robust recovery from the 2008 recession or ever returned to pre-recession prosperity.

Second, the state's conservative Republican governor made dramatic cuts to the state's investment in public education, public services and infrastructure, and Wisconsin's job growth rate remained a consistently dismal 1.6 percent, ranking 44th in the nation.[8] Further examination of these figures indicated virtually no rural job growth in Wisconsin, in either the agricultural sector or in small, one-industry towns.

Third, Congress waged war on the food stamp program nationally and Wisconsin's majority Republican legislature followed suit with an ugly, broad-spectrum assault on the state's poor. Cutbacks in nearly all programs that low-income people in Wisconsin have historically relied upon, including food stamps, medical assistance, occurred. This translated into more poor people receiving fewer benefits and in smaller dollar amounts, which was particularly devastating for the rural poor.

Fourth, Wisconsin was one of only a few states nationwide that refused federal Medicaid money, deciding instead to cut off medical assistance to 92,000 low-income Wisconsinites. The state expected these individuals to buy medical insurance through the Affordable Care Act's insurance exchange. Most will not be able to afford to do this, which will result in escalating medical care costs hospitals will be forced to write off. As a result, support jobs in Wisconsin's health care sector will disappear, hurting the poor in rural areas the most.

Fifth, Wisconsin led the nation in new jobless claims, a trend that began several years earlier and has not reversed. Complicating the unemployment problem further, Congress failed to extend the 26-week unemployment benefit period. This was a crushing blow to rural areas which relied mostly on manufacturing jobs that were already in long-term, continuing decline. As a result, many more unemployed, particularly in rural areas, lost the safety net extended of unemployment assistance provided. When their benefits expired, most found themselves further impoverished.

Sixth, Wisconsin has significant tribal land with limited potential for future economic development. The poorest county in the state is populated almost entirely by Native Americans living on reservation land and who have been very poor for generations.

Finally, selecting Wisconsin for the dubious honor of exemplifying poverty in the rural Midwest was a practical choice. While I haven't lived here long enough to be labeled a bona-fide local, I've lived in rural Wisconsin a long time, and held a newspaper job that positioned me very well to observe and grasp the intricate and complex lives of the rural poor.

Unlike my previous book, which was guided by a certain set of theoretical assumptions, I took a "go where it leads me" approach to writing this one. In other words, I followed the story line. Thus, the book is based, to a considerable extent, upon my years as a journalist working for a small, rural newspaper. I learned a lot about how life really happens in rural areas because I was, so often, at the scene of whatever was going on.

My academic poverty researcher career came into play when I realized that existing theories of rural American poverty are, in my view, weak, so I had nothing to fall back on other than my ability to pay attention, and I became pretty good at it.

Hands-on research of the sort I engaged in for this book frequently requires that the identities of individuals and places be protected. And while Prescott's reticence to talk about the poor went deeper than most people I spoke with, I sensed few were willing to "give me the whole story." Answering my questions was too much like talking about family, which, because so many rural people are related to one another, is what most rural communities are—and families don't air their dirty laundry in public. Looking at it from this perspective made it easier to understand why finding out what I wanted to know was going to be difficult, and also led me to conclude that there is an ugly underside to rural life no one really wants to acknowledge or talk about.

I did find some poor families willing to talk with me. What I did not find was a definable culture of rural poverty existing among the rural Midwestern poor. The reason for this, I believe, is that the rural Midwest is very "white" and neither racial nor ethnic diversity is found in nearly the numbers seen in larger urban areas. There are no particularly outstanding differences in language, dress, behavior or food preferences among the majority of rural Midwesterners that set them apart from each other, making them all "mainstream rural folks."

Despite my assurances of anonymity most interviewees didn't want their conversation tape-recorded or their names, and sometimes their locations, revealed. I willingly agreed to these terms because frequently it meant that I'd get better information. The result is that all of the incidents and stories in this book are true, but the locations where they occurred and identities of the individuals involved, are protected. Appendix One details the framework for gathering primary data on the rural poor.

Without question, this work represents a feminist, woman-eyed view of the Midwestern rural human experience, and a man seeing the same things might tell an entirely different story. But, maybe not. In rural communities men and women are strong and equal partners, both in business and in life, and are generally in common agreement about the things that really matter. They tend to share equally in the good and the bad that befalls their family, their community, and their neighbors. While women and men might describe the emotions surrounding an experience differently, they will likely both agree on the basic facts. This was also true of the interviews I did—a pattern of irrefutable basic facts emerged from everyone I talked to, and these helped me to grasp what I strongly suspected, as well as what I was unable to find out, about rural poverty.

To the extent that no research is value-free, and researcher bias is unavoidable, I readily acknowledge that much of what I have seen, heard, and learned about poverty over the years has been filtered through an educated, white female psychological lens clouded by a lifetime living as a member of the upper middle-class. I don't know what being poor "really feels like" and sometimes people who are living in poverty just don't have words to describe the experience. Consequently, readers will have to rely on my ability to describe what I saw and heard to help them grasp the struggles of Midwestern rural life, as lived within the legacy of its pioneer homesteading history and current economy, in a meaningful way.

Finally, there are three important caveats to this book on rural poverty:

First is that Native American poverty must be part of any conversation about Midwestern poverty. There are 334 active Native American Indian reservations in the United States today. All are managed by a sovereign tribal government, in cooperation with the Federal Bureau of Indian Affairs, which is a branch of the U.S. Department of the Interior. About one third of American Indians, totaling 700,000 individuals in the United

States, live on U.S. government–designated reservations. About half are concentrated on the ten largest reservations, several of which are located in the Midwest.

Reservations vary dramatically in terms of their size, population, proximity to urban centers, cultural beliefs and practices, and economy. Despite such variation, reservations share a similar history and face similar contemporary challenges. At the forefront of these challenges is poverty. In 2010, the poverty rate on American Indian reservations was 28.4 percent, compared with 22 percent among all American Indians (on and off reservations), and 15.3 percent among all Americans.[9] In addition to high poverty rates, low educational and employment levels, poor health care, substandard housing, high alcoholism rates and deficient economic infrastructures hinder reservation life.

Failing to, albeit briefly, discuss the plight of today's American Indians, who suffer the most recalcitrant poverty and are among the poorest of the Midwestern rural poor, would be an unforgiveable error of omission. While this book makes note of the Native American tribal history that has resulted in their intractable poverty, a truly in-depth discussion of Native American poverty deserves a book of its own.

Second is the issue of immigrant and migrant labor. Relative to California, Texas, and other southern border states, migrant and both legal and illegal immigrant labor is not as pervasive in the rural Midwest. Unquestionably there are issues with these populations in some rural areas of the Midwest, but they are best discussed from an anthropological perspective and on a regional, case-by-case basis.

Third is that I went into this project assuming there was a grass ceiling in American agriculture similar to the glass ceiling found in other American businesses, and that women farmers would, like women everywhere, work as hard as men and earn less than their male counterparts. I uncovered no substantial evidence to support this. While women farmers comprise about 14 percent of all farmers and tend to have somewhat smaller farms than men, many are equally, or more successful, particularly in the Midwest. Saying this, rural farm wives working in partnership with their husbands often work harder than their husbands, sometimes earning significantly more money than their husbands are able to earn as a farmer. Because theirs is a partnership, no one keeps score, but an outside observer cannot help but notice how hard farm wives work. Frequently they hold down a full-time, off-farm job in addition to keeping the financial records for the farm, helping with chores and raising the kids. In both a physical and mental sense farm women are the hardest-working women I have ever met.

With this in mind, unless it is relevant to a particular topic, throughout this book, no specific distinctions between male and female farmers will be drawn.

This Book

> *Rural Americans are a special people. Their labor puts food on our table and fuel in our gas tanks.... Their spirit of community inspires us all.* —Tom Vilsack, U.S. Secretary of Agriculture

Unlike other books on rural poverty, which tend to be small case studies confined to a particular region or focused on a single economic crisis, this book takes a macro approach to rural poverty and attempts to illuminate the big picture of Midwestern rural life and the context out of which rural poverty arises. The focus is on the farm economy as the backbone of the rural Midwest, because agriculture dominates the social and economic life of rural Midwestern towns. Local small-town businesses rise and fall on the farm economy, and occasionally on small manufacturing enterprises, but unlike urban centers, where diverse employment opportunities abound, in rural areas agriculture is everything.

The book also sheds a different light on rural poverty from that found in most previous work on the subject. This is because, over many years living in a rural community, I have repeatedly been astonished to find that most rural poor are amazingly adept at surviving their circumstances. Many don't view themselves as particularly disadvantaged, don't see money as the only key to their happiness and don't feel they need a lot of it. They find great satisfaction in simple things and feel tremendous pride in being able to manage their lives on their own terms, and if this includes surviving on a poverty income, so be it. As a result, Midwestern rural poverty often blends in more than it stands out.

Following this introductory chapter, Chapter 1 offers a discussion of the definitional problems facing any researcher attempting to work with rural poverty as a social problem, and why the usual definitions of poverty don't necessarily apply to the Midwestern rural poor.

Chapter 2 provides a brief history of the American Midwest and how land became so important to rural America. Chapter 3 profiles the demographics of the 12 Midwestern farm states that are the focus of this book. (Maps showing the areas of greatest poverty in each state are found in the Maps of Poverty Regions in Midwestern States section of this book.) Chapter 4 explains the complexities of the farm economy and how every farmer is playing in the sandbox of a world economy that operates at the whim of forces around the globe and far out of his control. Chapter 5 describes 21st-century rural Midwestern America and how it became what it is today. Chapters 6, 7, 8 and 9 detail the daily lives of the rural poor in terms of community life, health care, crime, and education. Chapter 10 discusses the root cause of all forms of poverty and draws conclusions about the Midwestern rural poor going forward.

Maps of Poverty Regions in Midwestern States

On the following pages maps of each state identify the highest poverty counties for each of the Midwestern states. Missouri, Ohio, Michigan and South Dakota have the overall highest percent of rural poverty among the Midwestern states. Bearing in mind that children are poor because their parents are poor, six Midwestern states have rural child poverty rates above 20 percent, while in Illinois, Iowa, Nebraska, Ohio and Wisconsin the rural child poverty rate is slightly lower than the urban child poverty rate.

Illinois

Indiana

▨ Poverty 20% or higher
☐ Poverty 13% – 19.9%

Iowa

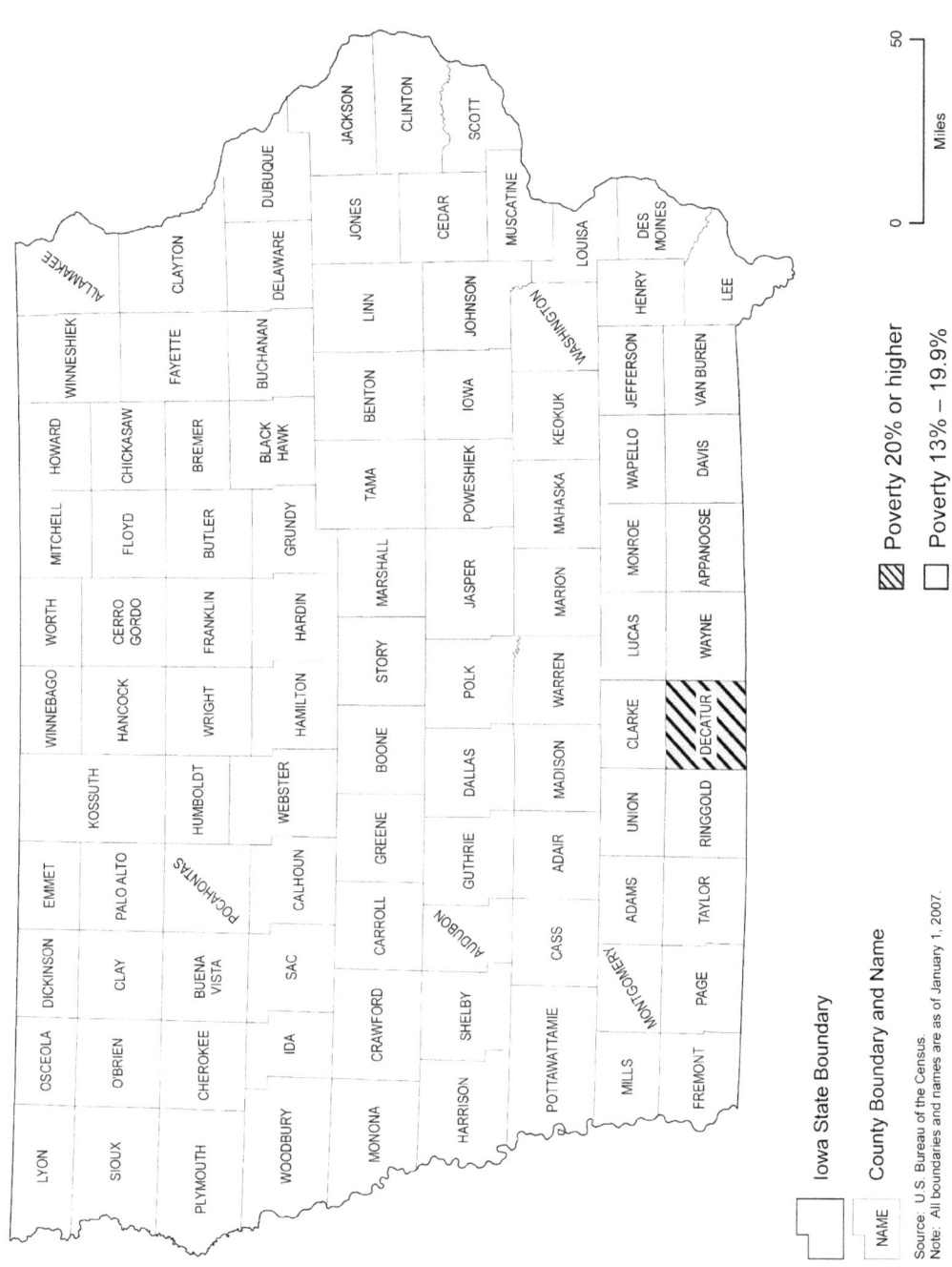

Kansas

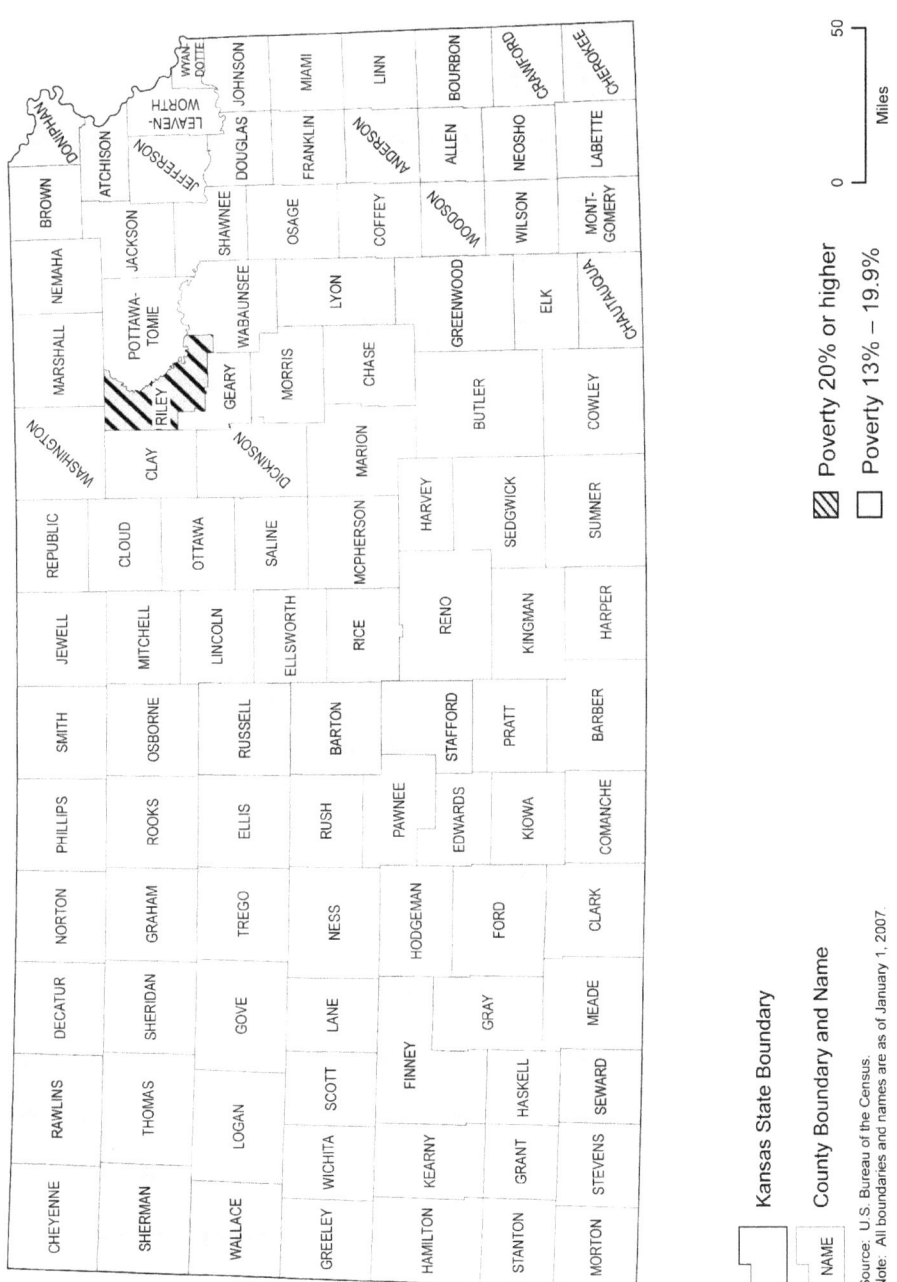

Michigan

Minnesota

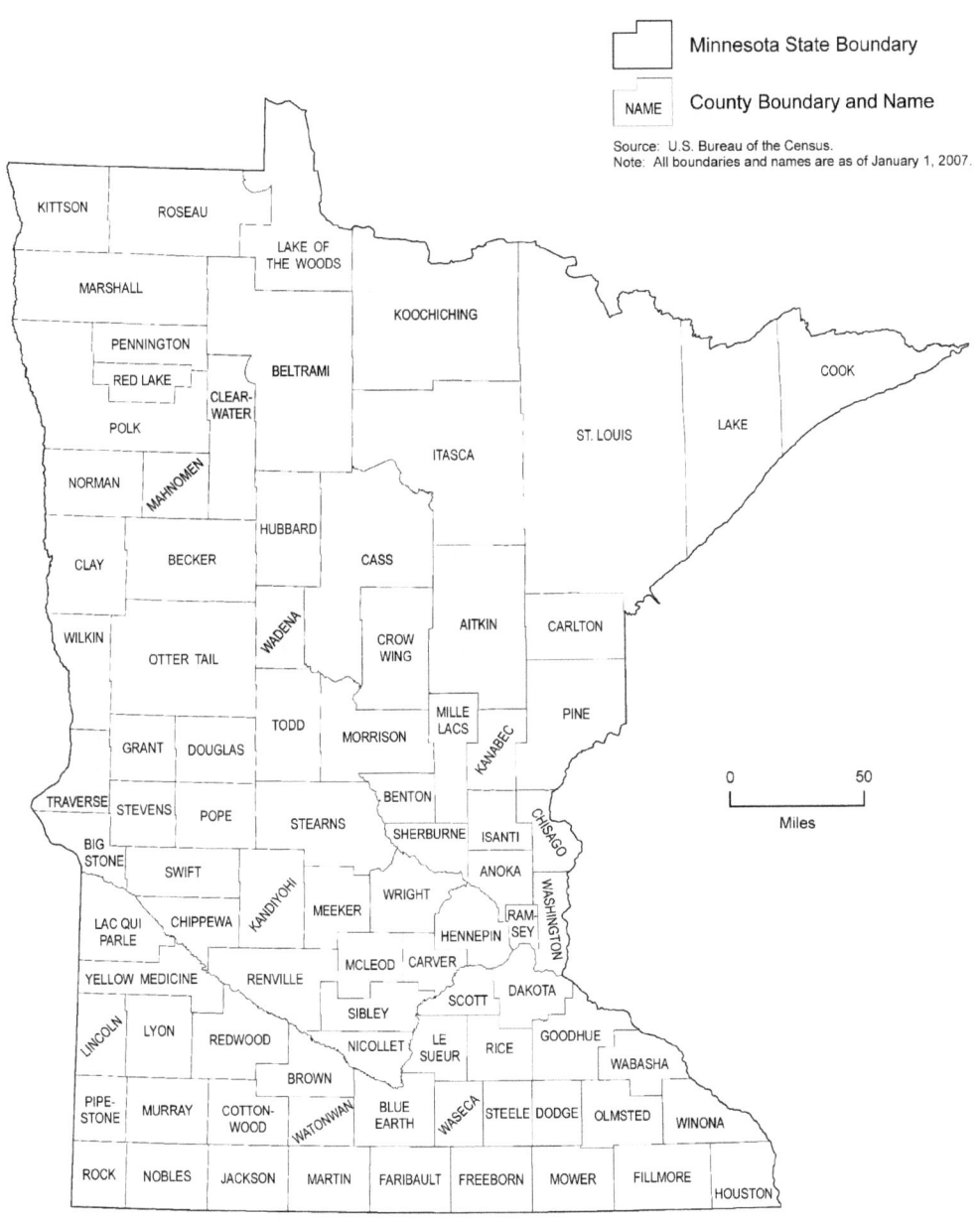

Missouri

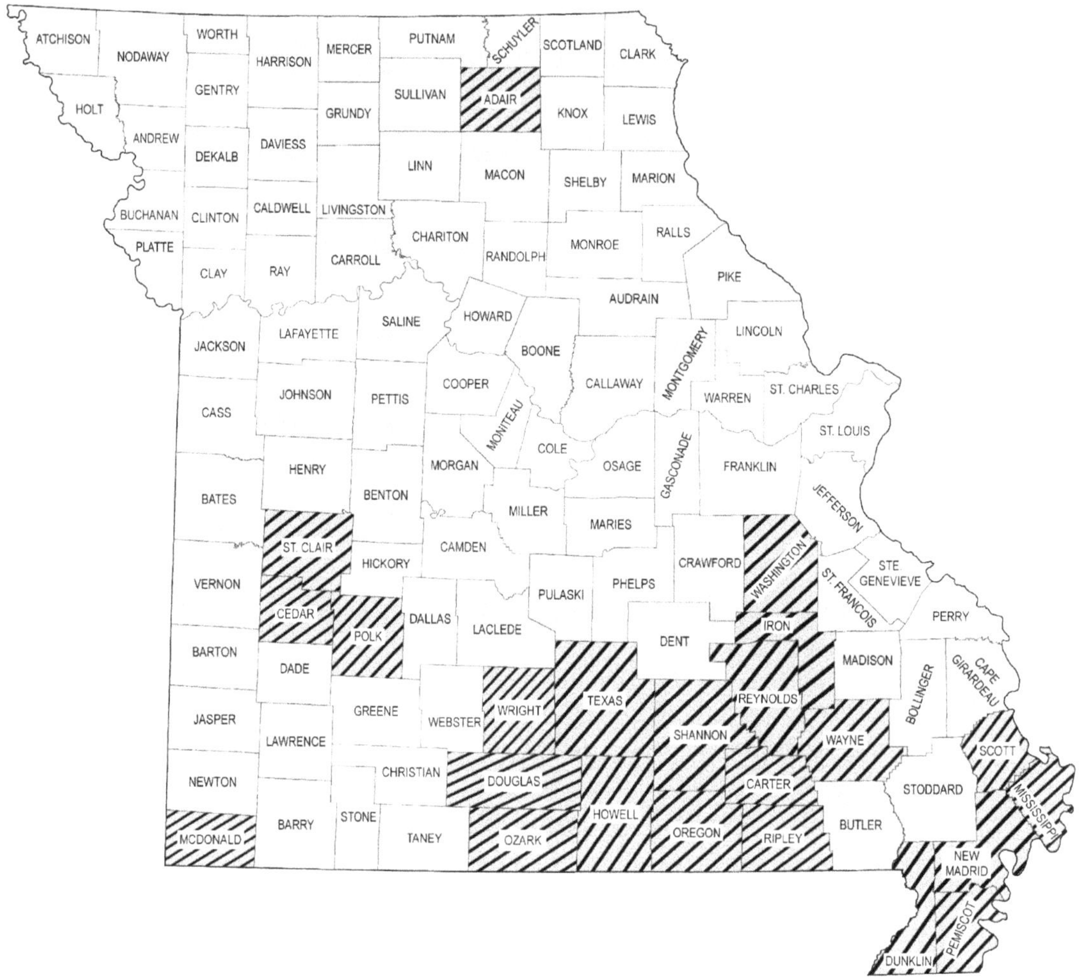

Missouri State Boundary

County Boundary and Name

Sources: U.S. Bureau of the Census, U.S. Department of Agriculture.
Note: All boundaries and names are as of January 1, 2007. For data collection purposes, the independent city of St. Louis is included in St. Louis County.

0 — 50 Miles

▨ Poverty 20% or higher
☐ Poverty 13% – 19.9%

Nebraska

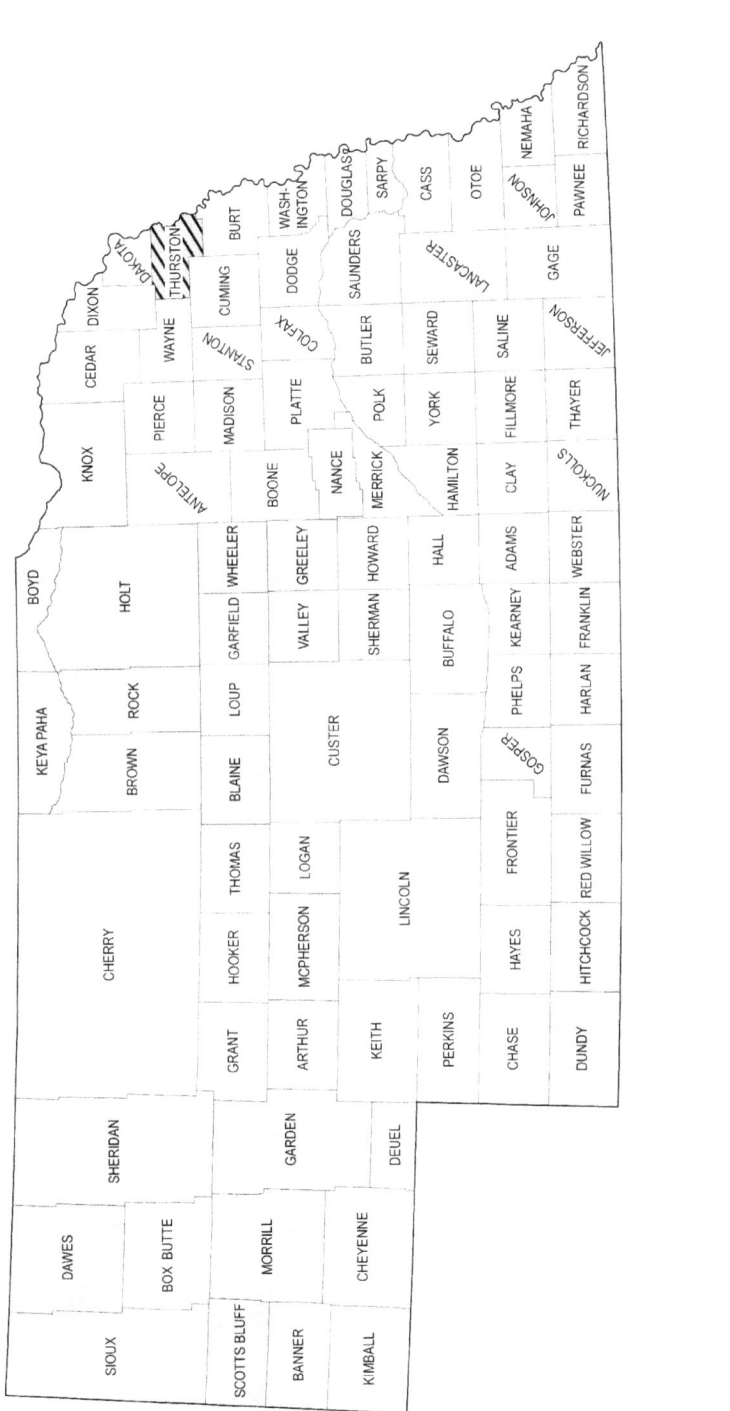

North Dakota

Ohio

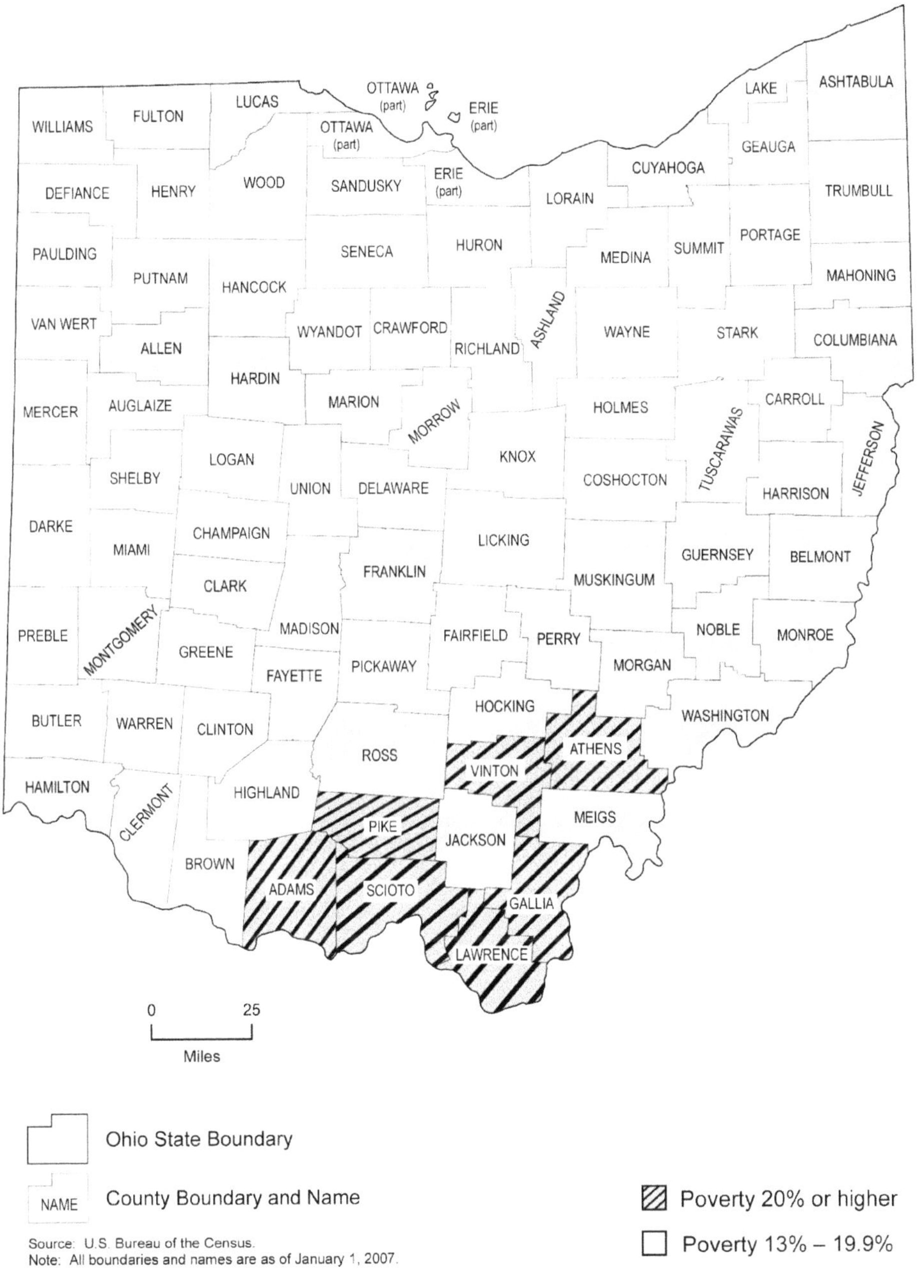

Source: U.S. Bureau of the Census.
Note: All boundaries and names are as of January 1, 2007.

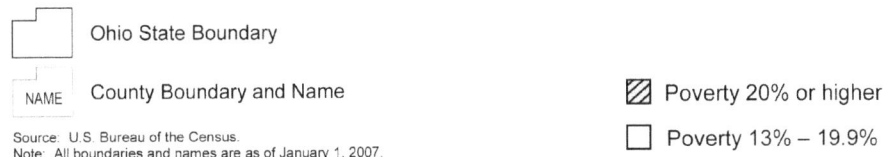

South Dakota

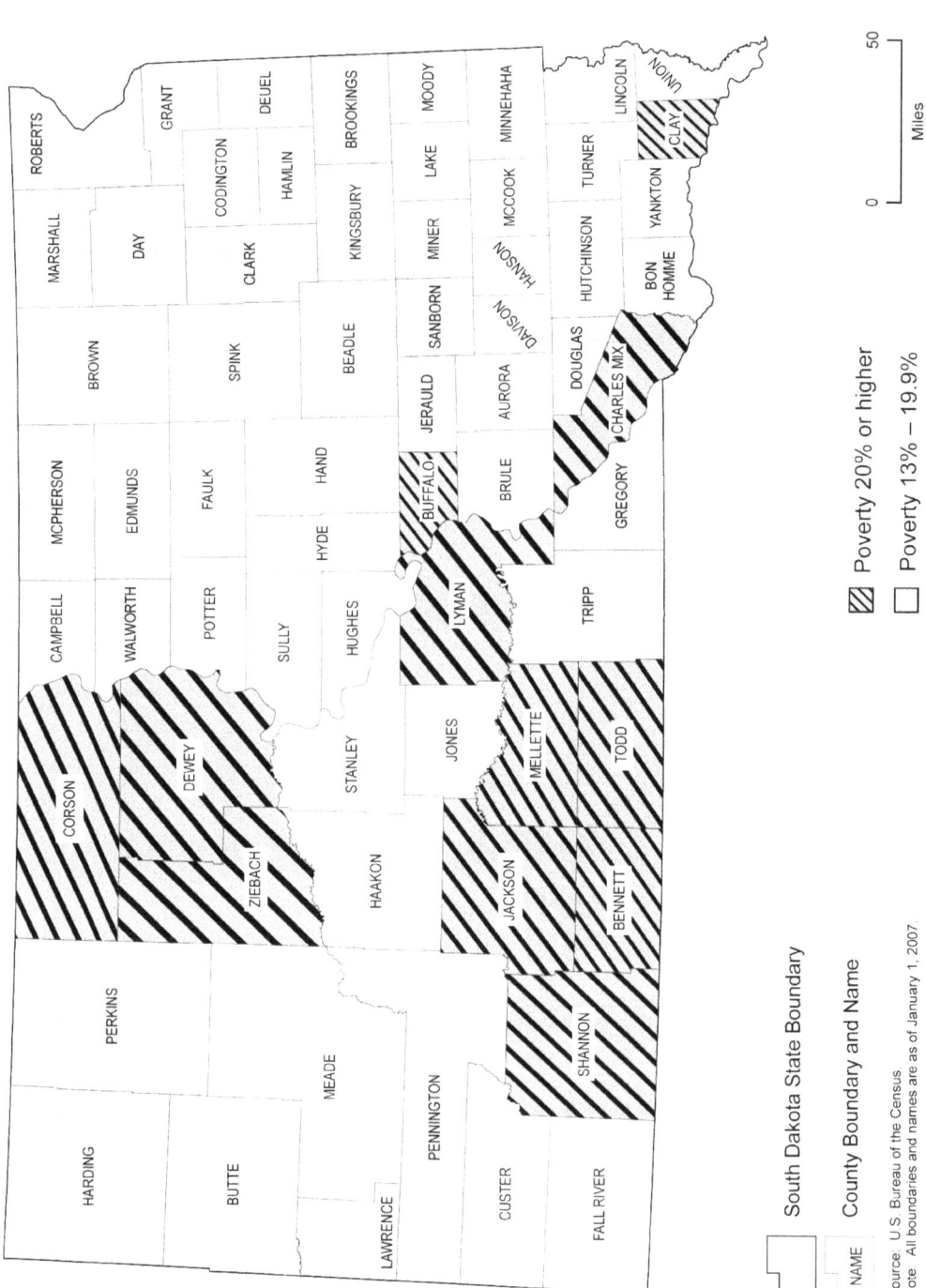

Maps of Poverty Regions in Midwestern States 41

Wisconsin

1

We Ain't Got Much, But We Got Plenty

Understanding Rural Poverty When the Usual Criteria Don't Apply

> *My dad, a life-long farmer, often said, "It's no disgrace to be poor, but it can be mighty inconvenient at times."* —Jerry Apps, Wild Rose, Wisconsin

That the concept of poverty is generally consistent across rural and urban areas seriously complicates an examination of rural poverty because so many rural poor don't self-define as being poor. And even though poverty always portrays human life as characterized by a sustained lack of resources, capabilities, choices, security and the social or personal power necessary to attain a minimally acceptable standard of living, in many rural areas, the poor don't think of themselves in these terms. This significantly obscures rural poverty.

Another complication is that a rural farmer classified as poor in 2010 because of a bad crop year may not meet even one of the definitional criteria for poverty the next year, or for many years thereafter. Another farmer may have serious cash flow problems for a couple years because of mediocre crop returns and unusually high, one-time farm operation costs yet be worth six, or even seven, figures on paper, because his land values are solid. But if land values drop, that same farmer can find himself in catastrophic, often near-fatal financial difficulty.

And, while strictly speaking, household income is a consistent measure of poverty, regardless of place of residence, it has long been believed that being poor in a less densely populated rural area is, in terms of overall quality of life, "better" than being poor in an urban area. There is some truth to this because inhabitants of rural areas can grow and preserve their own food, which is much cheaper (and healthier) than buying it; housing costs are less; garage and church rummage sales abound as rich sources of very inexpensive used clothing and household items; and kinship networks (extended family, church) take care of each other in a myriad of ways that factor into the poverty equation. Locally owned businesses in small communities are more likely to extend credit, even when they shouldn't, and nearly every male knows at least the basics of how to fix most things.

Further, in rural communities everybody knows everybody else, and if they have lived in the area long enough are probably related to them. It's pretty hard to turn your back on a friend, relative, or high school classmate who's come up against hard times, and most folks in small rural communities won't do it. Instead, they help each other out, so even if you're poor and don't have much, whatever "much" means, somehow, you've got enough.

Regardless, for everyone, being poor includes an absence of opportunities to improve one's life or to access civil, cultural, economic, political and social resources. In other words, poverty is not just economic, it is an all-encompassing way of life defined by many characteristics, including a dearth of food, clothing, shelter, and health care, and extreme inconvenience. And defining poverty, particularly in rural areas, encompasses many clusters of meaning, all leading to some level of hardship that is always greater than mere inconvenience.

Precisely Defining Rural Poverty

> *Poverty is not a single, easily identifiable condition; it is a fluctuating set of circumstances.* —World Bank Participatory Poverty Assessments

The usual terms employed when discussing poverty don't work very well when applied to rural poverty, which can't be neatly tied up in a tidy bundle of definitions that, when applied, give a clear picture of the issue. In other words, poverty means different things according to circumstances, location, and individual perception.

In Europe the poor are defined as anyone whose income falls below 60 percent of the median for the individual country. Great Britain uses three poverty measures: one relative, one absolute and another, broad indicator of material deprivation, such as whether a child's family can afford to have a birthday celebration. The United Nations uses a range of indicators, including schooling and life expectancy. In the U.S., poverty is defined exclusively by annual income above or below a certain amount determined annually by a fixed formula and does not consider other "softer" variables that determine areas of deprivation and desperation caused by insufficient income.

At its core, the definition problem is bedeviled by two competing, contradictory viewpoints: one directs the social sciences to assign an arbitrary poverty measure and criteria-based definition to the concept of poverty; the other favors working from the perspective of the poor themselves, allowing them a voice in determining which diverse sets of circumstances and views of poverty have meaning for them. The following discussion will explore both.

What the Social Sciences Say about Defining Poverty

> *The lack of definition in our definition of poverty ... helps to answer the question of how the richest country in the history of the world could have so many people living in a state of deprivation.* —Thomas Edsall, *The Opinionator*

The social sciences have been less concerned with defining poverty than with figuring out what causes it. As a result, social scientists have remained fairly comfortable with a simple, arbitrary definition of poverty that automatically sorts individuals and families into categories of income above or below a predetermined poverty line. This line is determined by a formula that has been in place since 1963 and was originally developed using the U.S. Department of Agriculture (USDA) economy food plan for families of three or more persons.[1] The formula is based upon the assumption that an average family spends one third of its income on food, so the dollar cost of the USDA economy food plan was multiplied by three and adjusted for family size.[2] The result was that anyone whose family income fell at or below this figure was deemed poor. The three-times-the-cost-of-the-food plan calculation was only done once; since 1963, poverty thresholds have been updated annually, using the Consumer Price Index.

While no one would argue against defining poverty as being much more complicated than applying the standard formula, the concept is nearly always cast in terms that reference income, and most household income is from earned wages. This one indisputable fact ties poverty directly to the health and well-being of local labor markets and is an area where it is possible to draw clear distinctions between rural and urban environments.

In simplest terms, the rural labor market tends to be smaller, less well-paying, and less stable than its urban counterpart. Further, the extent to which a population is comprised of able, working-age people is an important indicator of labor force vitality and potential employment opportunities, and rural areas, having smaller, less dense population distributions, frequently can't measure up. Additionally, the labor force trajectory, measured by the age and training composition of the rural population, helps predict future economic health for rural areas. Overall, rural labor-force participation tends to remain fairly flat in most areas of the country.

In 2009 the White House Council of Economic Advisors looked at the average age composition in high-density rural and low-density rural counties in 1970 and 2000.[3] The under age 20 population has declined since 1970, while the proportion of the population in the prime working ages (20–49) has increased; however, the population of prime-age workers continues to be substantially lower in rural counties, meaning that less cash flow and disposable income is available to the local community.

The overall share of the U.S. population living in rural counties has been steadily declining over time, with high-density rural counties experiencing particularly sharp declines. From 1900 to 1970, rural counties lost nearly 0.3 of a percentage point of the U.S. population per year; from 1970 to 2008, this trend continued, albeit at a slower rate, ultimately costing rural counties almost 0.1 percent of the U.S. population annually. In 1900, about 40 percent of the population lived in a county that would be classified as rural in present-day America, whereas today that share has dwindled to half this amount.[4]

An additional measure of a robust labor force is the share of the working-age population (25–64 years old) healthy enough to be counted as potential labor force participants. The Federal Social Security Disability Insurance (SSDI) program, which provides monthly cash benefits to people who are unable to work due to a disability, is one indicator of labor force strength. In 2008, disability insurance enrollment as a share of potential labor force participation was 6.5 percent of working-age adults in high-density rural areas and 5.7 percent in low-density rural areas, compared with 3.9 percent in urban areas.[5] Thus, the average rural resident was significantly more likely to be enrolled in SSDI than his or her urban counterpart. Because individuals enrolled in

SSDI are unlikely to exit from the program, these disparities are likely to impact future labor force capacity.

In their critical review of the social science literature on rural poverty, Bruce Weber, Leif Jensen, Kathleen Miller, Jane Mosley and Monica Fisher point out that[6]:

- Nationwide poverty rates are highest in the most urban and the most rural areas and are higher overall in the rural areas.
- High-poverty counties tend to be geographically concentrated in certain regions of the country and included among these are the Indian reservations located in the Great Plains.
- County-level poverty rates vary on a rural-urban continuum, with rates being lowest in suburbs adjacent to urban areas and highest in remote rural areas not adjacent to metropolitan areas.
- High poverty and persistent poverty are disproportionately located in rural areas.

In 1999 about one in six (15.7 percent) rural counties had poverty rates above 20 percent, while only one in twenty (4.4 percent) of urban counties had poverty rates above 20 percent. About 13 percent of all counties had persistently high poverty rates and 95 percent of these counties were rural.[7]

These statistics support the notion that poverty tends to be repetitive and cyclical, meaning that some people move into, and out of, poverty, as defined by the federal poverty guidelines, many times during their life. They also raise the question of whether there is "something about rural areas" that isn't found in urban areas, thus increasing the likelihood of poverty. In other words, how important is "place" in determining whether, all other things being equal, an individual will be poor?

In a case study of rural poverty, Janet Fitchen examines the relationships the poor in one rural county have with existing social institutions (schools, county offices, existing labor market) and concludes that these institutions are relatively isolated from each other—a condition both the poor themselves and these institutions contribute to and maintain.[8] Further, this isolation is a major player in creating and sustaining desperate economic circumstances for the individuals involved.

Other researchers[9] examined the good-job—bad-job continuum as a structure affecting economic well-being in rural areas and determined, not surprisingly, that good-job households fared considerably better than bad-job households.[10] Due to the security, and social connections that come with having a steady, well-paying job, unquestionably, good-job households are better positioned to engage in other economically beneficial pursuits. From this viewpoint good-job households are doubly advantaged because they can continue to increase their economic well-being, while bad-job households are doubly disadvantaged by being employed in poorly paying jobs and not having the same opportunities to increase their income as those holding better jobs.

To date, social scientists have been unable to make a definitive determination about whether anything beyond demographic characteristics (gender, age, ethnicity, educational level) and local economic context make it more likely that persistent poverty will be found more frequently in rural areas. However, based simply on the economic context of rural areas, conventional wisdom suggests this would be the case. And every snapshot of rural poverty, regardless of the lens through which the problem is viewed, reveals that, on average, rural residents have notably lower incomes than urban residents. So while the rural poverty rate decreased between 1979 and 1999, the poverty rate in the average rural county is still at least several percentage points above those observed in urban counties.

And notably, the cost of living is higher in urban areas, thus wages tend to be higher. Ideal measures of income and poverty would adjust for these differences, but often do not.

Poverty Defined as Substandard Consumption

> *Poverty is a standard of consumption which is below what is generally considered to be a decent minimum.*—Stein Ringen

Defining and measuring poverty by analyzing consumption patterns is the darling of the political right because the notion assumes that the government is doing its job and programs such as Medicaid, food stamps, and income assistance are working. In this scenario there is no need to do anything differently in the public policy arena, nor is there any need to "worry" about the poor, because they are being taken care of effectively. Additionally, because they must first purchase what they consume, the poor have enough money to be active participants in the prevailing economic system.

According to researcher Stein Ringen, using consumption rather than income to define poverty assumes that, over time, consumption is much more stable than income, and that current consumption patterns are likely representative of past patterns, thus combine to form a lifetime pattern.[11] This is even more true in the case of farmers who depend on the weather for their income, and hence have a more volatile income pattern. "If you know that farmers are often relatively poor, then this issue is all the more salient for poverty measurement," explains statistician Filip Spagnoli, who also suggests that, when queried, people are more willing to be forthcoming about their consumption than their income and tend to remember spending more accurately than income.[12]

Using consumption to measure poverty has a definite downside. "If you want to measure how much people consume, you have to include durable goods and housing," Spagnoli says, adding that consumption of those goods is difficult to measure because it's difficult to value them. For example, if a household owns a house, an estimation of what it would cost to rent that particular house must be added to the total consumption of that household in order to make it possible to compare consumption patterns among individuals or households, some of whom rent rather than own a home. "You can't make poverty statistics if you don't make such comparisons, and then you have to do the same for cars, etc.," Spagnoli explains.

Another difficulty in measuring consumption as a means of defining poverty is that, in rural areas, households usually consume a lot of what they themselves produce on the family farm. This is difficult to value correctly. And, different people and households have different consumption needs, depending on their age, health, employment status, etc. "It's not clear to me how these different needs are taken into account when consumption is measured and used as an indicator of poverty," Spagnoli says.

Testing the consumption thesis is one way to define and measure poverty. University of Chicago economist Bruce Meyer and his colleague James Sullivan compared those who qualify as "poor" based on income and those who qualify as poor based on consumption across 25 indicators of household well-being, including assets, health insurance, number of bathrooms in the home, whether the family owned a dishwasher and other appliances, computer access and whether the head of the household is a university graduate.[13] They found that those who are "poor" by the consumption definition of poverty are worse off in 21 of the 25 categories of household well-being. Researchers explained the outcome, saying, "Some of those who fall below the poverty line when these are not considered, in the official income-before-taxes poverty measure, rise above the poverty line when these are included. In addition, consumption poverty better captures those who don't have other resources to fall back on, so those, whose income is temporarily low enough to fall below the poverty line, but have other ways to keep their consumption from falling as much, don't show up as falling below a consumption-based poverty line." Speaking to the political implications of these findings, Meyer adds that "the poverty rate is often cited by policymakers, researchers and advocates who are evaluating social programs that account for more than half a trillion dollars in government spending."

Defining poverty according to consumption patterns, rather than as a condition of unacceptable hardship, takes the moral sting out of the problem. It's harder to define someone as poor when they are actively consuming material goods, which implies they have money to spend and are making decisions about how to spend it. However, the importance of recognizing the moral implications surrounding poverty as a societal condition is not to be dismissed, because to acknowledge poverty implies a moral imperative to do something about it, and a definition of poverty that does not include moral elements makes it much easier for politicians to tread lightly over the problem. The only effective way to argue against poverty as a condition of unacceptable hardship is to take an entirely different view of poverty—one that assumes the poor have money to spend and then defining the extent of their problem according to how they spend it.

Poverty Defined as Income Insecurity

> *There can be no real individual freedom in the presence of economic insecurity.*—Chester Bowles, U.S. Under-secretary of State

If economic security is having a reliable job that guarantees enough income to meet the cost of basic necessities, including food, clothing, housing, health care and transportation without having to rely on public subsidies, economic insecurity is the absence of the ability to do any of these things on a predictable and regular basis. Data vary widely on how many Americans are affected by economic insecurity, which is a relatively new term in the poverty conversation. However, if the definition includes experiencing forced unemployment at any time during an adult's working life, a year or more spent relying on government assistance programs such as food stamps, or having an income below 150 percent of poverty, the risk of economic insecurity rises to 79 percent of all working Americans, and if current economic uncertainty continues, will rise to 85 percent by 2030.[14] The interesting caveat in these figures is that current income insecurity data terminology refers mostly to whites, who are often believed to be more invisibly poor than their African American or Hispanic counterparts, are more often dispersed in rural small towns, and disproportionately include the elderly who comprise large numbers of rural poor.

Using a series of measures of income security, Table One provides a report card of economic security conditions in the Midwestern states.[15] Notably the Midwest does very poorly overall in terms of job quality and Missouri, Indiana and North and South Dakota have the lowest overall scores. These findings do not bode well for the rural Midwest's economic future, where jobs are few and low-paying.

Table One: Midwestern States Income Security Report Card

State	Income	Job Quality	Public Assistance	Education	Assets	Worst Score	Best Score	Overall Score
IL	C-	D	C+	C	B	F 1a	A+ 1b	C
IN	D+	D	C	D+	C+	F 2a	A 2b	C-
IA	C+	D+	C+	C	B-	F 3a	A+ 3b	C
KS	C+	D	C-	C	B-	F 4a	A+ 4b	C
MI	C-	D	C+	C	C	F 5a	A- 5b	C-
MN	C+	D+	C	C	B-	F 6a	A 6b	C
MO	D	D-	B-	C	C+	F 7a	A 7b	C-
NE	B-	D-	C	C-	B-	F 8a	A 8b	C
ND	D-	D	D+	C+	B	F 9a	A+ 9b	C-
OH	C	D	C	C	B	F 10a	A+ 10b	C
SD	C-	D	D+	C	C	F 11a	A+ 11b	C-
WI	C+	C	C+	C+	B-	F 12a	A+ 12b•	C+*
Midwest Average	C-	D	C	C	B-			C

1a. State pension funding; 1b. Medicaid asset eligibility limits
2a. State tax credit; 2b. mortgage fraud laws
3a. Mortgage fraud laws; 3b. state expenditures per child
4a. State pharmacy program; 4b. Medicaid asset eligibility limits
5a. Child care subsidy rates; 5b. job placement rate
6a. Minimum wage; 6b. mortgage fraud laws
7a. Child care subsidy rates; 7b. mortgage fraud laws
8a. Per child income eligibility limit; 8b. housing trust funds
9a. Real estate tax relief; 9b. per capita workforce funding
10a. Elder Medicaid safety net; 10b. asset eligibility limit for temporary assistance for needy families (TANF)
11a. Housing trust funds;11b. unemployment benefits exhaustion rates
12a. Medical, pregnancy & disability leave; 12b. Medicaid asset eligibility limit
*Since these data were collected Wisconsin has opted out of Federal Medicaid funding, severely restricting the number of persons eligible for Medicaid. If this were factored into WI's scores, the results would be lower.

How the Poor Define Poverty

> *Bein' Poor's real hard ... and nobody understands just how hard hard gets ... hell, nobody even cares.*—Odessa, Women and Poverty in 21st Century America

Much of the work in rural poverty has occurred under the auspices of the World Bank and focuses primarily on economically underdeveloped nations and the third world. All of these studies acknowledge that there are many different definitions and concepts of poverty, but each takes a slightly different approach to examining the problem by including the concept of well-being, which is both an objective and subjective, self-report measure.

In general terms, well-being refers to whether households or individuals have enough resources or abilities to meet their needs; to the distribution of income, consumption or other attributes across the population; and to vulnerability, including the risk of falling deeper into poverty in the future. Thus, to be poor is to suffer a pronounced decline in well-being linked primarily to not having sufficient income or consumption ability to rise above a predetermined, adequate threshold. This view sees poverty primarily in monetary terms, but also considers the possibility that consumption can be issue-specific. For example, an individual can be house poor, food poor, or health poor, meaning either that most of their income goes toward one thing leaving little else to meet other needs, or that the individual lives in poor housing conditions, does not have enough food, or is in poor health.

The World Bank definitions of poverty encompass hunger, lack of shelter, being sick and not being able to see a doctor, not having access to school and being unable to read, not having a job, fear for the future, and living one day at a time. Poverty is also losing a child to illness brought about by unclean water, lack of political and personal power, no access to social services, and lack of representation and freedom. Taken together, these variables focus broadly on the capability of the individual to function in society, and poor people often lack key capabilities, as revealed by inadequate income, lack of education, or poor health.

Robert Chambers, a research associate at the Institute of Development Studies at the University of Sussex, together with others, questioned the definitions of poverty and posed the question of who should determine those definitions?[16] They argue that no one knows more about poverty than the poor themselves, thus they should define the problem rather than having a definition of their life in poverty imposed upon them by social scientists and others with little or no familiarity with the realities of the condition they are proposing to critically examine.

Accordingly, in 2002 the World Bank published a paper *Voices of the Poor: Can Anyone Hear Us,*[17] in which the poor themselves describe their plight in terms of suffering relationships. Because relationships are central to a person's belonging, identity, and ability to meet other socio-emotional needs, this is an important consideration when defining what it means to be poor. An individual's relational fabric is his or her means for navigating social norms, accessing resources and mobilizing the skills of others toward common goals. Who you know matters a great deal in any context, including that of a poor man (or woman) navigating his (or her) way out of poverty, or trying to survive while in it.

Other findings from this study of rural poverty include:

- Dependence was mentioned by 40 percent of the respondents, with some of them noting that a poor person always has to "seek out others" or "work for somebody else."
- Marginalization was noted by 37 percent, who defined a "poor person" as one who was "alone," had "no support," did "not feel involved in anything," or was "never consulted."
- Scarcity was included in the poverty definitions by 36 percent, who used statements such as having "nothing to eat," a "lack of means to meet clothing and financial needs," a "lack of food, livestock and money," and "having nothing to sell."
- Restrictions on rights and freedoms were associated with poverty by 26 percent

of respondents, who stated that "a poor person is someone who does not have the right to speak out" or "someone who will never win a case or litigation against someone else."
- Incapacity was mentioned in connection with poverty by 21 percent, including being unable to make decisions, to feed or clothe oneself, or to act on one's own initiative.

Only 36 percent of the poor described poverty in terms of material scarcity, which strongly suggests that "money isn't everything" and that using income level as a primary indicator of poverty is a seriously flawed notion that fails to measure several very important aspects of what being poor actually means. Equally important, while these data come from third and fourth world nations, they identify universally applicable variables that are relevant to rural poverty everywhere, including the American Midwest.

Twelve Clusters of the Meaning of Poverty

Poverty does not have a single meaning. It has a series of meanings linked through a series of resemblances.—Paul Spicker

Understanding how different visions and perceptions of poverty weave together is an enormous task, according to Professor Paul Spicker, who says "poverty needs to be seen as a composite concept embracing the range of meanings."[18] In Spicker's model the core of poverty is defined as "unacceptable hardship" affected by material conditions (patterns of deprivation, unmet needs, limited resources), economic circumstances (standard of living, inequality, economic position), and social position (lack of entitlement and basic security, exclusion, dependency and lower social class position). He points out that "it may be that the issues which poor people point to are not the issues that other people think of as being part of poverty, but these issues still matter to the people they affect."

Some have suggested that this approach to understanding and defining poverty represents a more philosophic approach to the problem than a sound application of scientific methodology to systematically study the problem. Feminist researchers, who believe in an interactive approach to research that includes research subjects as interactive collaborators, quickly take issue with this point, arguing that the task of defining poverty must be undertaken in ways that include the poor themselves, and that the definition of poverty should not be imposed upon the poor by outsiders trying to define a problem they personally don't suffer and have no direct knowledge of.

Ultimately, how poverty is defined is determined by the lens through which it is viewed and through which all data on the topic are filtered. Concerning rural poverty specifically, the most solid conclusions from the above discussion are first to recognize that definitions of poverty that work well in urban areas are seriously lacking when applied to rural areas because the fundamental differences between urban and rural poverty are extreme. Second, the emotional content of a poor person's life is extremely important, and any definition of poverty that relies solely on income or consumption misses that aspect entirely. Third, by any definition, poverty is living a life of unacceptable hardship.

Measuring Poverty

> *The judgment we had was that several of the decisions that were still embod_ied in the [poverty] measure were just woefully inappropriate—like the fact that nothing like the earned income tax credit could affect the poverty rate, that the in-kind transfers that were a large part of the effort that the nation makes can affect the measure of poverty because of the definition. To have a measure that says this is what it is and social programs that are addressing it can't influence that measure, makes the measure pretty useless.*—Robert Michael, Harris School of Public Policy Studies, University of Chicago

One of the biggest challenges researchers and others face when attempting to gain a greater understanding of poverty is answering the question of how to measure it when there are widely varying opinions about how to define it. And everyone agrees that before poverty can be measured, it must be defined in quantifiable, measurable terms. This makes using income level defined in dollars to determine whether someone is poor or not poor a very attractive notion.

The federal poverty line (FPL) threshold at or below which an individual is considered poor is determined by the U.S. Census Bureau. The poverty threshold figure is used for statistical calculations of the number of people in poverty, and employs a detailed forty-eight cell matrix of weighted thresholds that vary by family size, number of children, number of adults in the household, and whether or not any household members are elderly.

The FPL guidelines are issued through the U.S. Department of Health and Human Services and are used primarily for administrative purposes when determining poverty assistance program eligibility. Eligibility guidelines vary by family size, and some poverty programs accept persons having incomes up to 200 percent of the FPL. By this measure, an individual or household income falling at or below fifty percent of the poverty guideline for household size is categorized as living in extreme poverty.

Each year, poverty guidelines are issued in late January or early February, having been calculated from calendar year data two years previously. For example, the 2008 FPL was calculated from 2006 poverty threshold data, issued in August 2007, and updated to reflect the 2007 consumer price index. Thus, the 2008 FPL guidelines are approximately equal to 2007 poverty thresholds for most family sizes.

Some states have attempted to adjust the FPL by assessing a statewide standard of need. Wisconsin examined this concept in 1984, making use of both expenditure analysis (consumption) and subjective questions about well-being sent to over 1,800 households.[19]

The findings validate the FPL as an approximate measure of the standard of need for a family of four, but point to some special circumstances that increase household need: urban residence, the presence of teenagers in the household, and a household having two adults rather than one. These findings suggest that, in rural areas, a dollar can be stretched further than in an urban area—a notion many poverty researchers have had a "gut feeling" about for a long time.

Most states use the current year FPL as their basic guideline for determining a wide array of services to the poor. And some programs use multiples, up 200 percent of the FPL, as the guideline for service eligibility. Table Two below illustrates the

2013 income guidelines that define whether an individual or household is poor, as well as the multiples of income eligibility requirements for the various social assistance programs. The poor are not exempt from Federal income tax filing obligations, regardless of their income, but they are eligible to receive a federal earned-income tax credit.

Table Two: 2013 Poverty Guidelines[20]

Number of persons in family unit*	Annual Income (100% of poverty)	50% of poverty	125% of poverty	150% of poverty	175% of poverty	200% of poverty
1	$11,490	$5,745	$14,362	$17,235	$20,107	$22,980
2	$15,510	$7,755	$19,387	$23,265	$27,142	$31,020
3	$19,530	$9,765	$24,412	$29,295	$34,177	$39,060
4	$23,550	$11,775	$29,437	$35,325	$41,212	$47,100
5	$27,570	$13,785	$34,462	$41,355	$48,247	$55,140
6	$31,590	$15,795	$39,487	$47,385	$55,282	$63,180
7	$35,610	$17,805	$44,512	$53,415	$62,317	$71,220
8	$39,630	$19,815	$49,537	$59,445	$69,352	$79,260

*The per-person increase for households having more than eight persons is $4,020.

Poverty guideline figures are not the figures the Census Bureau uses to calculate the actual number of poor persons. Instead, the Census Bureau uses a set of income thresholds that vary by family size and composition to determine who is in poverty.[21] For example, in 2010 the poverty threshold figure for a family of four with no children less than 18 years of age was $22,541, while the figure for a family of four with two children under 18 was $22,162, $379 less, the implication being that younger children require fewer resources to sustain them. The array of major federal programs using various multiples of the FPL guidelines to determine eligibility is vast.[22]

The FPL is also utilized by non-profit and for-profit initiatives that aim to serve the poor, privately funded faith-based programs, informal community efforts, public-private anti-poverty projects and other poverty programs that do not use or depend upon federal or state tax dollars. Most reach into rural areas, but not at the level generally found in urban settings, particularly when offering a program requires a funding match by local units of government.

The primary problem with using the FPL to determine who is in poverty and who is not is embedded in the formula from which the FPL is derived, which many feel is obsolete and presents an unfocused, confusing picture of the problem. Food spending is a flimsy reference point when indications are that groceries account for less than 8 percent of American's household spending.[23] Further, the FPL does not account for financial benefit derived from assistance programs available to the poor and does not account for regional variations (i.e. south versus north; urban versus rural) in the cost of living.

Nevertheless, the FPL calculation endures as a useful measure of poverty because it is straightforward, easy to use, and leaves no doubt about where an individual or household falls on the poverty continuum when poverty is defined according to income.

Measuring Poverty Another Way

> *Ideal measures of poverty should: (1) measure comparative historical variation effectively; (2) be relative rather than absolute; (3) conceptualize poverty as social exclusion; (4) assess the impact of taxes, transfers, and state benefits; and (5) integrate the depth of poverty and the inequality among the poor.—*
> David Brady, Hoover Institute Senior Fellow

In 1995 the National Academy of Sciences (NAS) developed an alternative measure of poverty that includes both cash and in-kind income and subtracts taxes and non-discretionary work-related and out-of-pocket health expenses from total income. The NAS measure is a fluid, more complex measure of poverty than is presently used and requires more intricate estimates of both poverty thresholds and household expenses.[24] Specifically, the alternative measure recommends the following calculation for a family's resources[25]:

- Cash income, including earnings, government assistance from disability, welfare programs, and income generated from assets;
- Capital gains;
- Values of benefits received from the Supplemental Nutrition Assistance Program (food stamps), the Women, Infants and Children Program, the Low Income Home Energy Assistance Program, housing assistance and free and reduced-price school lunch;
- Federal and state income and payroll taxes;
- Refundable federal and state tax credits;
- Work-related expenses;
- Child support payments;
- Out-of-pocket health expenses.

The NAS Alternative Poverty Measure (APM) estimates family resources as the sum of cash income plus federal government in-kind benefits (including tax credits) that families can use to meet their food, clothing, shelter and utility needs, minus taxes, work expenses and out-of-pocket medical expenses—and significantly changes the poverty rate in America. For example, the 2008 official poverty rate for female-headed households is 31.4 percent. Using the APM, this figure increases to 32.3 percent when out-of-pocket medical expenses are subtracted from income and to 34.7 percent when out-of-pocket medical expenses are included in the poverty expenditure thresholds.[26]

The APM poverty threshold calculation estimates the cost of food, clothing, shelter and utilities and adds an additional 20 percent for other expenses. This threshold is adjusted for regional differences in cost of living and whether a family owns or rents its home. Included in the assessment of whether a family can meet its basic expenses, the SPM counts cash income, food stamps, tax credits and participation in other government assistance programs minus payments, work expenses and out-of-pocket medical expenses to arrive at a household income.

According to the APM, in 2006 a family of four would be poor if its annual income was at or below $21,818 without factoring in out-of-pocket medical expenses. However, if out-of-pocket medical expenses are factored into the threshold measure, the same family is poor if its annual income is at or below $23,935.[27]

Urban Institute researchers point out that compared with the conventional definition of poverty the number of persons living below 50 percent of the FPL is less under the NAS definition of poverty because the NAS definition includes some of the key benefit programs that target very low income families.[28] Using the APM threshold, many more people live just above the poverty threshold (100–150 percent of poverty) than the official definition suggests. Additionally the combination of taxes, child care expenses, and other work-related expenses included in the NAS poverty measure places some moderate-income, working families into the category of "near poor."

Applying the APM to 2009 data, 15.7 percent of all Americans were poor compared with 14.5 percent using the FPL formula. However, including government program support in the income calculation resulted in a decrease in the number of those living in extreme poverty. Other changes were that the number of rural poor dropped from 17 percent to 14 percent while the number of elderly living in poverty increased from 9.9 percent to 16.1 percent, in part due to higher medical expenses among this age group.[29]

The first official National Academy of Sciences APM was released in the fall of 2011 and is intended to be released yearly thereafter, in conjunction with, and in the same detail as the 2010 income and poverty statistics contained in the existing official poverty measure. However, it is not intended to replace the existing FPL.

It is possible that some poverty programs will adopt the APM as their official poverty guideline for allocating program resources. However, at this time Congress does not intend that the alternative, supplemental poverty measure entirely replace the formula currently in place. Critics of the APM take issue with pegging household expenses at 33 percent of all household spending, claiming that the formula measures inequality rather than poverty.

"Some [formulations] explain poverty as the outcomes of fixed demographic characteristics over which the individual has no control (race, gender, age, disability)—demographic characteristics that are the result of past, often constrained, choices (education, marital status, number of dependents, employment status, occupation) and exogenous area characteristics that define local economic opportunities (unemployment rate, job growth rate, industrial employment mix, occupational employment mix) and location of residence (rural or urban). Some studies also include variables intended to capture the effects of policy on poverty outcomes," explain Bruce Weber, Leif Jensen, Kathleen Miller, Jane Mosley and Monica Fisher.[30]

Food Insecurity

Food insecurity is a simple idea. A food insecure household sometimes doesn't have the financial resources to provide food for all of its members. It's a more common problem than you think. In 2010, nearly 50 million American households were listed as food insecure. As you can imagine, when you're worried about having enough money to buy food for your family, whether or not the food you do manage to buy is making you fat is probably not a top concern. Bad food is better than no food. —Morgan Clendaniel, Editor, CoEXIST

Because the classic model of poverty is based upon the assumption that an average family spends one third of its income on food, the United States Department of Agriculture (USDA) has determined that measuring food insecurity is an effective addition to attempts to ascertain the level of poverty a family or individual is living with regardless of income.[31] The term is defined in the context of limited or uncertain availability of nutritionally adequate and safe foods or limited or uncertain ability to acquire acceptable foods in socially acceptable ways.

Unlike the FPL or APM, which are based upon hard data, placement on the food security continuum is determined by the household's self-reported, subjective responses to a series of questions about behaviors and experiences associated with difficulty in meeting food needs. Some view food insecurity as a measure of hunger.

Households that reduce the quality, variety, and desirability of their diets, but the quantity of food intake and normal eating patterns are not substantially disrupted, are usually classified as having low food security. Households having very low food security are those in which, at times during the year, eating patterns of one or more household members were disrupted and food intake reduced because the household lacked money and other resources for food.

Households reporting three or more conditions that indicate food insecurity are classified as "food insecure." The three least severe conditions that would result in a household being classified as food insecure are worry over whether their food would run out before they had money to buy more; the food they bought didn't last, and they didn't have money to get more; or household members couldn't afford to eat balanced meals. To be classified as having "very low food security," households with no children present must report at least the three conditions listed above, in addition to indicating that adults ate less than they felt they should and cut the size of meals or skipped meals and did so in three or more months.

Table Three profiles the rural population, percent of total population that is classified as rural, poverty rates and food insecurity levels for the 12 Midwestern farm states. Nearly one third of the total population of the Midwestern states qualifies as rural, and in every state the per capita income is lower and the overall poverty rate is higher in the rural counties than in urban or suburban areas.[32]

Table Three: 2010 rural population, income, poverty, and food insecurity in 12 Midwestern States [33, 34]

State	Rural population/ percent of total population	Rural poverty rate	Rural child poverty rate	# Counties with poverty rates ≥20%	# Counties with poverty rates 13–19.9%	Percent of rural population reporting low food security	Percent of rural population reporting very low food security
IL	1,674,572 13%	14.5%	21%	5	35	13.3%	4.5%
IN	1,404,331 21.5%	14.7	21	1	22	13.2	5.4
IA	1,321,044 43%	12.5	15	1	16	12.0	4.7
KS	1,034,260 36%	14.9	18	1	30	14.5	5.2
MI	1,847,839 19%	17.0	22	2	43	14.2	5.6

State	Rural population/ percent of total population	Rural poverty rate	Rural child poverty rate	# Counties with poverty rates ≥20%	# Counties with poverty rates 13–19.9%	Percent of rural population reporting low food security	Percent of rural population reporting very low food security
MN	1,428,648 27%	12.4	14	0	9	10.2	4.3
MO	1,614,756 27%	18.8	25	23	64	16.0	6.7
NE	755,464 41%	12.5	14	1	18	13.3	4.9
ND	354,087 52%	12.9	17	3	10	7.8	3.1
OH	2,234,325 19%	16.1	20	7	30	15.5	6.4
SD	448,637 54%	17.2	21	12	19	12.7	5.3
WI	1,545,994 27%	13.1	15	1	6	13.1	4.7
Total/ Av. %	15,663,957 31.6%	14.7%	18.6%	57	302	13.0%	5.1%

None of the poverty measures used to assess rural poverty in the United States consider definitions of poverty that include variables other than those that can be quantified in monetary terms, and none attempt to get at the nuances of hardship and deprivation that a life of poverty entails. For the Midwestern rural poor, hardship level reveals the most about poverty, and hardship is a highly individualized, frequently changing variable that is extremely difficult to precisely determine and stabilize. Any discussion of rural poverty needs to bear this in mind.

2

Living off the Land

A Brief History of Rural Midwestern America

Farming's in your blood—no matter how bad things get, you keep on farming, because you can't not do it.—Jeanie Lewis, rural Wisconsin farm wife

Late on a Monday afternoon in the spring of 1986, during the week I would need a midterm examination typed and my largest research grant renewal application finished up, with 26 copies in the mail by Friday, my secretary requested the rest of the week off. Darlie lived on a 240-acre family farm 37 miles from campus, down the County Line Road. To make ends meet her husband long distance trucked and she worked in the secretarial pool at the university where I was a research professor. A normal day for her was getting up at 4 A.M., doing chores, getting the kids to the school bus, and being in the office by 8. She didn't take a lunch hour so she could leave early to get back home in time to complete the nightly chores the kids had already started after they returned from school, and have dinner on the table by 6:30. In the winter she worried about the kids working outside after dark, and she wanted to be sure she was the one to finish up in the barn.

I asked Darlie why she hadn't mentioned wanting the week off sooner so I could've planned better. She explained that until yesterday the weather forecast was "iffy" but now it looked like the front wasn't coming this far north so it was going to be a good week to plant after all. "I want to get the corn in by the time my husband gets back on the weekend," she explained, adding that he'd been on the road ten days.

"You'll be planting at around $2.83 a bushel and will be lucky to get $2.40 by fall. Coming up that short, you'd be better off not planting at all," I said. "I know," she answered quietly, "but Jim's dad has been planting our land every spring for over sixty years, through good and bad. When he turned the farm over to us, he made us promise to do the same; it'll kill the old man if we don't."

Darlie took the time off and I forgot about the extra work her need to plant that particular week caused me, but I never forgot our conversation. "Every farmer's a gambler," she told me later. That explanation of why, for most farmers, deciding whether or not to plant is never a decision at all was the first time I really understood that farmers are next year people. They always believe that if things go bad this year, they'll surely get better next year. This is how hard farming really is.

Go West Young Man—A Brief History of Rural America's Early Days

> *It is America's right to stretch from sea to shining sea. Not only do we have a responsibility to our citizens to gain valuable natural resources, we also have a responsibility to civilize this beautiful land.*—Congressman Robert Winthrop (Whig, MA)

The notion of stretching from sea to shining sea was fueled by a powerful belief in Manifest Destiny, the notion that a young United States of America was divinely ordained to expand across the continent.[1] With its religious overtones, the Manifest Destiny concept gave rise to the notion that the new nation had a future destined by God, and this destiny included unlimited expansion of its borders. It was an old idea.

The mistaken belief that it was God's will that America encompass the entire continent, and then willfully control and populate the country as they wished, fueled a sense of entitlement that resulted in a massive, prolonged land-grab. Conceiving of God as having the power to sustain and guide human destiny, expansionists convinced themselves they were being divinely led toward a utopian future. "It was white man's burden to conquer and Christianize the land," explains historian Stephen Demkin.[2] Believing in divine guidance and the call to build a City of God has justified much of American expansionism, at all costs, throughout much of the nation's history up to the present day.

While some expansion enthusiasts were driven by what they considered God's will; others saw Manifest Destiny as the historical inevitability of American dominion over all the open land between the Atlantic and Pacific oceans. Because the idea of exploring new territory was a romantic and exciting one, there wasn't much holding anyone back from embarking on such an intriguing adventure.

Either way, a Manifest Destiny philosophy would allow America to grow into a bigger, stronger nation, thus reviving interest in territorial expansion. Missionary zeal drove many politicians and government officials toward the irresistible temptations arising from seemingly boundless, sparsely settled land lying just beyond the nation's existing borders. Economic interests, driven by a growing desire to develop trade with the Far East, prompted the drive westward and brought with it exciting visions of opening new trade routes.

Intensifying expansion fever renewed fears that foreign intervention along its borders could impair the security of the United States. The easiest way to quiet these fears was to conquer land beyond the borders and expand American territories. As a result, going to war to get what it wanted became an enduring and forceful American policy. Influential newspaper editor John L. O'Sullivan, in an attempt to explain America's thirst for expansion and to present a defense for America's claim to new territories, wrote:

> the right of our manifest destiny to over spread and to possess the whole of the continent which Providence has given us for the development of the great experiment of liberty and federative development of self government entrusted to us. It is right such as that of the tree to the space of air and the earth suitable for the full expansion of its principle and destiny of growth.[3]

But Manifest Destiny had a dark side, and the resulting damage it brought about inflicted profound historical trauma on the American Indian population occupying the land those believing they were sent by God wanted to conquer and possess. Driven by what was perceived as their God-given right, white men felt justified in destroying anyone, and anything, that dared interfere with the national goal of claiming, protecting and developing western lands. The wide path believers in Manifest Destiny cut as they pushed westward draws a profoundly ugly picture of mass destruction of Indian tribal organizations, stolen land, Indian confinement to reservations, and genocide.

The ugly underside of Manifest Destiny was the white man's belief that his settling the land and destroying the civilization of the native people was preordained—and entitled. The arrogance that flowed, and continues to flow, from the Manifest Destiny philosophy was exemplified when American Imperialist Senator Albert T. Beveridge rose before the U.S. Senate to announce:

> God has not been preparing the English-speaking and Tectonic peoples for a thousand years for nothing but vain and idle self-admiration. No! He has made us the master organizers of the world to establish system where chaos reigns.... He has made us adepts in government that we may administer government among savages and senile peoples. Theodore Roosevelt, John Cabot Lodge, and John Hay, each in turn, endorsed with a strong sense of certainty the view that the Anglo-Saxon [Americans] was destined to rule the world. Such views expressed in the 19th century and in the early 20th century continue to ring true in the minds of many non–Indian property owners. The superiority of the "white race" is the foundation on which the Anti-Indian Movement organizers and right-wing helpers rest their efforts to dismember Indian tribes.[4, 5]

The settlements that extended across the Western territories promised that the American dream of freedom and independence that naturally arises from a seemingly limitless land would be realized. This, coupled with an agrarian spirit and unquestioning belief in Manifest Destiny, produced an attitude that nothing was going to stand in the way of progress. In the name of this doctrine, Americans believed they had the right, thus claimed the power to take whatever land they wanted and use it for their own benefit.

It is against this backdrop that the Western Frontier advanced. Journalist Horace Greeley, who favored the Manifest Destiny philosophy, and saw the fertile farmland of the West as an ideal place for people willing to work hard for the opportunity to succeed, wrote an editorial encouraging Civil War veterans to take advantage of the Homestead Act and colonize the public lands west of the Mississippi River. "Washington is not a place to live in," Greeley wrote in 1865. "The rents are high, the food is bad, the dust is disgusting and the morals are deplorable. Go West, young man, go West and grow up with the country." Many followed Greeley's advice, and soon after the first chapter in the long history of rural poverty was written.

The Louisiana Purchase

> *They will steal anything, and call it purchase.*—William Shakespeare, *Henry V*, Act 3, Sc. 2

Manifest Destiny's popularity enabled the rationale for the Louisiana Purchase, justified the war with Mexico, and was used to convince Congress to acquire all the land the nation could lay its hands on, beginning well before westward expansion opened the door to agricultural development. While conquering the west was viewed as the obvious solution to many of the nation's growing problems of poverty and unemployment characteristic of the big Eastern cities, it was during Thomas Jefferson's presidency that interest in expanding the young nation increased dramatically.

Jefferson sent James Monroe to France to help Robert R. Livingston complete the negotiations for the acquisition of New Orleans and West Florida. Instead, the French emperor, Napoleon I, offered to sell the entire Louisiana colony. Monroe was a clever and skilled negotiator and on April 30, 1803, the United States agreed to pay France $11.25 million plus cancel $3.75 million in debts, for 828,000 square miles of land west of the Mississippi River known as the Louisiana Territory. The final cost after the 6 percent interest payments to France was approximately $23.5 million dollars for 529,920,000 acres of land (four cents per acre), and remains as the greatest real estate deal in American history.[6]

Hearing of this, retired Revolutionary War General Horatio Gates wrote to President Jefferson on July 18, 1803, "Let the land rejoice, for you have bought Louisiana for a song."

The acquired land stretched from the Mississippi River to the Rocky Mountains (including Denver) and from the Gulf of Mexico to the Canadian border, nearly doubling the size of the United States and making it one of the largest nations in the world. Eventually thirteen states and parts of two Canadian provinces were carved from the Louisiana Territory.[7] The government had more land than it knew what to do with, and without much forethought, it opened the door to active exploration and settlement of the west. To facilitate frontier growth, the federal government began systematically displacing the indigenous Native American populations and taking possession of vast amounts of land stretching for thousands of miles between the Mississippi River and the Pacific Ocean.

The economic development policy driving this massive land acquisition was based upon a "do it because we can do it" attitude that had little regard for either the land itself or those who were already living on it. Instead it was about becoming bigger and better than everyone else.

Eventually the government had to make some formal decisions about what to do with its large, unoccupied land holdings. Politically, selling public land was viewed as a means to generate revenue for the government rather than as a way to encourage settlement. However, an individual was required to purchase a full section of land at the cost of $1 per acre for 640 acres (one square mile.) The investment needed to purchase these large plots and the massive amount of physical labor required to clear the land for agriculture were often insurmountable obstacles, so few attempted it.

By 1800, the minimum lot was halved to 320 acres, and settlers were allowed to pay in 4 installments, but prices remained fixed at $1.25 an acre until 1854. That year, federal legislation was enacted establishing a graduated scale that adjusted land prices to reflect the desirability of the plot. Plots that had been on the market for 30 years, for example, were reduced to 12½ cents per acre. Soon after, extraordinary bonuses were extended to veterans and those interested in settling the Oregon Territory, making homesteading a viable option for some.

Nevertheless, national public-land-use policy still made land ownership financially unattainable for most would-be homesteaders. Those who survived the trip westward found themselves far from home, unable to afford the land they hoped would provide their new livelihood, and unable to return. They survived as best they could, but their dreams of prosperity were shattered. Eventually pressure to change land policy arose from the evolving national economy, new demographics, and the shifting social climate of 19th-century America.

Prior to the war with Mexico (1846–48), people settling in the West demanded "preemption," an individual's right to settle land first and pay later (an early form of credit). Eastern economic interests opposed this policy because of fears that the cheap labor base (which encompassed the current poverty class) available for factory work would be severely diminished. And, during the 1830s and 1840s, rising prices for corn, wheat, and cotton enabled large, well-financed farms, particularly the plantations of the South, to force out smaller ventures, a situation not unlike what is occurring today as corporate farming pushes out family farms. Displaced farmers began looking westward toward unforested country that offered what they believed was an opportunity for more affordable development.

The Homestead Act Legislation

> *An allusion has been made to the Homestead Law. I think it worthy of consideration, and that the wild lands of the country should be distributed so that every man should have the means and opportunity of benefitting his condition.*—President Abraham Lincoln

After the 1846–48 war with Mexico ended, a number of political developments came together to support the growth of the homestead movement. Economic prosperity drew unprecedented numbers of immigrants to America, many of whom also looked westward to begin a new life. Homesteading opportunities launched a massive westward migration, populating the nation with Scandinavian, German, Irish and other immigrants of northern European origin seeking the chance to own land and find prosperity. New canals and roadways enhanced transport options, reducing western dependence on the New Orleans harbor, and the repeal of England's corn laws[8] opened new markets to American agriculture.

Despite these developments, legislative efforts to improve homesteading laws faced opposition on multiple fronts. Northern factory owners feared a mass departure of their cheap labor force and Southern states worried that rapid settlement of western territories would give rise to new states populated by small farmers opposed to slavery. Preemption[9] became national policy in spite of these regional concerns, but supporting legislation was stymied. Three times—in 1852, 1854, and 1859—the House of Representatives passed homestead legislation, but on each occasion, the Senate defeated the measure. In 1860, Congress finally passed a homestead bill providing Federal land grants to western settlers, but President James Buchanan refused to sign it.

As Southern states seceded from the Union, thus eliminating the slavery issue from the legislative debate, the Homestead Act finally passed.[10] President Abraham Lincoln signed it into law on May 20, 1862, and in so doing, opened the door to the largest free-enterprise initiative in American history. No government program before or since has ever afforded a opportunity of this magnitude to American citizens on their own soil, and with almost no strings attached.

The new land ownership policy provided an applicant, at no cost, ownership of a plot of undeveloped federal land, typically 160 acres, anywhere west of the Mississippi River. The new law flowed from an expression of the free soil policy favored by northern legislators who wanted individual farmers, rather than slave owners, to own and operate their own farms. The legislation established a three-fold homestead acquisition process: filing an application, improving the land, and filing for deed of title. Any U.S. citizen, or intended citizen who had never borne arms against the U.S. government, could file an application to lay claim to 160 acres (one quarter square mile) of surveyed U.S. government land.

A homesteader was required to be the head of the household or at least 21 years old. After filing a claim, the homesteader had to live on the land for the next five years, working to improve it by building a "twelve-by-fourteen" dwelling and growing crops. After five years, the homesteader could "prove up" by filing for his deed of title, which involved submitting proof of both residency and of having completed the required improvements, to a local land office. Local land offices forwarded the paperwork to the General Land Office in Washington, D.C., along with a final certificate of eligibility. Valid claims were granted deeds to the land free and clear, after paying a small registration fee.

Land title could also be acquired after a six-month residency and trivial improvements, provided the claimant paid the government $1.25 per acre, or $200 per 160-acre quarter section. After the Civil War, Union soldiers were allowed to deduct the time they served in the Union Army from the land acquisition residency requirements.

Immigrants, farmers without their own land, single women and former slaves also could qualify, as long as they could pay the 18 dollar filing fee. And while having the money to live and to finance building a home and proving up the land was often problematic, it was still an opportunity bulging with possibility for those willing to try it.

Not surprisingly, some land speculators took advantage of a legislative loophole caused when the law's language failed to specify whether the "twelve-by-fourteen" dwelling was to be built in feet or inches. Others hired phony claimants or bought abandoned land. The General Land Office was underfunded and unable to hire a sufficient number of investigators for its widely scattered local offices, and overworked, underpaid investigators were often susceptible to bribery.

Despite the ease with which vast amounts of land could be acquired, the realities of life on the frontier presented tremendous challenges for the men and women who dared risk it. Unresolved problems with the Native population, who resented being displaced from land that had been theirs for their entire history, persisted, and bloody conflicts between the Indians and the settlers were common. Never-ending wind, blizzards, and plagues of insects threatened crops. There were few trees to provide wood for solid structures, forcing many to build homes from sod. Limited fuel and water supplies rendered cooking and heating extremely difficult. Almost to a person, the settlers were poor in the extreme, but their commitment to forge a new life, coupled with remarkable ingenuity, kept them going anyway.

Diaries of the early pioneer women reveal a relentless determination and tenacity that helped them to survive loneliness, prairie fires, locusts, cowboy shootouts, Indian raids, blizzards and difficult domestic lives. In 1899, following a miscarriage she endured alone, Kansas homesteader Martha Farnsworth writes:

> Home and not feeling at all well. Johnny I know loves me dearly but every little thing offends him and it seems like I so often offend, tho' always without knowing it. I've already shed many bitter tears ... a most unhappy girl. I am not a bit well and can't bear

to have him so cross at me; it is enough to tear the heart right out of a person, for I love him and it is dreadful to be treated so by one, who should treat you the best.

A few days later, after having prepared a warm meal for her husband and awaited his return for several hours, she writes again:

> I was happy that I had our little home so cheerful and waiting patiently for his coming, but one, two hours passed—and I began to cry with uneasiness as the presentment came into my heart that all was not right—and the hours dragged by till he was more than four hours late, when at last I heard his welcome step, but when the door opened and I went to give him my welcoming kiss he staggered into the room drunk. Oh! God have mercy on my wretched, miserable life. Oh! The disgrace and shame of having my dear, dear Boy come home in such a condition. Only a bride yet and this so soon. Oh! what is my life to be. How could my boy do so. Oh! dear God take me from this world before I ever see my boy drunk again. Oh! What a time I had with him.[11]

Life on the frontier was difficult in other ways. S. N. Hoisington, also writing from the Kansas frontier in 1872, describes the fate of one homesteader:

> A man by the name of Johnson had filed on a claim just west of us and had build a sod house. He and his wife lived there two years, when he went to Salina to secure work. He was gone two or three months and wrote home once or twice, but his wife grew very homesick for her folks in the east and would come over to our house to visit mother.
> Mother tried to cheer her up but she continued to worry until she got bed fast with the fever. At night she was frightened because the wolves would scratch at the door, on the sod and on the windows. So my mother and I started to sit up nights with her. I would bring my revolver and ammunition and axe, and some good-sized clubs.
> The odor of the sick woman seemed to attract the wolves and they grew bolder and bolder. I would step out, fire off the revolver and they would settle back for a while when they would start a new attack. I shot one through the window and found him lying dead in the morning.
> Finally the woman died and mother laid her out. Father took some wide boards that we had in our loft and made a coffin for her. Mother made a pillow and trimmed it with black cloth, and we also painted the coffin black.
> After that the wolves were more determined than ever to get in. One got his head between the door casing and as he was trying to wriggle through mother struck him in the head with an axe and killed him. I shot one coming through the window. After that they quieted down for about half an hour, when they came back again. I stepped out and fired at two of them but I only wounded one. Their howling was awful. We fought these wolves five nights in succession, during which time we killed four grey wolves and two coyotes. When Mr. Johnson arrived home and found his wife dead and his house badly torn down by wolves he fainted away.... After the funeral he sold out and moved away.[12]

While not all homesteaders were men and not all women homesteaders were married, all possessed a profound courage and faith in themselves unimaginable in the technology-driven 21st century. Their desire to own land was so strong these settlers left families behind, not knowing if they would ever see them again, and traveled westward into an unknown place and unpredictably harsh life for which they had no prior experience or preparation.

A woman who wanted to farm was generally advised to marry a farmer, and men interested in homesteading were keenly aware of the need for a good, strong wife who could labor beside him in the fields, cook and keep house, bear and raise their children without assistance, nurse him through the effects of accidents, snake bites, drunken brawls and other unfortunate mishaps, and work to build frontier communities necessary to sustaining a livelihood far away from the nearest town.[13] These circumstances, where a woman's contributions and cooperation with her husband was necessary in order for a man to succeed, gave women great social power on the advancing western frontier, pushing them closer to an equal partnership with their husbands than any other life would have afforded them. This same partnership between a farmer and his wife still exists in the rural Midwest today.

Despite the great temptation to romanticize the pioneer spirit, day by day life on the frontier was very much harder than most women ever anticipated when they left home and family ties to embark upon a westward adventure. Pulitzer Prize winning Nebraska writer Willa Cather writes realistically of pioneer life in several of her books, frequently extolling the strengths and successes of frontier women. *My Antonia*, published in 1918, vividly portrays the story of a pioneer woman whose strengths and passions are memorably rendered, and is widely recognized as one of Cather's finest novels.[14]

Similarly, *O Pioneers*, tells a compelling story of a Nebraska frontier woman whose farming abilities and success surpass her brothers.[15] Published in 1913, Cather persistently contended that the land is the hero of *O Pioneers*!—making it fundamentally a story of the wild becoming civilized. Each character in the story attempts to make their land livable and each can be judged based on an ability to work with the land rather than against it. Alexandra explains that "the land belongs to the future, Carl; that's the way it seems to me. How many of the names on the county clerk's plat will be there in fifty years? I might as well try to will the sunset over there to my brother's children. We come and go, but the land is always here. And the people who love it and understand it are the people who own it—for a little while."

As time wore on, it became evident that the smaller section size, which enabled more land to be purchased, took its own toll. While 160 acres may have been sufficient for an eastern farmer, it was not enough to sustain agriculture on the wide open, dry land of the Great Plains, and scarce natural vegetation made raising livestock on both the plains and the prairie difficult. As a result, in many areas, the original homesteader did not stay on the land long enough to "prove up" and claim ownership.

The Transcontinental Railroad

> *The one moral, the one remedy for every evil, social, political, financial, and industrial, the one immediate vital need of the entire Republic, is the Pacific Railroad.*—Rocky Mountain News, 1866

Six months after the first Homestead Act was passed, the Railroad Act was signed and the railroad companies were given taxpayer-funded government bonds and enormous tracts of land with which to build. They hired lobbyists to encourage the politicians in Washington to keep the subsidies flowing by exchanging stocks for votes. Since the government was funding construction, the companies were in no hurry to link their lines; in the first two and a half years of work, the Union Pacific line was still only 40 miles outside Omaha, Nebraska, giving rise to calls for more workers to speed up the construction process.

In May 1866, after General Greenville Dodge, a hero of the Union Army, took control as chief engineer, the United Pacific finally began to move westward. Native Americans, including members of the Sioux, Arapaho and Cheyenne tribes, understandably threatened by the white man's prograss in driving an "iron horse" across their lands, launched bloody attacks on the railroad workers. Still, the Union Pacific moved relatively quickly across the plains, compared to the slow progress of its rival company through the Sierra Nevada Mountains. Ramshackle settlements popped up wherever the railroad went, turning into environments where drinking, gambling, prostitution and violence flourished, eventually creating the enduring mythology surrounding the "Wild West."

In 1865, after struggling with retaining workers and under pressure to complete the Central Pacific railroad line, construction chief Charles Crocker began hiring Chinese laborers from among the more than 50,000 Chinese immigrants who were living on the West Coast, many having arrived during the California Gold Rush. This was a controversial hiring practice because the Chinese were considered an inferior race. Crocker's justification to his critics was "They built the Great Wall of China, didn't they?" The Chinese laborers proved to be tireless workers, so Crocker hired more of them. By 1867 more than 14,000 Chinese had become America's newest slaves, toiling under brutal working conditions as they attempted to cross the rugged Sierra Nevada mountain range.

Eventually the new railroad connected existing rail lines in the east with rail lines up and down the Pacific Coast, making most of the continent much more accessible. The railroad provided homesteaders a welcome and convenient means for transportation when previously they had traveled west by covered wagon, mule, or horse. The trains brought mail from "back home" to the settlers much more frequently and reliably than the Pony Express, helping to encourage further westward migration.

New immigrants were also lured westward by railroad companies eager to sell off excess land at inflated prices. The new rail lines provided ready access to manufactured goods, and catalog houses like Montgomery Ward offered farm tools, barbed wire, linens, weapons, and even houses delivered via the rails. The railroad also made it possible for farmers to transport larger quantities of wheat, corn and livestock to market, where the sales prices were higher. Over time rapid changes in transportation eased the hardships homesteaders faced, and those who persevered were rewarded with lucrative new economic opportunities.

The Pacific Railroad constituted one of the most significant and ambitious American technological feats of the 19th century, following in the footsteps of the Erie Canal in the 1820s and the Panama Railroad successfully crossing the Isthmus of Panama in 1855. The transcontinental line served as North America's vital link for trade, commerce and travel that joined the eastern and western halves of the late 19th-century United States. It cemented the ambitious nation's belief in Manifest Destiny and the "divine right" of its people to ride the great iron horse toward economic expansion coast-to-coast, at any cost.

The railroad also established the nation's future economic infrastructure by eliminating far slower and more hazardous stagecoach lines and wagon trains. The developing steam engine provided the technology for much faster, safer and cheaper transportation of emigrants who had previously traveled around the horn to get to the Pacific Coast and commercial goods. The railroads, bankers and the U.S. government in the East promoted a worldwide migration to the United States to enhance agricultural progress by the sale of land-grant lots and then provided farmers with the needed transportation for their crops, minerals and timber.

The railroad united the country in ways nothing else had ever done. Railroads served the North in its Civil War efforts, paved the way for faster Western expansion, and built the fortunes of influential men. And it was the largest government-subsidized economic development initiative of the 19th century, thus setting the stage for various forms of government subsidies to emerge in the future.

Inland Waterways

> ... you'll always know your neighbor and you'll always know your pal if you've ever navigated on the Erie Canal.—Low Bridge

The opening of the Erie Canal in 1825 completed an all-water shipping route across the Great Lakes linking the Midwest to the seaport of New York City. For the first time Midwest agricultural products could be shipped more places, more directly than transporting them on the Mississippi and Ohio Rivers. In 1848, the Illinois and Michigan Canal breached the continental divide spanning the Chicago Portage and linking the waters of the Great Lakes with those of the Mississippi Valley and the Gulf of Mexico. The Saint Lawrence Seaway (opened in 1862, widened in 1959) linked the Midwest to the Atlantic Ocean.

Inland canals in Ohio and Indiana constituted another important waterway system, which connected with Great Lakes and Ohio River traffic. The commodities the Midwest funneled into the Erie Canal down the Ohio River allowed New York City to overtake both Boston and Philadelphia as the largest center of commerce on the eastern seaboard, opening new markets for Midwestern agriculture and manufacturing.

This Land Is My Land—Western Expansion and America's Indigenous People

> I wish it to be remembered that I was the last man of my tribe to surrender my rifle.—Lakota Chief Sitting Bull

As white settlers pushed westward, repeatedly driving the indigenous people from lands they had lived on since their beginnings, clashes between Native American tribes resisting this invasion and settlers intent upon claiming the land as their own were inevitable. Settlers believed it was their God-given right to claim Indian land, and the government agreed—and neither gave any thought to the consequences.

"The more we can kill this year the less will have to be killed the next year, for the more I see of these Indians the more convinced I am that they all have to be killed or be maintained as a species of paupers," declared General William Tecumseh Sherman, referring to the Plains Indians.[16] In 1864, Union troops killed several hundred Indian women and children at the Sand Creek Massacre in Colorado. The U.S. Army also fought the Sioux Wars in the Black Hills of the Dakota Territory during the 1860s and 1870s. In 1876, General George Armstrong Custer made his infamous last stand during the Battle of Little Bighorn. All 264 of Custer's troops fell at the hands of Chief Sitting Bull and his warriors in a battle that epitomized the intensity with which the native population resisted invasion by white settlers.

Public outrage over the military catastrophe at Little Bighorn brought thousands more cavalrymen to the area. Over the next year they relentlessly pursued the Lakota, who had split up after the Custer fight. These splits forced chief after chief to surrender, but Sitting Bull remained defiant. In May 1877 he led his band across the border into Canada, beyond the reach of the U.S. Army, and when General Alfred Terry traveled north to offer him a pardon in exchange for settling on a reservation, Sitting Bull angrily sent him away.

Four years later, after finding it impossible to feed his people in a world where the buffalo was almost extinct, Sitting Bull finally surrendered. On July 19, 1881, he had his young son hand his rifle to the commanding officer of Fort Buford in Montana, explaining that in this way he hoped to teach the boy "that he has to become a friend of the Americans."

Sitting Bull requested a reservation of his own on the Little Missouri River near the Black Hills and the right to cross back and forth into Canada whenever he wished. He was denied both; instead he was sent to Standing Rock Reservation, where his reception provoked fears that he might inspire a fresh uprising. Consequently, the Lakota tribal chief and his followers were sent further down the Missouri River to Fort Randall, where they were held for nearly two years as prisoners of war.

Finally, on May 10, 1883, Sitting Bull rejoined his tribe at Standing Rock. The Indian agent in charge of the reservation, James McLaughlin, was determined to deny the great chief any special privileges and forced him to work in the fields. Unfazed, Sitting Bull knew his own authority, and when a delegation of U.S. senators came to discuss opening part of the reservation to white settlers, he spoke forcefully, though futilely, against their plan.

Meanwhile, the U.S. Army fought the Nez Percé in the Pacific Northwest after the Tribe's leader, Chief Joseph, refused to relinquish the Nez Percé's lands to white settlers. The Nez Percé were eventually defeated and resettled to Kansas. In the New Mexico Territory, the Apache Tribe, led by Geronimo, fought bravely but failed to protect their homelands and were eventually relocated to the Oklahoma Territory and rural areas of the Southern United States.

Meanwhile, back in Washington it had become clear the U.S. government had to "do something about the Indian problem."

The Dawes Act

> *The Dawes Act was a way to break up the whole tribal structure of Native American nations. Instead of saying you are a group of people, all of a sudden you are individual landowners, you are Americans. And so it was designed to break up community, to civilize people, make us farmers, and also break up our tribal structure.* —Charlotte Black Elk

On February 8, 1887, a few months short of twenty-five years after the original Homestead Act legislation was enacted, Congress passed the Dawes Act,[17] authored by Senator Henry Dawes of Massachusetts. A strong believer in the power of owning private property, Dawes claimed that to be civilized was to "wear civilized clothes ... cultivate the ground, live in houses, ride in Studebaker wagons, send children to school, drink whiskey [and] own property," the implication being that anyone who did not do these things was an uncivilized savage—an unfortunate description many felt fit the Indian population perfectly.

Also known as the General Allotment Act, the Dawes legislation granted the president of the United States staggering power to further weaken the tribal nations by breaking up reservation land, currently held as common land by tribal members, into small allotments to be parceled out to individuals. Native Americans registering on a tribal roll were allotted small parcels of reservation land. "To each head of a family, one-quarter of a section; to each single person over eighteen years of age, one-eighth of a section; to each orphan child under eighteen years of age, one-eighth of a section; and to each other single person under eighteen years now living, or who may be born prior to the date of the order of the President directing an allotment of the lands embraced in any reservation, one-sixteenth of a section...."[18]

Most of the land allotted to the Indians under this new policy included desert or near-desert lands unsuitable for farming. Additionally, the techniques of self-sufficient farming were much different from their tribal way of life. Many Indians did not want to take up agriculture, and those who did want to farm could not afford the tools, animals, seed, and other supplies necessary to get started. There were also problems with inheritance. Often young children inherited allotments that they could not farm because they had been sent away to boarding schools. And when several people inherited an allotment, the size of the holdings became too small for efficient farming.

Despite this legislative effort the native Indian population continued fiercely resisting removal from their native lands. Hundreds of Native Americans died at the Battle of Wounded Knee in 1890, during the army's attempt to end the Ghost Dance Movement—a Native American movement that challenged white dominance in society and called for a return to the traditional native culture and ways of life.

Finally, in 1893 President Grover Cleveland appointed the Dawes Commission to negotiate with the Cherokees, Creeks, Choctaws, Chickasaws, and Seminoles, who were known as the Five Civilized Tribes. As a result several laws were passed that allotted a share of common property to members of the Five Civilized Tribes in exchange for abolishing their tribal governments and recognizing state and federal laws. In order to receive the allotted land, members were to enroll with the Bureau of Indian Affairs (BIA). Once enrolled, the individual's name went on the "Dawes rolls."

Over a 30-year period federal policy toward the Native Indian population shifted from war, treaties and reservations to breaking up reservations into individual land allotments. Sincere, well-meaning individuals reasoned that if an Indian adopted white clothing and ways, he would gradually drop his "Indian-ness" and be assimilated into the white population that was invading his world. It would then no longer be necessary for the government to oversee Indian welfare in the paternalistic way it had been obligated to do, or to provide the meager annuities that were keeping Indians in poverty and in a subservient social position. In other words, the more the Native Indian people became like their invading oppressors, the better off they would be.

The purpose of the Dawes Act and the subsequent acts that extended its initial provisions was purportedly to protect Indian property rights, particularly during the land rushes of the 1890s, but in many instances the results of enforcing this legislation were vastly different. In reality the U.S. government, in order to make room for increasing numbers of white settlers, set about herding defeated Native American populations onto reservations located on the poorest land in the Dakotas, New Mexico, and Oklahoma.

The land allotment policies enabled by the Dawes Act were revised many times during the legislation's forty-seven-year history, but displacing the Indian population continued. Prior to 1887, when the Dawes Act was legislated, Indians held over 150 million acres of land. When the law was finally repealed in 1934, Indian land had shrunk by two-thirds, to 48 million acres, rendering nearly three quarters of the Indian population either entirely without land or without enough land to sustain them.

The Dawes Act represents a massive failure of U.S. domestic policy that stripped Native tribes of their land and livelihood, and sentenced them to perpetual victimhood. As a result of America's unwavering belief in Manifest Destiny, coupled with the growing capitalist hunger for westward expansion (and legislation to support it) Native Americans, through no fault of their own, were sentenced to a future they had no say in configuring, on land that could not sustain them. The law did nothing to help Indians find new means to sustain their culture or way of life, thereby creating the most enduring and devastating poverty that currently exists in 21st-century America.

National Indian Defense Association

All the Indians pray to God for life, and try to find a good road, and do nothing wrong in their life. This is what we want to pray to God. But you did not believe us.—Chief Sitting Bull

The political argument for Indian land allotment articulated by the white leaders supporting the Dawes Act reflected a firm conviction that economic expansion, and all that comes with it, was vital to strengthening the seams holding the nation's social fabric together. However, not everyone agreed that displacing Native Americans off their land for purposes of furthering profit-motive, capitalist-driven economic development was a good idea.

Quaker populist Thomas Bland led a coalition of both whites and Indians to form the National Indian Defense Association and organize opposition to the Dawes Act Land Allotment Policy. "The desire to become rich has become a mania, a species of insanity, which is both epidemic and contagious," Bland wrote in fierce opposition to the notion of displacing small town rural networks of local farmers who assisted one another in a myriad of ways.[19] Bland, prophetically, feared the effects of big business and finance being allowed to penetrate a young, developing agrarian society, and relentlessly attacked what he believed were "corrosive effects" of unrestrained land acquisition, particularly by whites who obtained this land by displacing the native inhabitants—an act Bland considered profoundly immoral, because the Indians had no say in it.[20]

"The tacit admission, or rather the positive statement that 'No power on earth can keep the whites from dispossessing the Indians' is the opinion, alone, of the foes of justice," Bland wrote. "It is the last argument of those who favor extermination of the Indians…. It is true that the Indians are, in most cases, surrounded by selfish, grasping, and vicious whites … it is not true that this government cannot protect them in their rights, if it will."[21]

Mainstream American political thought of the day supported Bland's agrarian view of the importance of private property and a strong work ethic, but not enough to guarantee the success of the National Indian Defense Association. Although Bland was unsuccessful in stopping the land allotment legislation, the ideology he represented ultimately became the basis for the enduring opposition to corporate capitalism's invasion of rural America which is still expressed today, and which is largely responsible for impoverishing family farmers.

The Morrill Act—The First Federal Aid to Higher Education

Poverty must not be a bar to learning and learning must offer an escape from poverty.—President Lyndon Johnson

Most homesteaders brought little or no knowledge of farming with them when they set out to claim and then live off the land. Few had any formal education or understanding of the curvature of their homestead land, the composition of the soil, the effects of weeks of sub-zero temperatures and blinding blizzards in winter, floods and ravaging tornadoes in spring, droughts and crop-eating insects in summer, timing the fall harvest season, or the insidious effects of wind blowing without cease, all the time. If homesteaders were going to succeed at farming, they needed some means of obtaining information about how to farm under the conditions they found themselves in. Without this, the homesteaders lack the necessary tools for success.

While there is no evidence that the federal government was aware that many homesteaders had no knowledge of farming, the 1862 Morrill Act,[22] sponsored by Senator Justin Morrill of Vermont, ultimately proved to be vital to successful farming. The legislation laid the foundation for a national system of state colleges and universities, eventually known as land-grant schools, focused on agriculture, mechanics and domestic sciences (home economics) as the centerpieces of their curriculums.

Beginning in 1887, Congress also funded agricultural experiment stations and various categories of agricultural and veterinary research under the direction of the land-grant universities. Today these research centers conduct scientific investigations to solve problems and suggest improvements in the food and agriculture industry. Experiment station scientists work closely with farmers, ranchers, suppliers, processors, and others involved in food production and agriculture.

The Morrill legislation also set forth the means for establishing a system of public schools on the Great Plains.[23] That this legislation occurred shortly after the Homestead Act is probably coincidence rather than intentionally, carefully thought-through government planning.

However, the government did adhere to a philosophy that "knowledge is necessary to good government" and as public lands were surveyed into six-mile square townships, a one-square-mile section in each township was reserved for the support of public schools. The land itself was rarely used for school construction but rather was sold off, with proceeds used to fund the school program. The system invited misuse by opportunists, and substantial portions of the educational land-grants never benefited education. Nevertheless, land-grant support became vital to providing education to most American children who could never hope to attend private or charity-supported schools.

Sometime later Congress recognized the need to disseminate the knowledge gained at the land-grant colleges to farmers and homemakers. The Smith-Lever Act of 1914 started federal funding for a cooperative extension service, sending the land-grant universities' experts into every county of every state, bringing with them the latest research-based information about farming and rural living. However, in 1972, when the cooperative extension services embraced U.S. Agriculture Secretary Earl Butz's get-big-or-get-out philosophy, and encouraged farmers to buy more land when borrowing money was easy, thousands of farmers received very bad advice that ultimately cost them their livelihoods.

State colleges brought higher education in all forms, and across all subject matter areas, within the reach of millions of students, and taken together, the Morrill and Smith-Lever legislation reshaped the nation's social and economic fabric, particularly in rural areas. Without these institutions of higher education, poverty in rural America would be unimaginably worse than it is.

The Frontier Thesis

> *The existence of an area of free land, its continuous recession, and the advance of American settlement, explain American development.* —Frederick Jackson Turner

In 1893 historian Frederick Jackson Turner advanced the argument that the origin of the distinctive egalitarian, democratic, aggressive, and innovative features of the American character was deeply rooted in the American frontier experience. He stressed the significance of the settlement experience in moving the frontier line ever forward, noting the profound effect this had on pioneers leaving home to proceed westward into unknown territory and an unfamiliar, unpredictable life. According to Turner, by releasing Americans from European mindsets and ending prior customs of the 19th century, the advancing frontier established a new level of personal freedom. Turner elaborated on the theme in his advanced history lectures and in a series of essays published over the next 25 years.[24]

Others, including Theodore Roosevelt, who argued that the battles between the trans–Appalachian pioneers and the Indians had won the west and forged a "new American race," began embracing Turner's ideas and exploring the meaning of the frontier.[25] Roosevelt's emphasis on the importance of the frontier in shaping American character influenced the interpretation found in thousands of scholarly histories of the west and his model of sectionalism as a composite of social forces, such as ethnicity and land ownership, gave historians the tools to use social history as the foundation for nearly all social, economic and political developments in American history.

After the West Was Won

> *Whether the whites won the land by treaty, by armed conquest, or, as was actually the case, by a mixture of both, mattered comparatively little so long as the land was won. It was all-important that it should be won, for the benefit of civilization and in the interests of mankind.* —President Theodore Roosevelt

By 1900 much of the prime low-lying alluvial land[26] along rivers had been homesteaded, prompting an update to the original homestead legislation. The Enlarged Homestead Act was passed in 1909 to enable dryland farming,[27] thus increasing the number of homesteads to 320. Farmers began accepting more marginal land, particularly in the Southern Great Plains, because it could be irrigated. This attracted a massive influx of new farmers who knew precious little about farming and lacked even a passing acquaintance with Mother Nature. These were exceptionally hard working people, but due to ignorance of the land they failed in their efforts to live off of it.

Inappropriate cultivation techniques coupled with misunderstandings about the ecology of the region and cyclic drought led to immense land erosion and eventually to chronic crop failures, setting the stage for lives of chronic rural poverty to grip homesteaders and the generations who followed them. Throughout it all, the federal government continued its legislative efforts to encourage western expansion.

The Stock Raising Homestead Act

> *That the Secretary of the Interior is hereby authorized, on application or otherwise, to designate as stock-raising lands subject to entry under this Act lands the surface of which is, in his opinion, chiefly valuable for grazing and raising forage crops, do not contain merchantable timber, are not susceptible of irrigation from any known source of water supply, and are of such character that six hundred and forty acres are reasonably required for the support of a family.*—Section 2, Stock Raising Homestead Act

The Stock Raising Homestead Act was enacted in 1916, enabling settlers to obtain 640 acres of public land deemed to be of no value except for livestock grazing and growing forage to feed cattle. Over 70 million acres of public lands were privatized under this law.

A key provision of this legislation was that the homesteader gained ownership of the surface land but the federal government retained the mineral rights, meaning the provisions of the 1872 Mining Law applied and Stock Raising Homestead Act lands were opened to mining even though the surface land was privately owned. As a result, anyone had the right to enter these lands, prospect and file a mining claim, and then file a plan of operations to mine with the Federal Bureau of Land Management. The Act was later amended to require the surface land owner to be notified of the intent to enter, but even today a landowner cannot prevent entry or stop mining from occurring on his or her property.[28]

Between 1862 and 1934 the federal government granted 1.6 million homesteads and distributed 270,000,000 acres (420,000 sq mi) of federal land for private ownership, a total of 10 percent of all lands in the United States. About 40 percent of the applicants who started the homesteading process were able to complete it and obtain clear title to their homestead land. The passage of the Federal Land Policy and Management Act of 1976 repealed the Homestead Act in the 48 contiguous states but granted a ten-year extension on claims in Alaska.

Land Use Politics

> *The old ways may have been good enough before, but they don't work now. Set aside conventional wisdom and embrace land use politics.*—Dwight Merriam, The Complete Guide to Zoning

Across history land management politics have been contentious, and across the lawless frontier abuses of the land laws were common. Although the intent of the Homestead legislation was to grant land for agriculture, in the arid areas east of the Rocky

Mountains and west of the Appalachian Range, 640 acres were generally not enough to sustain a viable farming operation. In the absence of well-managed irrigation projects, people manipulated the provisions of the act to gain control of resources, especially water.

Commonly, an individual, acting as a front for a large cattle operation, filed for a homestead surrounding a water source, under the pretense that the land was to be used as a farm. Once the homestead was granted, other cattle ranchers would be denied the use of that water source, effectively closing off the adjacent public land to competition. This method was also used by large businesses and land speculators to gain ownership of timber and oil-producing land. Because it charged royalties for extracting these resources from public lands, the federal government was complicit in this scheming.

Homesteading schemes such as this were generally pointless for land containing "locatable minerals," such as gold and silver, which could be controlled through mining claims under the 1872 Mining Act, for which the federal government did not charge royalties. Further, the government had no systematic method to evaluate claims under the homestead acts. Land offices relied on affidavits from witnesses that the claimant had lived on the land for the required period of time and made the required improvements. In practice, often these witnesses were bribed or otherwise colluded with the claimant. And, although not necessarily fraudulent, eligible children of a large family often claimed nearby land. After a few generations, a family could build up a sizable estate that included ownership of vast amounts of land—and water rights.

While the homestead allotments were criticized as being too small for the environmental conditions on the Great Plains, one homesteader alone, using 19th-century animal-powered farming methods, could not have cultivated the 1,500 acres later recommended for dryland farming. Some scholars believe the acreage limits were reasonable when the legislation was written but reveal how poorly understood the physical conditions of the plains were.

The Grange Movement

> *We will rally round the Grange,*
> *We will rally once again,*
> *Shouting the Farmer's cry of Freedom,*
> *We will rally to the Grange,*
> *Our rights to maintain,*
> *Shouting the Farmer's cry of Freedom.*
> *—Anthem of the Grange Movement*

Beginning in the decade following the Civil War, U.S. Department of Agriculture employee Oliver Kelley, fearful of the ignorance surrounding sound agricultural practices, organized the Patrons of Husbandry to bring farmers together for educational purposes and as a social outlet. The organization eventually divided into local units called "Granges" and was the first national effort to politically organize farmers.[29]

Farmers were drawn to the Grange Movement by the need for unified action against the monopolistic railroads and grain elevators (often owned by the railroads) that charged exorbitant rates for handling and transporting crops and other agricultural products. By 1870 nine states had Granges. By the mid–1870s nearly every state had at least one Grange, and national membership reached close to 800,000. As its membership grew, the Grange Movement became increasingly political.

In 1871 Illinois farmers were able to get their state legislature to pass a bill fixing maximum rates that railroads and grain-storage facilities could charge. Minnesota, Wisconsin, and Iowa later passed similar regulatory legislation. These laws were challenged in court, and what became known as the "Granger cases" reached the U.S. Supreme Court in 1877. The court, with Chief Justice Morrison Remick Waite writing for the majority, upheld the state legislation on the grounds that any private enterprise that affects the public interest is subject to governmental regulation.

Meanwhile, independent farmers' political parties began appearing across the country. All were outgrowths of the Grange Movement and at their meetings farmers were urged to vote only for candidates who would promote agricultural interests, including restrictions on the monopolistic practices of railroads and grain elevators. When necessary, the Grangers fielded their own candidates.

The rise of the Greenback Party[30] brought about a precipitous decline in the original Grange movement. Other agricultural protest efforts, coupled with ill-advised farmer-owned cooperatives that manufactured agricultural equipment, had sapped much of the movement's strength and financial resources. By 1880 membership in the Granges had dropped off to slightly more than 100,000.

The Grange movement rebounded in the 20th century, especially in the eastern part of the country. The National Grange, as it is called, remains a fraternal organization of farmers and takes an active stance on national legislation affecting the agricultural sector.

The National Farmers' Alliance

In things essential, unity; in all things, charity; to develop a better state, mentally, morally, socially and financially, and to suppress personal, local, sectional and national prejudices. —Motto of the National Farmers' Alliance

The National Farmers' Alliance, formed in 1889, carried the Grange movement deeper into politics by embracing several originally independent organizations formed from 1873 onwards. The movement reached its greatest power about 1890, in which year twelve national farmers' organizations were represented in conventions in St. Louis, and the six leading ones alone probably had a membership of 5,000,000. As with the Grange, concrete remedial legislation for agricultural or economic ills was mingled with principles of lofty idealism and vague radical tendency.

The Alliance advocated for the education of the agricultural classes in the science of economical government in a strictly non-partisan way and favored the abolition of national banks, the free coinage of silver, a "sufficient" issue of government paper money, and revising tariff regulations. Less common demands included an income tax, debt tax, and government loans on lands. Pure food legislation, abolition of landholding by aliens, reclamation of unused or unearned land grants (to railways, e.g.,), and either rigid federal regulation of railways or other means of communication or government ownership was also favored.

In 1889–1890 the Alliance, as a non-partisan political movement, developed astonishing strength. It captured the Republican stronghold of Kansas, brought the Democratic Party to vassalage in South Carolina, revolutionized legislatures even in conservative states like Massachusetts, and seemed likely to completely dominate both the South and the West. All its work in the South was accomplished within the old-party organizations, but in 1890 the demand for an independent third party, for which various consolidations since 1887 had prepared the way, became more intense.

By 1892 the core strength of the farmers' organizations was united in the People's Party (more generally known as the Populist Party), which had its beginnings in Kansas in 1890, and received national recognition in 1892. This party emphasized free silver, income tax, an eight-hour day, reclamation of land grants, government ownership of railways, telephones and telegraphs, popular election of federal senators, and the use of voter referendums as a means for determining how taxpayer dollars should be spent.

In the presidential election of 1892 the People's Party cast 1,041,021 votes (of a total 12,036,089), and elected 22 presidential electors, the first chosen by any third party since 1856. In 1896 and 1900 the People's Party "fused" with the Democratic Party in the presidential campaign. During this period the greatest part of the People's Party was split and reabsorbed into the two major political parties from which its membership had originally been drawn.

Both the Alliance and Populist movements were built on the idea of "ethical gains through legislation" but locally the movements were often plagued by eccentric ideas, narrow prejudices, and weaknesses in economic reasoning. Consequently the Farmers' movements were much misunderstood, abused and ridiculed. Nevertheless, they accomplished a vast amount of good. This was particularly true for the Grange, which prepared the way for establishing local rural and mobile libraries, reading courses, lyceums, farmers' institutes (a steadily increasing influence) and rural free mail delivery (inaugurated experimentally in 1896 and adopted as part of the permanent postal system of the country in 1902).

These rural movements were responsible for agricultural exhibits and an improved agricultural press, encouraging and increasing profit from the work of agricultural colleges. They enabled establishment of a vast array of services provided by the U.S. Department of Agriculture. And, by demanding equal rights to all, they opposed granting special privileges to anyone.

Much of the effort focused on an extraordinary lessening of rural isolation, improving farmers' opportunities, irrigating the semi-arid West (adopted as a national policy in 1902), and enacting pure-food laws (1906) and the interstate-commerce law of 1887. Other successful legislative efforts included the railway rate laws of 1903 and 1906, the Department of Commerce and Labor law of 1903, and the Anti-trust laws of 1903 and later.

Owing to the relatively rapid frontier expansion, in the 1800s the United States was simultaneously both a developing and undeveloped country and, like today, on specific political questions each economic area reflected its own peculiar interests. Nevertheless, the broad Farmers movements were the beginning of widespread, ongoing and effective protest against "the menace of privilege" in the United States.

Teddy Roosevelt and Land Conservation

> *There can be no greater issue than that of conservation in this country.*—President Theodore Roosevelt

In 1889 the Oklahoma Territory became the last remaining reserve of useful public land opened for settlement. Because the remaining unoccupied lands were largely either arid or mountainous, in 1890 the director of the Census announced that a western frontier no longer existed. It had long been believed that the supply of new lands and natural resources in the United States was inexhaustible and limitless. A bitter debate followed the Census Bureau's announcement—and continues today. Profiteers argue that America should exploit its resources to the fullest for as long as possible while conservationists believe in sustaining supply over a longer time and preserving natural beauty.

By the turn of the 20th century several environmental issues were glaringly evident. Forest lands were severely depleted and farmland fertility was spent, having been exhausted by overuse. As a result, much of the nation's farmland was only marginally productive. Most concerning of all, water rights in the arid west had increasingly come under private control, limiting farmers' access to this valuable resource and inviting bribery, as well as other forms of criminal activity.

President Theodore Roosevelt, a sportsman and naturalist, sided emphatically with the conservationists, pushing for legislation devoted to changing the way America used its land, especially in the West.[31] Rep. Francis G. Newlands of Nevada became the prime moving force behind efforts to extend federal assistance to farmers and ranchers who worked the arid lands of the West. Under the Newlands Reclamation Act, passed in 1902, the Land Reclamation Service, later to become the Bureau of Reclamation, was established. This measure, along with subsequent legislation, sold public land to finance dams, placed thousands of new acres under cultivation and positioned the federal government front and center in the water distribution debate in the West.

Meanwhile, between 1903 and 1907 Roosevelt launched 24 reclamation projects, 21 on the settlement land and three on Indian reservations.[32] All focused on means of irrigating western farm and grazing land. "The conservation of natural resources is the fundamental problem. Unless we solve that problem it will avail us little to solve all others," Roosevelt insisted in a speech to the Deep Waterway Convention in Memphis, Tennessee, on October 4, 1907.

The broad-reaching positive effects of Roosevelt's land reclamation efforts cannot be understated. By bringing water to arid land he made it useful for farming, grazing, and human habitation, thus enabling sustainable economic development for homesteaders throughout the West.

The Dust Bowl—Mother Nature's Terrorist Act

The only difference between here and the Sahara Desert is ain't no damned fools tryin' to farm in the Sahara.—Dust Bowl–era farmer

The Dust Bowl era, when the Great Plains dried up and literally blew away, was a dramatically pivotal moment in the history of American agriculture. Sixty-mile-per-hour winds creating dust clouds 6,000 feet high and 200 miles wide blew relentlessly across the Great Plains region for nearly a decade, breaking the hearts and spirits of homesteaders who, a few short years earlier, had been prosperous grain and livestock farmers. The Dust Bowl was an environmental disaster of biblical proportions, and its impact is both difficult to describe and impossible to exaggerate. "The chickens went to roost in the middle of the day because the dust storms made it so dark they thought it was night," said Herman Goertzen of Henderson, Nebraska, reflecting on the hardscrabble life that was the Dust Bowl era.[33]

The Dust Bowl years began in the early 1930s when severe drought conditions overtook an unusually wet period that had encouraged settlement and cultivation in the Southern Great Plains. A region that included the flatlands of eastern Colorado and eastern New Mexico, the Oklahoma and Texas panhandles, and northward from the western half of Kansas suddenly dried up. Without natural vegetation to anchor the soil in place, it became friable, turning to fine, powdery dust. For the next several years prevailing winds out of the west blew mega-tons of sand and dusty topsoil eastward past Chicago to Buffalo, Boston, Cleveland, New York City and Washington, D.C, steadily depositing rich, fertile Midwestern soil into the Atlantic Ocean.

In one 12-month period, just one series of bad dust storms stripped enormous amounts of topsoil from already desiccated South Dakota farmland. A strong, two-day dust storm removed massive amounts of Great Plains topsoil and later that winter red snow fell across New England. These immense dust storms—given names such as "black blizzards" and "black rollers"—eventually involved more than 100,000,000 acres of American prairieland. Clouds of dust were so big and so thick they obscured the sun and reduced visibility to less than 12 inches, imposing major ecological and agricultural damage.

The infamous Black Sunday dust storm that occurred on April 14, 1935, packed 60 MPH winds. "The impact is like a shovelful of fine sand flung against the face," journalist Avis D. Carlson wrote in a New Republic article. "People caught in their own yards grope for the doorstep. Cars come to a standstill, for no light in the world can penetrate that swirling murk.... We live with the dust, eat it, sleep with it, watch it strip us of possessions and the hope of possessions. It is becoming real."[34]

Farmers' favored agricultural methods during this time period did not include crop rotation, fallow fields, cover crops or other techniques such as soil terracing and wind-breaking trees to prevent wind erosion—all missteps that created the conditions for large-scale soil erosion to occur. The widespread deep plowing and other soil preparation methods to enable agriculture had virtually eliminated the native grasses that held the soil in place and helped retain moisture during dry periods. Farmers left fields bare over winter months, when winds in the High Plains are at their worst, and burned the stubble as a means to control weeds prior to planting, thus depriving the soil of organic nutrients and surface vegetation to hold it in place.

For eight long years great clouds of dust blew across the Great Plains. It came in a yellowish-brown haze from the South and in rolling walls of black from the North. Dust and dirt covered everything, inside and outside, and the simplest acts of life—breathing, eating a meal, taking a walk—were no longer simple. Children wore dust masks to and from school, women hung wet sheets over windows in a futile attempt to stop the dirt from coming inside their houses, and farmers watched helplessly while their crops blew away and their livestock died.

"The dispossessed were drawn west—from Kansas, Oklahoma, Texas, New Mexico; from Nevada and Arkansas, families, tribes, dusted out, tractored out. Car-loads, caravans, homeless and hungry; twenty thousand and fifty thousand and a hundred thousand and two hundred thousand. They streamed over the mountains, hungry and restless—restless as ants, scurrying to find work to do—to lift, to push, to pull, to pick, to cut—anything, any burden to bear, for food. The kids are hungry. We got no place to live. Like ants scurrying for work, for food, and most of all for land, " wrote Nobel Prize–winning novelist John Steinbeck in 1939, in his famous story of the Dust Bowl era, The Grapes of Wrath.[35]

Identified as the "most extreme natural event in 350 years," the Dust Bowl was an agricultural catastrophe that greatly intensified the effects of the Great Depression on Rural America. Always believing things would get better next year, farmers responded to falling cash crop prices and sinking commodity markets by planting more, because farmers' answer to everything has always been to plant more. But this time it didn't work. Bad weather, low crop prices and poor farming techniques conspired to push many farmers under, despite their best efforts to avoid losing their farms. Meanwhile, Plains residents, especially in Kansas and Oklahoma, frequently succumbed to dust pneumonia or malnutrition.

Life in Midwestern America had turned uglier than anyone ever imagined it could, and no one saw it coming. Not only did farmers not want someone telling them how to farm, they discovered they didn't understand Mother Nature's complex personality very well either. They were trying to implement an agricultural system unsuitable to the land they were trying to farm. Many farmers fought against Mother Nature rather than working with her—and, as she always does, Mother Nature won out. Eventually, just as the Great Depression was gaining a grip on the rest of the nation, banks foreclosed on these farms.

By 1940 2.5 million people had abandoned their farms in Oklahoma, Arkansas, Missouri, Iowa, Nebraska, Kansas, Texas, Colorado and New Mexico and headed for California. Many were tenant farmers who, upon arriving, became migrant workers. But for many leaving only made their lives worse. They lost the ability to farm and with it some measure of economic independence when there was a good year. Formerly prosperous farmers became the new farm laborers dependent upon whatever wages the growers are willing to pay. The exiled farm family's economic circumstances, if anything, became worse. There was no opportunity to improve their lives because they didn't now, nor would they ever be able to, own land again.

Great clouds of dust relentlessly blowing up on the western horizon season after season was not enough to cause 75 percent of farmers to give up. Despite the harsh conditions, they desperately hung on, or died trying. Fiercely proud, independent people, they were simply unable to leave the place where they were born and had grown up, where they wanted to raise their own children, where their kin were buried and where, on a clear day, wide open spaces stretched out beneath blue skies far into the distant horizon. But not giving up meant farmers had to accept government help, even though doing so went against everything they believed in.

The New Deal: Government Responds to a Growing National Crisis

> *You can blaspheme Almighty God all you want to, but you damned well better not ever say one single word against Roosevelt.* —Jerry Shakeshaft, Topeka, Kansas

President Franklin Delano Roosevelt truly understood what their land meant to the descendants of the homesteading pioneers, and how desperate their lives had become. During the first 100 days of his first term in office he wrote legislation designed to conserve soil and restore the ecological balance of nature on the Great Plains—with the intent of allowing these farmers to keep their beloved land.

But the wind had already been blowing great quantities of soil across the nation for nearly two years and no government program, no matter how well thought out or intended, could neither stop nor reverse the damage. Regardless, Roosevelt believed he had to try, and within six months following his inauguration he ordered Interior Secretary Harold L. Ickes to establish the Soil Erosion Service (SES).[36] After Congress declared soil erosion a "national menace" in 1935, the SES was transferred and reorganized under the Department of Agriculture and renamed the Soil Conservation Service (SCS). The SCS developed extensive conservation programs that retained topsoil and prevented irreparable damage to the land. Farming techniques, including strip cropping, terracing, crop rotation, contour plowing, and cover crops, were advocated and farmers were paid to practice soil-conserving farming techniques.

Roosevelt also quickly declared a four-day bank holiday, during which time Congress drafted the Emergency Banking Act of 1933, stabilizing the banking industry, which had been decimated in the Crash of 1929. This legislation restored faith in the banking system and curtailed banking practices that had haunted farmers since banks, seeking profit sources, became involved in agriculture. A few months later the Emergency Farm Mortgage Act allotted $200 million for refinancing mortgages to help farmers facing foreclosure. The Farm Credit Act of 1933 chartered local banks and established local credit associations.

In the fall of 1933 over six million young pigs were slaughtered to stabilize hog prices. With most of the meat going to waste, public outcry forced immediate creation of the Federal Surplus Relief Corporation (FSRC). The FSRC diverted agricultural commodities (apples, beans, canned beef, flour and pork products) to relief organizations to be distributed through local channels. Cotton goods were eventually included to clothe the needy as well.

In 1934 Congress approved the Frazier-Lemke Farm Bankruptcy Act restricting the ability of banks to dispossess farmers in times of distress. Originally effective until 1938, the act was repeatedly renewed until 1947, when it expired. Roosevelt signed the Taylor Grazing Act, which allowed him to take up to 140 million acres of federally owned land out of the public domain and establish carefully monitored grazing districts. One of many New Deal efforts to reverse the damage done to the land by overuse, the program was able to slow land deterioration, but couldn't undo the historical damage, and by the time it was implemented over 125 million acres of cropland had lost its topsoil.

In 1935 the federal government formed a Drought Relief Service (DRS) to coordinate relief activities. The DRS bought cattle in counties that were designated emergency areas, for $14 to $20 a head. Those unfit for human consumption—more than 50 percent at the beginning of the program—were destroyed. The remaining cattle were given to the Federal Surplus Relief Corporation to be used in food distribution to hungry families nationwide. Although it was difficult for farmers to give up their herds, the cattle slaughter program helped many of them avoid bankruptcy. Most believed the government cattle buying program was a God-send to desperate farmers, as they could not afford to keep their cattle, and the government paid a better price than they could obtain in local markets.

In 1935 Congress passed the most important legislation of the Great Depression, the Emergency Relief Appropriation Act, which provided $525 million for drought relief, and authorized creation of the Works Progress Administration (WPA), which would eventually become the Civilian Conservation Corps (CCC) and employ 8.5 million people.

In his second inaugural address on January 20, 1937, Roosevelt told the country, "I see one-third of the nation ill-housed, ill-clad, ill-nourished ... the test of our progress is not whether we add more to the abundance of those who have much; it is whether we provide enough for those who have too little." This statement was the prelude to the WPA's Shelterbelt Project, which called for large-scale planting of trees across the Great Plains, stretching in a 100-mile-wide zone from Canada to northern Texas, with the singular purpose of protecting the land from erosion. Farmers were paid to plant and cultivate native trees such as red cedar and green along fence rows separating properties. The project was estimated to cost 75 million dollars over a period of 12 years. When disputes arose over funding sources (the project was considered to be a long-term strategy, and therefore ineligible for emergency relief funds), FDR transferred the program to the WPA, where the project had limited success. Nevertheless, the extensive re-plowing of land into furrows, planting trees in shelterbelts, and other conservation methods resulted in a 65 percent reduction in the amount of soil lost.

However, the drought continued. By the end of the 1930s over 75 percent of the topsoil had blown away from many Great Plains regions and by 1940 counties that had experienced the most significant levels of erosion saw a greater drop in agricultural land values. The per-acre value of farmland had declined by 28 percent in high-erosion counties and 17 percent in medium-erosion counties, relative to land value changes in low-erosion counties. Even over the long-term, the full agricultural value of the land often failed to recover. In highly eroded areas, less than 25 percent of the original agricultural losses were recovered. The economy adjusted predominantly through large population declines in more-eroded counties during the 1930s through the 1950s.

But there was wide variation in the degree to which the land was degraded, and aside from the short-term economic consequences caused by erosion, there were severe long-term economic consequences of the Dust Bowl, which persisted, in part, because of farmers' failure to switch to more appropriate crops for highly eroded areas. Because the amount of topsoil had been severely reduced, it would have been more productive to shift from food crops and grain (namely wheat) to animals and hay. But during the Depression and through at least the 1950s, there was limited relative adjustment of farmland away from activities that became less productive in more-eroded counties.

Some of the failure to shift to more productive agricultural methods was related to ignorance about the benefits of changing land use. A second explanation is the high rate of bank failures in the Plains states. Because banks failed in the Dust Bowl region with a higher rate of frequency than in the rest of the country, it was harder for farmers to gain access to the credit they needed to fund a shift in crop production; consequently, animal operations and hay field production increased only slightly. Even if they knew about the benefits of changing land usage, the incentive for farmers to switch immediately was relatively small.

The Civilian Conservation Corps

> *If it hadn't been for Roosevelt establishing the CCC [Civilian Conservation Corps] I don't know what a lot of young guys would've done ... he saved the nation.* —Jerry Shakeshaft

Roosevelt had campaigned on the promise of a New Deal for America. "Give me your help, not to win votes, but to win this crusade to restore America to its own people," he repeated time and again throughout months leading up to his successful election.[37]

During his first 100 days in office Roosevelt, eager to make good on his campaign promises, approved several measures beyond those directly affecting distressed agriculture. The speed with which New Deal programs moved through the political morass toward implementation reflected a miraculous level of cooperation among all the agencies and branches of the federal government politicians today can only dream about.[38]

Roosevelt didn't want to keep a hungry, downtrodden, sad and desperate nation waiting, and he truly believed that "we're all in this together" and that the only way out of it was together. His appeal resonated with a downtrodden, desperate and anxious nation thirsty for someone to lead it out of its massive economic depression. Wise politicians rolled up their sleeves and got to work putting people back to work. Out on the Great Plains this meant building roads, implementing better farming practices, and planting trees to break up the incessant eastward wind, with nothing stopping it between the Rocky Mountains and the Appalachian Range—and finding men to do the work.

The Emergency Conservation Work Act (ECW), better known as the Civilian Conservation Corps (CCC), was a centerpiece of the New Deal, and remains the largest job creation program in the nation's history. Roosevelt, brilliantly, recruited thousands of unemployed young men, enlisted them in a peacetime army, and sent them to battle the erosion and destruction of the nation's natural resources. He connected young men with the land in an effort to save them both, and it worked.

Also known as Roosevelt's Tree Army, the CCC set about renewing the nation's decimated forests by planting an estimated three billion trees between 1933 and 1942. This was crucial, especially in states affected by the Dust Bowl, where reforestation was necessary to break the wind, hold water in the soil, and hold the soil in place. The CCC's reforestation program was so far reaching that it was responsible for more than half the reforestation, public and private, accomplished in the nation's history. Harley Jolley, who joined the CCC in 1937, described the situation this way:

> We had not taken care of our country. We had not taken care of our land. No basic scientific farming to speak of. Farm this, gut it and move on. Farm this, gut it and move—that's what we did. We're talking 150-plus years of no care, of very poor care. I can remember playing in gullies two stories high. That was my playground. But it was a bad thing, because that meant all that erosion and that much good land gone. The soil erosion we were losing annually was enough to load a series of boxcars seven times around the earth. That's a lot of dirt. Part of it goes back to the big timber companies of the '20s and '30s, cutting and cutting and cutting, leaving slash. Slash would burn, storms would come, floods would come, and down the river goes our good fertile soil. The end result is it caught up with us, total impact, in 1930s, big, big, big-time impact with the resulting disaster.[39]

Eligible young men flocked to enroll in the CCC, and the participation requirements were designed to ensure broad eligibility. Sound physical fitness was mandatory because of the hard physical labor required. The only other requirements were that a man be unemployed, unmarried, and between the ages of 18 and 26, although age and marital status limitations were eventually relaxed to include Spanish American War and World War I veterans. Enlistment was for six months, although many reenlisted time and again because $30 a month, with mandatory $25 allotment checks sent home to the man's family, was a very attractive employment option at the time. A further social benefit of the CCC, many politicians believed, was that the CCC resulted in a 55 percent reduction in desperation crimes committed by the young men of that day.[40]

The program enjoyed great public support. As the CCC became better known, the camps became accepted and even sought after because they stimulated regional economies and provided communities with improvements in forest activity, flood control, fire protection, and overall community safety. Camps were set up in all states, as well as in Hawaii, Alaska, Puerto Rico, and the Virgin Islands. CCC enrollment peaked at the end of 1935, when there were 500,000 men located in 2,600 camps in operation in all states. California alone had more than 150 camps. More than 90 percent of enrollees participated in some facet of the CCC's educational program and as a result more than 40,000 illiterate men were taught to read and write.

Early in 1933 the CCC extended enlistment coverage to about 14,000 American Indians whose economic circumstances were deplorable and had mostly been ignored. Ironically, before the CCC program ended, more than 80,000 Native Americans were paid to help reclaim the land that had originally belonged to them.

By 1942, there was hardly a state that could not boast of the benefits of permanent CCC projects. The CCC worked on improving millions of acres of federal and state lands, as well as parks. New roads were built, telephone lines strung, and trees planted. CCC projects included:

- more than 3,470 fire towers erected;
- 97,000 miles of fire roads built;
- 4,235,000 man-days devoted to fighting fires;
- more than three billion trees planted;
- 7,153,000 man-days expended on protecting the natural habitats of wildlife; 83 camps in 15 Western states assigned 45 projects of that nature;
- 46 camps assigned to work under the direction of the U.S. Bureau of Agriculture Engineering;
- more than 84,400,000 acres of good agricultural land received manmade drainage systems (Indian enrollees did much of that work);
- 1,240,000 man-days of emergency work completed during floods of the Ohio and Mississippi valleys;
- disease and insect control;
- forest improvement—timber stand inventories, surveying, and reforestation;
- forest recreation development—campgrounds built, complete with picnic shelters, swimming pools, fireplaces, and restrooms.[41]

Five hundred CCC camps were under the control of the Soil Conservation Service and focused on erosion control. By Roosevelt's design, the CCC worked on projects that were independent of other public relief programs, and although other federal agencies, such as the National Park Service and Soil Conservation Service, contributed, the U.S. Forest Service administered more than 50 percent of all public work projects for the CCC. The effects of the CCC were felt for decades after its inception.

As the depression receded and the job market picked up, businessmen indicated a preference for hiring a man who had been in the CCC, and the reason was simple: employers believed that anyone who had been in the CCC would know what a full day's work meant, and how to carry out orders in a disciplined way—and they were correct.

Although there was still work to be done, following the Japanese attack on Pearl Harbor, it became obvious that any federal project not directly related to the war effort was in jeopardy. A joint committee of Congress recommended that the CCC be abolished by July 1, 1942. Technically, however, this did not occur; instead, Congress refused continued funding. Eventually, $8 million was set aside to cover all costs of liquidation, and the War Department, Labor Department, and Civil Aeronautics Administration were given first opportunity to acquire CCC properties for the war effort. Ultimately, the War Department claimed the majority of the equipment.

Unquestionably the Civilian Conservation Corps was both one of the most successful New Deal programs of the Great Depression and among the most effective public policies in all of American history. It existed for fewer than 10 years and left a legacy of good roads, sturdy bridges, and other needed infrastructure throughout the United States. Between 1933 and 1941, the CCC put more than 3,000,000 unemployed men back to work.

More than any other New Deal agency, the CCC is considered to be an extension of Roosevelt's personal philosophy, which reflected a profound understanding that the ability to earn a living is integral to a man's personal self worth in a deep, fundamental way. Accordingly, Roosevelt was not interested in putting people on the dole as the chief means of helping the desperate. Instead, he was determined to preserve the pride of American workers, and he concentrated on creating jobs by creating a massive revitalization of the nation's economy, with a view toward putting Americans back to work.

Farmers, and most of the rest of the nation, saw Roosevelt as their savior, and in very many ways he was. "Sometimes your grandmother had an extremely difficult time telling the difference between Roosevelt and God," my father told me.

Making the Best of Hard Times: World War II and Future Agricultural Expansion

> *One front and one battle where everyone in the United States—every man, woman and child is in action. That front is right here at home, in our daily lives.—President Franklin Roosevelt*

When America entered World War II, the entire nation went to war. Men signed up to fight, and women volunteered to support the war effort in every imaginable way. Some baked cookies to load on troop trains rolling through the small towns scattered across the Great Plains, picking up draftees; rolled bandages for the Red Cross; and knit woolen liners for soldiers' helmets during France and Germany's freezing winters. Other women went to work in factories producing wartime goods.

Whereas before the war agriculture was one of the largest employment sources in the nation, the outbreak of World War II presented the rural Midwest with new challenges. Many farm hands left farm labor to pursue better-paying jobs in the factories that supported the war effort. The war demanded that farmers produce more, with less help. They had to keep American soldiers in Europe and the South Pacific fed, while meanwhile, at home, the government rationed food and fuel.

Farmers committed to remaining in farming responded to the call for more production by putting their wives and children to work alongside them on the farm when their hired hands signed up for the military. Farmer organizations complained about labor shortages, and Congress responded by enacting draft deferments for farmers and farm workers who were "necessary to and regularly engaged in an agricultural occupation." Nevertheless, the farm worker exodus was already well underway and eventually became so acute the government brought German and Italian prisoners of war to be used as Midwest farm labor, and created a women's land army to provide additional farm workers.

With no guarantee that the men who returned from the war would ever go back to farming, the nation was forced to find new ways to create well-paying employment opportunities that met the continual, ongoing need for food. And, as feared, most of the hired men who went off to fight didn't return to farming after the war ended. In some ways that didn't matter nearly as much as it could have, had major technological advances in farming not occurred during the time they were gone. In spite of severe rationing of needed raw materials, farm implement manufacturers made significant improvements to tractors and other machinery. And during this time the government wisely maintained agricultural price supports to avoid a post-war farm recession, so farmers had enough disposable income to purchase additional equipment and reduce their reliance on hired help.

Among the most important programs pushing agriculture into the future was the New Deal's Rural Electrification Administration (REA), which enabled low-cost loans to impoverished rural areas and brought electrical power to the remote rural landscapes. By allowing for improved communication through telephones and mechanization of many farming operations, such as threshing, milking, and hoisting grain for storage, farming became more efficient.

But ever cautious farmers took to modernization slowly, realizing that technological advances, while making American agriculture the envy of the world, also had a down side by rendering idle hundreds of thousands of farmers and farm hands. Recalling the moment when he threw the switch sending the first electrical current down the Tennessee Valley farm region, REA administrator Norman Clapp said he turned to the farmer standing next to him and asked what he thought of finally having access to all the benefits of electrical power? "Got along fine without it," was the reply. Nevertheless, electricity made agricultural expansion infinitely easier and allowed farming to become more productive.

For those who had decided to keep "toughing it out," their efforts paid off. By the time World War II was in full force, Midwest climate problems had quieted, the programs to improve both farm prices and the soil were in full effect, and cash crops were once again in high demand to support the war effort.

Unquestionably the government programs that enabled agriculture to survive the Dust Bowl, the Great Depression, and World War II changed rural America in very profound ways. The young men who returned from the war were profoundly changed, and so were the women who had supported the war effort. Those who went to work in the factories that supplied the war effort abruptly lost their jobs when the war ended and returning soldiers needed civilian employment. Young men who left the farm to defend the nation knew how hard farming was and didn't necessarily want to return to that life if other options were available.

But in the end, many of them did return to the land that their families had owned for generations. What they didn't realize at the time was how hard farming was going to become.

3

America's Heartland

Life in the Midwestern Farm States

> *Agriculture is the backbone of our economy—and the one thing that can bring our nation down is our dependence on foreign countries for food and energy.*—Congressman John Salazar (D-CO)

Agriculture is the cultural and economic centerpiece of the Midwest, otherwise affectionately known as the nation's breadbasket. It's the place where a large portion of our food is grown, where "Midwestern values" endure and people, no matter their economic circumstances, are deeply rooted in fertile black soil and lack of pretense. "I tried to leave here once, right after college," Iowa farmer Don Hayes told me, "but I got so homesick for wide open spaces and a good visit with the neighbors I came back home for the 4th of July and never left again."

The Midwestern United States is America's heartland. Each of the 12 Midwestern states contains both large, population-dense metropolitan areas and vast expanses of rich farmland, occasionally interrupted by a small town comprised of two, maybe three thousand people. These are what are commonly referred to as "rural areas."[1]

Mostly for public policy reasons, the Midwest is sometimes divided into the East North Central States (Wisconsin, Michigan, Illinois, Indiana and Michigan); the Great Lakes States (states that come in contact with one of the Great Lakes), which include Illinois, Indiana, Michigan, Ohio, Minnesota, and Wisconsin; the West North Central States (North Dakota, South Dakota, Wisconsin, Iowa, Minnesota and Nebraska); and the Great Plains States (states that are located within the Great Plains region of the country), which include Iowa, Kansas, Missouri, North Dakota, Nebraska, and South Dakota. Some states fall into more than one group, which can have political implications, as when regulations around Great Lakes water usage were being configured. The 2012 U.S. Census report puts the total population of the twelve Midwestern states at 65,377,684.[2]

Illinois is the most populous among the Midwestern states and is home to the third largest city in the nation: Chicago. Located on the southern Lake Michigan shoreline, Chicago has a population of 2,707,000 and a population density of 11,482 persons per square mile.[3] Other Midwestern cities with a population above 500,000 are Indianapolis, Indiana; Columbus, Ohio; Detroit, Michigan; and Milwaukee, Wisconsin. Detroit, with a 32.5 percent poverty rate, is the poorest city in the country, followed by Cincinnati (27.8 percent), Cleveland (27 percent), St. Louis (26.8 percent) and Milwaukee (26.2 percent). Large portions of Ohio, Michigan, northern Illinois and northern Indiana are primarily manufacturing rather than agriculturally based economies and are often referred to as "The Rust Belt."

As manufacturing jobs have declined agriculture has become the biggest driver of local Midwestern economies, accounting for billions of dollars worth of exports and thousands of jobs. The area has some of the richest farm land in the world and is known primarily for grain, cattle and hog farming. The tall grass prairie has been gradually converted into one of the most intensive crop-producing areas in North America and today less than one tenth of one percent of the original land cover of the tall grass prairie biome remains.

Iowa, Illinois, Minnesota, Wisconsin, Nebraska, and Missouri comprise "The Corn Belt." Because of agricultural land use intensity, Illinois and Iowa rank 49th and 50th among the 50 states in total remaining uncultivated land. The region's rich black soil enables farmers to produce abundant harvests of cereal crops, such as corn, wheat, and oats, and is why the entire Midwest grain belt region is referred to as "the breadbasket of the nation."

Midwestern Values

> *Here in the Midwest, we enjoy sex but not nearly as much as an ear of freshly picked sweet corn.* —Garrison Keillor

"Midwestern values" is a term frequently tossed into any conversation about life in America's heartland and native Midwesterners proudly adhere to the simple values they believe in and hold dear—an honest day's work for an honest day's pay; frugality; trustworthiness in word and deed; modesty; lack of pretense; willingness to step up and lend a helping hand; intolerance for injustice or suffering; and having one's name, reputation and character be their most cherished possessions. They have an aversion to shiny objects, flashy ways, consumerism, political spin, and fast talkers. They are, in equal measure, grateful for good food, good health, love of family, shelter, friends, and community.

Those living in rural areas work hard at being dependably good neighbors, pull together when trouble comes, and are satisfied with a simple waste-not-want-not life. No matter how bad things are now, endlessly optimistic rural Midwesterners know that sooner or later things will get better. Meanwhile, they gain great personal strength from their ability to remedy most everything, including whatever ails you, your dog, your horse, your calf or your vegetable garden. They shy away from hedonism, are most satisfied with the things they grow or make themselves and are not pleasure seeking. "As I've often said, Wisconsin's greatest strength continues to be the dedicated, hardworking people of our state. They go to work every day, pay their taxes, and raise their kids with good, solid Midwestern values," explains former Wisconsin governor Jim Doyle.

As idyllic as life in the Midwest sounds, it has a downside. The weather is harsh—rainy falls and early frosts can make harvesting difficult, animals have to be cared for in subzero cold winters, sometimes spring never shows up at all, and summers, particularly in the Corn Belt, where the corn crop itself emits enough moisture to thicken the air to an almost unbreathable level in July and August, are uniformly hot and humid. Blizzards lasting days can bring everything to a standstill, including airports, interstate highways, schools and businesses, depositing so much snow it takes a week to dig out. Spring tornados can level a community in seconds and a summer hailstorm can strip the leaves entirely off a corn crop, making it useless even as silage.

And not everyone who lives in the Midwest necessarily subscribes to the ethic of Midwestern values, partly because they're transplants from somewhere else, and partly because people can become greedy, ruthless competitors, engage in unfair business practices, or otherwise forget about what being a good neighbor really means. And, although on a smaller scale, the rural Midwest has the same problems big cities everywhere have—crime, violence, illegal drugs, poorly performing public schools, unemployment, and crumbling infrastructure. Nevertheless, Midwesterners generally tend to be simple, hardworking and uncomplicated—some might even say naïve—folks who try hard to live by the "do unto others as you would have them do unto you" philosophy.

What "Rural" Really Means

City people—they may know how to street fight but they don't know how to wade through manure. —Melina Marchetta, On the Jelicoe Road

Living in a metropolitan area usually guarantees plenty of safe drinking water, a working sewer system, promptly snow-plowed streets, speedy access to medical care and other services, and the security of knowing that, if you collapse while mowing your front lawn, or fall off your roof, within minutes someone with a cell phone will walk by and call 911. Rural life isn't nearly this secure.

In addition to knowing, from a very early age, exactly how to successfully wade through manure, rural people live entirely different lives from their urban counterparts. Rural folks drill their own wells and then must remember to test them regularly to be sure the drinking water isn't contaminated by nitrates or other farm chemicals; they lay a septic field and hope it both drains properly, and that nobody puts too much bleach in the washing machine, killing the bacteria that keeps the septic system functioning properly; and they must watch that the propane tank doesn't get too low and that propane prices don't suddenly skyrocket in the middle of winter. And they travel slippery snow-covered county roads that might not get plowed all winter.

If you roll your tractor chances are nobody will know about it until you fail to show up for dinner. Even if someone does find you sooner, it will take a while for the volunteer rescue squad to get to you, and even longer to transport you to the nearest hospital, which might be fifty or more miles down a two-lane road congested with tractors, manure spreaders, combines and semis. The hospital probably won't have the latest medical equipment or be up to date on current emergency medical practices.

When examining rural life and rural poverty it's important to bear in mind that living in a rural area is, for most people who do it, a freely chosen way of life. Nearly everyone in Anytown, Rural USA could live and work somewhere else, but they don't want to, because most rural people, and all farmers, would rather work for themselves and take their chances on the financial outcome than to work for somebody else, at a wage somebody else determines, and according to someone else's rules. This is a population willing to face the unpredictability that accompanies farming and the inconveniences of rural life rather than put up with crowded urban living and somebody else telling them what to do. They want quiet and plenty of space surrounding them and cherish the freedom to make their own decisions.

Rural people need land under their feet every single day of every season of the year, in the same way they need food, clothing and water. Too many days off their land throws them out of sorts, and leaving their animals is no different than leaving their kids, and sometimes more upsetting. "I was gone for a week once, and worried the whole time about my cows—whether they were getting milked the right way or were upset and missed me talking to them..." a rural Wisconsin dairy farmer told me, seriously meaning every word.

For rural people, milking a cow, driving their tractor, hoeing the garden or climbing on their horse to check their fences frequently take care of whatever is on their mind. If things get really bad they'll walk their fence row from one end to the other, talking things over with their dog.

The Nuts and Bolts of Farm Finances

> *In the past 40 years, the United States lost more than a million farmers and ranchers. Many of our farmers are aging. Today, only nine percent of family farm income comes from farming, and more and more of our farmers are looking elsewhere for their primary source of income.* —Tom Vilsack, U.S. secretary of agriculture

"Historically, successful farmers are those who are comfortable with risk-taking, possess unwavering faith in the future and believe that no matter what happened this year, next year will be better. They also have a good business sense, respect the environment, love their families, and possess an entire tool box of skills ranging from how to repair a tractor to tending for a sick animal, from knowing which crops to plant to knowing when to harvest the corn—and much more..." explains rural historian Jerry Apps, who makes two points critical to understanding how farming works: First, it's a risky and unpredictable means of earning a living, and second, it's a business that rises and falls on factors the farmer has little control over—the weather and market prices being two big ones.

How a farmer bankrolls his operation explains a lot about life in typical rural communities. The mechanics of farm finances readily reveal how a farmer can fall into and then climb back out of poverty, or get into financial trouble so deep it follows him the rest of his life.

Not uncommonly farmers have cash flow problems that require them to borrow money to short-term finance their year-to-year operations, so farm operating loans are set up to meet expected annual farm operating costs. Maturity dates attempt to match the farm operation's cash flow and the farmland is used as collateral. In the best case scenario the farmer is able to repay the loan from the farm profits in the same year the loan is taken out.

The LIBOR Indexed Variable Rate (London InterBank Offered Rate) known as the LIBOR Average usually represents the lowest rate available for farm credit. Interest rates on these loans move up or down every 30 days, depending on the movement of the LIBOR index. The LIBOR one–Year Fixed Rate is set for 12 months then resets at the end of the 12-month period to a 30-day variable rate. When the loan resets, it is possible to move it into another one-year fixed rate period.

Fixed rate loans are more expensive than variable rate loans but eliminate the concern about rising interest rates during the loan's lifetime. A farmer who takes out a variable rate loan is gambling that interest rates will remain stable or fall, and not rise, during the lifetime of the loan.

Farm operating loans are available through local banks or the USDA Farm Service Agency (FSA), whose available funds are allotted by Congressional appropriation.[4] Farm operating loans may be used to purchase livestock and feed, farm equipment, fuel, farm chemicals, insurance and other operating costs, including family living expenses, minor improvements or repairs to buildings or to refinance certain farm-related debts, excluding real estate. Operating loan funds cannot be used to finance nonfarm enterprises, including earthworms, exotic birds, tropical fish, dogs or horses used for non-farm purposes (racing, pleasure, show and boarding).

The maximum loan amount for a direct farm operating loan with no cash down payment requirement is $300,000. However, a lien is placed against the farmer's land to guarantee the loan. FSA also makes microloans of up to $35,000 available to smaller, non-traditional and specialty niche farming operations, such as organic farms or wind energy operations.

The problem with borrowing money to do business year over year is that if profits are not sufficient to pay off the operating loan in full each year, it continues forward into the next year. Assuming additional operating money is needed the following year, the farmer borrows more money, usually at higher interest rate because he's carrying over prior year debt. If another bad crop year ensues, the farm falls further into the red, and too many bad crop years in a row, bad agricultural markets, or issues in the wider economy that keep farm prices low can create a situation whereby the farmer accumulates considerable debt, to the point of owing more money than his land is worth. When this occurs the bank refuses to lend him more money, effectively shutting down his farm operation. Alternatively, if land values drop below the amount of debt the farm has against it, the loan is called in. Both scenarios force the farmer to sell off his land, thereby losing his farm.

Because the costs of doing business on a farm increase steadily, it is a rare farmer that is entirely debt free, even when crops and livestock operations are profitable and land values hold steady or rise. However, most farmers are willing to live with the debt rather than deal with the crushing blow of having to sell off land that has been in their family for generations and has been planted or ranched every year, through good and bad times.

Few farmers get rich farming, but most believe that if they stick with it long enough they'll average out a decent enough living to stay afloat over time. Unfortunately, staying afloat is all many farmers can manage when the average medium-sized farm is 350 acres, with an additional 50 head of dairy cattle or other livestock equivalent, and the average annual farm income, after expenses were subtracted from revenue, is $35,000.[5] This number has not varied significantly in recent years and, absent any additional off-farm income, a family of four living entirely on this amount has a total income between 125 percent and 150 percent of the federal poverty line.

As a result of low on-farm incomes, in recent years, 85–95 percent of farm household income has come from off-farm sources. The relative importance of off-farm income varies considerably from farm to farm, but even in a good market year many farmers are satisfied if the farm pays for itself and rely upon off-farm income to support their families.[6]

Land Values

Sure, this is my land, but the bank owns most of it.—Kansas farmer

A farmer regards the ability to live off the land as a deeply spiritual endeavor and undeniable proof of strength of character. He likes to cultivate both the soil he plants and the illusion that having the right combination of skill, good luck and hard work guarantees success. And because land is a fixed entity limited in quantity and there will never be more land than there is now, land is both a natural resource and a uniquely stable asset that will always, in the farmer's eyes, have substantial value. This belief can lead to a false sense of security because land values increase and decrease as a result of sometimes freakish combinations of circumstances far beyond the farmer's control.

The perfect example of wildly unpredictable land values is the agricultural economy of the 1970s and 1980s, when commodity prices were high and interest rates were low, enabling farmers to follow the "get big or get out" philosophy and borrow more money, purchase more land to enlarge their operations and grow more crops.[7] Because farm land was producing a highly valuable product, and there was a hungry market eager to buy farmland at top dollar, agricultural land values soared to record highs. Then the farm economy crashed, bringing land values crashing down too. Although the land itself hadn't changed in any way, the value of what it was able to produce had changed dramatically, and suddenly land was no longer an economic engine producing a high value product.

While farmland values have generally trended upward in recent years, so have the costs associated with farming, which have bumped up against a tighter money-lending market and greater difficulty obtaining farm loans to meet operational and household needs. Many factors affect the likelihood of current trends continuing, including current and future demand for food and energy source crops, which help support farm income.

According to USDA Economic Research Service researchers Cynthia Nickerson, Mitchell Morehart, Todd Kuethe, Jayson Beckman, Jennifer Ifft and Ryan Williams, "stable farm incomes could keep farmland values at or above their current levels."[8] However, a largely unpredictable combination of increasing interest rates, increasingly volatile agricultural markets, and/or sharp reductions in or elimination of government subsidy programs all have the ability to destabilize farm income and could result in loss of farmland value.

Current interest rates on borrowed money are relatively low, but their stability rests on sensitivity to many factors out of the agricultural sector's control, including the impact of shifts in monetary policy, tightening credit as the wider economy recovers from the recent recession, and rising risk premiums on loans generally. While the overall farm economy is not highly leveraged at this time, if interest rates increase rapidly, farms that are heavily indebted might have serious difficulty servicing their loans, thus risking foreclosure.

Alternatively, some farmers own small amounts of land and lease additional land to farm, in effect borrowing someone else's land to grow crops without transferring ownership or equity interest in the property to the person leasing it. Agricultural leases are either cash or crop share leases. The cash lease involves a cash payment of either a specified sum or an amount determined by a formula in exchange for the use of farmland. The tenant pays the farmland owner a certain amount of rent regardless of the crop yields or prices. This is called tenant farming, and the tenant farmer has the sole responsibility for making the management decisions regarding land production.

A typical crop share lease agreement between the landowner and share crop farmer specifies that each receive a predetermined percentage of the crop based on their contributions to production. Both the landowner and farmer supply part of the equipment and inputs such as seed, fertilizer, and chemicals. In contrast to a straight forward cash lease, in a crop share lease the landowner and the farmer share management responsibilities regarding land production. The rent share usually ranges from one third to one half, depending on local custom and on the proportional contributions of the share crop farmer and the landowner.[9]

Although the cash lease and the crop share lease are the most common farming leases, a farmer-tenant may also enter into a livestock share, labor share or flexible-rent lease with a landowner. Given the average farm size, the fact an economically viable farm operation (one having no off-farm income) would have to plant between 2,000 and 3,000 acres of row crops annually and raise an additional 500–600 sows or other livestock,[10] coupled with the fact that not many farmers can afford to purchase and maintain that much land, it's understandable that sharecropping or tenant farming is common.

Retiring Off the Land—The Plight of the Rural Elderly

> *Most farmers don't ever retire, and most don't want to, but even those who do want to usually can't. They just work till one day they drop.*—Jeanie Lewis

Residents of rural areas tend to be somewhat older than urban populations, and rural communities have disproportionately higher elderly (65+) and near-retirement age (50–64) groups relative to the working age population.[11] While the overall percent of the population living in rural counties has declined steadily in recent years, the percent of elderly within the rural population has trended upward.

The elderly as a population group have higher than average poverty rates, and elderly women in particular tend to be considerably poorer than women generally.[12] These facts significantly complicate the picture of rural poverty picture.

Most of the rural elderly have lived in their community all, or nearly all, their lives, and don't want to leave their friends and extended family networks when they retire. "Most farm women move into town when their husbands die. Maybe the son keeps up the operation, or maybe they sell out and pay everything off, but either way, an awful lot barely scrape by," says Wisconsin farm wife Jeanie Lewis. The "aging in place" issue many rural elderly desire is an important factor in rural poverty because Social Security (SS) retirement benefit income is often the only income source they have and it isn't enough to keep those with no money to supplement their SS income above the poverty line.[13,14]

In 2009 SS income accounted for 9.3 percent of the total income in rural counties, compared to only 5.5 percent of the total U.S. income and 5 percent of urban and suburban income.[15] Further, 23.6 percent of the total rural population receives some kind of SS income (retirement, disability, survivor) compared to 16.7 percent nationwide.[16] Sixty-six percent of the rural SS income is paid to retirees; the remaining is paid as survivor or disability benefits. Because persons eligible to receive these benefits are not usually mobile, most of this income is spent in the local community.

SS retirement benefits average about 42 percent of former wages and are not intended to be a retiree's sole source of income. However, this often turns out to be the case, particularly in rural areas. Because of lower lifetime earnings, these individuals have been unable to accumulate additional, liquid retirement savings. Instead, for many rural residents, personal savings and "other" retirement funds, if there are any, are tied to land values. Many older farmers told me their land "is my 401K."

If land values are low at the time of retirement, when the land is sold off, there won't be as much retirement money available as there would be in higher land value years. Additionally, this "retirement savings scheme" is tied directly to the amount of land one owns, as the following example, which is valid only for the elderly who own debt-free land they are able to sell off at retirement, illustrates:

> In 2,000 Iowa had 393,000 residents receiving an average of $695 per month in SS payments.[17] If an Iowa farmer owns 100 acres of debt-free land valued at $2,000 per acre[18] the land sale would generate $200,000 before taxes. Assuming $100,000 of this amount goes toward moving off the farm and buying a house in town, the remaining $100,000 comprises his/her retirement savings. Withdrawing the annual recommended 5 percent from retirement savings generates an additional $416 per month income, for a total monthly income of $1,111 ($13,340 annually.) This places this farmer's annual retirement income, assuming he resides in a two-person household, well below the poverty line.
>
> If the farmer's wife worked on the farm her entire life, and did not pay into SS for herself during this time, she is not receiving any SS payment of her own. If land values happen to have dropped to $1,500 per acre at the time this farmer needs to sell, the amount of additional retirement money he has to work with is automatically reduced by 25 percent, before taxes. If this farmer has debt against his land, the amount he has to retire on is further reduced by the amount he owes the bank.
>
> If the farmer's wife produced off-farm income during her working years, she may have pension or Social Security benefits. More than likely hers was a lower-wage job, so her post-retirement income, while helpful, is not substantial, and if her husband dies, she loses a substantial portion of his Social Security income.

This example illustrates the reason so many elderly rural women find themselves living out their remaining years in poverty, and it points out the danger of depending upon agricultural land as a 401K retirement savings plan. It also assumes a land-owning farmer wants to sell his land at retirement, and not all do.

In reality, retirement for most farmers is inextricably woven into a complicated legacy involving their family history and their land, and hard choices have to be made. All of the assets are tied into the land and the farming operation, and they have to figure out how they will manage during their elderly years, when their children have families of their own they need to support.

The retirement picture is entirely different for those who farm on leased land and own little or none of their own, a group whose numbers continues to increase.[19] These farmers will not have land equity to cash in at retirement, thus face an even bleaker retirement.

Generational Land Transfers

> *A farm family business is not the product of a single generation, or single family. It is intimately tied to the intergenerational land transfer process amongst many interconnected families.*—Roy Roper and Rabel J. Burdge, *Family Life Cycle Disruption in Rural Communities*

Bearing in mind that rural wealth is tied directly to varying land values, and that farming is a small business operation whose profit margin also varies unpredictably, rural land owners face enormous difficulties both in accumulating wealth and transferring land to family members. The profoundly deep emotional ties farmers have both to their land and to their families, coupled with their intense desire to "keep the farm in the family," immeasurably complicate generational land transfers. For many, keeping family land is so important it surpasses good business sense and ultimately contributes significantly to rural poverty. Simply speaking, it works this way:

"Farmer Smith" and his wife raise five children on the farm. His son Joe begins farming with his dad at around age 20, when he marries and starts a family of his own. This arrangement may continue for many years—or not. Joe may decide he wants to strike out on his own and takes out a loan to buy a small, start-up farm, intending to expand as time goes on. If he does this, he begins to accrue debt immediately.

Another possibility is that after several years Farmer Smith becomes disabled by illness or is otherwise unable to continue farming and Joe takes over the entire farming operation, which now must support his own family as well as both elderly parents. The farm can't support two families so Joe's wife takes a full-time job off the farm, as well as helping on the farm. This works some years, but other years Joe has to take out a loan to meet operating costs, and the profits aren't always sufficient to pay the loan back in its entirety. Over time debt builds up.

Meanwhile, Joe's other four siblings have scattered and are engaged in non-farming occupations. When Joe reaches about age 50 both parents die, and ownership of the farm passes equally to the five siblings. For Joe to continue farming he must buy out his siblings' share of their inheritance. If, at this time, the farm operation and land is valued at $300,000, Joe must come up with $240,000 in cash, which he does not have, because all the assets are tied up in the farmland and operations. "This is like receiving a pie after everyone else had taken their slice," explains anthropologist Kathryn Dudley, adding that many families who "face off across the kitchen table" to figure out how to proceed make decisions that put the farm, and family relationships, at risk.[20]

The land is already indebted by previous operational loans, and if Joe takes out $240,000 more debt against it to buy out his siblings who, fairly, want their share of the inheritance, he places his farm operation in serious financial jeopardy. His choices are to enlarge his operation in hopes of supporting a larger debt load; selling off some of the land, thereby reducing the size of his operation, but also reducing the size of the mortgage he has to take out against the remaining acreage; cutting some kind of deal with his siblings that might include leasing some of the land and allowing them the proceeds; entering into a land contract purchasing arrangement with his siblings[21]; finding some way to increase off-farm income enough to meet a much larger mortgage payment; or selling the farm outright and splitting the proceeds five ways, after all the debt against it is reconciled.

None of these options is appealing because Joe will either have to assume a very heavy debt load at age 50, knowing he'll never get far enough out from under it to avoid passing it along to his own children, or be forced off the farm and into a job market he's not equipped to enter. If the siblings all want to keep the farm in the family they may agree to a land contract arrangement with terms Joe can manage, but which still places more debt on Joe's shoulders. If some of the siblings agree to a land contract arrangement and others do not, they have to work through a major disagreement. And if Joe defaults on his land contract payments to his siblings, they have to deal with that problem, which risks the demise of the sibling relationships. In the end, there are no good solutions that will keep Joe out of incurring additional debt and still allow his siblings to each receive their share of their land inheritance.

In the best case scenario, Farmer Smith, with the agreement of all the children, sells the farm operation to Joe on a land contract, with a balloon payment due in five or ten years. Assuming Joe keeps up the payments, Farmer Smith uses some of the balloon payment to pay the non-farming siblings their inheritance, and hopefully still has some left for himself in retirement. And the debt on the farm is reduced to the cost of operating loans.

All the possibilities in this example involve families doing business among themselves which is not always an agreeable process. While family members are not likely to force foreclosure on a sibling who is struggling and fails to make his loan payments, defaulting on the loan will very likely create tension among those involved. And sometimes it is the sibling who doesn't participate in the land contract buyout agreement who comes out best because he/she insisted on their share of the land inheritance at the time the last parent died. In this situation Joe takes out a conventional loan to buy this sibling out. If land values crash, debt mounts and Joe's operating loan needs become more than his land is worth, the bank can refuse to lend Joe more money, or call in his outstanding loans. Joe's land will be sold off to pay the bank –a situation in which everyone, except the sibling who received his/her share up front, loses everything.

Farming is a risk-fraught business. The chances of falling into poverty loom large among farmers and small business people whose enterprises depend on agriculture, and the chances of getting back out of poverty once anyone in a rural area falls into it, is small. Success and failure rise and fall on the same, largely unpredictable and uncontrollable events—weather, the commodities markets, the local and world-wide economy, interest rates, government trade and agricultural policies, and luck.

Public Policy Fails and Midwestern Native American Poverty Endures

> *When the lands colonized by the Europeans became the United States and wealth was measured in material terms and money, the relatively minimalistic Native Americans suddenly found themselves at the mercy of the almighty dollar.*—Dante McAuliffe, Pine Ridge Indian Reservation

Native American poverty is not the traditional American poverty whereby workers are poor because they don't get paid enough and wages are kept low to increase profits for the companies that employ them. Keeping the Indian population poor provides no direct benefit to the scheme of American free-enterprise, profit-motive capitalism that caused the problem in the first place. It is not difficult to understand why Native Americans have the problems they do—they live in a country that stole everything from them and has refused to give anything back. Indians were remanded to barely inhabitable land and left there because politicians don't care enough to do anything about it, because their relationship with the federal government is complicated, because they don't have mandated representation in Congress, and because they don't vote in appreciable numbers, and thus have great difficulty entering into any political arena to negotiate for their needs or advocate for themselves.

Sadly, portraits of Native American poverty paint the ugliest possible picture of rural Midwestern America, because theirs is the nation's most dire poverty—a circumstance that became the nearly unavoidable Native American manifest destiny the moment they were sentenced to life on reservations more than one hundred years ago. The difference is that while the white man believed their manifest destiny was ordained by God, Native Americans believe their manifest destiny arose from the evil white man.

That the unabated greed of expansionist America in the 1800s plunged the Native American population into a depth of poverty from which most tribes have never recovered is not news.[22] What is profoundly disturbing is that the devastating effects of this public policy agenda crafted over a century ago still endures as profound historical trauma for Native Americans and has never been made right.

In 2013, Shannon County, South Dakota, was the poorest county in the United States and encompasses the Pine Ridge Indian Reservation, home to 40,000 members of the Oglala Sioux Indian Tribe. These are the poorest of America's poor, who live overcrowded lives in rotting, mold infested trailers, and suffer the extraordinary problems that come with high alcoholism and drug abuse rates, youth gangs, poor health, lack of employment opportunities and excessive school dropout rates.

The average annual per capita income in Shannon County is $8,000. Ninety percent of the county budget relies on federal government transfer payments and $70 million of the tribe's $80 million annual budget depends upon federal program allocations. The median income on Pine Ridge is between $2,600 and $3,500 a year. About 97 percent of Pine Ridge residents live below the poverty line. Other statistics indicate[23]:

- Unemployment rates between 80 and 90 percent;
- Average per capita income of $4,000;
- Eight times the national rate of diabetes;
- Five times the national rate of cervical cancer;
- Twice the rate of heart disease;
- Eight times the national rate of tuberculosis;
- Alcoholism rates estimated as high as 80 percent;
- One in four infants born with fetal alcohol syndrome or its effects;
- Suicide rates more than twice the national rate;
- Teen suicide rate four times the national rate;
- Infant mortality is three times the national rate, and life expectancy on Pine Ridge is the lowest in the United States and the second lowest in the Western Hemisphere. Only Haitians have a lower life expectancy, and Haiti is considered a third (or fourth) world nation.

When the 2012–13 Congress adopted sequestration measures, the Native American population was once again raped and pillaged by government policies.[24] None of the programs aiding the Native American population, including money allocated through the Departments of Interior, Health and Human Services and Agriculture, was included on the sequestration exemptions list. Consequently, the federal program cuts are delivering yet another blow to the Native American population. Vital social programs such as Meals on Wheels, which delivers food to housebound elderly, school budgets, Head Start and health services have disappeared.

The tribes' position is that they should be exempt from the sequestration policy because the money they receive from the federal government is part of the nation-to-nation treaty obligation the U.S. government agreed to when it took away their land. Viewed from this perspective, the program cuts fracture existing legal and moral agreements with the Native American population. "It's one more reminder that our relationship with the federal government is a series of broken promises," says the Rev. George Winzenburg, a Catholic priest who presides over the Red Cloud Indian School at Pine Ridge.[25]

Tribal Governance

> *We were told that they wished merely to pass through our country ... to seek for gold in the far west.... Yet before the ashes of the council are cold, the Great Father is building his forts among us.... His presence here is ... an insult to the spirits of our ancestors. Are we then to give up their sacred graves for corn?—*
> Chief Red Cloud (1822–1909), Oglala Sioux Nation

Historically Native Americans have always, with very good reason, felt misunderstood and have never trusted that their treaty agreements with the United States would be honored. Because American Indians are citizens of their tribal nations as well as the United States, and those tribal nations are characterized under U.S. law as "domestic dependent nations," a special relationship exists that creates a particular tension between rights granted via tribal sovereignty and rights that individual Indians retain as U.S. citizens. The tension over this "dual citizen" status was far more extreme before Native Americans were uniformly granted U.S. citizenship in 1924, but continues within the U.S. colonial context even today.

With the passage of the Indian Civil Rights Act (ICRA) in 1968, also called the Indian Bill of Rights, Native Americans were guaranteed many civil rights previously withheld from them, including:

- Rights to free speech, press, and assembly
- Protection from unreasonable search and seizure
- Right of criminal defendant to a speedy trial, to be advised of the charges, and to confront any adverse witnesses
- Right to hire an attorney in a criminal case
- Protection against self incrimination
- Protection against cruel and unusual punishment, excessive bail, incarceration of more than one year and/or a fine in excess of $5,000 for any one offense
- Protection from double jeopardy or ex post facto laws
- Right to a jury trial for offenses punishable by imprisonment
- Equal protection under the law and due process

While these protections are extremely important to the tribal populations, none of them provides a clear roadmap leading them out of deep, persistent poverty.

Individual Midwestern State Farming Profiles

> *Farming looks mighty easy when your plow is a pencil, and you're a thousand miles from a corn field.*—President Dwight D. Eisenhower

At the beginning of the westward advancement there were no boundaries anywhere in the wide open spaces and thousands of miles that comprised the Midwest. Eventually the area was divided up, first into territories and later into states; and land use, which varied by state or territorial boundary, were put into place.

Over time each state developed its own culture and personality but remained part of Middle America, the nation's heartland, with its characteristic values and vast, deeply entrenched agricultural economy. North Dakotans may differ from South Dakotans or Iowans, but not as much as New Englanders differ from Southerners or Californians differ from everybody.

Besides being a tough way to earn a living no matter where one lives, agriculture throughout the Midwest shares certain common traits[26]:

- Land ownership has tended to remain stable, but areas having more cropland tend to have a higher percentage of rented land.
- The average age of farmers is 57 and this number is creeping up. The number of farmers over age 75 and still farming is increasing and the number of younger farmers (under age 25) dropped 30 percent between 2002 and 2007. During this same time period the number of women farmers increased by nearly one-third.
- The majority of farms are still small-business operations with annual sales of less than $10,000. Most individually owned agricultural enterprises, in order to operate in the black, rely on off-farm income.
- Farm operators on larger farms (sales >$250,000 per year) tend to be younger, are more likely to report farming as their primary occupation, and are less likely to work off the farm. However, during the five years between 2002 and 2007, the number of primary occupation farmers decreased by 19 percent.
- Most livestock farmers try to grow at least a portion of their own feed (silage) in order to reduce production costs and increase their profit margin.
- Other than corporate enterprises, most individual and partnership farms diversify to include more than one category of inventory, while corporate farms are more likely to focus on a single crop or livestock operation.

The Great Lakes states differ from the Great Plains states in both geography and access to water for irrigation. The Grain Belt states' economy focuses primarily on agriculture while the Rust Belt states have been, until recently, manufacturing centers. And while, in large areas of the Midwest, the percentage of farmer-owned land exceeds 50 percent, because of the large amount of cropland, the region tends to have a greater percentage of rented land than is available in other rural areas.[27]

Tables One, Two and Three describe the agricultural profiles common to each of the 12 Midwestern farm states. Commonly a single farm produces more than one commodity, and it is not unusual for a farmer to both raise livestock and grow feed crops.

Tables One and Two are self-explanatory; in Table Three the difference between total cropland and harvested cropland is partially explained by the amount of land enrolled in a government program that pays farmers not to plant or to rotate certain crops, and/or by an individual farmer's decision not to plant because he fears commodity prices will be too low, or other factors impede his ability to plant in a particular year. Irrigation farms are less vulnerable to drought, while farms that do not irrigate are more vulnerable to variations in weather; however, the cost of irrigating must be figured into overall farm operations, making this type of farming more expensive.

Table One: 2007–2011 Farm Demographics[28]

Farm Profile	IL	IN	IA	KS	MI	MN
No. of farms	76,860	60,938	92,856	68,531	56,014	80,839
Acres in farmland	26,775,100	14,773,184	30,747,550	46,345,827	10,031,807	26,917,962
Average farm size in acres	348	242	331	707	179	332
No. of farms <180 acres	47,605	45,246	51,525	31,156	44,151	46,293
No. of farms >180 acres	29,255	15,692	41,331	37,375	11,863	34,546
Total cropland farms	67,431	51,283	82,785	55,272	48,592,	71,970
Total cropland acres	23,707,699	12,909,002	26,316,332	28,216,064	7,803,643	21,948,603
Harvested cropland farms	54,185	41,743	63,672	43,553	37,868	53,943
Harvested cropland acres	22,611,443	12,108,940	23,799,380	20,917,000	6,859,081	19,267,018
Irrigation farms	2,388	2,391	1,287	5,957	5,078	2,918
Irrigated acres	474,454	397,113	189,518	2,762,748	500,428	506,357
Farms w/profit <$25,000	41,944	39,452	42,479	39,636	40,765	46,601
Farms w/profit >$25,000	34,916	21,486	50,377	25,895	15,249	34,391
Family/individual farms	65,748	52,553	77,452	55,706	48,687	70,055
Partnership farms	6509	4,614	6,990	5,549	4260	6,227
Corporate farms	3433	2,976	6,509	2,774	2,494	2,848
Other farm type	1,170	793	1,905	1,502	573	1,862
Average operator age	56.2 years	55.0	56.1	57.7	56.3	55.3
Percent of full-time farm operators	48%	42%	52%	47%	44%	48%

Farm Profile	MO	NE	ND	OH	SD	WI	12-State
No. of farms	107,825	47,712	31,970	75,861	31,169	78,463	806,038
Acres in farmland	29,026,573	45,480,356	39,674,586	13,956,563	43,666,403	15,190,804	342,586,715
Average farm size in acres	269	953	1,241	184	1,401	194	425
No. of farms <180 acres	69,300	18,955	8,723	42,403	10,727	54,521	470,605
No. of farms >180 acres	38,535	28,757	23,247	33,458	20,442	23,942	338,443
Total cropland farms	86,299	40,798	29,378	64,775	26,625	68,478	693,686
Total cropland acres	16,405,595	21,486,025	27,527,180	10,832,772	19,094,311	10,116,279	226,363,505
Harvested cropland farms	69,585	34,715	20,408	54,790	21,902	54,105	550,469
Harvested cropland acres	12,980,113	18,169,876	22,035,717	9,991,007	15,278,709	8,884,628	192,902,912
Irrigation farms	3,613	17,128	795	2,402	1,627	2,907	48,491
Irrigated acres	1,199,981	8,558,569	236,138	37,959	373,842	377,291	15,614,398
Farms w/profit <$25,000	78,784	18,898	15,436	51,751	13,302	50,715	479,763
Farms w/profit >$25,000	29,041	28,814	16,534	24,110	17,867	27,748	326,428
Family/individual farms	94,818	29,848	28,079	66,382	26,633	68,138	684,099
Partnership farms	8,202	3,616	2,834	5,737	2,658	6,386	63,582
Corporate farms	3,063	3,571	560	2,956	1,421	3,333	35,938
Other farm type	1,742	677	467	786	457	606	12,540
Average operator age	57.1	55.9	56.5	55.7	55.7	55.0	56.0
Percent of full-time farm operators	42%	60%	58%	43%	60%	47%	49.3%

Sixty-seven percent of the total Midwest farm acreage is in cropland, and 75 percent of all Midwest farms are cropland farms. Eighty-five percent of Midwestern farms are family or individually owned. Overall, there are less than one million operating farms supporting the entire 12 state Midwestern farm economies.

Table Two outlines the 2007–2012 livestock inventory for the Midwestern states. Farms identified as sale farms are those raising cattle or hogs to sell to other farm operations. Farms raising cattle or hogs to sell to other farm operations, rather than taking their livestock to market, are identified in the "sale" commodity category.

Table Two: 2007 Livestock Inventory[29]

Commodity	IL	IN	IA	KS	MI	MN	MO	NE	ND	OH	SD	WI	12-State
Cattle & calf farms	18,397	18,463	29,690	30,017	14,454	24,685	58,645	21,414	10,508	26,105	15,667	35,125	202,170
Inventory	1,231,105	875,350	3,982,344	6,669,163	1,048,206	2,395,217	4,292,702	6,576,950	1,811,523	1,272,402	3,687,728	3,373,923	37,216,613
Beef cattle farms	14,753	12,668	20,809	25,776	7,848	14,410	51,289	18,223	9,667	17,398	13,802	14,775	221,418
Inventory	429,111	235,299	904,100	1,516,374	109,500	399,768	2,089,181	1,889,842	930,023	293,757	1,649,492	169,820	10,616,267
Dairy farms	1,217	2,023	2,390	776	2,647	5,148	2,621	493	402	3,650	656	14,158	36,181
Inventory	99,667	166,149	215,391	115,634	344,233	459,752	110,358	54,410	26,479	271,938	86,243	1,249,309	3,199,563
Sale cattle & calves	16,046	15,088	27,535	27,565	11,631	22,122	52,060	20,218	10,025	21,438	15,171	30,193	269,092
Inventory	894,593	637,951	3,635,880	8,738,281	603,609	1,586,705	2,462,198	7,620,019	1,109,460	793,955	2,745,227	1,513,662	32,341,540
Hog & pig farms	2,864	3,420	8,330	1,454	2,691	4,382	2,999	2,213	350	3,718	959	3,188	36,568
Inventory	4,298,716	3,669,057	19,295,092	1,885,252	1,032,054	7,652,284	3,101,469	3,268,544	181,679	1,831,084	1,490,034	436,814	48,142,079
Sale hogs & pigs	3,063	3,790	8,758	1,542	2,930	4,748	2,971	2,482	351	4,505	1,042	3,516	39,698
Inventory	13,196,581	9,523,891	47,279,443	4,712,306	3,316,183	22,815,512	9,073,468	10,880,227	675,808	5,881,107	4,487,708	1,085,793	132,928,027
Poultry farms	260	399	598	158	725	940	644	206	75	791	85	1,238	6,119
Inventory	325,036	37,072,109	10,257,286	26,941	4,027,972	47,948,383	279,937,641	4,893,959	14,442	49,656,074	272,986	48,804,252	483,237,081

The largest livestock inventory is poultry; however there are fewer poultry farms than any other Midwestern farm type, indicating that individual poultry farms are large confinement operations. While the largest livestock market inventory is hogs, the greatest number of livestock farms overall raise beef cattle. Those farms that sell cattle and hogs to other farmers maintain large livestock categories. And some farmers maintain more than one category of livestock.

Table Three numerates the total crop inventory for the Midwestern states. Silage grain, commonly corn or sorghum, is fermented high-moisture fodder that can be fed to cud-chewing animals such as cattle and sheep or used as a biofuel feedstock. The grain is fermented and stored in a process called ensilage, ensiling or silaging, and is usually made from grass crops, including corn, sorghum or other cereals, using the entire green plant (not just the grain). Silage can be made from many field crops and is stored either by placing cut green vegetation in a silo, piling it in a large heap covered with plastic sheeting, or wrapping large bales in plastic film. Corn also is the main feedstock used for producing ethanol fuel in the United States, which is produced by means of ethanol fermentation and distillation.

Forage acres are parcels of pasture land set aside for grazing, most often by cattle, sheep and hogs. Some farmers seed their pastureland to insure the availability of food for their grazing animals; others rely on the native grass and other vegetation.

Table Three: 2007 Crop Inventory for Major Crops[30]

Commodity	IL	IN	IA	KS	MI	MN
Corn (grain) farms	38,260	24,400	50,095	11,236	13,768	30,976
acres	13,096,231	6,362,576	13,842,282	4,200,000	230,668	7,700,000
Corn (silage) farms	2,296	2,120	4,967	1,665	3,352	7,998
acres	75,247	105,937	220,646	350,000	297,381	435,506
Wheat (all) farms	9,416	5,058	577	22,630	6,263	6,727
acres	891,567	362,571	29,512	7,900,000	523,153	1,526,000
Oats (grain) farms	1,006	568	3,056	874	2,181	5,499
acres	24,165	7,948	66,651	25,000	55,046	110,000
Barley (grain) farms	46	37	86	157	376	1,126
acres	738	493	2,815	6,000	12,953	60,000
Sorghum (grain) farms	731	78	40	11,379	26	3
acres	76,601	8,938	2,113	2,000,000	658	36
Sorghum (silage) farms	58	52	51	1,779	125	13
acres	1,169	796	837	85,000	2,635	145
Soybean farms	33,945	21,973	41,524	13,232	10,461	27,040
acres	8,293,711	4,783,821	8,612,810	3,750,000	1,715,427	7,020,000
Forage land acres	593,186	625,898	1,125,565	2,450,000	1,160,467	2,098,000

Commodity	MO	NE	ND	OH	SD	WI	12-State Total
Corn (grain) farms	15,375	22,812	5,809	24,436	12,198	27,505	276,870
acres	3,070,000	4,830,000	2,348,171	3,606,246	4,445,368	3,250,847	66,982,389
Corn (silage) farms	1,704	2,671	1,707	3,928	3,928	15,338	51,674
acres	69,353	160,000	180,634	182,935	383,599	732,636	3,193,874
Wheat (all) farms	7,640	8,037	12,303	11,485	7,163	5,422	102,721
acres	680,000	1,964,302	8,428,462	732,106	3,324,778	280,464	26,642,915

Commodity	MO	NE	ND	OH	SD	WI	12-State Total
Oats (grain) farms	459	885	2,513	2,800	1,702	7,934	29,477
acres	8,000	35,108	257,021	46,348	124,743	166,794	926,824
Barley (grain) farms	56	35	4,855	210	205	1,104	8,293
acres	1,531	1,777	1,384,689	2,994	28,761	23,645	1,526,396
Sorghum (grain) farms	1,085	1,901	0	16	394	11	15,664
acres	33,000	236,607	0	1,203	129,413	242	2,488,811
Sorghum (silage) farms	174	444	17	122	191	138	3,164
acres	6,533	20,376	1,222	2,718	17,983	2,201	141,615
Soybean farms	18,388	16,620	5,779	23,892	9,862	14,513	237,229
acres	5,200,000	3,834,855	3,073,981	4,236,337	3,222,872	1,363,124	55,106,938
Forage land acres	3,770,000	2,563,515	2,525,213	1,156,523	3,239,947	2,797,497	24,105,811

The largest Midwestern grain crops are corn, soybeans and wheat. More Midwestern farms grow corn than any other grain, but as is true with livestock, many farmers grow more than one crop type, so it may be included in more than one grain category.

Appendix Two identifies the counties in each of the Midwestern states having poverty rates greater than or equal to 20 percent and counties having poverty rates between 13 and 19.9 percent, which is above the national poverty rate.

Other demographic data indicate that 88 percent of the rural residents are Caucasian, the overall educational attainment at all levels is slightly less than for urban areas, and per capita income averages 71 percent of that of urban residents.[31] The unemployment rates tend to exceed the ongoing national average and the average non-farm income is less than 50 percent of their urban counterparts.

The rural Midwest experiences a significant shortage of health care professionals and the infant mortality rate is considerably higher than in urban areas. And notably, while 14 percent of independent farmers nationwide are women, the states with the lowest percentages of women principal farm operators are in the Midwest, with women making up less than 10 percent of all farm operators in four Midwestern states: South Dakota (7.7 percent), Nebraska (8.4 percent), Minnesota (9.1 percent) and Iowa (9.1 percent). However, 13.4 percent of all Missouri farmers are women, and the state is home to the largest number of women farmers (12,754) among the 12 Midwestern states. Missouri is also the poorest among the Midwestern states.[32]

4

Feeding Candy to the Cows

The Rural Midwestern Farm Economy

> *Although they are some of the hardest working folks I know, rural Americans earn, on average, $11,000 less than their urban counterparts each year. And they are far more likely to live in poverty ... because most of the persistent poverty in the nation is found in rural areas.*—Tom Vilsack, U.S. Secretary of Agriculture (2008–present) and former Iowa governor

"Cattle farmers struggling with record corn prices are feeding their cows candy instead," headlined a 2012 news article about the rising costs of corn, a mainstay of bovine feed.[1] "It has been a practice going on for decades and is a very good way for producers to reduce feed cost, and provide less expensive food for consumers," said Ki Fanning, a livestock nutritionist with Great Plains Livestock Consulting, Inc. in Eagle, Nebraska, adding that this is an efficient way to feed cattle during drought years and when the price of corn gets too high—up to $315 per ton. By comparison, a ton of ice cream sprinkles can be purchased for as little as $160.

"As the price of corn has climbed, farmers either sold off their pigs and cattle, or they found alternative feeds," explains Mike Yoder, a dairy farmer in Middlebury, Indiana, also quoted in the article. He feeds his 400 cows bits of candy, hot chocolate mix, crumbled cookies, breakfast cereal, trail mix, dried cranberries, orange peelings and ice cream sprinkles, which are blended into more traditional forms of feed, like hay. According to Yoder, a cow whose diet consists of three percent sugar will increase its milk production by three pounds per day—a not insignificant amount.

Not surprisingly, the practice is subject to the laws of supply and demand, and Yoder said he's seen the price of sprinkles rise from $160 per ton, which is about half the price of corn, to about $240. But he still buys the candy. "Farming is a game of inches sometimes, or half-inches. Every little penny you can find to save, you do," he says.

Saving a penny here and a penny there describes the Midwest farm economy perfectly. Farmers try their best to save money any way they can, penny by penny, and still survive—or at least not fall so deeply into poverty they have no reasonable hope of ever getting out.

Economic Life in the Rural Midwest

> My father asserted that there was no better place to bring up a family than in a rural Midwest environment.... There's something about getting up at 5 a.m., feeding the livestock and chickens, and milking a couple of cows before breakfast that gives you a lifelong respect for the price of butter and eggs.—Bill Vaughan

Although faced with the responsibility of being the major producer of the nation's food supply, the number of Midwestern farms has steadily declined since 1935.[2] The number of currently working farms in the Midwest has dropped from 806,038 to 772,630 (6 percent) in the last five years, a loss of 34,142 farms. Midwestern farmers operate 36 percent of the total number of farms nationwide, and the number of working farms in the Midwest continues to decline, making the Midwest rural agricultural economy, at best, fragile.[3]

The Midwest Rust Belt

> By the 1980s, the Rust Belt became what the Dust Bowl had been to an earlier generation—a symbolic name for a devastating economic change.—Dictionary of American History

The Rust Belt is an effective description of a quickly declining industrial heartland dominated by the heavy manufacturing and steel industries that were abandoned and went to rust. Geographically the term refers to an economic region of the Midwest, which includes Illinois, Indiana, Michigan and Ohio, that depends primarily upon manufacturing both as the chief source of employment and a source of supplemental, off-farm income. And while the Rust Belt includes many large, densely populated urban areas, its workforce comes from nearby rural areas.

When the U.S. steel industry collapsed during the 1970s and 1980s the U.S. worldwide market share of manufactured steel dropped 8 percent in 20 years, causing the loss of a staggering 260,000 well-paying, benefit-rich manufacturing jobs that have never returned.[4] In Youngstown, Ohio, the closure of three steel mills eliminated nearly 10,000 high-paying jobs. Detroit fell victim to a collapsing automotive industry, causing that Midwestern city to become the poorest in the nation.[5] Many of these jobs were lost following the execution of the North American Free Trade Agreement (NAFTA)[6] between the United States, Mexico and Canada; the rest succumbed to the recent recession.

While manufacturing jobs appear to be very slowly trending upward, it will take a long time to recover from job losses that ranged up to 56 percent in some regions of the Midwest. And unlike previously, new manufacturing jobs are not necessarily high-wage jobs.[7] This is important for two reasons: First, fewer rural residents graduate from high school or go onto college than their urban counterparts, so overall the earning power of working adults in rural areas is diminished, and most who are employed are low-wage earners.

Second is the issue of workforce quality. The availability of a skilled labor force is paramount in any manufacturer's decision to locate a production facility in a rural area, and rural areas generally have fewer skilled workers, making them less attractive locales for new manufacturing plants.

For rural areas that rely upon manufacturing jobs, when these jobs disappear re-employment options are slim. Rural communities tend to have only one manufacturing plant of any kind and draw employees from a wide area, and if the plant closes, workers have nowhere else nearby to look for work, creating a larger pool of potential workers than available jobs. This also creates a population of long-term unemployed, who are less attractive hires when a job becomes available.

The loss of manufacturing jobs devastated the economies and budgets of states where these jobs had been located. As a result, services normally provided by states, including Medicaid, Community Service Block Grants for anti-poverty and low income help programs, and other types of government assistance, shrank dramatically, leaving financially struggling rural people with nothing to grab onto.[8]

The Grain Belt Economy

It's far too easy for Americans to forget that the food they eat doesn't just magically appear on a supermarket shelf.—U.S. Senator Christopher Dodd

Indiana, Illinois, Missouri, Ohio, Iowa, Kansas, Minnesota, North and South Dakota, Nebraska and Wisconsin comprise the Midwest Grain Belt, which produces over $100 billion in grain and another $100 billion in livestock annually.[9,10] This region not only feeds the nation, it produces significant amounts of bio-fuel, which is an important player in America's efforts to become energy independent.

In production volume terms, Iowa, for example, harvested 55 million tons of grain in 2010, and over the previous five years averaged 57 million tons per year.[11] By comparison, Canada's five-year average is 49 million tons for the entire nation. While Canada has more than 30 million acres in grain, mostly wheat, Iowa has only 13 million acres in grain, mostly corn. The yield-per-acre difference is huge—just 1.4 tons in Canada versus more than four tons in Iowa.

Iowa also produced 13 million tons of soybeans in 2010. During the same period China produced 15 million tons, mirroring Iowa's average production figures over the past five years.[12] However, Iowa has less than 10 million acres in soybeans, while China has 22 million acres; thus Iowa's yield-per-acre is 1.4 tons, exactly double the 0.7 tons per acre China produces.

Obviously Iowa, sitting in the heart of the Grain Belt, owns and occupies a phenomenally productive piece of agricultural real estate. This rich farmland enabled the United States, with only 4 percent of the world's population, to produce a remarkable 40 percent of the world's corn, the leading grain, and 35 percent of its soybeans—until 2012 when a nationwide drought took its toll on corn and other crops.[13]

The Grain Belt also produces other crops, including barley, hay, oats, sorghum, and wheat, as well as having a lucrative dairy and livestock industry. Table One illustrates the total Midwest crop value of production for the principal Grain Belt crops for 2012, the most recent year for which data are presently available:

Table One: 2010 Midwestern States Crop Values Summary[14]

State	Field/Misc. crops ($1,000s)	Fruit/nut ($1,000s)	Commercial vegetables ($1,000s)	Total crop value ($1,000s)
Illinois	16,105,750	33,365	47,835	16,186,950
Indiana	8,113,550	13,994	90,470	8,217,964
Iowa	17,240,048	2,228	1,156	17,243,432
Kansas	7,801,835	5,250	*N/A	7,807,085
Michigan	3,815,502	308,891	257,380	4,381,773
Minnesota	12,231,134	12,571	117,961	12,361,666
Missouri	5,489,307	21,060	13,444	5,523,811
Nebraska	11,539,490	N/A	N/A	11,539,490
North Dakota	7,503,696	N/A	N/A	7,503,696
Ohio	6,034,433	48,563	153,997	6,236,993
South Dakota	6,201,746	N/A	N/A	6,201,746
Wisconsin	4,373,009	211,150	152,691	4,736,850
**Midwest Total	$106,449,500	$657,072	$834,934	$107,941,456
% of U.S. Total	68%	3%	7%	57%
**U.S. Total	$157,543,382	$21,902,400	$11,927,629	$189,370,975

*NA: data not available;
**Putting these numbers in perspective, one trillion equals one thousand billion, thus $189,370,975,000,000 which is the total 2010 U.S. crop value, is 189 trillion, 370 billion, 975 million dollars, over half of which is produced in the Midwestern states. To illustrate the magnitude of these numbers, $233 stacked is 1 inch, $1 million is 333 feet or 11/3 football fields, and $1 billion (1000 million) is 333,000 feet or just over 63 miles.

In 2010 the Midwestern states produced 68 percent of the nation's field and miscellaneous crops, 31 percent of the fruit and nut crops, 7 percent of the commercial vegetables and 57 percent of the total crop value. The overall U.S. total represents an increase of 20 percent and 11 percent respectively, over 2009 values for field and miscellaneous crops and fruit and nut crops, a 3 percent decline in commercial vegetable values, and a 17 percent overall increase in these crop values nationwide. However, in 2012–13 many areas of the Midwest experienced a relentlessly severe drought and the U.S. Drought Monitor[15] updates show little indication that the drought will abate soon. Climatologists say two or three winters of an absurd amount of snowfall followed by heavy spring rains are needed to reverse the intense and dangerously dry conditions.

Corn. Corn is grown on over 400,000 U.S. farms, making the United States the largest corn producer in the world. In 2000, the United States produced almost ten billion bushels of the world's total 23 billion bushel crop. Grain corn accounts for almost 25 percent of the harvested crop acres in this country; corn grown for silage[16] accounts for about 2 percent of the total harvested cropland, or about six million acres.[17]

About 80 percent of all corn grown in the United States is consumed by domestic and overseas livestock, poultry, and fish production.[18] The crop is used as ground grain, silage, high-moisture, and high-oil corn. About 12 percent of the U.S. corn crop results in foods that are either consumed directly (e.g., corn chips) or indirectly (e.g., high fructose corn syrup). It also has a wide array of industrial uses, including ethanol, a popular oxygenate in cleaner burning auto fuel.

Soybeans. In 2000 approximately 2.8 billion bushels of soybeans were harvested from almost 73 million acres of U.S. cropland, roughly equivalent to that of corn grown for grain.[19] Over 350,000 farms in the United States produce soybeans, accounting for over 50 percent of the world's soybean production and $6.66 billion in soybean and product exports.

Soybeans produce 56 percent of the world's oilseed and are also used to create a variety of products, the most basic of which are soybean oil, meal, and hulls. Soybean oil, used in both food manufacturing and cooking, represents approximately 79 percent of all edible oil consumed in the United States.[20] Soybean oil is found in anti-corrosion agents, soy diesel fuel and waterproof cement. Over 30 million tons of soybean meal is consumed as livestock feed in a year, and the hulls are used as a component of cattle feed rations.

Alfalfa. Alfalfa is the primary hay crop grown in the United States, exceeding 150 million tons per year. Hay is produced mainly for domestic consumption, although there is a growing export market. The most common exports are timothy, some alfalfa, Sudan grass, and Bermuda grass hay.[21] Hay crops also produce seeds that can be used for planting or as specialized grains.

Wheat. Over 240,000 farms in the United States produce wheat, which is about 13 percent of the world's wheat, and supplies about 25 percent of the world's wheat export market. About two-thirds of total U.S. wheat production comes from the Great Plains.[22]

Wheat is classified by time of year planted, hardness, and color (e.g., Hard Red Winter (HRW). The characteristics of each class of wheat affect milling and baking when used in food products. Of the wheat consumed in the United States, over 70 percent is used for food products, about 22 percent is used for animal feed and residuals, and the remainder is used for seed.

Sorghum. In the United States, grain sorghum is used primarily as an animal feed but is also used in food products and as an industrial feedstock. Some farmers grow sorghum as a hedge against drought. This water-efficient crop is more drought tolerant and requires fewer inputs than corn. Kansas, Texas, Nebraska, Oklahoma, and Missouri produce most of the grain sorghum grown in this country. The United States exports almost half of the sorghum it produces and controls 70 percent to 80 percent of world sorghum exports.

As much as 12 percent of domestic sorghum goes toward ethanol production and its various co-products. With demand for renewable fuel sources increasing, demand for co-products like sorghum DDG (dry distiller's grain) will increase because of sorghum's favorable nutrition profile.

Industrial products that utilize sorghum include wallboard and biodegradable packaging materials. However, worldwide, over half of the sorghum grown is for human consumption.

Rice. Just over 9,000 farms produce rice in the United States and none are in the Grain Belt. U.S. rice production accounts for just over 1 percent of the world's total, but this country is the second leading rice exporter with 18 percent of the world market. About 60 percent of the rice consumed in the United States is for direct food use; another 20 percent goes into processed foods, and most of the rest goes into beer.[23]

The total field and miscellaneous crop production values for the most common Midwestern crops produced nationwide during the period 2009–2011 are illustrated in Table Two. Oats, barley and rice dropped 11 percent, 15 percent and 18 percent, respectively, from previous years. All others increased, and the total U.S. field and miscellaneous crop value increased 26 percent during this three-year period. Variations in crop values indicate the quality of the crop year combined with market fluctuations.

Table Two: Total 2009–2011 Field and Miscellaneous Crop Production Values for the Most Common Midwestern Crops[24]

Crop	2009 $1,000s	2010 $1,000s	2011 $1,000s	Increase/Decrease $1,000s/%
Barley	972,173	691,666	822,151	150,022/-15%
Corn	46,734,066	64,643,295	76,464,126	29,730,060/+64%
Hay	14,715,599	14,656,191	17,749,495	3,033,896/+21%
Oats	208,473	217,498	186,338	22,135/-11%
Millet	25,460	52,419	53,706	28,246/+111%
Rice	3,209,236	3,183,213	2,631,681	577,555/-18%
Rye	34,471	37,401	49,180	14,907/+43%
Sorghum	1,207,111	1,617,851	1,284,777	7,666/+6%
Wheat	10,654,115	12,827,254	14,367,556	3,713,441/+35%
Soybeans	32,145,207	37,546,840	35,784,360	3,639,153/+11%
Total	$109,905,911	$135,473,628	$149,393,370	+$40,917,081/+36%
Percent of U.S. Total	87%	86%	87%	

Farmers who grew corn, millet, wheat or rye had consistently good years during this period, while the others were not as prosperous, and those who grew barley, oats or rice lost money. However, crop production values increased by 36 percent and overall the farm economy grew by 27 percent during this period while, at the same time, the rest of the U.S. economy was experiencing a sluggish recovery from a significant recession. The largest beneficiaries of this growth were corporate farming enterprises; overall rural poverty rates remained basically unchanged and, in some areas, increased during this time period.

Livestock

> *We're moving from a commodity economy where a kernel of corn is a kernel of corn is a kernel of corn to an ingredient economy where there will be a kernel of corn that will be designed for fuel and food and there will be a kernel of corn designed for livestock.* —Secretary of Agriculture Tom Vilsack

Across history, the livestock industry has played an important role in the American economy, beginning with the industry following the advancing western frontier. But because success depended on both the environment and the weather, many homesteaders failed in their attempts to raise livestock all the way to market. A bad corn year meant less food for hogs, resulting in early butchering, lighter weight, and lower prices. A sustained drought meant poor grazing for cattle and sheep, resulting in lower quality meat and poor market value. Diseases such as hog cholera or tick fever could decimate a farmer's entire stock, leaving him completely devoid of income.

In the industry's early days animals were slaughtered on an "as needed" basis, but as farmers became more proficient, they sold their best animals at market and killed the others off each winter, rather than bear the cost of feeding them. While non-market animal parts were used for various animal products, the practice generated a great deal of animal waste.

As farmers and ranchers realized that grain-fed cattle yielded a higher grade beef than free range, grazing cattle, commercial interests took hold of the livestock industry. Huge feed lots capable of supplying as many as 50,000 animals per year emerged and by the mid 1960s the government estimated that nine million cattle were being raised in feedlots.[25] However, fluctuations in the wider economy, coupled with bad weather, can cause feed prices to increase, cutting into profits. And animals raised in confinement are more subject to diseases which, if they occur, can wipe out an entire stockyard.

Today, beef cattle, dairy cattle and hogs are the primary livestock raised in the Midwest and, in addition to meat and dairy products, are sources of various animal byproducts having many commercial uses. Other types of livestock raised for commercial sale generally do not rise to the production levels beef and dairy cattle and hog operations enjoy, however poultry (chickens, turkeys, ducks, geese), sheep, goats, rabbits, alpacas and llamas are raised in significant numbers. All are food sources and most have dual value in other commercial markets. For example, sheep, llamas and alpacas produce wool, geese produce down feathers, and rabbit fur is used in clothing. Nevertheless, beef cattle, dairy cattle and hogs dominate the economic marketplace.

Farmers nationwide must comply with a variety of local, state and federal regulations as they raise livestock and grow crops, and government food safety regulations carefully monitor the livestock industry. Regardless, certain dangers remain, and animal rights groups have attacked the livestock industry, particularly animal confinement practices, and the use of chemicals and growth hormones to preserve meat and generate greater yields has raised concerns among food safety experts.

Meat Processing

> *Forests and meat animals compete for the same land. The prodigious appetite of the affluent nations for meat means that agribusiness can pay more than those who want to preserve or restore the forest. We are, quite literally, gambling with the future of our planet for the sake of hamburgers.* —Peter Singer, *Animal Liberation*

As the livestock industry expanded, so did the meatpacking industry, which has been the sight of some of the worst working conditions in the history of American labor. Despite the regulations put into place with the 1938 Fair Labor Standards Act, working in a meatpacking plant is still a difficult, backbreaking job. And because it very directly affects the nation's food supply, meat packing has been among the more controversial agribusinesses.

Iowa Beef Processors, Inc. (IBP) was the United States' biggest beef packer and its number two pork processor. In 1967 IBP introduced boxed, vacuum-packed beef and pork, packaged in smaller portions, which was a significant departure from the traditional method of shipping meat as whole carcasses. The boxed meat saved energy and transportation costs by eliminating the shipment of fat, bones and trimmings.

In 2001 IBP was acquired by Tyson Foods for $3.2 billion in cash and stock and relocated to South Dakota. A $24-billion operation, Tyson manages most of the nation's meat supply and provides about 25 billion pounds of chicken, beef, and pork per year to McDonald's, Wal-Mart, and most major supermarket and restaurant chains in the United States. The company has, on occasion, manipulated the nation's food supply.

In 2007 Tyson recalled 40,000 pounds of beef sold at Wal-Mart stores in 12 states after samples tested at its Texas plant revealed potentially deadly E. coli O157:H7 contamination. This same year Tyson began labeling and advertising its chicken products as "raised without antibiotics." After being advised by the USDA that Tyson's use of bacteria-killing gonophores in unhatched eggs constituted antibiotic use, Tyson and the USDA compromised on rewording Tyson's slogan as "raised without antibiotics that impact antibiotic resistance in humans." Tyson competitors Perdue Farms and Sanderson Farms sued, claiming that Tyson's claim violated truth-in-advertising/labeling standards. In May 2008, a federal judge ordered Tyson to stop using the label.

A few months later, USDA inspectors discovered that Tyson was also using the antibiotic gentamicin in eggs. USDA undersecretary for food safety Richard Raymond claimed that the company hid the use of this antibiotic from federal inspectors and that the use of this chemical is standard industry practice. Tyson agreed to voluntarily remove its "raised without antibiotics" label in future packaging and advertising.

Beef Cattle

Raising beef cattle was hard work, but when we sold out and moved into town, I really missed seeing them out the kitchen window ... they were like old friends who showed up every day to say hello.—Lu Mayard

According to 2011 USDA data, Texas was number one, and Kansas, Nebraska and Iowa were second, third and fourth in the nation with regard to beef production.[26] Colorado was fifth, and, together, these five states produce more than 50 percent of the total value of U.S. sales of cattle and calves. Additionally, according to the USDA Agricultural Census Data,[27] in the United States:

- 2011 cattle inventory was 92,582,400/head;
- The economic impact of the beef cattle industry was $44 billion in farm gate receipts; the number of herds was 742,000 and included 30.9 million beef cows and 26.7 million feeder calves[28];
- According to the U.S. Meat Export Federation, 2011 beef exports equaled $4.08 billion for 2.35 billion pounds of beef exported to Mexico, Canada, Japan, Hong Kong and Taiwan[29];
- The cost of production, from 1990 to 2003, included feed yard cost of grain: $261/head; in the past four years, feed yard cost of grain has increased to $494/head;
- Average producer age: 58, up from 56 in 2002;
- U.S. productivity advantage: domestic cattle inventory: 7 percent; domestic beef production: 20 percent;

- 33.5 million head of cattle harvested under USDA inspection; 26 billion pounds of beef harvested under USDA inspection; average weights at slaughter: steers—830 lbs., heifers—769 lbs., bulls—893 lbs., cows—617 lbs.
- Total livestock production cost: $54.8 billion;
- Per capital spending on beef in 2009: $261.90 (47.8 percent of per capital spending on all meat).

During the years 2000–2009 yearling cattle sold in May averaged a $23.84/head higher return than ones sold in July. How much would production efficiency have to decline to make March sales less profitable than July sales? In a $99.43/per hundred weight (cwt)[30] fed cattle market, death loss would have to be almost 3 percentage points higher (i.e., 4 percent rather than 1 percent), or the steer would have to eat 16 percent more $3.50/per bushel corn, or, assuming 30¢/head/day yardage, the steer would have to be on feed an additional 91 days. Thus, it is unlikely that July returns will exceed those of May sales. However, it can happen, and it is important for all livestock farmers to evaluate the current market environment in addition to past averages and to recognize the rapidity, and unpredictability, surrounding the rise and fall of both prices and profits.

Dairy Cattle

All our cows had names, and they all knew where their milking stalls were ... there wasn't any warmer place in the barn on a cold winter morning than sitting on a milking stool talking to old Bessie.—Jerry Apps

The American dairy industry has undergone significant change in recent years. According to USDA data total milk cow production nationwide between 2001 and 2009 declined by one third, down from 97,460 dairy cow operations in 2001 to 65,000 in 2009.[31] However, during this same time period the Midwest dairy industry continued to be productive, as Table Three illustrates:

Table Three: Changes in Midwest Milk Production 2001–2009[32]

State	Milk Production (million lbs.)	Increase/Decrease (million lbs.)
Illinois	1,925	-95
Indiana	3,383	+816
Iowa	4,379	+594
Kansas	2,488	+878
Michigan	7,968	+2,098
Minnesota	9,019	+207
Missouri	1,568	+301
Nebraska	1,203	+37
North Dakota	309	-259
Ohio	5,192	+897
South Dakota	1,892	+522
Wisconsin	25,239	+3,040
Total	**64,656**	**+9,390**

Confounding these findings is that while milk production increased 15 percent, the number of milk cows only increased 1 percent, from 9.1 million head in 2001 to 9.2 million head in 2009. Half the Midwestern states saw decreases in herd size and half saw increases. However, among the top dairy producers, only Michigan saw an increase in herd size.[33] Two states, Illinois and North Dakota, experienced decreased milk production during this period, while the other ten experienced increases, for an overall eight-year increase of 14 percent.

Wisconsin, Minnesota and Michigan are second, third and fourth in milk production nationally, producing 13.9 percent, 4.8 percent and 4.2 percent of the total milk weight. California leads the nation, producing 21 percent of the total milk weight, and reflects two industry trends: westward movement and an increase in the number of large dairy operations.

While the number of dairy operations has declined since 2001, the number of large operations having herds of 500 or more milk cows has increased by 20 percent. As the number of large dairy operations has steadily increased so has their share of milk production.

In 2009 operations having more than 500 head of cattle accounted for 60 percent of total milk production, an increase of 39 percent over 2001. Total production in the smaller herds declined 24 percent because of a 35 percent decrease in the number of dairy operations and a 31 percent decrease in inventory. At the same time, the output from larger dairy operations increased by 74 percent, due to an increase in the number of operations, having a greater share of the total inventory of dairy cows, and increased milk production per cow.

Over the last decade, milk prices have fluctuated between $12.18 and $19.21 per hundredweight (cwt). Because of increased feed costs since 2005 the general trend in the annual milk-feed ratio,[34] which is an indicator of milk production profitability, has been downward, primarily because of increased feed costs, coupled with dropping milk prices since 2009. If the ratio is 3.0 or greater it is generally considered profitable to purchase feed and produce milk.

Despite historically high milk prices in 2007 and 2008, the milk-feed ratio still remained low because of high feed prices. In 2009 the milk-feed ratio dropped again, in spite of lower feed prices, because milk prices dropped 30 percent, a trend that continues. And, the last time the milk-feed ratio reached 3.0 was in 2005; it has now been below that critical value for nearly 10 years.

The overall dairy industry trend is toward increasing numbers of larger operations having a greater share of milk cow inventory and, accordingly, of milk production. Although in 2009 the large operations accounted for only 5 percent of all operations, they owned 56 percent of the milk cow inventory and produced 60 percent of all milk.

"The thing about running a dairy farm is that no matter what, those cows gotta get milked morning and evening. Your mother-in-law can get hit by a train, your kid can wreck the car, or you can break your leg, but you still gotta milk the cows and if the electricity goes out, you gotta do it by hand, even if it takes all night ... everybody tries to help out in a crisis, because one way or another, them cows gotta get milked," explains dairy farmer wife Jeanie Lewis, adding, as an afterthought, that "one problem with rural kids participating in high school sports is that they aren't home to help with the milking."

Hog Operations and Pork Production

> *I'd say one of the biggest livestock controversies in recent years is hog confinement. Animal rights people hate it, the neighbors don't want to be downwind of a hog operation, and the waste management issues are a big, big problem.—*
> J. Patrick Reilly, *The Dodgeville Chronicle*

Twenty years ago hog farming was mostly a small farrow-to-finish[35] effort that included raising both hogs and crops. Today the hog industry is dominated by production contracts awarded to large operations that produce hogs on several different sites, each specializing in a single phase of production, and animal confinement.[36] This shift in production style has changed the economics of hog production dramatically.[37]

Hog production varies significantly by region. During the 1992–98 period production shifted from the Heartland (Illinois, Indiana, Iowa, Kentucky, Missouri and Ohio) where most hog production has traditionally occurred, to the Southeastern states.[38] However, the growth in hog operations in the Southeast slowed considerably after 1998 because the North Carolina State Legislature, in response to environmental concerns, placed a moratorium on expanded hog operations. Almost immediately Midwest hog operations gained a greater share of contract production.

Hog industry restructuring has, among other things, resulted in heightened environmental risks and nuisance impacts, and forced hog producers to either adjust the size and organizational structure of their operations or close down. Today hog facilities with a capacity of 2,500 or more hogs are considered by the Environmental Protection Agency (EPA) to be concentrated animal feeding operations (CAFOs) subject to point source pollution permit requirements.

More than the cattle industries, hog farming has raised concerns about the environmental integrity of rural communities in areas dependent upon farming as their primary economy. In addition, widespread controversies over animal welfare have precipitated drops in pork prices, which are good for consumers, but challenged hog farmers to make up for low pork prices by economies in organization and production.

While the hog inventory remained stable, the number of hog farms fell by more than 70 percent between 1992 and 2004.[39] The average hog operation grew from 945 head in 1992 to 4,646 head 12 years later, resulting in 80 percent of the hog inventory being held by operations having 2,000 or more head. Fifty percent of the total hog inventory belonged to hog operations totaling 5,000 or more head.[40] During the same period specialized operations increased their share of output from 55 percent to 77 percent; farrow-to-finish operations fell 47 percent to 18 percent of the total hog operation output; and contract production operations increased 25 percent, accounting for more than two-thirds of total production.[41] Contract operations were larger than independent operations and more likely to specialize in a single production phase.

The logistics of hog farming revolve around the age of the pigs, feeding ration and operating expenses. Cost estimates are derived from estimated monthly returns from finishing feeder pigs—hogs purchased at 50 lbs. or as 10–12 lb. weaned pigs. Values of both feeder and weaned pigs are determined by the average delivered price for lots of 750 (or more) head.

Fifty lb. pigs are immediately placed in a finishing facility and expected to gain about 1.55 lbs. per day until they reach market weight (270 lbs.), which takes about 147 days. Weaned pigs are placed in a nursery facility until they reach 50 lbs. and are then transferred to a finishing facility.

Each feeder pig that grows to market weight is expected to consume 9.3 bushels of corn, 87 lbs. of soybean meal and 32.5 lbs. of dried distiller grains. Weaned pigs are expected to consume 10.2 bushels of corn, 120 lbs. of soybean meal, and 32.5 lbs. of distiller grains during their finishing process. Both are given vitamin and mineral supplements, which make up 2 percent of their total rationing needs. Expected death loss is 3 percent for feeder pigs and 6 percent for weaned pigs.[42]

Table Four summarizes operating costs for finishing feeder pig production facilities.

Table Four: Operating Costs for Finishing Feeder Pig Production Facilities[43]

	Per 50 lb. pig	Per weaned 10–12 lb. pig
Health maintenance	$3.99	$4.15
Labor*	$2.75	$3.67
Administrative costs	$1.50	$2
Manure handling**	$1.90	$2
Utilities	$1.57	$2.57
Total per pig	**$11.71**	**$14.57**

*Labor requirements are assumed to be 0.08 hours per pig finished @ $22/hour plus benefits.
**Each feeder pig produces about 190 gallons of manure during its growth period.

Transportation costs include the expense of trucking 148 finished hogs to a packing facility at a base per mile trucking fee of $2.50 per loaded mile, plus an additional 20 percent fuel surcharge when the price of road diesel fuel surpasses the $1.20 per gallon threshold. The minimum transportation cost per head is $1.68.[44]

Hog confinement facilities are expensive to build, must be maintained and repaired, and involve annual insurance and tax payments. The building/equipment cost ratio is 70:30 and operational confinement facilities are expected to last approximately 25 years; equipment needs replacing about every 10 years. Fifty-pound feeder pigs are placed in 9,600 space finishing facilities valued at $1.9 million. A $450,000, 4,000-head nursery must be added to cost estimates for weaned pig finishing operations. The cost split for the nursery operation is 65/35.

When hogs reach the market weight of 270 pounds they are sold for the average weekly price paid in Iowa–Southern Minnesota as determined by the Livestock Market Information Service based on USDA data. The average market hog price is multiplied by 74 percent to make the conversion to live hog price. Cull hogs[45] are assumed to comprise 3 percent of the total market hog volume and are discounted 45 percent per head. Final sales values are adjusted by 98.4 percent to account for lighter weight cull hogs.

Table Five summarizes 1992–2004 feeder-to-finish (weaned pigs-to-market) hog production activity, indicating the profitability of hog production.

Table Five: Feeder-to-Finish Hog Production Productivity 1992–2004[46]

Item/Region	1992 %	1998 %	2004 %	Average Annual Growth Rate 1992–2004 %
Share of feeder-to-finish farms				
Heartland*	54.7	55.9	48.9	53.16
Southeast**	15.2	9.6	10.7	11.83
Other Regions***	30.1	34.5	40.4	35
Share of feeder-to-finish output				
Heartland	57.9	35.4	45.2	46.16
Southeast	20.1	32.3	24.7	25.7
Other Regions	22.0	32.3	30.0	28.1
Mean farm output (hundredweight gain)	cwt	cwt	cwt	
Heartland	1,716	5,399	11,313	
Southeast	2,333	20,771	25,074	
Other Regions	1,097	10,516	12,933	
Feed productivity◊	cwt	cwt	cwt	Annual Growth Rate 1992–2004
Heartland	0.286	0.314	0.764	8.5
Southeast	0.281	0.443	0.629	6.9
Other Regions	0.243	0.313	0.625	8.2
Labor Productivity†	cwt gain	cwt gain	cwt gain	
Heartland	2,070	3,019	6,187	9.6
Southeast	2,237	6,151	6,918	9.9
Other Regions	2,584	2,919	5,373	6.3
Capital Productivity‡	cwt gain	cwt gain	cwt gain	
Heartland	0.091	0.097	0.238	8.3
Southeast	0.099	0.156	0.0252	8.1
Other Regions	0.075	0.111	0.234	9.9
Other inputs productivity§	cwt gain	cwt gain	cwt gain	
Heartland	0.327	0.491	0.541	4.3
Southeast	0.456	0.359	0.485	0.5
Other Regions	0.248	0.491	0.490	5.8

*Illinois, Indiana, Iowa, Kentucky, Missouri, Ohio
**Alabama, Arkansas, Georgia, North Carolina, South Carolina, Virginia
***Colorado, Kansas, Michigan, Minnesota, Nebraska, Oklahoma, Pennsylvania, South Dakota, Tennessee, Texas, Utah, Wisconsin

◊ cwt gain per cwt feed.
† cwt gain per unit of hog enterprise labor; labor input is a weighted index of paid labor plus unpaid household labor that uses the labor expenditure shares for paid (observed) and unpaid (estimated) labor as weights.
‡ cwt gain per dollar—the estimated cost of replacing existing capital equipment (barns, feeding equipment, etc.).
§ Actual cost expenditures for veterinary services, bedding, marketing, custom work, energy and repairs.

Overall, hog production contracts continue to be associated with higher farm productivity and helped encourage the recent industry growth. Productivity gains contributed to about a 30 percent reduction in hog prices at the farm gate and resulted in lower food prices.[47]

The Iowa State University Extension Marketing Office summary of estimated hog and cattle production returns for 2000–2009[48] calculates estimated returns for five livestock enterprises each month, providing a snapshot of hog and cattle production economics. While the estimates constitute pencil production because they do not factor in production uncertainty due to weather or poor animal health, they do account for actual prices associated with input and output. Estimates also provide a long-term, ongoing benchmark to monitor the economic environment in which livestock producers operate.

The estimated returns calculation ignores production differences associated with feeding at different times of the year (weather, mud, etc.). It does account for purchase and sale prices and feedstuff purchase prices weighted by when the feed was consumed. A producer can then ask whether performance differences due to time of year offset the buy-sell advantages?

Overall, farrow-to-finish producers have had a profitable 10 years, with an average return of $4.20/head. The range in returns varied by almost $92.25/head, from -$45.43 to $46.82. Sixty percent of the months were profitable for selling hogs. Highest monthly returns were made on hogs sold during May through August, the time of seasonally higher prices. November and January had the lowest average return, but was profitable in 30 percent of the past 10 years. About 27 percent of the months had returns between -$10 and $10/head. The 2009 marketing year was very challenging for many producers, with an average loss of $26.04 per head.[49,50]

Author Osha Gray Davidson quotes an Iowa hog farmer describing large-scale animal confinement operations.[51] "They call it economic development, but they don't realize the consequences. It's just unbelievable the smell that comes off of there. Remember, I've raised hogs. I know what hog manure smells like. This is different. It's unbelievable. Within three miles are 6,400,000 chickens and 26,000 hogs. Now it's one neighbor against another."

Poultry

> *Uncle Sam expects you to raise hens and keep chickens. Every back yard in the United States should contribute its share to a bumper crop of poultry and eggs in 1918. In Time of Peace a Profitable Recreation—In Time of War a Patriotic Duty.*—U.S. Department of Agriculture advertisement, 1918

Poultry farming is focused on raising domesticated birds, most often chickens, turkeys, ducks and geese, for the purpose of harvesting the meat or eggs for food. Poultry are farmed in huge numbers. More than 50 billion chickens are raised annually as a food source, both for their meat and their eggs. Chickens raised for eggs are laying hens while chickens raised for meat are broilers.

At any given time, the poultry inventory in the United States is about 1.97 billion birds.[52] In recent years poultry has been a growth industry within American agriculture because the common availability and lower cost of poultry has made it a common and popular meat product. In the 1980s and 1990s growing concerns over the cholesterol content of red meat resulted in increased consumption of chicken. Broilers currently grow to market weight in six to seven weeks, and in the United States the use of growth hormones to accelerate the growth rate and reduce production costs is illegal.

Eggs are produced on large egg ranches where the parameters of environmental impact are controlled. Chickens are exposed to artificial light cycles to stimulate egg production year-round. In addition, it is a common practice to induce molting through manipulation of light and the amount of food they receive in order to further increase egg size and production. On average, a chicken lays one egg a day for a number of days (a "clutch"), stops producing eggs for one or more days, then begins another production cycle. In 1900, average egg production was 83 eggs per hen per year; in 2000, due to light manipulation and selective breeding, average egg production increased to over 300 per hen. The egg-producing period begins when the hen is about 18–20 weeks old (depending on breed and season) and laying hens are butchered after their second egg-laying season.

From the farmer's point of view, eggs are a cash crop on par with currency because egg production peaks in the early spring, when farm expenses are high and income is low. However, production expenses are increasing rather dramatically, rising 67 percent during the five-year period between 2002 and 2007 and now averaging $61,000 per farm.[53]

In 2007 family farms made up more than 90 percent of all poultry operations, but accounted for only 31 percent of inventory and 70 percent of total sales. In contrast, corporate poultry farms make up only 4 percent of all poultry operations but account for more than 52 percent of inventory and 28 percent of sales. Broilers account for the largest portion of the poultry inventory, followed by layers and turkeys.

Table Six outlines the 2010–11 poultry sales value and U.S. production rank among all fifty states for the 12 Midwestern states. Ohio, Missouri, and Minnesota rank seventh, ninth and tenth among all 50 poultry-producing states. The total Midwestern poultry sales value approaches six billion dollars.

Table Six: 2010–11 Poultry and Sales Value, and U.S. Production Rank for the 12 Midwestern States.[54]

State	Sales ($1,000)	U.S. Rank/ 50 states
IL	1,849	18*
IN	887,196	15
IA	872,263	17
KS	69,807	35
MI	288,212	n/a
MN	1,045,674	10
MO	1,265,166	9
NE	165,265	27
ND	28,496	39
OH	624,299	7
SD	140,798	30
WI	375,284	23
Total	$5,764,309	

*Illinois ranks 18th in egg sales only; they do not report their total poultry sales; n/a: data not available.

Agribusiness Industries

> *The word agriculture, after all, does not mean "agriscience," much less "agribusiness." It means "cultivation of land." It is only by understanding the cultural complexity and largeness of the concept of agriculture that we can see the threatening diminishments implied by the term "agribusiness."* —Wendell Berry, The Art of the Commonplace

Agribusiness refers to farming engaged in as a large-scale business operation embracing the production, processing and distribution of agricultural products and the manufacturing of farm machinery, equipment and supplies. The term has two distinctly different connotations, depending on context.

Within the agriculture industry, agribusiness is a widely used generic term that combines agriculture and business activities and usually refers to the range of activity involved in modern food production. It also refers to the primary agricultural-related businesses underpinning all of American agriculture, including farm implement sales and manufacturing, farm chemical manufacturing, meat processing, waste management, ethanol production and wind farming.

Among critics of large-scale, industrialized, vertically integrated food production, agribusiness is synonymous with corporate farming. The term carries a negative connotation and is often contrasted with smaller family-owned farms. Negative connotations are also derived from the juxtaposition of "business" and "corporation" by critics of capitalism or corporate excess.

Examples of agribusinesses include seed and agrichemical producers such as Dow Agro Sciences, DuPont, Monsanto, Cargill and Syngenta. Other agribusinesses include AB Agri (part of Associated British Foods) animal feeds, biofuels, and micro-ingredients; Archer Daniels Midland, which processes and transports grain; John Deere, a farm machinery producer; Ocean Spray, a farmer's cooperative; Iowa Beef Processors; and Purina Farms, which has created an agritourism farm.

Environmental Protection and Agricultural Waste Management

> *Waste not-want not means converting waste agricultural biomass into energy that can provide a decentralized energy source in rural areas while simultaneously achieving a cost effective solution to waste disposal, and a reduction in greenhouse gas emissions.* —United Nations Environmental Programme

An agricultural establishment daily produces many types of waste, and effective waste management is surprisingly complicated as well as a major part of successful farming and a significant line item on the expense side of all farm operations budgets. Sometimes livestock waste management, particularly for animal confinement operations, also includes careful nutrient management whereby animals are fed diets that reduce animal waste production.

Effective agricultural waste management is a complicated, comprehensive endeavor that significantly impacts the environment. Any definition of a "good farmer" always includes some reference to how well he manages the waste associated with his farm operation.

The National Agriculture Compliance Assistance Center (NACAC), managed through the U.S. Environmental Protection Agency (EPA) with the support of the USDA, offers comprehensive information about pesticide control and waste management that are both environmentally protective and agriculturally sound.[55] The NACAC is part of EPA's Office of Compliance and focuses first on providing information about EPA's own requirements. The center relies heavily on existing sources of agricultural information and established distribution channels to provide growers, livestock producers, and other agribusinesses a means of easy access to its resources.

The USDA and other agencies provide educational and technical information on agricultural production, but assistance in complying with sometimes complex, and often costly, environmental requirements surrounding pesticides, animal waste management, ground and surface water contamination, containment and solid or hazardous waste has not been as readily accessible.

Livestock and Grain Markets

The farmer is the only man in our economy who buys everything at retail, sells everything at wholesale, and pays the freight both ways.—President John F. Kennedy

The marketplace is where producers and buyers meet to conduct the business of selling and buying agricultural products. Unlike earlier times, when farmers sold mostly locally, today they must operate in a world economy that directly influences the worth of whatever they produce. Livestock producers are less vulnerable to the weather fluctuations that affect grain farmers, but not entirely immune from the effects of a bad weather year, particularly if the issue is drought, which diminishes the grazing capability for sheep, goats and cattle.

Livestock Markets

There is no good reason for our livestock producers to have limited market access. Our beef is the best in the world, and we need to be allowed to reach all global markets.—Conrad Bums

Most livestock is sold at auction, and nine factors come together to determine livestock auction prices[57]:

- Increasing feed costs. The 2012 Midwest drought reduced grain and oilseed yields, pushing up feed prices for livestock producers. During the summer of 2012 corn and soybean meal (both important protein sources for cattle feed) prices increased 60 percent and 25 percent respectively.
- Global demand. A growing middle class in China and India has created an increased demand for meat. The United Nations Food and Agricultural Organization estimates[56] that 50 percent more food will need to be produced by 2030 to meet growing global demand as the world population reaches nine billion by 2040.
- Weather. Severe drought in 2011–12 resulted in shortages of animal feed and grass, causing ranchers to bring their animals to market sooner, and at a lighter

weight, because thinning out herds rather than bearing the cost of feeding large herds through the winter made better economic sense. The 2011 beef cattle slaughter was 15 percent higher than the previous five-year average resulting in the next year's calf drop being at its lowest level in 60 years.
- Competition. Beef prices are negatively impacted by pork and chicken prices because these alternative protein sources are less expensive to produce, thus cheaper for consumers to purchase.
- Global trade restrictions. Ten percent of U.S. beef is imported and taxed according to the exporting country's tariff rate, leading to higher consumer prices.
- Reduced livestock weight. When production costs are high; producers sell at lower weight, resulting in less production, lower revenues for producers, and increased consumer prices.
- Food safety. Food safety concerns, such as those that arose over Bovine Spongiform Encephalophy ("Mad Cow Disease"), negatively impact meat prices and result in bans of certain exports. When this occurs, excess supply drives prices down.

Milk Pricing

> *I would like to restore your right to drink raw milk anytime you like.... It's cheaper.*—Congressman Ron Paul (R-TX)

Historically, milk pricing has been a highly volatile topic made more complicated by the fact that cows produce milk regardless of falling prices and a dairy farmer can't shut his cows off until prices rise. As a result, dairy farmers have been known to dump milk when prices fell too low—an action that has not been viewed sympathetically by either consumers or the government agency that sets milk prices.

Over the past 125 years, a complex pricing system has evolved to deal with the problems of milk production, assembly, and distribution.[58] The various government and private institutions making up the system are designed to work together to ensure that the public gets the milk it wants, while dairy farmers get the economic returns needed to provide the milk. The complexity of the system, however, has baffled many and led to numerous misconceptions. Briefly:

Economic theory posits that the milk pricing system must balance the supply of milk with the demand for milk, but the physical uniqueness of milk and the inability to preserve it for long periods complicates the pricing arrangements that are available for other products or commodities.[59] A complex mix of public and private pricing institutions has arisen as producers, processors, milk marketers, and consumers have grappled with milk's fragile and short shelf life.

In the U.S. milk pricing involves a wide variety of pricing regulations based on public policy decisions. Some of these regulations include milk price supports, federal milk marketing orders, import restrictions, export subsidies, domestic and international food aid programs, state-level milk marketing programs, and a multi-state milk pricing organization. Nongovernment pricing institutions, the dairy cooperative being a major example, also influence milk pricing. And, as the dairy industry has become less regulated in recent years, the use of futures markets has engendered considerable interest.

In almost all cases, the major intent of public pricing policies is to somehow influence producer (farm) milk prices, and, for 50 years, price supports have been the backbone of the pricing system for milk and dairy products. The milk support price underpinned the entire price structure for bulk milk sold by farmers either directly to processors or through cooperatives. USDA's Commodity Credit Corporation (CCC) stood ready to buy as much butter, nonfat dry milk, and cheddar cheese as manufacturers wanted to sell at specified support purchase prices. These prices were calculated to return at least the announced milk support price to the farmer. However, until the 1996 Farm Act, interest in developing alternatives to the support purchase program was minimal or nonexistent.

Federal milk marketing orders are concerned primarily with the orderly marketing of raw fluid-grade milk from the producer to the processor. Legal and technical language make the orders complex to read and understand, and underlying the entire pricing system is the link between prices for various milk classes and the wholesale prices of manufactured dairy products.

University of Wisconsin agricultural economists Ed Jesse and Bob Cropp further explain the role of the government in basic milk pricing as follows[60]:

Federal order pooling allows producers to receive a common price for their milk components regardless of how their milk is used. Total producer milk value under the pooling order is the sum of the following elements:

- Total hundredweight milk × producer price differential (PPD) at location[61]
- Protein pounds × protein price
- Other solids pounds × other solids price
- Butterfat pounds × Class IV/butterfat price
- Total hundredweight milk × somatic cell adjustment expressed in terms of hundredweights of milk.

Producer prices will differ according to milk composition, milk quality and the location of the receiving plant. To illustrate extremes, consider two producers, each shipping 100,000 pounds of Grade A milk to a handler regulated under the Upper Midwest Federal Milk Marketing Order during the month of April 2003. The PPD at the base zone for April 2003 was $0.46 per hundredweight, decreasing to $0.26 in the outermost zone. Producer A ships to a plant in Harvard, IL (Class I differential = $1.80; PPD = $0.46). A operates a Jersey herd with April 2003 tests of 4.5 percent butterfat, 3.7 percent protein and 6.0 percent other solids. The herd somatic cell count was 110,000. Producer B milks Holsteins and ships to a plant in Grand Forks, ND (Class I differential = $1.60; PPD = $0.26); B's April 2003 tests were 3.2 percent butterfat, 2.8 percent protein and 5.7 percent other solids. Somatic cell count was 420,000.

Under these conditions, Upper Midwest federal order milk values for Producer A would be calculated as follows:

Pricing element	Units	Rate	Value
Producer Price Differential	1,000cwt.	0.46	460.00
Protein	3,700 lbs.	1.8006	6,662.22
Other Solids	6,000 lbs.	(.0008)	(4.80)
Butterfat	4,500 lbs.	1.1503	5,176.35
Somatic Cell Adjustment	1,000 cwt.	1320	132.00

Total value: 12,425.77

Value per cwt: 12.43

Producer B's milk value as determined from the federal order pricing elements would be calculated somewhat differently:

Pricing element	Units	Rate	Value
Producer Price Differential	1,000	Cwt. 0.26	260.00
Protein	2,800 lbs.	1.8006	5,041.68
Other Solids	5,700 lbs.	(.0008)	(4.56)
Butterfat	3,200 lbs.	1.1503	3,680.96
Somatic Cell Adjustment	1,000 cwt.	(.0392)	(39.20)

Total value: 8,938.88
Value per cwt: 8.94

While the rates of payment for milk components are the same for each producer, the federal order payment per hundredweight differs because of components that are the same for each producer, because of different milk composition, and because of different locations. Producer B actually receives $0.47 per hundredweight less than the Class III price for April 2003, mainly because lower butterfat and protein values relative to the standards used to compute the Class III price more than offset the producer price differential.

According to Jesse and Cropp, what dairy producers receive from their milk purchaser is usually different from the federal order calculation. "Most producers receive various premiums and deductions. Some premiums and deductions are associated with specific milk characteristics. Many plants have quality payment schedules that reward or penalize producers according to standard plate count (SPC) and somatic cell count (SCC)...." They also note that producers may receive "extra-order" payments: premiums for other milk characteristics (e.g., volume premiums) or payments for milk quality or protein beyond what is required by federal order pricing rules. Producers may also be paid under a different pricing arrangement, for example via a cheese yield formula. However, the total producer payment cannot be less than what would be calculated using the federal order pricing elements.

The Dairy Price Support Program

> *There's also the "milk cliff." And if we fall off that cliff, the price of milk could go up to $7 a gallon. It's an average of $3.56 now, so why would we let that happen?*—Matthew Zeitlin

The Dairy Product Price Support Program (DPPSP) began as the Milk Price Support Program (MPSP) and is legislatively mandated. The secretary of agriculture is authorized to carry out this program under the CCC borrowing authority. The MPSP was established on October 1, 1949, by the Agricultural Act of 1949 to provide farmers a parity level of income. The program has been modified over the years but continues to support prices for dairy farmers, and provisions for inventory control and other programs have been added.

The MPSP has never paid farmers directly but purchases dairy products from processors and vendors to allow farmers to be paid the mandated support price for their milk. As Jesse and Cropp explain it:

From time to time, prices for butter, cheese and nonfat dry milk are affected by the federal dairy price support program. The support program operates through a standing offer by USDA's Commodity Credit Corporation (CCC) to purchase unlimited quantities of butter, nonfat dry milk and cheddar cheese at specified purchase prices. The purchase prices are derived from the announced support price for milk, currently $9.90 per hundredweight for milk of average butterfat test (3.67 percent) and $9.80 for milk testing 3.5 percent butterfat. The milk support level is specified in federal legislation. Formulas involving product yields are used to mathematically translate the support level for milk into associated CCC purchase prices for the dairy products eligible for purchase. These formulas use roughly the same yields and make allowances as the formulas used to price milk under federal milk marketing orders, thus linking the two federal programs. The resulting purchase prices should financially allow a reasonably efficient plant making the eligible products to pay farmers the announced support price.[62]

Grain Markets

Pretty soon, with the iPad, I'm going to be able to trade right from my tractor during planting.—Illinois grain farmer

In marketing terms, grain refers to raw wheat, oats, barley, sorghum, corn and rice that is bought and sold on the commodities market where producers and manufacturers meet to trade in raw materials, like grain, which will be used to manufacture products like flour. Grain is traded mostly as grains futures, which establishes a set price for anticipated grain harvest.[63] The futures contract guarantees a price if the market price for grain collapses or all or part of the crop fails.

The grain industry rises and falls on the economic principles of supply and demand that play out in the commodity markets. Grain prices are heavily influenced by weather, which is entirely unpredictable, yet directly affects crop output. A ferocious hail storm can wipe out an entire grain crop in less than half an hour; a heavy thunderstorm can flood a cornfield in minutes; days and days of hard spring rain can wash out a newly planted field; heavy fall rains or early snow can ruin a harvest; and a drought kills everything because no crop can grow without water. Better weather conditions in grain-producing markets create more supply, which lowers the price. Conversely, if the weather is poor and grain crops are compromised, supply falls and prices rise.

Demand is also influenced by demand increases due to population growth in emerging markets, defined as those countries or markets that are experiencing rapid growth. The higher the growth, the higher grain prices rise. When trying to estimate the expected price of harvested grain, it is necessary to examine grain prices over the last two years and look for trends that are not explained by weather or changes in emerging market demands.

Ten factors influence grain prices[64]:

- Weather. Drought, flooding and freezing all have the capability to reduce grain supply, which can cause dramatic increases in essential grain crops. The 2012 U.S. drought, considered the most widespread in half a century, is expected to negatively impact production of key grains such as corn and soybeans, resulting in record high prices for those commodities.
- Global demand. Like the livestock industry, the grain industry is influenced by

the growing middle class in China and India, which has created an increased demand for commodities as well as for meat to meet the need for approximately 50 percent more food availability by 2030.
- Biofuel policy. Due to federal government mandates, 40.6 percent of the corn crop (five billion bushels) are used for ethanol production, diminishing supply for other uses to the lowest level in 15 years.
- Limited cropland. Due to development and increased non-food growing use, cropland is being lost at an unprecedented rate at the same time food prices are increasing.
- Government policy. Policies such as tariffs to support domestic production reduce competition, limit supply available for international trade and impact prices. During 2010–2011 Russia's ban on wheat exports reduced global supply by 15 million metric tons.
- Disease. Diseases and pest infestations cause shortages in both grain and livestock availability, which shrink the food supply. On average, roughly 35 percent of global crop production fails each year due to disease and various insect problems.
- Energy costs. High oil prices drive up the costs associated with bringing food to market, and these costs are passed on to consumers.
- Declining grain reserves. Grain stocks to usage ratios were at record low levels in 2012, meaning grain inventory is decreasing globally as more grain is needed to meet rising demand.
- Macroeconomic factors. A strong U.S dollar relative to European and other currencies has a dramatic effect on commodity prices. Economic woes in Europe and slowing growth in China played a significant role in 2012 commodity markets, and are expected to continue as major influences in 2013.
- Geopolitical conflicts. Political unrest can disrupt productivity, impacting supply and commodity pricing. During 2012 wheat prices spiked as a direct result of political protests in Egypt, one of the world's largest wheat importers.

Table Seven illustrates the market value of all agricultural products sold in the Midwestern states in 2007, the most recent year for which complete data in all categories are available. The total market value for Midwestern agricultural products is 127 billion dollars.

Table Seven: 2007 Market Value of All Agricultural Products Sold in Midwestern States[65]

State	Crop value (in $1,000s)	Livestock value (in $1,000s)	State total (in $1,000s)
IL	10,876,415	2,452,692	**13,329,107**
IN	5,319,019	2,952,272	**8,271,291**
IA	10,343,585	10,074,511	**20,418,096**
KS	4,887,212	9,525,971	**14,413,183**
MI	3,329,928	2,423,291	**5,753,219**
MN	7,048,913	6,131,554	**13,180,467**
MO	3,494,938	4,017,988	**7,512,926**
NE	6,843,325	8,662,710	**15,506,035**

State	Crop value (in $1,000s)	Livestock value (in $1,000s)	State total (in $1,000s)
ND	5,038,521	1,045,697	6,084,218
OH	4,109,722	2,960,490	7,070,212
SD	3,383,497	3,186,953	6,570,450
WI	2,669,326	6,298,032	8,967,358
Midwest Total value	$64,344,401	$59,732,161	$127,076,661

In terms of agricultural production, Iowa, Nebraska and Kansas are the overall most productive Midwestern farm states. Iowa and Nebraska are tied in having the second lowest poverty rates (12.5) among the Midwestern states, while Kansas is fourth. All three states claim only one rural county having a poverty rate greater than 20 percent. Michigan, South Dakota and Ohio are the least agriculturally productive among the Midwestern states. South Dakota and Michigan are the second and third poorest among their counterparts; South Dakota has 11 rural counties with poverty rates above 20 percent, while Ohio has seven and Michigan has two.

Missouri, the poorest among the Midwestern states, ranks ninth in overall agricultural productivity. The state has the greatest number (24) of rural counties with poverty rates above 20 percent and the greatest number (64) of rural counties with poverty rates ranging between 13 and 19 percent.

While the market value for Midwestern livestock and crops is substantial, nearly all of the profits flow directly into the pockets of corporate agriculture. Average Midwestern family farmers receive far, far fewer of these dollars.

Pesticides and Organic Farming

> *Before we eliminate pesticides and go back to organic agriculture, somebody is going to have to decide which 50 million people in the world we are going to let starve.* —Earl Butz, U.S. Secretary of Agriculture (1971–76)

When Rachel Carson wrote *The Silent Spring* in 1962 she launched an assault on agricultural chemicals and pesticides that endures today.[66] Dedicated to Albert Schweitzer, who said, "Man has lost the capacity to foresee and to forestall. He will end by destroying the earth,"[67] Carson confronted an enormous and extremely lucrative agribusiness industry that produces farm chemicals guaranteed to increase crop production. Not surprisingly, in the "kill the messenger" tradition, she was mercilessly vilified.

Widely regarded as a meticulous scientist, Carson set about to lay bare the harmful effects of herbicides and pesticides, arguing that their unrestrained use would eventually render the planet unable to sustain any life forms, including human. She identified chlorinated hydrocarbons and organophosphates as the culprits leading to bird and fish kills, human nervous system disorders, and human death from various environmentally induced diseases, including cancer. Pointing out that, at one time, herbicides were thought to be safe for animals, she proposed that herbicide use led to surface and ground water contamination. She explained that water treatment facilities could not make water safe because multiple chemicals in catch basins interact to form toxic compounds and carcinogens, thereby creating cancer hazards from polluted water.

Chemical treatment of the soil, which is essential to farming, also, according to Carson, almost certainly leads to destruction of biologically beneficial organisms, thereby upsetting the ecosystem balance and destroying wildlife. She also accused the government of grossly underestimating the dangers of pesticides for humans and wildlife, and of aerially spraying vast agricultural areas without prior public notice, ignoring the possibility for chemical residue in food grown in areas where pesticides and insecticides were in common use. Carson strongly believed, and set out to prove, that using chemical treatments on plants and insects was going down a path that, once embarked upon, could not be turned back, and that the price of trying to completely control nature was not only too high, but was also an idea conceived in arrogance.

Medical literature is replete with evidence that Carson was unequivocally correct. A 1993 summary article in the Western Journal of Medicine states that:

> Epidemiologic studies document that work in the agricultural sector is associated with many occupational health hazards. Exposure to organic dusts and airborne microorganisms and their toxins may lead to respiratory disorders. The burden of exposure-related chronic bronchitis, asthma, hypersensitivity, pneumonitis, organic-dust toxic syndrome, and chronic airflow limitation can be diminished by appropriate preventive measures. The contribution of exposures to agricultural chemicals to cancers and neurodegenerative disorders is being investigated. Some studies document that farmers and those in related industries are at higher risk for the development of cancer of the stomach, soft tissue sarcoma, non–Hodgkin's lymphoma, and multiple myeloma. Chronic encephalopathy and Parkinson's and Alzheimer's diseases are being studied in relation to agricultural chemicals. The possible carcinogenicity and neurotoxicity of pesticides emphasize the need to promote the safe use of chemicals. Another area for health promotion programs is disabling injuries and traumatic deaths. Farm accidents are important because of their frequent occurrence among young people and disturbing fatality rates. Other health issues of concern in these industries include skin diseases, hearing loss, and stress.[68]

Over time it was proved that one of the worst pesticide dangers came from dichlorodiphenyltrichloroethane, better known as DDT.

The war between environmentalists and exploiters of the natural world persists. Legislation to curb pesticide and herbicide use has had mixed results, due in part to lax enforcement and poor design. An often cited example of failure is that four times more endangered species continue to decline in population than do those that increase in numbers.

Critics of government regulation say this is evidence that the endangered species legislation has failed. By this logic, hospitals should be eliminated, because people die in them. Nevertheless, particularly in the arena of corporate agriculture, the approach has been to beat nature into submission rather than try to work with the natural environment in biologically sustainable ways.

Wind Farming

> *Using wind to generate electricity is a great idea, as long as you only need electricity when the wind is blowing and can do without it the rest of the time.—* Don Hayes

Wind is abundant in many rural areas of the United States and harnessing wind energy is an extremely popular notion among energy independence enthusiasts because it uses a naturally occurring resource to meet a critical need. However, from a job creation point of view, locating a wind farm in a rural area as an economic development initiative is not particularly lucrative because once the wind farm is set up it operates on its own, thus creating no new jobs. However, a farmer can lease land to an energy company for purposes of erecting wind turbines and will receive regular payments from the energy company that buys the electricity the wind farm generates.

Logistically, it works this way: wind is a form of solar energy caused by the uneven heating of the atmosphere by the sun, the irregularities of the earth's surface, and the rotation of the earth. Wind flow patterns are modified by the earth's terrain, bodies of water, and vegetative cover. This wind flow, or motion energy, when "harvested" by modern technology, can be used to generate electricity, thereby mechanically generating power that can be used for specific tasks (such as grinding grain or pumping water.) Alternatively, a generator can convert this mechanical power into electricity to send power where it is needed.

Wind turbines looking very much like aircraft propeller blades turn in the moving air and power an electric generator that supplies an electric current. Simply stated, a wind turbine is the opposite of a fan. Instead of using electricity to make wind, wind turbines use wind to make electricity. The wind turns the blades, which spin a shaft connected to a generator and produces electricity.

Wind energy is a free, renewable resource, so no matter how much is used today, the same supply will exist in the future. Wind energy is also a source of clean, non-polluting electricity and, unlike conventional power plants, emits no air pollutants or greenhouse gases. According to the U.S. Department of Energy, in 1990, California's wind power plants offset the emission of more than 2.5 billion pounds of carbon dioxide, and 15 million pounds of other pollutants that would have otherwise been released into the atmosphere.[69] It would take a forest of 90 million to 175 million trees to provide the same air quality.

Even though the cost of wind power has decreased dramatically in the past 10 years, the technology requires a higher initial investment than fossil-fueled generators. Roughly 80 percent of the cost is the machinery, with the balance being site preparation and installation. If wind-generating systems are compared with fossil-fueled systems on a "life-cycle" cost basis (counting fuel and operating expenses for the life of the generator), however, wind costs are much more competitive with other generating technologies because there is no fuel to purchase and minimal operating expenses.

Compared to fossil fuel power plants, using wind power to generate electricity has relatively little impact on the environment. But wind turbines are unsightly, and concerns over the noise produced by the rotor blades, and about birds and bats having been killed by flying into the rotors, are common. Most of these problems have been resolved or greatly reduced through technological development or by proper wind propeller placement, but this does not take away their negative visual impact on an otherwise serene landscape.

The major challenge to using wind as a source of power is that it is intermittent and does not always blow when electricity is needed. Wind cannot be stored (although wind-generated electricity can be stored using batteries) and wind can't be harnessed to meet the timing of electricity demands. Good wind sites are often located in remote locations far from areas of high electric power demand (such as cities) and getting the electricity to where it is needed can be costly.

Wind resource development can compete with other uses for the land, and those alternative uses may be more highly valued than generating electricity. However, wind turbines can be located on land that is also used for grazing and planting crops without taking up very much land space.

Farmer Cooperatives

When farmers cooperate, society benefits.—Farmer's Cooperative Society, 1907

In agriculture, broadly speaking there are three types of cooperatives: a machinery pool, a manufacturing and marketing cooperative, and a credit union.

- Machinery pool: A family farm may be too small to justify the purchase of expensive farm machinery, which may be only used irregularly, for example during planting or harvesting; instead local farmers may get together to form a machinery pool that purchases the necessary equipment for all the members to use.
- Manufacturing/marketing cooperative: A farm does not always have the means of transportation necessary for delivering its produce to the market, or its small production volume may place it in an unfavorable negotiating position with respect to intermediaries and wholesalers. In these situations a cooperative will act as an integrator, collecting the output from members, sometimes undertaking manufacturing and delivering farm output in large aggregated quantities downstream through the marketing channels.
- Credit union: Farmers, especially in developing countries, can be charged relatively high interest rates by commercial banks or even not have access to banks. When providing loans, these banks are often mindful of high transaction costs on small loans or may refuse credit altogether due to lack of collateral—a very acute problem in developing countries. To provide a source of credit, farmers can group together funds that can be loaned out to members. Alternatively, a credit union can raise loans at better rates from commercial banks due to the cooperative having a larger associative size than an individual farmer. Often members of a credit union will provide mutual or peer-pressure guarantees for repayment of loans. In some instances, manufacturing/marketing cooperatives may have credit unions as part of their broader business. Such an approach allows farmers to have a more direct access to critical farm inputs, such as seeds and implements. The loans for these inputs are repaid when the farmer sends produce to the manufacturing/marketing cooperative. Many farmers rely on credit cooperatives as a source of financing for both working capital and investments.

The agricultural cooperative, also known as a farmers' co-op, is a business model that enables farmers to pool their resources in certain areas of activity.[70] A broad typology of agricultural cooperatives distinguishes between agricultural service cooperatives, which provide various services to their individual members, and agricultural production cooperatives, where production resources (land, machinery) are pooled and members farm jointly. Examples of agricultural production cooperatives include collective farms in former socialist countries, the kibbutzim in Israel, and collectively governed community shared agriculture efforts.

Cooperatives as a business organization are distinct from the more common investor-owned firms (IOFs). Both are organized as corporations, but IOFs pursue profit maximization objectives, whereas cooperatives strive to maximize the benefits they generate for their members.

Agricultural cooperatives are created in situations where farmers cannot obtain essential services from IOFs (because the provision of these services is judged to be unprofitable by the IOFs) or when IOFs provide the services at terms disadvantageous to the farmers (i.e., the services are available, but the profit-motivated prices are too high). In economic theory, the former situations are characterized as market failure, or missing services motive. The latter circumstances drive the creation of cooperatives as a competitive yardstick or means of allowing farmers to build countervailing market power to oppose the IOFs. The concept of competitive yardstick implies that farmers, faced with unsatisfactory performance by IOFs, may form a cooperative whose purpose is to force the IOFs, through competition, to improve their service to farmers.

Most agricultural cooperatives are service cooperatives, focused either on supply cooperative or marketing cooperative activities. Supply cooperatives provide their members with inputs for agricultural production, including seeds, fertilizers, fuel, and machinery services. Marketing cooperatives undertake transportation, packaging, distribution, and marketing of farm products (both crop and livestock).

While the economic benefits are a strong driver in forming cooperatives, this is not the sole consideration. In fact, it is possible for the economic benefits from a cooperative to be replicated in other organizational forms, such as an IOF, but important strength of a cooperative for the farmer is that farmers retain control over the governance of the association, thereby ensuring they have ultimate ownership and control of their product. The profit reimbursement (either through the dividend payout or rebate) is shared only amongst the farmer members, rather than shareholders as in an IOF.

Agricultural supply cooperatives aggregate purchases, storage, and distribution of farm inputs for their members. By taking advantage of volume discounts and utilizing other economies of scale, supply cooperatives bring down the cost of the inputs that the members purchase from the cooperative, compared with purchasing directly from commercial suppliers. Supply cooperatives provide inputs required for agricultural production including seeds, fertilizers, chemicals, fuel, and farm machinery. Some supply cooperatives operate machinery pools that provide mechanical field services (e.g., plowing, harvesting) to their members.

A practical motivation for the creation of agricultural cooperatives is related farmers' ability to pool production and/or resources. In many situations within agriculture, it is simply too expensive for farmers to manufacture products or undertake a service. Cooperatives provide a means for farmers to join together in an "association," through which, as a group, farmers can achieve a better outcome, typically financial, than by acting independently, and have greater control over the marketplace.

This approach is aligned with the concept of "economies of scale" that results in a form of economic synergy whereby two or more agents work together to produce a result not obtainable by any of the agents independently.

While it may seem reasonable to conclude that the larger the cooperative the better, this is not necessarily true. Cooperatives exist across a broad membership base, with some cooperatives having less than 20 members while others have over 10,000.

A good example of an effective farmer cooperative is the Iowa Farmers Cooperative

Society.[71] Through its seven centers in northwest Iowa, the Farmers Cooperative Society offers its members/farmers a full range of agricultural growing and marketing products and services, including crop-storage facilities and business consulting. Its feedlot, with room for some 5,500 head of cattle, helps members buy and care for feeder cattle and provides discounts on grain for members. The co-op also operates a members-only building store in Sioux Center, Iowa, that sells hardware, lawn-care products, lumber, and paint, as well as brand-name home appliances.

Rural Small Business Enterprises

> *There's a lot more business out there in small town America than I ever dreamed of.*—Sam Walton, Walmart founder

Sam Walton correctly and prophetically observed that there is a lot of business to be done in rural areas, and he proceeded to systematically capture that economic market by building supersized department stores strategically located in rural areas where the only competition was small local businesses. Today, residents of most small towns are between 25 and 40 miles of a Walmart, where they can buy just about anything, including groceries, paint, hunting equipment, hardware, clothes, house wares, health supplies and prescription drugs. Without exception, these items are remarkably cheaper at the nearest Walmart than they would be at the local hardware store, variety store, grocery store, or pharmacy, because Walmart buys wholesale in quantity, creating the ability to sell cheaper than the local mom and pop store, and it provides a convenient, full-service, one-stop shopping experience.

"Walmart changes every town it's in, and all the other towns within 25–30 miles, and it's never for the better," local newspaper publisher Pat Reilly says. "People are surprisingly fickle when it comes to their money, and they don't seem to have a lot of loyalty to local small businesses if they can buy cheaper somewhere else." Reilly is correct, to a point. Walmart did drive the local hardware store in his town of 6,000 out of business. The local pharmacy survived until a Walgreens came to town; so far the local grocery store is still hanging on.

However, seven miles away, in a town of 2,500, the local hardware and grocery stores are "doing OK," according to Chamber-Main Street president Gail Buss. "The last thing we want to [see] happen is to lose our grocery or hardware store to Walmart ... sure, buying locally is a little more expensive, but it's also handier, and people realize folks in this area who don't farm have to make a living too."

While the local hardware store is important, the local grocery store might be just a little more important, because they'll deliver to the shut-ins living in the community. "We sure don't want our grocery store going away, even if it is a little more expensive ... it's still convenient for the small stuff, and if somebody wants to do a really big shopping they have a choice about going here or to Walmart," says lifetime rural resident Lucille Meyers. What she doesn't point out is that in the local grocery store, food often stays on the shelf just a little too long, choices are severely limited, and most items cost, on average, at least a dollar more than at Walmart. This price difference makes the seven-mile drive worthwhile, particularly for the poor and those on fixed incomes.

The local pharmacy is a slightly different story. The pharmacist knows the local folks by their first names, and if they're homebound, sick, or living alone, he'll drop their prescriptions off on his way home from work, which also gives him a chance to informally check on how they're doing. Walgreens is less expensive and will mail prescriptions, but this often takes a few days and doesn't work in an immediate health crisis situation. Walmart doesn't mail locally, but they are the cheapest of all, and are open the most hours per week. Furthermore, the local pharmacy operates like any other local retail store and is not open nights or Sundays, which can be a problem when someone's baby needs cough syrup or a fever reducer and can't wait.

Hardware stores stock just about everything imaginable, their advice is free, and is usually spot on. "The hardware store and the post office are the two social centers in town where you find out what's going on," Buss explains.

Hardware store owner Mitch Michaels, who grew up in the family business, acknowledges that his store is more expensive than Walmart and says he's keenly aware of the competition, but tries to find ways to compensate. "I have a pretty liberal return policy, and one of us will usually go over to somebody's house and look at the problem before we sell them the fix ... and we do stuff like consult on paint colors and do a quick turn-around on odd jobs, like replacing a broken window or mending a screen, which we do ourselves.... I think people appreciate that."

The biggest problem facing all rural small businesses is extending credit. "We're willing to do it," Michaels says, "but we don't carry much cash reserve and can get into a real bind if people don't pay their bills on time. Most of our customers pay up and support us every way they can, but unlike the bigger guys, all it takes is one big delinquent account to throw us into a tailspin."

In a world where it's all about competition, it takes intentional effort from an entire community to keep small businesses afloat. This means buying a car from the local dealership, even if it isn't the best deal, buying farm equipment from the local implement dealer and using the local bank to finance big ticket items. School district administrator Joe Burton explains it this way: "We put a lot of services out for bid, including school milk, fuel and service for the school buses, and janitorial services. I'm obligated to save the district as much money as I can on these things, and a lot of the time the local bid is the highest one. What I usually recommend is splitting the contracts. Half the year we buy milk through the local grocery store and the rest of the time directly from the dairy distributor; half the gas comes from the local station, even though it's several cents a gallon more than the gas station over by the highway, and we try to use the local mechanic for routine bus maintenance and small repairs. The school board and the local community know we could do it cheaper, but we all want the school to be a good business partner in the community, and in return, the community supports our fundraisers and is more likely to look favorably on a referendum for equipment or facilities."[72]

Burton understands that often the local school is the largest employer in a small community and functions as the center of social connections among community members. And many parents of his school children are employed locally. "A few years back we decided to build a new gym because, after we started letting senior citizens come free to the games, we couldn't accommodate even half the parents, grandparents, and other family members who wanted to watch the kids play basketball—and that referendum passed nearly unanimously, on the first try ... and was about much more than just a new school gym—it was about maintaining a thriving local school, which is a large business account for several area small businesses."

Rural towns are also peppered with one-of-a-kind specialty enterprises, mom and pop restaurants and taverns beloved by the locals but of little interest to anyone else. Most of the time these businesses do not make much money and slide back and forth between operating in the black and operating in the red several times during a given year.

Regardless, small business owners try hard to give back to the community that supports their businesses. In rural Arena, Wisconsin, a local beer maker donates the spent grain from his beer-making business to area farmers as animal feed. "It's extra good for animals, especially the young ones," explained the brewery owner's mother, herself a local café owner at one time. The gesture also generates miles and miles of good will among neighbors and, as a result, the only beer Arena residents ever buy is the local stuff.

Farming's Risky, So Why Do It?

> *There seems to be but three ways for a nation to acquire wealth. The first is by war ... the second is by commerce.... The third is by agriculture, the only honest way, wherein man receives a real increase of the seed thrown into the ground, in a kind of continual miracle, wrought by the hand of God in his favor, as a reward for his innocent life and his virtuous industry.* —Benjamin Franklin

America sends her bounty all over the world, and satisfying world food demand is exactly what Midwestern American farmers do—and it begins on family farms and in the rural communities where they live. For these men and women, farming is not about the money and is more than a livelihood—it's a legacy shared with everyone and, in some way, we're all intimately connected to Midwest agriculture.

The economic bottom line in the rural Midwest is that it takes an intentional community effort to keep a community economically afloat, and even then, it's an ongoing struggle. Small businesses come and go at an alarming rate, and every failure means at least one person, maybe more, has lost their job and source of income. Farms have good years and bad years, and the wider small town economies prosper, or suffer, as a result. Nowhere else are people, their poverty, and their livelihoods so closely interwoven as occurs in rural America.

By the numbers, a snapshot of American agriculture looks like this[73]:

- To keep up with population growth more food will have to be produced in the next 50 years as the past 10,000 years combined.
- Today, the average U.S. farmer feeds 155 people. In 1960, a farmer fed just 26 people.
- Today's farmer grows twice as much food as his parents did—using less land, energy, water and fewer emissions.
- American farmers ship more than $100 billion of their crops and products to many nations.
- U.S. farmers produce about 40 percent of the world's corn, using only 20 percent of the total harvested land in the world.
- Farmers are a direct lifeline to more than 23 million U.S. jobs in all kinds of industries.
- In the past five years, U.S. farm operators have become more demographically diverse. The 2007 census counted nearly 30 percent more women as principal

farm operators. The count of Hispanic operators grew by 10 percent, and the counts of American Indian, Asian and African-American farm operators increased as well.

- One bushel of corn is 56 pounds. That means U.S. farmers produce an average of more than 9,000 pounds of corn per acre.
- If U.S. farmers used crop production practices from 1931 to produce an amount of corn equivalent to the 2008 crop, it would require 490 million acres—an area more than 120 million acres larger than the state of Alaska.
- Individuals or families own 82 percent of corn farms. Another 6 percent are family-held corporations.
- Less than 15 percent of U.S. corn acres are irrigated.
- Farmers today produce 70 percent more corn per pound of fertilizer than as recently as the 1970s.
- Corn farmers have reduced total fertilizer use by 10 percent since 1980.
- According to the USDA, one acre of corn removes about eight tons of carbon dioxide from the air in a growing season. At 180 bushels per acre this produces enough oxygen to supply a year's needs for 131 people.
- Corn production has marched steadily upward for decades while using fewer acres.
- American farmers produced the five largest corn crops in history during the past five years. Even after supplying food-makers, ranchers, ethanol producers and grain exporters, America will again be able to save 10 percent of this year's harvest for the future.
- Farmers today grow five times as much corn as they did in the 1930s—on 20 percent less land. That is still 13 million acres, or 20,000 square miles—twice the size of Massachusetts.
- The yield per acre has skyrocketed from 24 bushels in 1931 to 154 now, or a six-fold gain.
- Farmers in more than 30 U.S. states grow soybeans, making soybeans the country's second-largest crop in cash sales and the number one value crop export.
- Soy ink is used to print textbooks and newspapers.
- The soybean is the highest natural source of dietary fiber.
- The livestock industry is the largest consumer of soy meal.
- In 2008, soybeans represented 56 percent of world oilseed production, and 33 percent of those soybeans were produced by the American farmer.
- The United States exported 1.16 billion bushels (31.6 million metric tons) of soybeans in 2008, which accounted for 40 percent of the world's soybean trade.
- A 60-pound bushel of soybeans yields about 48 pounds of protein-rich meal and 11 pounds of oil.
- One and a half gallons of biodiesel and 48 pounds of soybean meal can be produced from one bushel of soybeans.

Benjamin Franklin makes a valid point when he observes that agriculture is one of three ways for a nation to acquire wealth, but becoming wealthy is not the reason farmers engage in the risky business of farming. Bill Schroeder of Reynolds, Indiana, explains it this way: "We're people just like everyone else. We care about what we do. We work very hard and we're proud of what we have. Farming is a way of life for us ... it's all we know."

5

Get Big or Get Out

Rural America Moves into the 21st Century

> *Thanks to production incentives that began with the 1973 Farm Bill and his [Earl Butz] fencerow to fencerow stump speech, federally subsidized, corn-based meats and sweets were the staples of my childhood, I grew up eating the bounty his policies left behind.* —Curt Ellis

Serving under President Richard M. Nixon and his successor, Gerald R. Ford, Earl Butz was the most powerful secretary of agriculture since Henry A. Wallace helped lead the nation through the Great Depression. Butz was also a forceful, sharp-tongued agricultural policy enigma who both bulldozed American agriculture toward the 21st century and engineered legislation sharply reducing all-important federal subsidies for small farmers.

By putting into place federal policies designed to pay farmers to keep some of their cropland and livestock out of production in the face of plunging market prices, Butz significantly changed the face of American agriculture. Yet, as an advocate of free market agricultural policy, he also encouraged farmers to produce more and to sell their surplus overseas, bringing them higher prices. "Plow up every bit of land you can get your tractor on, and plant fence row to fence row," Butz advised.

Farm income did rise during Butz's time in office, largely as the result of a huge grain shipment to the Soviet Union Butz brokered in 1972. However, at the same time grain was going to Russia, American consumers began paying significantly more for food at home, a fact Butz felt American consumers should both understand and willingly accept. Speaking before members of a farm credit association in Champaign, Illinois, in 1973, he remarked that if the average housewife did not have "such a low level of economic intelligence she would understand that the price of everything has gone up and you can't get more by paying less."

"Butz's power as secretary of agriculture seemed overwhelming," wrote Joel Solkoff. "He made one decision to sell the Russians massive quantities of grain that virtually overnight transformed the basic problem of U.S. agricultural policy from what to do with the surplus to how to make up for the shortage."[1]

Democrats in Congress criticized Butz, viewing him as a subsidy-cutter and voice of corporate agricultural interests at the expense of small farmers and consumers. Ultimately Butz was responsible for overturning most of the New Deal programs President Franklin Roosevelt had instituted to keep American agriculture from being plowed under by the Great Depression and saved struggling family farms hit by the massive tsunami of dirt that was the Dust Bowl.

Dubbed "King Corn," Butz ushered in an era of 1,000-acre corn farms and billion-bushel corn harvests, which worked to the tremendous advantage of big farm operations. Corporations were able to turn large profits based upon volume while simultaneously crushing small farm operations. Butz's policies were forcing the small family farmer out of business and onto the welfare rolls and, in five short years, Butz dramatically changed the face of rural Midwestern farming. Whether these changes were good or bad depends entirely upon who is asked.

When a Georgia peanut farmer no one knew much about assumed the U.S. presidency, Midwestern farmers believed that, because of his agriculture background, Jimmy Carter would be inclined toward farmer-friendly policies and continuing the pro-active trade practices favored by the Nixon and Ford administrations. Instead, Carter single handedly engineered the collapse of the American farm economy, first by instituting a new monetary policy and then by slapping an embargo on wheat sales to the Soviet Union following its invasion of Afghanistan. The first action, instituted by then Chairman of the Federal Reserve Board Paul Volcker, was intended to curb rising inflation by raising the federal funds rate.[2] Suddenly money became much more expensive to both lend and borrow.

The Russian wheat embargo struck a death blow to the economic heart of farmers, particularly those who had followed Butz's "get big or get out" advice and expanded their operations by leveraging their farms. They were producing vast quantities of wheat being sold to the Soviet Union at record high prices when the bottom dropped out. Farmers, justifiably, wondered why they had to suffer because the Russians had invaded Afghanistan and why no one had figured out what the embargo would do to the U.S. farm economy. Third generation Minnesota farmer Earl Hagendorf sees it this way:

> The biggest problem [in agriculture] I see is that the government jumps in—like when there's an issue with China over human rights. Suddenly we're going to boycott; we're going to hold back our product. Hell, that's none of their business! We're the ones who are producing the product, let us be. Fight with them on some other issue. But let us price our product and export our product and let's see what we can do. But every time you get some politician involved in some foreign country [farmers] suffer. Because we're the people held hostage, or our product is held hostage. Because of some State Department idiot. They have no concept of what farming is in the first place. And yet we're the people that get it taken out on. How often do they banish cars from a foreign country? Or refrigerators? Or computers? But our product gets it every damned time![3]

Hagendorf has a valid point, particularly considering that the wheat embargo was entirely unsuccessful in forcing Russia to do anything because plenty of other nations had wheat for sale at reasonable prices. The Russians quickly solved their pending shortage by buying wheat from European and South American sources, at cheaper prices. Who could've ever imagined that this action would affect farmers just as personally, and just as much, as Russian soldiers themselves marching across their fields, crushing newly-planted crops under their boots?

The 1980s Farm Crisis

> *The government got us into that mess, and then didn't do a damned thing to help get us out. Hell, even the Ag[ricultural] extension agents were telling us to borrow money to get bigger. Damned easy for them to say—they didn't have to pay it back.* —Iowa farmer

Federal farm programs from the 1930s through the 1980s were designed to aid and encourage commercial production, and the more a farm operation grew, the more federal assistance was available. It became profitable to produce commodities qualifying for subsidies, which invariably led to surpluses. While the subsidy programs sought to guarantee farm prosperity through manipulation of the market price, most often the result was to price American farm products out of the global market. As a result both the government and the average American taxpayer ended up having to subsidize food exports.

This was an era of easy credit for farmers and they borrowed money to buy up land as fast as they could, grew more and more grain, sold it at record high prices, and built up a huge grain reserve—all because they, mistakenly, as it turned out, trusted the government not to let them down. They remembered how Roosevelt's New Deal had saved the rural economy and believed the government had their best interests at the forefront of all agricultural policy decisions. They weren't at all concerned when the Soviet Union invaded Afghanistan in 1979.

When President Carter initiated the grain embargo against the Soviet Union, the sky fell. Farmers were left holding the bag in terms of a huge buildup of grain reserves and no market for it. Land values, farmers' only remaining asset, plummeted, because there was no market for what the land could produce. Having used their now far less valuable land as collateral, farmers had borrowed a lot of money to expand their farm operations, believing they would pay off these loans from profits generated by continuing high grain prices. It seemed like a safe bet because a year earlier the Soviet Union had been buying U.S. wheat as fast as farmers could grow it. Overnight American farmers couldn't give their wheat away, propelling them into deeper financial trouble than they ever imagined.[4]

Most farmers had eagerly participated in the boom times, when credit was easy and their product had historically high market value. They knew people had to eat, and they were growing food; they were participating in a perfect economic and successful marketing equation—producing a product for which there was an infinite need. They never saw the crisis coming—and most blamed the government for causing it. Minnesota farmer Steve Schroeder explains the farmer's perceptions this way:

> What was really kind of bad is that the government controls the economy. They raise the interest rates and what really hurt us is in 1980 they threw that embargo on us. We had our bins full of corn and we were figuring we could export it and get a better price and all at once they came along and whacked us. Jimmy Carter did that to us, and I'll never forget that day.... The government doesn't realize they make people very angry. There's a lot of people that feel abused by the system, and we did feel that way."[5]

Falling cash receipts from marketing commodities in the 1980s were offset by rising government subsidy payments. And lower inflation, lower energy rates, and declining interest rates lowered farm production expenses. Consequently, net cash farm income reached $44 billion in 1985—a record high. At the same time, between 1981 and 1986 there was a $300 billion decline in farm asset values, a loss of one-fourth of the total valuation.

President Ronald Reagan, being strongly against government interference in anything, and believing the agricultural markets would self regulate, backed away from decisive action to help farmers who had taken advantage of easy money and now found themselves deep in debt. On Reagan's watch thousands of farmers were displaced by overwhelming debt and lost their land, their homes, and the only livelihood they had ever known. Rural communities were changed forever simply because the government made money too easy for farmers to borrow, and then suddenly changed its mind and wanted its money back—immediately.

By the end of the 1980s, the federal government had moved ever closer to a "public utility" approach to farm policy. President Reagan's efforts to steer that policy into a market-oriented format were undermined by the severity of the farm crisis earlier in the decade, and ultimately it proved impossible for economic as well as political reasons. By the time the agricultural sector was beginning to recover in 1987, the Reagan administration's willingness to make hard choices in terms of farm policy had evaporated. Consequently, when Ronald Reagan left office federal agricultural policy remained an expensive burden on the American taxpayer.

Farmers weren't the only ones feeling the pinch of the rural financial crisis. The ripple effect of farmers suddenly in financial trouble widened to include small, local businesses in rural communities that depended upon the farmers' business. The local hardware store sold him fencing, the local gas station supplied his fuel, the local veterinarian treated his sick animals, the local doctor treated his kids' sore throats, and on it went.

Farming was the economic backbone of the rural Midwest, and when farmers got into trouble, everybody else did too. These businesses operated locally and did not draw from a wide geographic area and, as a result, they had no financial safety net to catch them when the farmers whose business they depended upon suddenly had no more money to spend.

The availability of easy money during the 1980s saw so much food being produced in the Midwest that plummeting crop prices were inevitable, because greatly increased supply far outstripped demand. This made farming for all but the largest players unprofitable. As farming became less economically viable for small farmers, the bottom fell out of agricultural land prices, making it extremely difficult for farmers to use their land as collateral to borrow needed operating dollars to maintain a positive cash flow.[6] Consequently, the entire agricultural economy imploded into ruin.

Because of the basic principles of supply and demand economics, there's probably little Reagan could have done to change the fact that on his watch real farm income dropped to the lowest level since the Depression, and interest charges on large loans farmers were encouraged to take out by willing, if not eager, lenders began swallowing up a formerly prosperous farmer's net income and cost thousands of family farmers their farms.

"Since the Reagan Administration took office my wife and I have lost half our net worth. It took us 20 years to build that up and three years to lose it," David Sprague, a Kansas wheat farmer said.[7]

The Farm Bill

> *Doesn't the Federal Farm Bill help out all these poor farmers? No. It used to, but ever since its inception just after the Depression, the Federal Farm Bill has slowly been altered by agribusiness lobbyists. It is now largely corporate welfare.... It is this, rather than any improved efficiency or productiveness, that has allowed corporations to take over farming in the United States, leaving fewer than a third of our farms still run by families.*—Barbara Kingsolver, Animal, Vegetable, Miracle

Every five years Congress is supposed to pass a comprehensive farm bill to oversee the affairs under the purview of the U.S. Department of Agriculture (USDA), including some welfare programs. This legislation is the primary agricultural and food policy tool of the federal government. And, thanks to Earl Butz, the farm bill has become one of the most politically contentious legislative efforts facing Congress in any year when a new farm bill is negotiated—so much so that the 2012 farm bill had been expired for two years before Congress was able to agree to the terms of the new one, which had only one legislative sponsor.

According to the American Farmland Trust, "The Farm Bill is where, every five years, Americans draw a compact to fight through drought, protect fragile farmland, restore our wetlands and keep our landscape healthy. It is where the nation comes together in the interest of a productive and sustainable farming industry." The Trust argues that agriculture is not a partisan issue and not about politics; it's about sound policy that benefits everyone.[8] While laudable, this position presents an unfortunately naïve view of the realities of American agriculture.

The Congressional Budget Office (CBO) estimates the total 10-year cost of the 2012 Farm Bill to be $968.2 billion.[9] Eighty percent of these dollars is being spent on nutrition, namely the food stamp program, which carries a $768.2 billion price tag. The remaining 20 percent is divided among price supports and crop insurance for commodity crops; conservation programs that affect land, water and soil use; agricultural exports and food aid, including humanitarian assistance to other nations; food assistance programs other than food stamps targeting the poor; direct and guaranteed loans to farmers and ranchers; forestry programs; programs promoting renewable fuels; and disaster insurance.

Farm Bill spending, as a percent of the total federal budget, is difficult to determine, but according to the CBO it's typically more than is spent on education and less than is spent on defense or social security. Sponsors of the 2012 Farm Bill claim it will save taxpayers $23.6 billion over the next 10 years, which is less than 2.5 percent of the total cost of the bill. Opponents say that isn't enough. "We don't often get the chance to reform farm policy, and unfortunately this bill is woefully short of what's needed," said Congressman Ron Kind (D-WI).[10]

The biggest changes in the 2012 Farm Bill over past bills involve a transition away from direct payments to farmers that were instituted in the 1990s and available to farmers regardless of whether they had a good year with high yields and high prices or a bad year when yield was poor and prices were low. The new provisions shift the balance of the farmer's income equation away from price supports toward risk management, minimizing the need for Congress to do ad hoc disaster legislation for farmers each time a catastrophic event occurs.

The Supplemental Nutrition Assistance Program (food stamps) became the whipping boy of both political parties during the 2012 farm bill negotiations, and the timing was bad. During the recession, food stamp demand naturally increased because people couldn't find jobs, said Jonathan Bader, program director for the Wisconsin Community Action programs, which administer aid in the form of housing assistance and food supplement programs in rural areas. "This legislation is very hostile toward low-income people ... it's like complaining to the fire department about their enormous water bill while they're fighting a wildfire," Bader remarked, adding that the 2012 farm bill represents seriously flawed legislation.[11]

Government Policy Gone Wrong

We're not growing quality here, we're growing crap!—Iowa farmer

Since the Great Depression the farm lobby has proved particularly lucrative for farmers, but over time it has had the unintended net effect of detaching agriculture from efficient production of good food consumers can purchase at a reasonable cost. This began to occur with the first omnibus farm bill, the Agriculture and Consumer Protection Act of 1973, passed during Butz's tenure as agriculture secretary.

This game-changing legislation adopted target prices and deficiency payments[12] as a tool to support farm income and reduce forfeitures of surplus stocks to the Commodity Credit Corporation (CCC).[13] It also reduced payment limitations from $55,000, set in 1970, to $20,000 for all commodity program crops.

The 1973 legislation went beyond authorizing farm commodity programs to include disaster payments and disaster reserve inventories; created the Rural Environmental Conservation Program; amended the Food Stamp Act of 1964 (P.L. 88–525), authorized the use of commodities for feeding low-income mothers and young children (the origin of the supplemental food program); and amended the Rural Development Act of 1972 (P.L. 92–419).

The federal agricultural production system Butz devised no longer paid farmers to refrain from overproducing—a system that kept crop prices high in the past; instead, it subsidized the creation of huge surpluses. As a result, the annual tsunami of cheap corn that resulted has become an essential ingredient in every fast food joint, in every processed food product on grocery shelves and in the feed of industrially produced poultry, pork and cattle.

Many believe Butz's expansionist policies, as reflected in the 1973 farm bill, did not have farmers' best interests at heart. By working with profit-hungry corporate interests Butz was able to flip the federal system of farm supports on its ear, thereby flooding the country with cheap food and altering the life and health of the nation in lasting ways, until today nearly everything in the typical American diet revolves around cheap corn. In reality, most Midwestern corn is not fit for human consumption because Butz tossed diverse, self-sufficient family farming to the wolves and opened the door to corporate takeover. Farms became bigger, more industrial, increasingly obsessed with a single crop, and increasingly dependent on government stipends. As consolidation plowed up family farms, swallowing up generations of agrarian tradition, the treasured, necessary human connection to the land, and to the food it produces, was severed.

"The name of the game now is 1,000 acres, a big tractor, genetically-engineered seeds and a tank of anhydrous ammonia fertilizer parked at the end of the rows. Once the seeds are planted, it's just a matter of watching the corn grow, spraying occasionally with pesticides and herbicides, then driving truckloads of corn to the local grain elevator, usually overflowing with grain well before the growing season is over," says Pat Schneider, reflecting on the pending 2012 farm legislation.[14]

Butz saw cheap food as a means of increasing American wealth, and acted accordingly. Some believe the true result of his cheap food agricultural policies is a national epidemic of obesity, skyrocketing health care costs and a generation that will, most likely, as a direct result of poor diet, have a shorter life span than its predecessor.

Farm Subsidies

> *A farmer on subsidies is part welfare bum, whereas a free-market farmer is a small businessman with a gun.* —Grover Norquist, founder, Americans for Tax Reform

Subsidy programs give farmers extra money for their crops and guarantee a price floor. For example, written into the 2002 Farm Bill was the guarantee that, for every bushel of wheat sold, farmers were paid an extra 52 cents and guaranteed a price of $3.86 per bushel from 2002 to 2003 and $3.92 per bushel from 2004 to 2007. If the price of wheat in 2002 was $3.80 per bushel, farmers would get an extra 58 cents per bushel (52 cents plus the six-cent price difference).

Depending upon who is asked, farm subsidies are either critically important insurance policies designed to keep farmers in business growing food or a government welfare system that freely allows farmers to live off the dole and lines the pockets of mega-rich farming corporations. Either way, subsidies have been a mainstay of the agriculture industry since the before the New Deal.

Direct payment subsidies were established in 1996 and originally intended to wean farmers off traditional subsidies that are triggered during periods of low commodity crop prices. While the beneficiaries of the subsidies have changed as American agriculture has changed, currently the United States pays around $20 billion per year in direct subsidies to farmers.[15] Known as "farm income stabilization," these subsidies have included one very important provision: direct payments are made without regard to the economic need of the recipients or the financial condition of the farm economy and corporate farming enterprises receive subsidies whether they need them or not.[16]

However, as tables one and two indicate, not all Midwestern farmers take advantage of direct subsidy payments, and those who do, do not receive large subsidy payments.

Table One: Midwestern Farm Subsidy Summary 1995–2011[17]
(b=billion; m=million)

State	Commodity	Crop Insurance	Conservation	Disaster	Total (billion)	Rural Poverty Rate	% of subsidy farmers
IL	$14.4b	$3.12b	$1.86b	$3.18m	$19.7	14.5%	74%
IN	$7.3b	$1.63b	$766m	$260m	$9.78	14.7	59%
IA	$16.9b	$3.47b	$3.63b	$587m	$9.78	12.5	81%

State	Commodity	Crop Insurance	Conservation	Disaster	Total (billion)	Rural Poverty Rate	% of subsidy farmers
KS	$9.07b	$2.96b	$2.27m	$1.13b	$15.4	14.9	68%
MI	$2.92b	$821m	$514m	$349m	$4.61	17.0	41%
MN	$10.1b	$3.35b	$1.96b	$722m	$16.2	12.4	70%
MO	$5.48b	$1.5b	$2.09b	$528m	$9.60	18.8	41%
NE	$10.5b	$2.79b	$1.47b	$807m	$15.6	12.5	73%
ND	$6.3b	$3.9b	$2b	$1.75b	$14	12.9	84%
OH	$5.05b	$1.14b	$791m	$375m	$7.36	16.1	50%
SD	$5.11b	$2.79b	$1.32b	$1.16b	$10.4	17.2	74%
WI	$4.3b	$1.03b	$902m	$352m	$6.65	13.1	60%
MIDWEST TOTAL	$97.43b	$27.37b	$17.31b	$8.02b	$139.08b	**14.7%**	64.4% av.

Notably, there is no evident correlation between individual states' rural poverty rates and the number of farmers receiving farm subsidy payments. Michigan and Missouri both have high rural poverty rates, yet only 41 percent of farmers in those states receive subsidies; 84 percent of Nebraska farmers and 81 percent of Iowa farmers receive subsidy payments, and both have lower rural poverty rates. Further, as Table Two indicates, the individual, per-year subsidy payment is not large enough to appreciably influence the income level of a struggling farm family.

Table Two: 1995–2011 Midwestern Subsidy Program Participation[18]
(b=billion; m=million)

	Corn	Soy	Conservation	Wheat	Disaster	Dairy	Environmental quality incentive
IL[1] Participants	213,027	174,788	82,228	111,163	54,737	3,256	7,983
$ amount	$12.4b	$3.8b	$1.7b	$704m	$318m	$88m	$68.4m
IN[2] Participants	11,017	86,483	38,507	65,164	27,852	3,368	5,087
$ amount	$6b	$2b	$643m	$367m	$260m	$77m	$59m
IA[3] Participants	173,557	128,327	101,420	0	62,965	6,693	11,165
$ amount	$14.9b	$4b	$3.5b	0	$587m	$158m	$127m
KS[4] Participants	72,805	69,118	67,590	160,230	92,629	1,484	11,033
$ amount	$3b	$931m	$2b	$5.5b	$1.2b	$41m	$133m
MI[5] Participants	50,313	19,156	18,491	37,101	21,850	5,954	2,832
$ amount	$2b	$639m	$354m	$361m	$349m	$212m	$81m
MN[6] Participants	90,115	60,827	65,008	47,946	49,104	17,064	10,010
$ amount	$7.9b	$2.9b	$1.7b	$1.6b	$722m	$378m	$131m
MO[7] Participants	90,382	76,197	48,833	87,296	77,972	4,645	0
$ amount	$2.9b	$1.7b	$1.8b	$888m	$528m	$92m	0
NE[8] Participants	104,980	70,645	35,678	66,198	1,633	0	11,411
$ amount	$9.2b	$1.7b	$1.2b	$806m	$37m	0	$165m
ND[9] Participants	28,445	15,318	40,659	61,056	47,666	0	6,790
$ amount	$1.3b	$978m	$1.8b	$5.3b	$1.7b	0	$95m
OH[10] Participants	86,415	66,498	33,588	67,892	330,049	6,410	7,066
$ amount	$3.6b	$1.7b	$623m	$624m	$375m	$177m	$71m

	Corn	Soy	Conservation	Wheat	Disaster	Dairy	Environmental quality incentive
SD[11] Participants	54,439	37,300	30,272	41,625	43,966	0	4,114
$ amount	$3.7b	$1.6b	$1.2b	$1.7b	$1.2b	0	$93m
WI[12] Participants	77,378	33,854	40,932	21,398	31,019	41,024	8,539
$ amount	$3.5b	$535m	$725m	$95m	$352m	$1b	$103m
Midwest Total							
Participants	1,052,873	838,511	603,206	767,069	841,442	89,898	86,030
$ amount	$70.4b	$22.48b	$17.25b	$17.95b	$7.63b	$2.22b	$1.126b

	Livestock	Wetland	Misc*	State Total	16 year Average $ per person	Average $ per year
IL Participants	22,250	192	27,500	49,942	$3,059	$191
$ amount	$36m	$31.8	$85m	$152.8m		
IN Participants	16,329	441	8,653	25,423	$1,990	$124
$ amount	$26m	$11m	$13.6m	$50.6m		
IA Participants	35,722	588	79,549	115,859	$1,174	$73
$ amount	$92m	$28m	$16.1m	$136.1m		
KS Participants	33,475	0	162,111	195,586	$874	$54
$ amount	$100m	0	$71m	$171m		
MI Participants	9,254	533	877	10,664	$7,295	$455
$ amount	$23.6m	$26.4m	$27.8	$77.8m		
MN Participants	26,317	0	29,102	55,419	$5,377	$336
$ amount	$7m	0	$291m	$298m		
MO Participants	55,677	0	66,093	121,770	$13,533	$845
$ amount	$148m	0	$1.5b	$1.65b		
NE Participants	32,098	367	57,924	90,389	$6,784	$424
$ amount	$198m	$38.5m	$376.7m	$613.2m		
ND Participants	17,940	0	88,990	106,930	$16,702	$1,043
$ amount	$124.6m	0	$1.66b	$1.79b		
OH Participants	20,204	0	33,767	53,971	$959	$59
$ amount	$32.3m	0	$19.5m	$51.8m		
SD Participants	26,319	30,272	42,571	99,162	$19,436	$1,214
$ amount	$256.4m	$1.2b	$471m	$1.93b		
WI Participants	21,329	362	56,482	78,173	$1,370	$16
$ amount	$50.5m	$33.4m	$23.2m	$107.1m		
Midwest Total						
Participants	316,914	32,755	653,619	1,003,288	$7,834.24	$489.64
$ amount	$1.094b	$1.37b	$4.55b	$7.86b		

*Oats, sorghum, sunflowers, barley, tobacco, sugar beets, cotton, rice, canola

1. Twenty-six percent of Illinois farms did not collect subsidy payments between 1995 and 2011. Of the 74 percent that did collect subsidies 10 percent collected 68 percent of all subsidies, totaling $11.2 billion over 17 years. The top 10 percent averaged $28,747 per year. The bottom 80 percent averaged $831 per year.
2. Forty-one percent of Indiana farms did not collect subsidy payments between 1995 and 2011. Of the 59 percent that did collect subsidies 10 percent collected 74 percent of all subsidies, totaling $6.06 billion over 17 years. The top 10 percent averaged $27,525 per year. The bottom 80 percent averaged $556 per year.
3. Nineteen percent of Iowa farms did not collect subsidy payments between 1995 and 2011. Of the 81 percent that did collect subsidies 10 percent collected 58 percent of all subsidies, totaling $11.8 billion over 17 years. The top 10 percent averaged $33,626 per year. The bottom 80 percent averaged $1,553 per year.
4. Thirty-two percent of Kansas farms did not collect subsidy payments between 1995 and 2011. Of the 68 per-

cent that did collect subsidies 10 percent collected 70 percent of all subsidies, totaling $8.67 billion over 17 years. The top 10 percent averaged $27,615 per year. The bottom 80 percent averaged $721 per year.

5. Fifty-nine percent of Michigan farms did not collect subsidy payments between 1995 and 2011. Of the 41 percent that did collect subsidies 10 percent collected 71 percent of all subsidies, totaling $2.69 billion over 17 years. The top 10 percent averaged $24,399 per year. The bottom 80 percent averaged $595 per year.

6. Thirty percent of Minnesota farms did not collect subsidy payments between 1995 and 2011. Of the 70 percent that did collect subsidies 10 percent collected 62 percent of all subsidies, totaling $7.95 billion over 17 years. The top 10 percent averaged 35,237 per year. The bottom 80 percent averaged $1,319 per year.

7. Fifty-eight percent of Missouri farms did not collect subsidy payments between 1995 and 2011. Of the 41 percent that did collect subsidies 10 percent collected 72 percent of all subsidies, totaling $5.8 billion over 17 years. The top 10 percent averaged $22,436 per year. The bottom 80 percent averaged $537 per year.

8. Twenty-seven percent of Nebraska farms did not collect subsidy payments between 1995 and 2011. Of the 73 percent that did collect subsidies 10 percent collected 62 percent of all subsidies, totaling $7.97 billion over 17 years. The top 10 percent averaged $36,494 per year. The bottom 80 percent averaged $1,340 per year.

9. Sixteen percent of North Dakota farms did not collect subsidy payments between 1995 and 2011. Of the 84 percent that did collect subsidies 10 percent collected 61 percent of all subsidies, totaling $6.17 billion over 17 years. The top 10 percent averaged $45,980 per year. The bottom 80 percent averaged $1,212 per year.

10. Fifty percent of Ohio farms did not collect subsidy payments between 1995 and 2011. Of the 50 percent that did collect subsidies 10 percent collected 70 percent of all subsidies, totaling $4.38 billion over 17 years. The top 10 percent averaged $22,872 per year. The bottom 80 percent averaged $577 per year.

11. Twenty-six percent of South Dakota farms did not collect subsidy payments between 1995 and 2011. Of the 74 percent that did collect subsidies 10 percent collected 62 percent of all subsidies, totaling $4.71 billion over 17 years. The top 10 percent averaged $37,375 per year. The bottom 80 percent averaged $1,383 per year.

12. Forty percent of Wisconsin farms did not collect subsidy payments between 1995 and 2011. Of the 60 percent that did collect subsidies 10 percent collected 64 percent of all subsidies, totaling $3.61 billion over 17 years. The top 10 percent averaged $19,290 per year. The bottom 80 percent averaged $692 per year.

The Farm Subsidy Controversy

> *Congress has once again proven itself incapable of producing a comprehensive Farm Bill that is responsive to family farmers and responsible to taxpayers.—*
> Congressman Ron Kind (D-WI)

No part of farm policy legislation is more controversial than subsidies. Veronique de Rugy, a senior research fellow at the Mercatus Center at George Mason University, presents compelling arguments for the reason farm subsidies must end.[19] "Farm subsidies benefit the rich and hurt the poor. They are massively expensive and hugely wasteful," she writes.

De Rugy's arguments in support of her position include the following:

- In 2012, the Department of Agriculture (USDA) spent $22 billion on subsidy programs for farmers.
- Only a handful of farmers reap most of the benefits from the subsidies: Wheat, corn, soybeans, rice, and cotton have always taken the lion's share of the feds' largesse.
- 10 percent of subsidized farms—the largest and wealthiest operations—have raked in 74 percent of all subsidy payments. Sixty-two percent of farms in the United States did not collect subsidy payments.
- Like most businesses, farms buy insurance policies to protect from potential losses, such as poor yields or declining prices. Unlike most businesses, farms can count on the government to pay about two thirds of the premiums, at a cost of $7 billion annually.
- Farm subsidies increase the cost of food by creating economic distortions. For

example, the USDA protects American producers against foreign competitors by imposing U.S. import quotas, and against low prices with a no-recourse loan program that serves as an effective price floor. As a result, since 1982 Americans have had to pay an average of twice the world price of sugar.
- Farm subsidies impact land values. Almost half of the country's farmland is operated by someone other than its owner. Those renters—especially young farmers who generally have higher borrowing costs to start with—face increases in both the price of renting and the cost of buying. In 2010 some 90,000 direct payments went to wealthy investors and absentee land owners.
- Price support programs such as marketing loans, conservation subsidies that pay farmers not to farm their land, export subsidies, which aid farmers in foreign sales, and countercyclical payments, which compensate for drops in crops' market prices all waste taxpayer dollars.

The good news, according to de Rugy, is that the current fiscal problems have made these subsidies politically unsustainable, forcing Congress to consider terminating them. However, history has shown that attempts to wean farmers from the federal programs have proved disastrous.

Brian Riedl, Grover Herman Fellow in Federal Budget Affairs at the Thomas R. Roe Institute for Economic Policy Studies at the conservative Heritage Foundation, expands on the anti-subsidy argument. According to Riedl, farm subsidies are intended to[20]:

- Alleviate farmer poverty, but the majority of subsidies go to commercial farms with average incomes of $200,000 and net worth of nearly $2 million.
- Raise farmer incomes by remedying low crop prices. Instead, they promote overproduction and therefore lower prices further.
- Help struggling family farmers. Instead, they harm them by excluding them from most subsidies, financing the consolidation of family farms, and raising land values to levels that prevent young people from entering farming.
- Be consumer-friendly and taxpayer-friendly. Instead, they cost Americans billions each year in higher taxes and higher food costs.

Riedl also claims subsidy payments are a solution seeking a problem and charges that advocates operate from a set of flawed justifications regarding farmer poverty, crop disaster compensation and maintaining a cheap food supply because farm subsidy formulas are designed to benefit large agribusinesses rather than family farmers. "Most farm subsidies are distributed to commercial farmers, who have six figure average incomes and seven figure land values," he explains. "If farm subsidies were really about alleviating farmer poverty, lawmakers could guarantee every full-time farmer an income of 185 percent of the federal poverty level ($38,203 for a family of four) for just over $4 billion annually—one-sixth of the current cost of farm subsidies," Riedl says.[21]

While farming can be very profitable, farmers are always one weather disaster away from losing their crops. Riedl believes this risk can be handled with basic crop insurance rather than with expensive annual government subsidies and that crop insurance markets, as well as futures and options markets, can balance good and bad years in a way that is cost-neutral over the long run. He admits that some economists contend that food markets would fluctuate wildly without farm subsidies and, in reality, food prices of both subsidized and unsubsidized crops are relatively stable.

"The percentage of family budgets spent on food has dropped from 25 percent to 10 percent since 1933 so any potential price instability would have an increasingly small impact on family budgets. Even if price stabilization was necessary, price support programs have largely been replaced by commodity subsidies that stimulate overproduction rather than stabilize prices," Riedl claims.[22]

Riedl also contends that farm subsidies do not contribute to lower food costs because two-thirds of food production is unsubsidized and thus relatively unaffected by subsidies. Of the remaining one-third, price reductions caused by crop subsidies are balanced by conservation programs that raise prices. Furthermore, food prices are based not only on crop prices, but also on food processing, transportation, and marketing costs. "Bruce Babcock, professor of economics at Iowa State University, has calculated that eliminating farm subsidies would have virtually no effect on food prices," Riedl notes.[23]

Subsidy proponents contend that they are vital to keeping farmers in business and sustaining the nation's food supply, making the issue a matter of national security, because without subsidies, American farm products would be replaced by imports, leaving the United States dangerously dependent on foreign-grown food. However, the United States currently grows more food than it needs to feed itself and exports a quarter of its production, Riedl explains, adding that the lack of subsidies "has not driven all beef, poultry, pork, fruit, and vegetable production out of America, nor would it drive away production of currently subsidized crops."[24]

There's also the matter of agricultural policies in other countries: Europe and Japan's farm subsidies bring American consumers food at below-market prices. Rather than enact trade barriers to prevent this, Riedl believes Americans should welcome the cheap imports and allow farmers to focus on producing the crops in which the United States has a comparative advantage. U.S. subsidies and trade barriers have had the net effect of raising prices for American consumers and thereby limiting any progress in free-trade negotiations. Further, two-thirds of all farm production—including fruit, vegetables, beef, and poultry—thrives despite being ineligible for farm subsidies.

Riedl contends that the most logical explanation for the persistence of farm subsidies is simple politics, and he makes a good point. Eliminating any government program is nearly impossible because recipients form interest groups that relentlessly, and effectively, defend the benefits they are receiving. Further, more than 90 percent of all subsidies are paid to just five crops (wheat, cotton, corn, soybeans, and rice) and the vast majority of crops are actually ineligible for subsidies. For subsidy-eligible crops, subsidies are paid per amount of the crop produced, so the largest farms automatically receive the largest checks, which is a huge public policy black eye for the farm subsidy program.

According to Wisconsin congressmen Ron Kind (D) and Tom Petri (R), $11.3 million in taxpayer-funded farm subsidies are paid directly to 50 billionaires invested in farm operations.[25] These mega-rich recipients of farm subsidies include Paul Allen, cofounder of Microsoft, and investment mogul Charles Schwab. "The recipients don't even have to be farmers," Kind and Petri say. "Some government farm checks have been sent to wealthy residents of Maple Bluff or Shorewood Hills[26] where no farms exist.... Crop insurance subsidies should be targeted to real farmers and dollar limited so farmers don't plant on land they otherwise wouldn't cultivate."

Kind and Petri also believe a 68 percent subsidy is too generous because it bumps up against the risk inherent in farming, or any other small business endeavor. "They [farmers] are going to plant in the most fallow and highly sensitive and most erodible land, knowing their losses will be covered," Kind said, adding that more scrutiny of federal payments is needed.

Other flaws in the subsidy program revolve around three major areas:

- Despite being called a "loan," the marketing loan program has the net effect of reimbursing farmers for the difference between a crop's market price and the minimum level that Congress sets every five to six years.
- Fixed payments are given to farmers based on their farms' historical production averages and are unrelated to actual current production.
- The countercyclical payments program functions somewhat similarly to the marketing loan program by subsidizing farmers up to a government-set rate. This rate is higher than the marketing loan rate and therefore represents an additional subsidy.

Riedl also charges the government with making contradictory farm policies. "After handing out commodity subsidies that pay farmers to plant more crops, Washington then turns around and pays other farmers not to farm 40 million acres of cropland each year—the equivalent of idling every farm in Wisconsin, Michigan, Indiana, and Ohio. The Conservation Reserve Program, which pays farmers to sign 10-year contracts pledging not to farm their land, is often promoted as supporting environmental stewardship. In reality, removing farmland to raise crop prices has been the program's central long-term justification. Paying some farmers to plant more crops and others to plant fewer crops simply makes no sense," he says, adding that the flawed logic does not end there.[27]

"Businesses calculate their revenues by multiplying the product's price by the quantity sold. Similarly, farmers calculate per-acre revenues by multiplying the crop price by the yield (crop volume per acre). However, farm subsidy formulas focus only on crop prices and simply plug in a historical yield measure for the quantity. This makes little sense. Revenues depend as much on the quantity sold as on the price, and these two variables often move in opposite directions, leading to one of two common scenarios:

- Surging yields flood the market with crops and cause prices to drop. Total revenues may increase, yet farmers still receive large subsidies simply because the price fell.
- Falling yields lead to crop shortages, pushing up prices. Total revenues may decline sharply, but farmers do not receive subsidies because Washington focuses only on the price increase and assumes that farmers are thriving…
- Driving small farmers out of business. Farm subsidies are promoted as assistance to family farmers. In reality, they finance the demise of family farms and prevent young people from entering farming. Economists estimate that subsidies inflate the value of farmland by 30 percent. High farmland prices make starting a farm prohibitively expensive for younger people, who would also have other expenses, including buying expensive equipment, seeds, and pesticides. With young farmers unable to enter the industry, the average age of farmers [is increasing]."[28]

Farm policy is supposed to help farmers recover income lost because of low crop prices; however, under the current system farmers can increase their subsidies by planting additional acres, which increases production and drives prices down further, thereby spurring demands for even greater subsidies. In other words, subsidies merely lower prices.[29] This is the policy equivalent of trying to use gasoline to extinguish a fire.

In a free market, low prices serve as an important signal that supply has exceeded consumer demand and that production should shift accordingly. By shielding farmers from the effect of low market prices, farm subsidies induce farmers to grow whatever government will subsidize, not what consumers really want or need. Further, agribusinesses often use their enormous farm subsidies to buy out smaller family farms. In what has been called the "plantation effect," family farms with less than 100 acres are being bought up by larger agribusinesses and converted into tenant farms.

Proponents of free-enterprise economics believe this consolidation is not necessarily harmful and may improve efficiency. They believe large agribusinesses are not villainous and often succeed because they can produce large quantities of food at low prices. Furthermore, the blame for the tilted distribution of farm subsidies lies with Congress, which writes the laws, rather than with the agribusinesses that cash the checks that they receive because of those laws.

Riedl describes "the scandalous distribution of farm subsidies" using the following example:

> One can imagine the result if Washington tried to solve poverty by creating a welfare program that applied only to workers in the fast food, cleaning, and retail industries. Everyone in those occupations would receive a government check, with the richest executives receiving the largest checks and the poorest workers receiving the smallest. Workers in other industries would receive nothing, no matter how poor they were. Obviously, such a policy would be nonsense, yet this exemplifies how farm subsidies are distributed. The government's solution to alleged farmer poverty is to subsidize growers of wheat, cotton, corn, soybeans, and rice while giving no subsidies to producers of fruit, vegetables, beef, poultry, and livestock. Because subsidies are paid per acre, the largest and most profitable farms receive the largest subsidies, while family farms receive next to nothing. Thus, a large, profitable rice corporation can receive millions while a family vegetable farmer receives nothing. Overall, farm subsidies are distributed with little regard to merit or need.[30]

While farm subsidies are promoted as helping struggling farmers, according to the USDA, the majority of farm subsidies are distributed to high-income, high-value commercial farm enterprises that need subsidies the least because, due to economies of scale, they are the most efficient. One-third of the $240 billion in annual farm production is eligible for farm subsidies, and five crops receive more than 90 percent of all farm subsidies,[31] which Riedl says is important for two reasons:

> First, those who assert that the absence of farm subsidies would cause massive poverty, rapid price fluctuations, and the eventual demise of the agricultural industry have not persuasively explained why the two-thirds of the industry that operates without subsidies has experienced none of these problems.
>
> Second, those who assert that farm subsidies are necessary to alleviate farmer poverty have not explained why favoring one crop over another [will solve the rural poverty problem].[32]

Those on both sides of the subsidy argument agree that taxpayers should not be required to finance the consolidation of small farms into large ones through farm subsidies. By raising land values and financing consolidation, farm subsidies drive out existing small farmers and prevent new farmers from entering the industry.

And, many farmers view subsidies as not all they are cracked up to be. They believe the best way to handle market forces is to back off and simply let free-market economic principles work, on their own, to bring commodity prices down, but will do so through innovation rather than compulsory subsidies.

However, if one farmer accepts subsidies, then others are forced to follow because the subsidized farmer can produce the product at a much lower price than those who are not accepting subsidies, effectively putting those who do not want to accept subsidies out of business.

Despite the controversy surrounding farm subsidies, subsidized farming creates a very predictable and stable farming system. It enables all farmers to have good equipment and to continue farming through both good and bad years. If farmers weren't subsidized, consumers would face dramatic price spikes due to something as singular as a bad harvest, and the cost of eating would potentially rise considerably. Current farm subsidies contribute large amounts of money towards the growing science of ethanol, which reduces carbon emissions and, from the human rights perspective, is good for the impoverished developing world, because staples like milk, wheat, and sugar are more affordable for those living in these regions.

The battle over a Farm Bill that protects both farmers and consumers from boom-and-bust cycles, keeps the United States competitive in the global agricultural market, encourages environmental stewardship and delivers sufficient savings to be fiscally responsible will continue beyond the current legislation—and the stakes for the Midwest farm belt are very high. American Farm Bureau (AFB) lobbyists believe the 2012 Farm Bill proposes significant reform. "The elimination of direct payments is a big deal," says AFB lobbyist Mary Kay Thatcher "It's real reform."[33]

However, Congressman Kind viewed the 2012 Farm Bill as so deeply flawed he voted against it. "It cuts another $8.6 billion from the nutrition title on top of previous cuts that have already been made, but gives huge taxpayer subsidies that go to a few large agribusinesses. It codifies historically high commodity target prices, so any slight dip in prices will result in huge payments going out that will quickly offset any savings found in the bill. It doesn't address the 'multiple entity' rule meaning that multiple farm managers working at the same farm can qualify for the same subsidies.... And while the elimination of direct payments is a welcome step towards reforming farm subsidy programs, in the case of this Farm Bill the majority of those savings are steered into new subsidy programs," he explains.[34]

Worse yet, Kind contends, this bill does nothing to reform the bloated crop insurance program. Allowing that program to continue would indirectly subsidize, on average, 62 percent of farmers' crop insurance premiums, reimburse insurance companies for their administrative and operating expenses, adjust premiums in order to produce a 14 percent return for crop insurance companies, and take the riskiest crop insurance policies off the companies' books.

And, according to Kind, as further evidence of the bill's fiscal irresponsibility, the federal government will continue to send nearly $150 million every year, courtesy of the American taxpayer, to the Brazilian cotton industry.

This is the enduring legacy of Earl Butz's "get big or get out" philosophy, and there is no sign it will fade into obscurity in the foreseeable future. Sadly Butz sentenced small farm operations, for generations to come, to a lifetime of enduring poverty.

Designer Farming—Organic and Biological Methods

> *The more we pour the big machines, the fuel, the pesticides, the herbicides, the fertilizer and chemicals into farming, the more we knock out the mechanism that made it all work in the first place.*—David Brower

In the 52 years since *The Silent Spring* was first published, scientists have continued to debate whether Rachel Carson overreacted when she claimed pesticides would prove deadly to the natural environment.[35] In 1996 a comprehensive, in-depth examination of whether Carson "was right" was published by the American Chemical Society, in cooperation with the United Nations Environment Programme.[36] Comprised of a series of papers by distinguished scientists, the overall result is remarkably sympathetic to Carson's views:

Was Rachel Carson right? In many respects, yes. In her time the environment was relentlessly assaulted by a society hoping for total control. Nature was not as self-cleansing as we believed. Many of Carson's predictions about environmental toxicity, human health effects, water contamination, and waste site problems have proved correct.

Was Rachel Carson wrong? In fewer respects, yes. Nature, not just humans, generates its share of carcinogens and other poisons. Nature and humans both use chemicals for their own advantage. Human life span is still increasing. Society has responded, and, of course, birds still sing. Biological controls alone have been able to replace chemicals only in a few special cases.[37]

Pesticides can often cope with pest problems as a sole control measure, but at an environmental cost and with the danger of the development of pesticide-resistant strains. Other control measures (e.g., host-plant resistance, biological control, etc.) often may not provide an acceptable level of control. The remaining gap then has to be filled. Thus, pesticides are still, and are likely to remain, a component in the majority of integrated pest management (IPM) programs where the threshold for pest damage is low. IPM, including some pesticide use, is the route by which it has become possible to reverse the pesticide treadmill in developing countries.

Today both organic and biological farming methods have taken hold, but neither can begin to compete with the agricultural mega-industry created and supported by Earl Butz. Despite the proven risks, industrial farming continues to thrive by using chemicals to produce bigger crops, and it is very difficult for a local farmer to compete in this arena. Nevertheless, some farmers strenuously object to taking those chances with the nation's food supply and are willing to settle for less in terms of farm production; others continue using chemicals and pesticides as an integral part of their farming practices.

The shift away from emphasis on chemicals in IPM does not detract from the logic and appropriateness of their use in a multiple, all-suitable-techniques strategy for sustainable pest control.[38] Scientists also point out that overreliance on pesticides continues in most countries but has been integral to agricultural progress in developing countries, where rural poverty abounds, and the only hope for ameliorating it rests with agricultural development.

Organically Grown Food—Good Farming, Clear Thinking, Right Living

> *It bothers me enormously, in the moral sense, that the organic food I grow, and eke out a small profit from, is only available to people able to afford to purchase it.*—Mike Irwin

Family-owned farms are the ones more likely to use sustainable farming techniques, protect the surrounding environment, maintain green spaces, use crop rotations and management for pest and weed controls, and apply fewer chemicals. In other words, they're doing exactly what 80 percent of U.S. consumers say they would prefer to support.

However, it's hard to make a living as an organic farmer who can generate some income by participating in this niche market, but produces a product that costs more than those produced by conventional means. Most organic farmers find it very difficult to make a living when their main sales outlets are local farmers' markets.

For many of these farmers, organic farming is a moral issue, and rather than sell out to industry standards they are willing to live on the edge of poverty because using organic methods "is the right way to farm." Additionally, organic farming is not as productive as conventional methods because resident insects do their damage and the soil is not as enriched.

Farmers who organically farm and sell locally must price their product competitively in order to generate sufficient sales, but many don't. As a result, participating in this small agricultural market does relatively little to relieve the chronic poverty facing many small farmers and local rural residents. In order to stay afloat organic farmers must charge premium prices and locals can't afford to pay that much.

Cost is also a problem in a different way. If imported apples cost 50 cents each at the local grocery store and locally grown apples cost $1.50, the extra dollar spent on the local apple is money not available to other local businesses in the small community where the orchard is located. And some foods are not suitable for production in a particular location, so importing them is the only way they can be available to local consumers. For example, trying to raise tropical fruit in a Midwestern climate would necessitate heating and artificially lighting a large greenhouse, which would be extremely costly, thereby putting the product far out of reach of the average consumer.

Another problem is lack of quality control. While most people say they prefer to buy locally, even when it doesn't make economic sense, a reality of the local food industry is that it is not carefully regulated. Local farmers can be just as dishonest as large-scale agricultural producers and, absent regulation, can do considerable damage in terms of food safety.

"'Localavoreism' is, at best, a marketing fad that frequently and severely distorts the environmental impacts of agriculture and is not as environmentally positive as people think," claim geographer Pierre Desrochers and economist Hiroko Shimizu.[39] "If the point is to help people of lesser means, the concept doesn't work because local food has to be priced competitively—otherwise it's a charity, not a business, and you don't build a strong local economy on charity," Desrochers says.

Irrigation Farming

> *About 94 percent of the nation's four major commodity crops—corn, soybeans, wheat and cotton—is grown on farmland that relies on rain for moisture.* —P. J. Huffstuter

Central to the uncertainties that surround Midwestern farming is how much rain will fall in a given year, and in what pattern. An extremely wet, rain-soaked spring delays planting and drowns out newly emerging crops. A dry spring creates problems with the seeds ever sprouting at all, and a hot, dry summer stunts plant growth. So does an excessively cold, wet summer. And too much rain late in the fall drowns out the crop before it can be harvested.

A farmer has no control over any of these circumstances and while he can hope for the ideal of rain when it's needed, as often as not, it doesn't always happen that way. As a result, one of the most valuable modern devices available to farmers is an irrigation system.

The High Plains Aquifer, a waterlogged area that stretches from South Dakota to the Texas Panhandle, has been the savior for Midwest farmers who have been able to tap into this water artery to irrigate their crops. Also known as the Ogallala Aquifer, part of the High Plains Aquifer System is a vast yet shallow underground water table aquifer located beneath the Great Plains. As one of the world's largest aquifers, it covers an area of approximately 174,000 miles (450,000 kilometers) in portions of eight states: South Dakota, Nebraska, Wyoming, Colorado, Kansas, Oklahoma, New Mexico, and Texas.

The Ogallala Formation underlies about 80 percent of the High Plains and is the principal geologic unit of the High Plains Aquifer. About 27 percent of the irrigated land in the United States overlies this aquifer system, which yields about 30 percent of all ground water used for irrigation in the United States. The aquifer system supplies drinking water to 82 percent of the 2.3 million people who live within the boundaries of the High Plains—and the lower part is drying up as a result of more intensive farming and continued drought. In west-central Kansas up to 20 percent of normally irrigated farmland along a 100-mile area of the aquifer has gone dry, and in other areas of Kansas there is no longer sufficient water to meet peak need during a typically scorching Kansas summer. When groundwater dries up, it is gone for good, and refilling the aquifer would take centuries of continual heavy rains combined with no draw-down.

The economic impact of having less available water is significant. For one thing, irrigated land produces higher yields than land that relies on natural rainfall, which can vary widely in a growing season. For another, farm towns in areas where farmers aren't producing as much tend to shrivel up. Those farmers who want to keep farming will adapt by shifting their emphasis to less thirsty crops or to animal operations, which don't use as much water. However, with the advent of bio-fuels, corn has become the biggest cash crop, and it drinks up a lot of water during a growing season. With corn prices being so consistently good, a lot of farmers want to grow it, and, if they can afford it, are willing to dig a deep well and invest thousands of dollars in irrigations systems to make that possible, even if the result is to severely deplete the aquifer they all depend upon.[40]

An unchanging reality of rural life, and rural poverty in the 21st century, is that no one who lives the rural lifestyle will ever be as wealthy as those who earn their living either on Wall Street or as part of the vast American corporate, industrial complex. Mother Nature is a whimsical and very unpredictable business partner who can't be fired, controlled, or moved to another department in the company; and no matter how much damage she does in any given year, the farmer remains always optimistic that "next year will be better." Maybe it will be better, and maybe it won't be. Next year's drought can shrivel a farmer's crops, or next year's excess rain and flooding can drown him out. Maybe the farmer will live below the poverty line for several years, but if Mother Nature has a cooperative streak, he probably won't be in poverty every year. And everybody knows Mother Nature is the decider.

6

Throwing Cow Chips for Entertainment

The Pluses and Minuses of Rural Community Life

Yea—I take a lot of pride in throwing cow poo.—Josh Sweeney,
2008 Iowa State Fair Men's Cow Chip Throwing Champion

I first discovered cow chips as a form of entertainment one dripping hot August afternoon, after I'd just crossed the Mississippi River into Wisconsin on my way to enter graduate school at the University of Wisconsin-Madison. This was my first "feet on the ground" trip across the Midwest, and it had been seemingly endless days filled with seemingly endless boring miles of flat land and corn fields.

Midday I stopped for gas at some small town I don't even remember the name of, and I glanced up to see a flimsy plastic banner strung across the main street announcing the "Annual Cow Chip Throwing Contest" the next day. I asked the gas station attendant what cow chips were and why people threw them? After he, and everyone else within hearing distance, stopped laughing, he looked toward my car, with its telltale license plate and asked me, "You mean they don't throw cow shit in California?" I shook my head no, and he proceeded to give me a motion by motion, detailed description of how one throws a cow chip, stopping every ten or so words to laugh again.

When we were finished he urged me to come back for the contest. "It's more fun than watching the Packers[1] on TV," he assured me, adding that I better come early, because they get quite a crowd. "In this weather, we'll probably run short on beer," he warned, suggesting I might want to bring some of my own.

By the time I got to Madison I was convinced that, despite its stellar reputation, coming to the "Berkeley of the Midwest" was a bad mistake. I called home and asked my dad to send money for a return trip immediately, explaining that "on top of everything else, they throw cow shit for entertainment!" He advised that, as long as I was already here, I should stay for the fall term, and give the place a fair chance. "I'm sure they do other things for fun besides just that," he laughed.

Eventually I found other things to entertain myself and went on to receive a great education. But I've never forgotten the sign greeting me in the first small Wisconsin town I encountered and, to my great surprise, over the years I discovered that cow chip throwing contests are common occurrences in the rural Midwest. Some places even have corporate throws involving small businesses competing against each other, similar to bowling league competition. There are also throws for kids divided by age group, adult throws for both men and women, and senior competition for those over 65.

And just last year I overheard two farmers in a café exclaim that the shortage of cow chips for this year's local cow chip throwing festival had reached a new level. "We have a crisis the Obama administration needs to step up and do something about," one said—and I honestly couldn't tell whether he was serious.

While I've not personally thrown cow chips, I have, admittedly not often, attended a throwing contest and can attest that, indeed, they are very entertaining—and winning one involves quite a bit more effort and concentration than one might imagine. "Cow chips aren't Frisbees, so people have to learn to avoid the temptation to throw them like that's what they are," explains Carl Bierman, who emcees the annual event at the Iowa State Fair.

Obviously there's a lot more to rural community life than throwing cow manure for entertainment, but no one can argue that they don't know how to do it, can do it well enough to make a competition out of it, and have learned to have fun using whatever resources are at their disposal.

Traits of Rural Communities

> *Rural towns aren't always idyllic. It's easy to feel trapped and be aware of social hypocrisy.*—Bill Pullman

In small towns the community itself wields great social influence, often dictating the appropriate means for surviving economic hardship or even for living in poverty. Generally acceptable coping strategies for the poor include getting help from family, taking any available job (or jobs) and keeping it, and living frugally. Unacceptable coping includes taking welfare, engaging in illegal activities, and failing to work at all. There appears to be a moral value system operating in small towns that tends to forgive the poor who try hard by working at whatever job they can find and harshly judges those who don't work and won't even try to find a job.

The working poor are held in higher regard, both by themselves and within the wider community, because even if they aren't making it, at least they're trying. For these folks, being poor is viewed as a conspiracy of bad luck and circumstances and not as a personal failing. These are the people who consider hard work valuable for its own sake, and in this way they are in agreement with the wider community who respects them for their efforts.

The economically destitute, non-working members of the community are often considered the "undeserving poor," because they are viewed as lazy and unwilling to even try to help themselves, and thus don't deserve a handout. Even those who suffer chronic addictions, which many of the rural poor do, are viewed negatively because "they don't have control over their lives," and little regard is given to the circumstances that brought them down. Being poor is not a problem in a small town, as long as you are trying to help yourself, but there isn't a lot of patience with those who don't try.

These moral judgments, based upon widespread American values of individualism and self-reliance, further harm the poor because the wider community of both poor and non-poor view them as personally deficient, responsible for their own misfortune, lacking motivation to improve their lives, and therefore unworthy of social support or assistance.

In rural communities, more than urban settings, accepting welfare assistance of any kind carries a heavy stigma. "We know a lot more people need our services than come here," the operator of a local food pantry in rural Wisconsin told me, adding that "they don't want anyone to know they're coming here because they're afraid people will look down on them.... Some people even waste gas driving to a pantry in another town, where they're pretty sure no one will recognize them."

Precisely because they are small and everyone tends to know everyone else, rural communities tend to make serious attempts at solving their own problems and prefer depending upon local units of government, or any government, as little as possible. In 2013, faced with funding cuts to the county aging and senior services, a local political group in Barron County, Wisconsin,[2] decided to hold a raffle to make up for cuts in funding to the Barron County Office on Aging and the Rice Lake Senior Center. The program is losing about $9,000 in funding, and the Senior Center is facing cutbacks in staffing and programs because of city budget cuts, and the county has nowhere to turn for additional revenue sources. Rather than let the local programs go down, local residents banded together to try to save them. Raffle tickets were $20 each and the goal was to raise $20,000, with the winner of the raffle receiving $10,000 and the remainder of proceeds split between the Rice Lake Senior Center and the Office on Aging, which operates the Meals on Wheels program.

This ability to "fix it yourself" coupled with an awareness of the interconnectedness of community members is a profound strength in rural areas, and what saves most, but not all, rural poor again and again is that they know how to find pick-up work, do odd jobs, for which they are paid off the books, and find all kinds of ways to earn extra money. Able-bodied elderly women will clean houses for cash, others make crafts local stores are willing to sell for them without taking a cut, and sell homemade jams, jellies and baked goods at the local farmer's market. Men cut wood, clear fields, plow snow, keep the parking lots of local businesses sanded and salted in winter, and show up at the grain elevator daily spring, summer and fall looking to get hired on as temporary help.

And both rural men and women hunt and fish, which is both recreation and vital to keeping food on the table. A good hunting and fishing season combined with a decent garden in summer followed by a productive canning season in the fall goes a very long way toward feeding many rural families, who find all kinds of ways to make their lives work, at least to some degree, most of the time.

When Trouble Comes, Raise Money

> *Fundraiser at Roxbury Tavern for Jerry Jones, 34, who suffered a bad stroke last month and can't work.... Saturday 4 to ???. First beer half price. Snacks provided.* —Sign on the door of Roxbury gas station

In a small town everybody knows everybody else, and when trouble befalls any one of the local residents, neighbors and local businesses pony up. Large jars are found on countertops all over the town and usually have a picture of the person and a few sentences describing their bad luck. Sometimes the same countertop has more than one jar, and the story is usually related to a medical crisis: "Laurie Jones, a 24 YO mom to two kids has been diagnosed with stage three stomach and kidney cancer and doesn't have health insurance. Laurie has had to close her home day care business. Donations will help with the cost of chemotherapy and radiation." People throw loose change or dollar bills into these jars. Even though these small donations can never be enough to offset the costs of the medical treatment, the recipient knows that the people in her community really do care about her.

"People in rural areas will come together to take care of each other and of someone in need who they don't even know as an act of faith.... It's a sacred act, just like it's a sacred act of faith when you entrust yourself to your neighbors," says Douglas Larson Sell, a small-town Lutheran minister. His church runs a local food pantry. Rural writer Jerry Apps agrees. "No matter what, they're your neighbors ... and you always do what you can to help them out...."

Other times, fundraising occurs for someone less financially needy but dearly beloved in the community. When a local veterinarian fell asleep at the wheel of his truck in the early morning hours, after sleeping all night in a barn awaiting the birth of a calf to a very valuable milk cow having a hard labor, the local community immediately organized a fundraiser. Everyone knew insurance would cover his truck and equipment loss, that he had adequate health insurance to pay his medical bills and could access money to live on while he recuperated, but the community felt compelled to "do something for Doc" because he had taken care of their herds and their pets for years.

The local bowling alley donated the space and agreed to sell beer on tap at cost, the local grocery store donated food and local women made pies and bars to sell—and the effort raised more than $3,000. "When my cows got milk fever Doc saved every one of them—and saved my operation.... I'd a gone clear under without him," a bow-legged old farmer said as he threw a hundred dollar bill in the jar.

Sometimes communities get very organized, as has happened when what started out as a fundraiser for a young high school wrestler who lost his leg to bone cancer expanded into an annual event that raises money to those in need in the community, for various reasons that aren't always medical. Recent recipients included Lori, who waitresses at Grandma's Café, where all the old timers meet for coffee every morning to talk about the weather. She was diagnosed with breast cancer and underwent a double mastectomy. The money she receives will be used to make up for lost tips and wages during her recovery and to help with medical expenses.

Another recipient, Bob, has been fighting lung cancer and chronic obstructive pulmonary disease, which has left him unable to run his one-man cement and construction business. The money he receives will be used to cover living expenses and medical costs not covered by Medicare.

The Johnson family returned from a weekend away visiting an ill family member to find their basement flooded following a particularly severe summer thunderstorm. Their furnace and hot water heater were destroyed, and because of a layoff, find themselves without the means to replace them. With help from the Thermal Company and several friends, they were able to purchase a furnace; the money they receive will be used to replace the water heater and repair the damage to their foundation.

David was diagnosed with a heart murmur and irregular heartbeat. Within a month, the doctor told him he would need to have an aortic valve replacement. After surgery, he had to take several months off work to recover and his wife, Rhonda, had to take time off from her job to care for him. David still experiences symptoms that limit his ability to work. The money David receives will be used to cover expenses incurred during his illness.

Aggie, the mother of seven children, has been fighting pancreatic cancer for five years. Today she is doing well, but the battle has left her family with considerable debt. Aggie is employed by the local school district and has health insurance, but the co-pay for each hospitalization she incurs is $5,000. Her funds will be used to help offset those costs.

Relative to more populous areas, fewer people in the rural communities have much money themselves, and while they try to put something into the collection plate at church every Sunday, most don't regularly contribute to large charities. Yet, they always turn out to help when the need is there. However, what is noticeable about who the community decides to help is that most often they are individuals perceived as hard workers down on their luck, are active members of a church or are connected to the community in some other way. The truly poor, who are more isolated, are rarely among the recipients of informal community-based charity efforts, often because people are distrustful of them.

"Sometimes people exploit the good will of the community ... and communities have very long memories," explains the Rev. John Herzog, who spent his ministerial career in small rural Midwestern towns. Herzog recalls an incident when a young family's duplex apartment burned to the ground in January and they lost everything. "They had at least three small children, and the father had been out of work for a while, so the parish and the wider community really stepped up with cash and household items. If I remember correctly, someone even offered them a place to stay rent free for a while ... and then it turned out that the man had set the fire intentionally." Asked what happened to the family, Herzog said he wasn't sure but imagined "the community dealt with it some way," implying that the man was ostracized for cheating community members out of money they didn't have to spare in the first place and eventually the family left town. "Nobody would trust him, or his wife, because they'd think she put him up to it, so the best thing was for them to move on ... neither one of them ever could've gotten work around here after that," Herzog explained.

"I wonder what happens to people in rural areas who are not church members?" asks sociologist Annette Kuhlmann. "Churches in small towns are very powerful—they define the local moral values and are the center of a lot of the social life that doesn't occur in the bars, and someone who is not participating in a church community can be very isolated." Churches also define the moral values of a town and understand the importance of living by the Golden Rule, but if someone breaks this rule, the community can be, as Herzog points out, ruthless in dealing with them.

Idealizing Isolation—The Dark Side of Rural Community Life

> *Ever since I've been here it seems like every year somebody gets crucified.... Someone has got to stand up and say, "Do you think we could be nice to each other this week?"*—North Dakota Catholic priest

Herzog would agree that sometimes small rural towns seem to fall under an evil spell, and when this happens things get vicious and depressing. "It almost always seems to involve the school," says Herzog.

Richard Critchfield agrees and writes that it is often the schools that are lightning rods for resistance to change because they are so well positioned to effectuate it.[3] He explains that schools suffer difficulties with insider/outsider thinking because they are the place where teachers (outsiders) go head to head with a small town's values and ideas (insider) around what students need to learn, and often the outsiders (teachers) become scapegoats in a place that can't come to terms with its own internal differences. These non-local teachers are "expelled" from the community for knowing what they know and trying to teach it. When this occurs the community is sentenced to more years of sameness, and the teacher finds a better job somewhere else.

Rural school superintendent Joe Burton says that the one thing he heard most often from parents when he announced his retirement and the school board began its search for a new superintendent was "I hope they don't hire somebody who wants to change things." Ultimately the school board hired from within the existing administrative structure of the school, and as a result, nothing changed at all. If it is true that outside influences are what stabilize institutions by guaranteeing their growth and survival, resisting these influences perpetuates mediocrity and sentences these institutions to a slow, often painful death.

There's also the matter of isolation. "By the time an isolated Plains town is 75 or 100 years old it may be filled with people who have come to idealize their isolation ... they become more provincial than they intended and have a difficult time maintaining a normal sense of the world 'outside,'" says writer Kathleen Norris. "People who never leave a place, or flee back to it after a quick try living somewhere else, frequently come to view the wider world as a place they need to protect themselves from, and the ideal way to do that is to maintain the familiar. As their frame of reference shrinks, so do their aspirations and ability to adapt to change—and this is the death of any living entity, including communities. "Because it can't look outward, the town begins to turn on itself, and a schismatic, ultimately self-defeating dynamic takes hold," Norris writes.[4] "To some extent wariness about change is a prairie wisdom ... and negative connotations abound. The sad truth is that the harder we resist change, and the more we resent anyone who demands change of us, the more we short-change ourselves."

Unquestionably, small towns need a degree of insularity to survive. Some have had to make do with so little for so long they have no illusions that they are necessary to the surrounding farm economy, but slightly larger towns—those with a population of 1,000–1,500—are just large enough to maintain that illusion. Nevertheless, while family remains important, the same isn't necessarily true for the community and insular thinking can become so deeply entrenched that towns turn away from those who are somehow different, including the poor among them. "I really blanched when the church council decided, after replacing the worn-out carpeting, to ban AA [Alcoholics Anonymous] meetings in our church basement and moved the food pantry to an outbuilding. They said they didn't want people who might spill things on the carpet, or have dirty shoes, using the room ... and I couldn't convince them otherwise. It was like keeping the carpet clean was more important than simple, inclusive Christian charity toward their fellow community members," a Lutheran minister in a rural town of 1,600 told me.

Keith Gunderson, a native South Dakotan and Lutheran minister understands how much outsiders are needed in rural communities, and how much the community rejects them, always to its own detriment. He and Norris both observe that the prairie landscape is naturally isolating and people living there don't need to connect. "Progress is an illusion and hope is folly," Gunderson says. "We are born, we live, we die. Leave us alone.... We who live in western Dakota look forward to the day when we will rest in some forlorn prairie cemetery with relatives and friends around us, the land and the weather forcing us to live in the light of that reality: we belong to the land."[5]

Why the Poor Make the Decisions They Make

> *Nobody gets to where I am without a mix of bad luck and bad calls.*—Linda Tirado

Linda Tirado is an articulate young woman who wrote an expansive essay presenting several reasons why the poor make what others consider bad decisions and published it on an Internet blog.[6] Tirado has been, during various periods of her life, very poor and she makes several valuable points about the life a poor person leads that contribute to a broader understanding of the unrelenting despair that surrounds them.

- Most poor are clinically depressed, and cannot get therapy, medication or social support. "We get told to 'get over it,'" Tirado says, "so we find ways to cope ... [with] thoughts that are never too far away, that creep up on us every chance they get, that prey on our better judgment when we are tired and stressed and weakened." What Tirado fails to articulate is that living with a chronically depressed state of mind takes tremendous energy, leaving little for accomplishing the necessary tasks of daily life and work.

  "Nobody gives enough thought to depression. You have to understand that we know that we will never not feel tired. We will never feel hopeful. We will never get a vacation. Ever. We know that the very act of being poor guarantees that we will never not be poor. It doesn't give us much reason to improve ourselves. We don't apply for jobs because we know we can't afford to look nice enough to hold them. I would make a super legal secretary, but I've been turned down more than once because I 'don't fit the image of the firm.' I am good enough to cook the food, hidden away in the kitchen, but my boss won't make me a server because I don't 'fit the corporate image.' I am not beautiful. I have missing teeth and skin that looks like it will when you live on [vitamin] B12 and coffee and nicotine and no sleep. Beauty is a thing you get when you can afford it, and that's how you get the job that you need in order to be beautiful. There isn't much point trying...."

- Rest is a luxury the poor don't get to enjoy. Most work more than one part time job, leaving little time for helping kids with homework, housekeeping chores, and other daily tasks. "I get up at 6 AM, go to school, then work, then I get the kids, then I pick up my husband, then I have half an hour to change and go to Job 2. I get home from that at around 12:30 AM, in bed by 3. I never get a day off from work unless I am fairly sick. It doesn't leave you much room to think about what you are doing, only to attend to the next thing and the next. Planning isn't in the mix," she says.

- "I know how to cook," Tirado explains, "but to do it requires a working stove, and pots, and spices, and you'll have to do the dishes no matter how tired you are or they'll attract bugs." Tirado says junk food is "a pleasure that we are allowed to have; why would we give that up? We have very few of them." She points out that eating peanut butter from the jar and buying frozen beef burritos because they were 12/$2 makes sense because she can't make them that cheaply. "Convenience food is just that. And we are not allowed many conveniences."

- Trying too hard to be middle-class is not a good idea, Tirado says. "It never works out well and always makes you feel worse for having tried and failed yet again." To prove her point, she points out that since the Patriot Act passed in late 2001, it's much harder to get a bank account, and without one, she spends a lot of time figuring out where to cash a check and get money orders to pay bills.

- "We're aware that we are not having kids, we're 'breeding,'" she notes. "We have kids for much the same reasons that I imagine rich people do … nobody likes poor people procreating, but they judge abortion even harder." Tirado also points out the closest Planned Parenthood is three hours away. "That's a lot of money in gas. Lots of women can't afford that." And if there is a clinic closer, there's a co-pay, so the poor won't go. "Low-cost and sliding scale sounds like money you have to spend," she explains.

- Nicotine is a stimulant. It's also expensive, but easily accessible and, according to Tirado, "the best option" because she is always exhausted. "When I am too tired to walk one more step, I can smoke and go for another hour. When I am enraged and beaten down and incapable of accomplishing one more thing, I can smoke and I feel a little better, just for a minute. It is the only relaxation I am allowed. It is not a good decision, but it is the only one that I have access to. It is the only thing I have found that keeps me from collapsing or exploding."

- Tirado also admits to making a lot of poor financial decisions and believe none of them will matter in the long term because she will never not be poor. "What does it matter if I don't pay a thing and a half this week instead of just one thing? It's not like the sacrifice will result in improved circumstances; the thing holding me back isn't that I blow five bucks at Wendy's. It's that now that I have proven that I am a poor person that is all that I am or ever will be. It is not worth it to me to live a bleak life devoid of small pleasures so that one day I can make a single large purchase. I will never have large pleasures to hold on to. There's a certain pull to live what bits of life you can while there's money in your pocket, because no matter how responsible you are you will be broke in three days anyway. When you never have enough money it ceases to have meaning."

- Poverty is so bleak it "cuts off your long-term brain," meaning that delaying immediate gratification in the interests of planning for a better future is not possible, Tirado explains. "It's why you see people with four different baby daddies instead of one. You grab a bit of connection wherever you can to survive. You have no idea how strong the pull to feel worthwhile is. It's more basic than food. You go to these people who make you feel lovely for an hour that one time, and that's all you get. You're probably not compatible with them for anything long-term, but right this minute they can make you feel powerful and valuable. It does not matter what will happen in a month. Whatever happens in a month is probably going to be just about as indifferent as whatever happened today or last week. None of it matters. We don't plan long-term because if we do we'll just get our hearts broken. It's best not to hope. You just take what you can get as you spot it … it's safer."

In truth, the poor often do make what appear to be "bad" decisions, but they are not necessarily made for the wrong reasons. Marge Jones, who lives in a rural town on the Iowa-Kansas border, explains her decision to quit her job after her husband lost his job: "He was so depressed I was afraid to leave him alone. The kids were really upset they weren't able to have the things they were used to having, and I felt I had to stay home and just take care of everybody emotionally.... I was afraid what might happen if I wasn't there."

The result of Marge's decision was that the family income dropped to zero, they lost their home and ended up living in an abandoned school bus. She was afraid to try to collect welfare or apply for food stamps because she feared that her children would be taken from her if the facts of their living situation came to the attention of child welfare authorities. Ultimately she and the children ended up in a homeless shelter, and her husband disappeared.

Similarly, Karen Dixon, who lives in a rural town about 50 miles from where her job is located, explains that she sold her car for $750 to pay her back rent so she wouldn't be evicted from a small, run-down apartment over the local tavern. That the car was her only means of transportation to her job didn't factor into the decision because she knew she'd be "out on the street" if she didn't come up with the rent money. Because this decision resulted in being fired from her job, Karen also ended up in a women's shelter. She was philosophical about this turn of events in her life. "I wasn't making it financially anyway—by the time I paid for child care, I didn't have enough money left to make the rent, and I couldn't find a cheaper place to live."

Both examples illustrate how the poor can find themselves between a rock and a hard place and all too easily fall into situations for which there are no good answers. Many crucial needs go unmet, income can vary widely month to month, and for those who are employed, mostly at low-wage jobs, their take-home pay doesn't cover their bills. Every decision they make is a balancing act, and it's nearly impossible to stay balanced on an unsteady, insufficient income.

A Culture of Rural Poverty or Exceptional Self-Reliance?

The regular poor probably never will move out of poverty.... Whether it's conscious or not, they're fine with a subsistence life.—Wally Orzechowski

Wally Orzechowski, executive director of the Southwest Wisconsin Community Action Program (SWCAP), believes a significant percent of the rural poor "are OK with poverty" as long as their basic needs are met. "These people live in 150 year old houses, cut the wood they burn for heat, grow their own food, use Medicaid for health care and get a job now and then," he says.

Most are not people applying to SWCAP because if they own any land they are among the asset rich—income poor, thus not eligible for most income-based assistance programs, and even if they don't own land, they've still carved out a lifestyle they view as satisfactory. "These folks figure out how to stay afloat and make it work all on their own," Orzechowski explains, adding that often these are the generationally poor who are resilient, know how to cope with adversity, have years of experience managing a life lived mostly below the poverty line and are used to dealing with chronic cash flow problems.

For others, family issues, lack of education and emotional stress are at the top of Orzechowski's list of reasons the people who engage the services of his programs are poor. "Being poor is enormously stressful—it makes you crazy," he says, "and under that kind of stress, making good decisions is almost impossible, and future planning is pretty much out of the question." The chief stressors Orzechowski identifies are a lack of income security, inadequate access to health and dental care, and lack of mental health services. "These people live crisis to crisis, and that wears anybody out."

The family issues are, according to Orzechowski, complex. "Younger people who can move away, do it, and they are the ones with the best skills that the community needs the most ... but unless they're going to inherit a debt-free family farm, and want to be a farmer, the truth is, they are best off leaving." The reality is that leaving isn't much of a choice for those with the ability to do it, particularly when most local jobs pay $15 an hour and the trend, Orzechowski believes, is away from good, decent-paying jobs gravitating toward rural areas. "You have to have a well-trained, skilled workforce already available to attract really good jobs, and most rural areas can't offer that to a company looking for a place to locate," he says.

Orzechowski also believes alcohol and drug use among rural families is underestimated, and that these are major contributors to "severe family dysfunctions" as well as issues like farm accidents and disabling illnesses. "Seventy percent of the local jail inmates have substance abuse problems," he says, adding that the biggest reasons his clients end up in jail is because of being arrested for a drunk and disorderly offense, shoplifting or petty theft, and everybody in town finds out about it. "People listen to police scanners like our parents used to listen to the radio," Orzechowski chuckles, "and when a call comes in, they know who lives at the address the cops are going to, and what they're going for. There are no secrets in small towns ... and people have to live with that."

He also believes the stigma of being poor is worse in small towns and rural areas than is found in larger cities. "Everybody thinks you're supposed to be tough and should just go work it off in the barn," Orzechowski explains, "but these people are working multiple part time jobs trying to piece some kind of income together when they have no permanent home, not enough food, sometimes they don't even have a car—and around here you can't exactly take the bus or call a cab to take you someplace, even if you did have the money to pay for it ... it can be ridiculously hard to pull out of poverty."

Rising Above Poverty and Making It

If you've ever really been poor, you remain poor at heart all your life.—Arnold Bennett

Despite the bleak picture of poverty Tirado and Orzechowski both paint, some rural poor do manage to rise above their circumstances. The general consensus among those who administer rural human service programs is that those who do succeed in pulling out of poverty have at least a high school education and dislike being poor enough to take low paying jobs they are overqualified for and work hard enough at them to be promoted, eventually building a solid employment record that leads to promotions and job security. "I tell clients to never, ever underestimate the importance of a solid record of being a reliable worker ... that's more important than what the job is they're doing," says Orzechowski. He adds that these are the people who take advantage of social programs designed to help them get ahead, but don't become dependent upon these programs.

Marsha Miller is one such person. She is 43 years old, married once and currently divorced, and has three children. Eight years ago, as a single mother with three children under age 12, she took advantage of an opportunity to live in a home built by a rural Habitat for Humanity (HFH) program.[7] HFH is a nonprofit, ecumenical Christian organization dedicated to eliminating substandard housing and homelessness worldwide and, by making adequate, affordable shelter a matter of conscience and action, HFH considers itself a ministry founded on the conviction that every man, woman and child should have a simple, decent place to live in dignity and safety.

Miller says she barely qualified for a HFH house. "When I initially applied, I was working two part-time jobs and was under the minimum income qualifications for the program. They fudged it a little and let me in." At the time she was on Medicaid and used other services such as food stamps and a food pantry.

Miller continued with her education, eventually obtaining a master's degree, and at the present time has a job with the state Department of Corrections, working as a counselor and psychologist. Her salary is about 300 percent of the poverty line for a family of four and includes health insurance. She describes a stable employment history and a significant salary increase, which has continued since 2009.

Today, Miller says that even though she makes a good living now, she doesn't have much disposable cash. She attributes this to being in school part time herself and having one child in college now. Asked how she decides which bills to pay in the months when she's stretched thin, she explains that she prioritizes needs over wants. She has managed to contribute to a savings account, and when several things in the house needed repairing at once, she was able to pay for it out of savings, without using a credit card. She is proud of her good credit history, which, she believes, provides "a good safety net," and recently, for the first time in her life, has started having savings automatically deducted from her paychecks to build a rainy day account. "I have my house, which is also a kind of savings account," she says. But her financial success has come at an emotional price.

"My family judged me harshly when I went with Habitat—they thought I was taking a handout. This caused a rift that hasn't ever fully resolved," Miller explains. Her extended family does not live nearby and she sees them only when she makes the effort. "I don't rely on them for anything … and sometimes they're an emotional drain on me," she explains, adding that they expected her to write a character reference for her brother when he was arrested for a crime while under the influence of alcohol. "My father was an alcoholic, one of my brothers struggles with alcohol and has legal problems as a result, and my sister has drug issues—my family resents me for having it the most together."

There are also abuse issues in Miller's background. She says her relationship with her eldest daughter's father was an abusive one, and that her parents' relationship was abusive but never talked about. Nevertheless, she was resourceful enough to acquire many skills to push her life forward. Asked how she managed to do as well as she has, she replied that she strongly believes in therapy and relied on it to get through some very difficult times. "I don't ever forget about what being poor was like, and I'm determined to give my kids a better life than I had," she smiles.

Often, moving forward out of adversity involves a large dose of personal resilience, which is the ability to work with adversity in such a way that one comes through it unharmed or even better for the experience. Resilience means facing life's difficulties with courage and patience—refusing to give up. It is the quality of character that allows a person to rebound from misfortune, hardships and traumas and is rooted in a tenacity of spirit—a determination to embrace all that makes life worth living even in the face of overwhelming odds. When one has a clear sense of identity and purpose, he or she is more resilient, because of the ability to hold fast to a vision of a better future.

Much of any individual's resilience flows from belonging to a community and having access to the relationships that allow individuals to lean on each other for support when needed. The traits that encompass resilience can be found in abundance in rural communities, which are comprised of people who take risks every time they plant a crop, not knowing what the growing season will bring, fix things to keep them working, take any pick-up job they can find, and get out of bed every morning because no matter how bad yesterday was, they have chores to do. Rural people face drought, flooding, freezing temperatures, sweltering heat, and unpredictable grain and livestock markets with equanimity and a sense of eternal optimism that no matter how this season turned out, things will be better next year.

Nevertheless, the question of why Miller was able to rise from the ashes of rural poverty while others cannot is not easily answered. Sometimes a successful exit from poverty results from a combination of good luck, personal resourcefulness, determination and catching a few breaks. Other times, as in Miller's case, it's the courage and willingness to leave a dysfunctional family behind and move forward despite them, coupled with a strong desire to give her children a better life, and the ability to find, and keep, a job.

"All parents want that better life for their kids, and for themselves," Orzechowski says, "but not all of them are able to make it happen, despite their best efforts.... Sometimes too much conspires against them, and the reality is that most of it isn't really their fault. That's when we step in and try to help them out."

7

Poverty Makes You Sick

The Rural Health Care Problem

> *Small rural health systems represent a variety of ever changing environments with two endangered species: hospitals and practitioners [, and] prescribing external remedies is far less important than understanding the lifestyle and habits of the patient.*—Robert C. Bowman, M.D.

Recently, on a blustery, mid-afternoon winter day, I watched a young couple in a battered old car, with two small children riding shotgun, pull into a gas station convenience store located on the main highway at the edge of town. They spent several minutes searching under their seats and sorting through their junk, collecting loose change. When they finally entered the store it took a long time to select several items, take them up to the cash register, ask how much each was, and determine whether they had enough money. They found they could only afford a large bag of potato chips and a can of chewing tobacco. "This is it for today," their father told the kids, handing the bag to the older child.

No one in the family looked healthy. The kids weren't energy machines jumping around nagging their parents to buy them something or another, the mother was severely overweight and the dad was too thin, and too nervous. None were wearing warm enough clothes and all of them had hacking, productive coughs of the sort that causes a healthy person to grimace, step back, and turn their face away.

I spent the next several days wondering about this family. I understood why they hadn't used their loose change to buy much needed cold tablets and knew the family had few options for self-treatment of obviously acute respiratory infections.[1] I returned to the gas station a few times, thinking I might see them again, and hoping they might talk with me for a while, but they never showed up when I was there. "People like them come through here every day," the store clerk shrugged, obviously not remembering the specific family I was asking about.

From the health care perspective alone, this family has nothing going for it. They are forty miles from the nearest hospital emergency room, which is their best hope for medical care because, by law, they would have to be treated regardless of their insurance status. But for this family the emergency room option didn't help them out much because they probably didn't have enough money for gas to get there, even if their car could make it, and it looked like it might not. This is why, sooner or later, poverty causes nearly everyone who is poor to get sick, often very sick, and sick people can't hold onto jobs.

For the rural poor, the picture is much bleaker because access to medical services in rural and remote areas is one of the most complex and difficult problems facing health care policy and practice. Certainly the issue of hospital quality and proximity is part of the rural health care problem, but so is practitioner ability and availability. In rural communities patients don't often have much choice about who will take care of their health care needs, and if the patient and local doctor don't hit it off, the patient either has to travel some distance to find another one or become much less inclined to seek preventative medical care at all.

As the cost of medical care generally has skyrocketed, small rural hospitals are increasingly unable to afford the latest medical equipment or to serve critically ill patients. It's not unusual for the "local" hospital to be 75 or 100 miles away, which is a long, long drive in an emergency, on a snowy night, or when you have less than a quarter tank of gas and no money.

Further, local first responders in small communities are volunteers having limited medical training and poorly equipped ambulances maintained by local community funds. In rural areas where farm and two-lane road highway accidents are common, emergency medical care, the success of which depends upon a quick and effective response, is an acute, frequently unmet need.

The Diseases of Rural Poverty

> *In the United States, there is a largely hidden burden of diseases caused by a group of chronic and debilitating parasitic, bacterial, and congenital infections known as the neglected infections of poverty.* —Peter J. Hoetz, M.D.

Sooner or later, poverty causes nearly everyone who is poor to get sick—and sick people have great difficulty navigating their way through life. Further, poor people suffer from chronic, disabling diseases at a much higher rate than the general population, have much greater difficulty accessing medical care when they get sick, frequently cannot afford needed acute care or maintenance drugs, and have even greater difficulty making healthy lifestyle choices, because they can't afford them. Poor people don't get annual health exams, can't afford gym memberships enabling them to exercise regularly, and don't have the time to do it anyway because they are often working two or three jobs, if they are working at all. Poor people eat what they can afford, not necessarily what is healthy for them, and do whatever they can afford to do to alleviate their chronically stressful life. Often this involves excessive alcohol and tobacco use, because both are relatively cheap and easy forms of self-medication for anxiety, depression and stress.

The common diseases the poor are known to suffer in greater numbers result from inadequate sanitation, contaminated water, poor nutrition, exposure to insect-borne diseases and poor health and dental care access. These conditions give rise to a higher incidence of asthma, alcohol and drug abuse, diabetes, obesity, high blood pressure, low birth weight babies, respiratory and skin infections, and cardiovascular disease among the poor. In other words, any disease a poor person suffers from is going to be worse for them than it will be for someone who is not poor, can afford regular health care, and can do the necessary things to improve their overall health status, including medical follow-up and management of chronic diseases such as diabetes and heart disease. The rural poor have all of these issues, plus the acute risk of farm and other accidents that can lead to permanent physical disability.

Rural residents are more likely to self-report fair to poor health status than are urban residents and are more likely to have experienced a limitation of activity caused by chronic conditions than urban residents. Obesity is 27 percent more common among rural residents than urban residents, as is diabetes, heart disease, and high blood pressure. Rural areas also have higher rates of late-stage cancer, attributed in part to residents being older, less educated and poorer, and to having little to no access to early detection cancer programs and services.[2]

"Sure rural folks eat a lot, and maybe more than we should, but we work hard on the farm, and get hungry—and there isn't a farm wife alive who isn't a real, real good cook," says Wisconsin farmwife Jeannie Lewis. "I suppose this can lead to health problems, but everybody's gonna die of something, and sometimes a good, hot meal is all you got to look forward to that day," she adds fatalistically.

While poor people and rich people suffer the same diseases, the poor have many fewer options for doing anything about getting better. According to Katharyn May, professor and dean of the University of Wisconsin—Madison School of Nursing, much of this is the fault of the American health care system, which is oriented toward crisis management rather than promoting wellness. There is a "huge difference" between what May terms "illness care" in the United States and "health care" in places having universal, publicly financed health and wellness care available to everyone. "Canada, for example, recognizes that it is much more efficient to emphasize self-responsibility for health, health maintenance, and disease prevention than to operate in a continual health crisis mode, which is the American model," May says.[3]

May claims that the reality of health and wellness is that it has relatively little to do with actual access to health care services, the implication being that those who lead healthy lifestyles will need to utilize the health care system less frequently and for less serious health problems than those who do not "take good care" of themselves. "Access to health care only explains about 10 percent of health outcomes," May said, adding that lifestyle habits (i.e., diet, exercise, wearing a seatbelt, moderate alcohol consumption) account for 40 percent; socio-economics predict another 40 percent; and physical environment (i.e., groundwater contamination) accounts for the remaining 10 percent.

Government Does, and Doesn't, Take Care of the Poor

> *Everybody should have access to medical care. And it shouldn't be such a big deal.*—Paul Farmer, M.D.

In 2010, after lengthy, contentious debates in a Democrat-controlled Congress, President Obama signed a health care reform bill intended to make health insurance both mandatory and affordable for all Americans. Despite intense Republican opposition, which did not end even after the U.S. Supreme Court found that the legislation was constitutional, the Affordable Care Act became the law of the land. Nevertheless, because U.S. health care is both profit-motivated and insurance-driven, insurance companies are still calling the shots regarding who gets health care, how they get it, and how much it will cost, and the insurance lobby has shown no signs of giving up this fight.

Currently the poor whose incomes are at or near the poverty line are guaranteed access to a broad spectrum of health care services administered through two government programs—Medicaid and Medicare. Both are governed and administered by the whim of public policy. Because of this, the ten-ton gorilla methodically attacking the federal budget is the combined costs of administering the Medicare and Medicaid health care programs,

Medicare provides guaranteed health care to everyone over age 65 and Medicaid is the chief vehicle for providing health care to both rural and urban poor. Medicaid costs are budgeted at $276 billion for 2013 and are expected to increase to $622 billion by 2022, an increase of 12 percent.[4] The largest portion of these dollars is spent caring for the impoverished elderly and disabled, a disproportionate number of which reside in rural areas. In 2013 Medicaid expenditures were about $10,255 per disabled enrollee and $11,840 per elderly enrollee.[5] By 2022 these figures are projected to increase to $17,764 and $19,373 respectively.

As a result of the political debates continually surrounding government-funded health care, for many Americans, particularly those who are medically indigent[6] almost nothing remains harder to guarantee over a lifetime, is further out of reach, or more politically driven than access to affordable health care. And, despite what May claims, in rural areas access to care is everything.

A New Era in American Health Care

> *Obamacare comes to more than two thousand pages of rules, mandates, taxes, fees, and fines that have no place in a free country."*—Congressman Paul Ryan (R-WI)

> *When we talk about health care, we always keep in mind that we are not just talking about saving money or increasing efficiency. We are also talking about providing a higher quality of life. When people are healthy, they miss fewer days of work and get more done. They spend more time at home and less time in doctors' offices. They can take care of their grandkids. They can play softball.... They can get a good night of sleep.*—Kathleen Sebelius, U.S. secretary of health and human services

P.L. 111–148, the Affordable Care Act, significantly changes the face of American health care by changing private health insurance eligibility rules in some important ways. The first is creation of a temporary high-risk pool that provides health coverage to individuals with pre-existing medical conditions, thereby forbidding insurance companies from refusing to provide health care coverage based upon medical history. Second, individual and group health plans are no longer allowed to place lifetime limits on the dollar value of coverage and may not rescind coverage except in cases of fraud. These provisions are very important in helping to prevent individuals and families from being plunged into poverty because of a catastrophic illness or other medical crisis that health insurance companies heretofore could refuse to pay for. The legislation requires an essential health care benefits package that provides a comprehensive set of services, covers at least 60 percent of the actuarial value of covered benefits, limits annual cost-sharing to $5,950 per individual and $11,900 per family, and mandates dependent child coverage up to age 26.

"The underinsured or uninsured don't get routine, preventative health care," explains family practice physician Aaron Dunn, who is also medical director of the Community Connections Free Medical Clinic in Southwest Wisconsin. "The new legislation will help because it guarantees a standard set of medical services, including preventative care, doctor, hospital, drug coverage and mental health coverage." What Dunn points out is true for everyone who can afford to buy health insurance from the insurance pool set up by states and regulated by market forces; however, the news is not so good for the poor, and not very good at all for the rural poor, because:

- Health insurance is still tied to employment, and if one is unemployed, self employed, or informally employed, which includes most rural poor, accessing the insurance purchasing pool is considerably more difficult.
- Companies with less than 25 employees do not have to provide health insurance coverage to their employees, and most employers in rural areas fail to meet the 25-employee requirement.
- While this legislation increased Medicaid eligibility to those whose incomes are at or below 133 percent of poverty, it sucker-punched the working poor whose incomes are between 134 percent and 200 percent of poverty. Not only are these individuals forced to assume the added cost of purchasing health insurance, they face stiff penalties if they do not comply.
- The penalty for failing to purchase health insurance is assessed through the Internal Revenue Service and is set at the higher of $95 or one percent of annual income for the first year, $325 or two percent of annual income for the second year, and $650 or 3 percent of annual income for the third year and thereafter.
- Tax subsidies are available to those whose income is below 200 percent of poverty and do not qualify for Medicaid, if the individual state they reside in sets up a health insurance exchange purchasing pool. Residents who live in states that have declined the federal Medicaid matching dollars will purchase insurance from a federal exchange. Subsidies designed to lower health insurance premiums, limiting the income percentage individuals or families will be forced to pay, are determined on a sliding fee scale. A family of four living at, for example, 150 percent of poverty won't have to pay more than four percent of their income for health insurance, which amounts to approximately $1,413 per year. A single person living on $30,000 per year, just under three times the poverty rate, qualifies for a subsidy of $112 per month, reducing a $321-per-month health insurance premium to $209, or $2,508 annually, dropping this person's income closer to twice the poverty rate. Because the subsidies are based upon reportable income, individuals who supplement their incomes in ways that result in cash payments, which is frequently the case in rural areas, will lose out on this opportunity.

ObamaCare critic Betsy McCaughey contends that some particularly poor counties, such as Ziebach, Shannon and Todd counties in South Dakota or Sioux County in North Dakota—among the poorest counties in the nation—won't even have an insurance pool option available because residents there are too poor to afford to pay any health care insurance premiums, so insurance companies won't bother with them.[7]

McCaughey also contends that insurance premium costs for state insurance exchanges will increase by as much as 150 percent and that these plans will restrict the choice of health care providers. She favors higher premium costs for those who smoke, have high cholesterol or are obese. "I believe setting premium rates based on behavior is a good thing," she says, adding that accepting personal responsibility for one's health is important.

The Affordable Care Act also offers all 50 states the option of expanding their Medicaid programs to cover the working poor who earn too much for Medicaid eligibility but whose incomes still fall below 133 percent of poverty. Nevertheless, according to a recent New York Times analysis, ObamaCare will leave out two-thirds of poor blacks and single mothers and more than half of low-wage workers who do not have insurance, the very kinds of people that the program was intended to help.[8] As is too often the case, the problem is political and directly tied to whether individual states accept the vast expansion of Medicaid and the associated federal Medicaid matches, even though the federal government will pay for 100 percent of the Medicaid expansion costs through 2016 and 90 percent of costs in the years thereafter.

Among the Midwestern states, Ohio, Indiana, Wisconsin, Nebraska, South Dakota and Missouri all have rejected the federal Medicaid match. With the exception of Missouri, all are governed by Republicans. The result is that people who can least afford to be in the position of not having health insurance are stranded because they have incomes slightly higher than poverty level, thus disqualifying them from Medicaid in its current form. These people will be forced into purchasing health care from an insurance exchange or face a penalty for failure to comply.

Current Wisconsin governor Scott Walker is one of several "red state"[9] governors who are trying to avoid the federal Medicaid match, which expands the state-funded Medicaid programs. However, Walker is the only governor who has been blaming ObamaCare for the decision.

If Walker gets his way, Wisconsin's plan will only cover residents who earn 100 percent of the poverty level or below—$11,490 a year for a single adult. Tens of thousands of Wisconsinites will be forced off completely subsidized health care onto the federal insurance exchange, where they can purchase private plans with a subsidy. To do this, Walker will give up federal funding that would cover 98,000 poor Wisconsin residents and cause another 179,000 who should have coverage to be denied.[10] This action will cost employers $36 million dollars at a time when the state has dropped from 11th to 44th in job creation. The same is true for the other five Midwestern states that declined the Medicaid expansion option. The poor in all of those states will be trapped into being forced to either pay for health insurance they can ill-afford or go without.

Medicare

> *One quarter of Medicare beneficiaries have five or more chronic conditions, sees an average of 13 physicians each year, and fills 50 prescriptions per year.*—Clayton M. Christensen

Forty-three million people across all socio-economic strata, including those who are poor, are enrolled in Medicare. This government insurance plan allows access to comprehensive medical care and a wide array of health services available both to the poor and non-poor alike. Most Medicare enrollees are over age sixty-five and the program plays a vital role in the spectrum of health care services available to poor women, because elderly women are far more likely than elderly men to be poor. Twenty-two percent of poor women are over age 65 and 12 percent of all women over age 65 are living at or below 100 percent of the Federal Poverty Line (FPL), with rates uniformly higher for non-married women.[11] Many of these individuals reside in rural areas.

Medicare has four components: hospital insurance, medical insurance, Medicare Advantage plans and a Part D prescription drug plan. However, Medicare does not cover every health care need and it does not pay the total cost for most health care services or supplies that are covered under the plan. The patient is responsible for the cost difference between what Medicare will pay for and what a hospital or physician charges for a procedure, which can be substantial, so those able to afford it carry private issue gap insurance designed to pay the difference between what a provider charges for health care services and what Medicare will reimburse. Medicare's hospitalization insurance program is cost-free to enrollees, but those wanting medical care coverage pay a small monthly premium that is automatically deducted from their Social Security check.

Another component of Medicare is the Medicare Advantage Plans, which generally operate as managed health care, preferred provider option health insurance programs having a fee-for-service requirement. At minimum, these plans must cover at least the same benefits covered under Medicare Parts A and B. However, the costs may be different and may include extra benefits such as coverage for prescription drugs or additional days in the hospital. Participants pay a premium for this plan but don't need an additional insurance policy that pays the difference between what a physician charges and how much Medicare reimburses for Medicare-covered services. Medicare Advantage Plans require that health care be obtained within a predetermined network of health care providers and are not generally within reach of the poor, particularly the rural poor.

Not all physicians participate in Medicare and some who do limit the number of Medicare patients they serve. Those who do refuse Medicare patients, a disproportionate number of which practice in rural areas, complain of low reimbursement rates and bulky paperwork issues they can't afford to hire staff to complete. Nevertheless, Medicare patients are generally satisfied with its provisions.

Politicians are reluctant to vote in favor of any legislation that will curtail Medicare benefits because the over age sixty-five population, who are the primary Medicare recipients, have a large, very effective Washington lobby through the American Association of Retired Persons (AARP) that acts to protect health care benefits for older Americans. Further, those over age sixty-five tend to be more politically active than other age groups and represent a substantial voting bloc.

Nevertheless, the 2010 health care reform legislation made substantial changes to the Medicare program. Some are cost containment measures designed to make the program more cost efficient to administer, some are aimed at promoting wellness, some are intended to make the prescription drug plan more affordable, and others affect direct services to patients. Between 2011 and 2015, physicians and surgeons practicing in health professional shortage areas will receive a 10 percent bonus, and qualifying hospitals in counties having the lowest quartile Medicare spending will also receive bonuses. Medicare coverage will also be expanded to include individuals who have developed certain health conditions associated with living in areas designated as environmentally

Medicaid

> *The Republican agenda is a radical vision in which Medicaid is slashed to the bone—in which we start to balance the budget on the backs of, literally, our most vulnerable citizens.* —Senator Al Franken (D-MN)

Medicaid is a jointly funded state-federal partnership aimed at providing medical care to the poor who do not receive Medicare benefits and is officially known as the Federal Medicaid Program.[12] Although the federal government establishes the general guidelines for the Medicaid program, individual states make their own determinations about the levels of services offered and states vary widely in the types of services they provide. After meeting the minimum federal health care requirements for mothers and children, states also decide for themselves who among these populations they will provide services to and what the services will be.

P.L. 111–148 expands Medicaid eligibility to include all non–Medicare eligible individuals under age 65 with incomes at or below 133 percent of the federal poverty line (FPL), and all newly eligible adults will be guaranteed a benchmark benefit package that meets the essential health care needs. To finance the expanded Medicaid coverage, states will receive 100 percent federal Medicaid funding for 2014–2016, 95 percent federal funding in 2017, 94 percent federal funding in 2018, 93 percent federal funding in 2019, and 90 percent federal funding for 2020 and thereafter. States are also required to maintain current income eligibility levels for children enrolled in Medicaid and the Children's Health Insurance Program (CHIP) through 2015. The new law also increases the Medicaid drug rebate percentage and provides greater incentives for physicians to participate in the program by increasing Medicaid payments for fee-for-service and managed care provided by primary care service providers to 100 percent of the Medicare payment rate for 2013–2014. States will receive 100 percent federal financing to cover the costs associated with increased payment rates.

Any poor woman of reproductive age who is a mother or legal caretaker of underage child(ren) and living in a family whose income falls at or below 100 percent of the FPL is eligible to receive health care at government expense through the Medicaid Program.[13] The federal matching rates for these services also vary, ranging from 50 to 76 percent, and are generally tied to an individual state's poverty level. Mississippi, having the highest poverty rate in the nation, receives the most federal Medicaid dollars.[14]

For poor women of childbearing age, it is frequently a pregnancy that first brings them into contact with the adult Medicaid health care system and programs providing prenatal care to the poor that are widely available. Notably, Medicaid is the only health care insurance program that does not consider being female a pre-existing condition that defines and regulates health care costs.

All states are required by law to offer free pre- and post-natal care to all pregnant women. Wisconsin is one of several states that has expanded their women's health care program to include reproductive health services and treatment for sexually transmitted diseases. The comprehensive Well Woman Medicaid Program offers mammograms and pap smears to women regardless of ability to pay. And, in recent years Medicaid coverage has been broadened to include children and their parents, pregnant women, and adults up to age 65 without dependent children whose incomes are up to 133 percent of the FPL based upon modified adjusted gross income.

Cost sharing credits to assist with paying ObamaCare health insurance premiums for employed individuals and families having an income between 133 percent and 400 percent of the FPL and refundable health care insurance premium credits to purchase health insurance through an insurance exchange are available. Cost sharing credits are designed to reduce the cost sharing amounts and annual cost sharing limits, which effectively increase the actuarial value of the basic health insurance plan benefits to 94 percent of actual plan value for those whose income is between 100 percent and 150 percent of the FPL and up to 70 percent of plan value for those having incomes between 250 percent and 400 percent of the FPL.

Premium credits are set on a sliding scale such that premium contributions are limited to 2 percent of income for up to 133 percent of the FPL and up to 9.5 percent of income for those having an income between 300 percent and 400 percent of the FPL. Neither of these subsidies take effect until 2014, allowing private insurance companies a five-year window to increase their premiums at a rate that does not necessarily reflect actual health care costs.

About one in five physicians nationwide refuse to accept new Medicaid patients, citing low reimbursement rates, long delays in receiving payment and complicated paperwork that costs them excessively in staff time needed to complete and submit the Medicaid claims.[15] Medicaid reimbursement rates, which are set by individual states, can be as low as 40 percent of the cost private insurance will pay for the same service.[16] As a result, increasing numbers of physicians feel they just can't afford to provide health care to Medicaid patients, thereby creating a crisis in health care delivery to the poor, even when there are programs in place to provide that care.

Other reasons physicians cite for being reluctant to treat Medicaid patients include the tendency for these patients to be "no-shows," thus creating non-revenue-producing gaps in the doctor's office schedule. Those physicians who do see Medicaid patients frequently limit the number of these patients they accept and often have long waiting lists for those appointments.

Despite the comprehensive services Medicaid in general, and Wisconsin Medicaid in particular, provides, the main reasons the program isn't more effective in improving the overall general health of the poor are that it doesn't provide for the ongoing, follow-up care needed to manage chronic illnesses, specialized care is nearly impossible to obtain because many specialists refuse Medicaid patients, and the Medicaid system itself is bulky and very difficult to navigate.

Most free or low-cost medical clinics that try to fill the Medicaid gap are devoted almost entirely to providing immediate care for a small spectrum of problems such as urinary tract infections, respiratory issues, skin problems and viral illnesses. Medical malpractice insurance issues prevent the attending, mostly volunteer physicians, from providing other than cursory care, yet nearly everyone they see suffers from chronic health problems, such as high blood pressure or uncontrolled diabetes, and needs further follow-up with a specialist.

Physician Aaron Dunn notes that many of the health problems his free clinic staff sees are chronic ones. "We see a lot of asthma and allergies, hypertension, and diabetes—and all of these need long-term, ongoing follow-up care." Dunn adds that the net result of no continuing patient follow-up is fragmented health care akin to putting a band-aid on a broken leg. "The care we can provide is inadequate to meet the need and simply doesn't fix the problem ... we're only open five hours per week, first come—first serve, so we can never meet all the needs that are out there." Additionally, volunteer medical personnel in the area, including some retired doctors and nurses, staff the clinic, and the cost of medical malpractice insurance, as well as restrictive terms of such insurance, significantly curtail the spectrum of services these health care professionals are able to provide in a free clinic setting.

Just as with the non-poor, the issue underlying most of the chronic illnesses the poor suffer from is obesity. According to a recent report released by the Wisconsin Department of Health Services, which mirrors national findings on the same issue, the poorer and darker you are, the more obese you're likely to be.[17] According to this report, 34 percent of Wisconsinites earning less than $15,000 per year are obese, compared to 23 percent of those earning more than $50,000 per year, and more blacks and American Indians are considered obese than are those in the white population. In reality, this is not news to most health care experts. However, getting a grip on this underlying health problem, which invariably leads to other, more severe medical conditions, has proven extremely difficult.

Another problem is that often chronic illnesses like hypertension or diabetes don't necessarily make people feel sick enough to prioritize their health management behaviors, thus making behavioral and medication compliance more difficult to achieve. Most successful, ongoing medical care occurs in a social context where patients develop an ongoing relationship with their health care provider that promotes self health management—and this just doesn't happen for Medicaid recipients because so often, because of a sudden medical crisis, they receive their care through emergency rooms. They'll never see the emergency room doctor again, so they have no incentive to follow his/her instructions. All these patients want is immediate relief from whatever problem caused them to go into the ER in the first place.

Unlike some states, Wisconsin provides dental care for those on Medicaid, and this is important because the connection between poor dental health and poor general health is undisputed. However, some dentists, like some physicians, are reluctant to treat Medicaid patients because the reimbursement rate is so much less than what they can earn from privately insured patients. This is particularly acute in rural areas where there are fewer dentists available and almost none who practice pediatric dentistry.

Appendix Three describes the spectrum of health care services available through the Medicaid program.

The Nuts and Bolts of Rural Health Care

> *I may be naïve, but I still think that a career in rural family medicine offers the best opportunity for the best doctors to be at their very best and have fun doing it and find those moments where they, too, will be dear and glorious.—* Robert Boyer, M.D.

Economic factors, cultural and social differences, educational shortcomings, lack of good rural health care policy and the sheer isolation of living in remote rural areas all conspire to impede rural Americans' struggle to lead a normal, healthy life. They also make it very difficult to convince physicians to settle in rural areas, particularly when they can earn more money elsewhere.

The health care picture in rural areas looks something like this[18]:

- Only about 10 percent of physicians practice in rural America despite nearly one-fourth of the population living in rural areas.
- Rural residents are less likely to have employer-provided health care coverage or prescription drug coverage, and the rural poor are less likely to be covered by Medicaid benefits than their urban counterparts.
- Although only one-third of all motor vehicle accidents occur in rural areas, two-thirds of the deaths attributed to these accidents occur on rural roads.
- Rural residents are nearly twice as likely to die from unintentional injuries, other than motor vehicle accidents, than are urban residents.
- Rural residents are also at a significantly higher risk of death by gunshot than urban residents.
- Rural residents tend to be poorer. On the average, per capita income is $7,417 lower than in urban areas, and rural Americans are more likely to live below the poverty level. The disparity in incomes is even greater for minorities living in rural areas. Nearly 24 percent of rural children live in poverty.
- People who live in rural America rely more heavily on the Federal Food Stamp Program; while 22 percent of Americans lived in rural areas in 2001, a full 31 percent of the nation's food stamp beneficiaries lived there.
- There are 2,157 Health Professional Shortage Areas in rural and frontier areas of all states and U.S. territories compared to 910 in urban areas.
- Abuse of alcohol and use of smokeless tobacco is a significant problem among rural youth.
- The rate of DUI arrests is significantly greater in non-urban counties. Forty percent of rural 12th graders reported using alcohol while driving compared to 25 percent of their urban counterparts. Rural eighth graders are twice as likely to smoke cigarettes (26.1 percent versus 12.7 percent in large metro areas).
- Between 57 and 90 percent of first responders in rural areas are volunteers.
- There are 60 dentists per 100,000 population in urban areas versus 40 per 100,000 in rural areas.
- Cerebral-vascular disease is reportedly 1.45 times higher in rural than urban areas.
- Hypertension is also higher in rural than urban areas.
- Twenty percent of nonmetropolitan counties lack mental health services versus 5 percent of metropolitan counties. In 1999, 87 percent of the 1,669 Mental Health Professional Shortage Areas in the United States were in nonmetropolitan counties and home to over 30 million people.
- The suicide rate among rural men is significantly higher than in urban areas, particularly among adult men and children. The suicide rate among rural women is escalating rapidly and nearly approaches that of men.
- Medicare payments to rural hospitals and physicians are dramatically less, for equivalent services, than are paid to their urban counterparts. This correlates closely with the fact that more than 470 rural hospitals have closed in the past 25 years.

- Medicare patients with acute myocardial infarction (AMI; heart attack) who were treated in rural hospitals were less likely than those treated in urban hospitals to receive recommended treatments and had significantly higher adjusted 30-day post AMI death rates from all causes than those in urban hospitals.
- Rural residents have greater transportation difficulties reaching health care providers, often travelling great distances to reach a doctor or hospital.
- Death and serious injury accidents account for 60 percent of total rural accidents versus only 48 percent of urban. One reason for this increased rate of morbidity and mortality is that in rural areas, prolonged delays can occur between a crash, the call for emergency medical assistance, and the arrival of a sometimes woefully undertrained, volunteer emergency medical services provider. These delays are related to increased travel distances in rural areas and personnel distribution across the response area. In rural areas, national average response times, from motor vehicle accident to EMS arrival, was 18 minutes, eight minutes greater than in urban areas.

Table One provides a summary comparison of rural and urban health care.

Table One: Comparing Rural and Urban Health Care[19]

	Rural	Urban
Percent of U.S. population	25%	75%
Percent of U.S. physicians	10%	90%
No. of specialists per 100,000 population	40.1	134.1
Population over age 65	18%	15%
Population below poverty level	14%	11%
Average per capita income	$19,000	$26,000
Non-Hispanic White	83%	69%
Adults with self-described poor health	28%	21%
Adolescent (age 12–17) smokers	19%	11%
Male (<age 24) death rate per 100,000	80	60
Female (<age 24) death rate per 100,000	40	30
Insured by private health insurance	64%	69%
Medicare beneficiaries	23%	20%
Medicare beneficiaries without drug coverage	45%	31%
Per capita Medicare expenditures compared to national average	85%	10%
Medicare hospital payment to cost ratio	90%	10%
Percent of poor receiving Medicaid	45%	49%

These figures point to several issues facing rural health care. First, compared to urban areas, significantly more rural elderly receive Medicare benefits, more rural Medicare recipients lack Medicare drug coverage, and per capita Medicare medical and hospital reimbursement costs, which the health care industry complains are woefully inadequate, make up a significantly greater proportion of overall rural medical and hospital cost reimbursements. This places rural hospitals in the unfortunate position of being unable to afford the latest equipment to treat critical care patients and sometimes they can't even afford vital health maintenance services or equipment, such as a kidney dialysis center. Anna Norris reports:

> Three days a week we had to drive 38 miles on the two lane to get Mickey to the nearest dialysis center, and we couldn't skip even if it was snowing so hard the road was slicker than a greased pig. We got up at four so we could leave at five A.M. to get there by 6:30 and the treatment took at least four hours on a good day, so we were lucky to get home by noon—and if things didn't go so well and they needed to keep him for a while we'd be lucky to get home by dark in wintertime. I think the reason Mickey quit dialysis was it was too much trouble—just too far to go and he felt it was too hard on me to do all that driving ... he died a week later.

Second, nearly half of all rural residents depend upon Medicaid, and evidence is that states that opted out of the federal match for Medicaid dollars will be faced with spending an extra billion dollars per year to treat individuals who cannot afford to cover the costs for their own health care.[20] Opt-out states are relying upon individual state indigent health care plans which, by law, must cover those below the poverty line, but don't have to provide health care coverage to those up to 200 percent above the poverty line who don't have health insurance coverage. Individuals falling into this category will be forced to enter the federal health insurance purchasing pool, whether or not they can afford it.

This decision is particularly devastating to rural areas where health care availability is already sparse and many people who float just above the poverty line have relied upon state funded health care. Rural hospitals with already small operating budgets are going to be faced with having, by law, to provide unreimbursed emergency medical care to more people who do not have insurance coverage but could have had it if their state had accepted the federal Medicaid matching dollars and expanded their Medicaid program accordingly.

Third, the physician shortage in rural areas is acute and includes a lack of both primary care physicians and specialists. The availability of federally mandated health insurance will result in millions of newly insured individuals seeking health care for the first time in years, swamping health care systems that are already short-staffed, particularly in rural areas. Illinois, Kansas, North and South Dakota and Ohio are all crafting plans, including medical school loan forgiveness, to make family practice in rural areas more attractive and granting pharmacists, and other health providers, greater decision-making ability.

Fourth, not everyone who is eligible for Medicaid signs up, and rural family practice physicians, whose patient population is often uninsured and sicker than insured patients, cannot ever earn as much as their urban counterparts or the amount earned by specialists who are paid by the procedure. Thus, convincing physicians to practice in rural areas remains challenging.

Due to the nature of their work and their unique risk profile, farm families have difficulty obtaining affordable coverage in the private insurance market. According to the Farm Bureau, farmers who don't purchase insurance through a spouse or second job face deductibles 183 percent greater than those with insurance from other sources. They also have less coverage for doctor visits and prescription drugs.[21]

"Farmers shouldn't have to choose between investing in new equipment to keep their operations profitable and health insurance for their family," former Wisconsin governor James Doyle says. Doyle has been a strong advocate for expanded rural health care insurance through BadgerCare, a state funded health insurance program, a position his successor, Scott Walker, disagrees with. Doyle rightly believes farmers are unfairly disadvantaged when applying for state funded health care because farm equipment depreciation income is counted against farmers when applying for health insurance. "Currently the value of a farmer's tractor or hay baler counts against them [farmers] when applying for BadgerCare. But those things aren't income. They don't help you pay the bills and they shouldn't be counted that way," Doyle said.

Hill-Burton Legislation

The Hill-Burton legislation authorizes financial assistance to public and other nonprofit medical facilities such as acute care general hospitals, specialty hospitals, nursing homes, public health centers and rehabilitation facilities. The Community Service Assurance under Title VI of the Public Health Service Act requires recipients of Hill-Burton dollars to make services provided by the facility available to persons residing in the facility service area without discrimination on the basis of race, color, national origin, creed or any other grounds unrelated to the individual's need for care. However, this legislation only requires that emergency care be administered to those unable to pay and allows a facility to refuse non-emergency care to anyone who cannot pay. Facilities receiving Hill-Burton funds must participate in Medicaid and Medicare programs unless they are ineligible to participate. These funds are vital to rural hospitals' ability to provide services.

Children's Health Insurance Programs (CHIP)

In addition to providing Medicaid program services, all states provide health insurance to children up to age eighteen through CHIP. In some states CHIP is part of Medicaid, in others it is separate, and some states combine the two. This program is specifically for children whose parents are not eligible for Medicaid but are unable to afford private health insurance. Generally this includes families whose income is at or below 200 percent of the FPL.

In 2009, the first full year of the CHIP legislation, 2.6 million additional children received medical coverage and offered states greater flexibility in eligibility criteria and program options. The 2010 CHIP Reauthorization Act increased program funding, including $100 million dedicated to outreach and enrollment services. An estimated five million children are thought to be eligible for the CHIP program, yet remain unenrolled.[22]

Farm Accidents

Not many people realize the high risks involved with farming. They envision a peaceful process of planting and harvesting, much like how it was done generations ago. Nowadays, however, the process is much more complex and involves lots of machinery, chemicals, and moving parts.—Attorney William J. Hayes

Agriculture is second only to mining as a hazardous occupation. Farmers are at very high risk for fatal and nonfatal injuries; and farming is one of the few industries in which family members (who often share the work and live on the premises) are also at risk for serious injuries. In 2010 approximately 1,823,000 full-time workers were employed in U.S. agriculture production. In that same year 476 farmers and farm workers died from a work-related injury, resulting in a fatality rate of 26.1 deaths per 100,000 workers.[23]

According to the U.S. Department of Labor tractor accidents on farms cause the highest number of fatalities with tractor overturns accounting for 44 percent of all tractor fatalities.[24] The accident rate for all farms is over six times greater than that for all other industrial occupations, and unlike other high-risk industries such as mining, there is no overall enforcement of safety regulations. The death rate for farm accidents has not changed appreciably since 1992 and, in real numbers, there has been a slight overall increase.[25]

"Most machines on a farm are very serious pieces of equipment, capable of chopping, shredding, gathering, etc. Metal moving parts on big tractors and other vehicles can spell disaster without proper protective gear. The catch is that seat belts and other protective measures are rarely required, and thus can be ignored quite easily," explains personal injury attorney William Hayes. National Safety Council data indicate that farm accidents and other work-related health problems claim as many as 1,300 lives and cause 120,000 injuries a year, most of which are preventable. Not surprisingly, males have a higher injury rate than females and hired workers frequently have higher injury rates than family members.[26]

"Me and my husband both got electrocuted in the milking parlor, and if it weren't that the neighbor girl saw it happen and called her mother, who knew how to do CPR, we'd both be dead now. We don't have no emergency responders around here—they'd have to come from up in Centerville which is maybe 40 miles from here ... think about that for a minute—first they'd have to put out the call, then wait for a driver and a couple EMT's to show up at the fire station, get organized, and then find their way all the way down to our place. We'd be lucky to see them in an hour," farm wife Mary Gotham told me.

Additionally, farmers must handle a variety of hazardous agricultural chemicals and other toxic and/or irritating substances and are also exposed to dust, sun, noise, and other health hazards. But most injuries are the result of machinery entanglements, farm structure emergencies such as grain bin or silo entrapments, electrocution, prolonged farm chemical exposures, spills and fires, toxic gas exposures and both farm animal and wild animal incidents. During the course of writing this book it was unusual for me to meet a farmer who wasn't missing at least one finger (or another limb), limped badly, or who had visible scars on his hands and face.

National Institute for Occupational Safety and Health (NIOSH) data indicate that four factors contribute to farming accidents: emergency preparedness, farm worker age, protective equipment, and equipment and machinery misuse.[27] "Hospital and emergency medical care are not usually available within a reasonable distance and the farmer and his family do not have the ability or time to deal with an emergency until professional help arrives," NIOSH experts explain, and Mary Gotham's story verifies. NIOSH reports that farm surveys indicate that the farm injury rate is highest among children under age 15 and adults over 65 year of age. Because the majority of farm accidents and fatalities involve the use of machinery, NIOSH also estimates that the use of protective equipment, such as seat belts on tractors, could prevent up to 40 percent of all farm work injuries.

Farming-induced illnesses are also significant. NIOSH has supported research and prevention programs addressing injuries and illnesses associated with agriculture, including pesticide exposure, pulmonary disease, musculoskeletal disorders, hearing loss, and stress-related difficulties. NIOSH also recognizes that substantial evidence exists suggesting that chronic exposure to farm chemicals increases the likelihood of farmers developing Parkinson's Disease and of farm wives developing breast cancer.

Both health care providers and patients in rural areas face obstacles that are vastly different from those in urban areas, and rural Americans face a unique combination of factors that create disparities in health care not found in urban areas. However, Katharyn May claims there are four prevailing myths surround rural health care: that it should be cheaper, that rural hospitals aren't as good as urban medical centers, that rural Americans are "naturally more healthy" than their urban counterparts, and that the rural population is shrinking.[28]

May believes rural health care delivery is "way too expensive" because health care service delivery is dominated by urban interests and the expectation that people will go to urban areas for medical care. "There is no evidence rural hospitals are not as good as urban ones, or that rural Americans are healthier, especially when considering that farming is a very high risk occupation and most farmers have inadequate health insurance coverage for health management, she said, adding that rural health care delivery is facing a scary future. "It's just not clear what's going to happen, but what we do know is that something will, because health insurance, particularly for the poor both in rural and in urban areas, simply isn't working." Added to this is that while the Medicare Reimbursement Modernization Act, which drives rural hospital care, has been a life-saver for rural hospitals, May cautions that embedded in this act are conditions and situations that can be interpreted in ways that will, over time, severely undermine rural health care delivery.

Teen Pregnancy and Reproductive Health Care

> *In my day when you got pregnant in high school you went to visit "Aunt Tilda" for a few months. Now getting pregnant before finishing high school's not such a big deal.* —Jeanie Lewis

> *I tried to get to the doctor at least once while I was pregnant—just to be sure everything was OK, although I'd have known if it wasn't.* —Anna Norris

Historically the teen birth rate in rural counties has been nearly one-third higher than urban and suburban locales (43 per 1,000 girls age 15 to 19).[29] However, the reasons for this are somewhat surprising. Teen pregnancy does not occur because teenagers in rural areas have sex with older men, have sex at younger ages, or necessarily marry younger than their urban counterparts. It's because they lack easy access to health care clinics that prescribe birth control and offer counseling; their parent's health insurance, if they have any, may not cover birth control; sex education in the rural public schools is often sparse; and abortion providers are hard to find. Both Jeanie Lewis and Mary Gotham believe rural teens get bored and lack good options for their free time and, as a result, "car sex just happens."

Why teens have sex, and do so without using effective contraception, is an ever-present question without a definitive answer. The United States has the highest rates of teen pregnancy, abortion, and childbirth among all industrialized nations, despite similar or higher rates of sexual activity in other countries.[30] Commonly accepted reasons for teens engaging in unprotected sex are that:

- Adolescents become sexually mature and fertile approximately four or five years prior to reaching emotional maturity.
- Modern culture sends many obvious and subtle messages that unmarried sex (particularly among teenagers) is common, acceptable, and even expected.
- Education about responsible sexual behavior (and the consequences of sexual intercourse) is not widely available, thus much of the information teens receive about sexual behavior comes from misinformed or uninformed peers.
- Contraception is not readily available in schools or other places teenagers frequent.
- Conservatives and anti-abortion, pro-life advocates have launched a massive public relations campaign against making contraception for women readily available, including lobbying against public funding for Planned Parenthood clinics, the largest single provider of reproductive health care services for women.
- Preventing pregnancy is the responsibility of the woman who is having sex, but teenage girls often have not grasped this and don't know what pregnancy prevention options are available to them.

Researchers have identified a number of other factors that contribute to adolescent pregnancy, including poverty, family history of adolescent childbearing, and childhood physical and sexual abuse.[31] Other predictors are early dating, which almost inevitably leads to early sexual involvement, dropping out of school, being the daughter of a teen mother, lacking a social support system and having few friends, lack of involvement in school, family and/or community activities, living in a community or attending school where early childbearing is the norm and not viewed as a cause for concern, and believing there is little or no opportunity for success in life. Some research also suggests the occurrence of a teenage pregnancy is related to a quest for love and acceptance.

Further confounding the adolescent pregnancy issue is that American culture is uniquely contradictory concerning sexual behavior. Media messages suggest sexual activity is normal for young and unmarried people, yet parents, schools, and government-funding criteria are all very reluctant to provide birth control devices or access to family planning information to teenagers who, by this age, are old enough to become parents. These mixed messages about a normal part of human behavior can easily result in an unplanned teen pregnancy and all the problems that come with it.

Infants born to teen mothers are more often premature and at greater risk for developmental problems, girls born to teen mothers are more likely to repeat this pattern and become teen mothers themselves, and boys born to teen mothers have higher arrest and incarceration rates than average. Infants born to teens are at higher risk of pre- and postnatal death, perinatal medical complications, low birth weight and prematurity, and retarded intrauterine growth. Finally, teen mothers are far more likely to have unhealthy habits that place infants at greater risk for inadequate growth, infection, and chemical dependence.

During 2005 and 2006, with the exception of youngest mothers (under age 15), birth rates increased for women in all age groups.[32] The birth rate for teenagers age 15–19 increased 3 percent, interrupting a 14-year period of continuous decline.

Sexual Politics and Women's Health Care

> *Medical and sexual politics collide in scientific reductionism—biological reductionism for [women] ... who are valued for their ability and willingness to raise children.* —Lisa Gannon

Barefoot and pregnant as a pre-destined lifestyle for women officially ended with Roe v. Wade in 1973, when the U.S. Supreme Court ruled that denying women access to safe abortions was a violation of their constitutional rights and made abortion legal. Nevertheless, the gigantic elephant in the room where women of childbearing age receive their medical care is the continuing and contentious public debate surrounding women's reproductive health care—namely the availability of family planning services, including access to safe, sterile abortion procedures. Despite having the legal right to terminate a pregnancy, abortion remains the most hotly contested public policy issues directly affecting women.[33]

The anti-abortion movement has been relentless in maintaining a widespread, highly emotional, exploitive and guilt-inducing public relations campaign in support of its position and socially isolating women who make the choice to abort an unwanted pregnancy. Much of its energy comes from the Religious Right and from the Catholic Church. The Knights of Columbus, an exclusively male fraternity within the Catholic Church, has taken on the anti-abortion issue as their primary social cause.

Unlike more populous areas, rural highways are littered with billboards proclaiming "abortion kills," and yard signs advocating the right to life and opposing abortion abound. Catholic cemeteries in rural areas have monuments, usually funded by the Knights of Columbus, to the unborn cleverly placed to be visible to anyone driving by.

Notably, many of the vocal pro-life, anti-reproductive choice, and anti-abortion advocates are men who have no relationship to, or obligation for, raising the children resulting from the pregnancies these men insist should continue. Pro-life, anti-choice advocates have gone so far as to object to the availability of emergency contraception to prevent a pregnancy from occurring as a result of unprotected sexual intercourse. And in some states pro-life pharmacists are allowed to opt out of dispensing over-the-counter morning-after contraception or filling prescriptions for the drug.

Currently North Dakota has the most restrictive laws governing abortion, which include a ban on the procedure after six weeks gestation. Wisconsin is almost on par, having recently signed into law provisions that severely constrict the ability of medical personnel to provide safe abortions. The pressing issue for rural women is the requirement that abortion providers have admitting privileges at a local hospital no less than 30 miles away, which not all do. And, when the local hospital is more than 100 miles away, or is Catholic and refuses abortion provider physicians admitting privileges, obtaining a safe abortion becomes much more complicated for a rural woman who lacks hospital choice. The other requirement, that of first obtaining an ultrasound before having an abortion, also complicates this aspect of women's health services because ultrasound equipment is expensive and not all rural hospitals or physician's offices have it.

Current federal Hyde Amendment legislation prohibits the use of federal funds for abortion services, except in cases of rape, incest, or an endangered mother's life. Nevertheless, in 2005 there were more than 1.2 million abortions (the most common surgical procedure performed on women), and estimates are that at current rates, about one third of all women will have had an abortion by age 45.[34]

The Hyde Amendment is not permanent law. Each year since 1977 it has been attached to Congressional appropriations bills, a political maneuver that insures Congress will continue to reaffirm its provisions and uphold its abortion restrictions. As a result, over time, the amendment has had an increasingly broad reach that includes Medicaid program limits on the availability of abortions for poor women. Seventeen states have circumvented the criteria set forth in the amendment by broadening the definition of "medically necessary" abortion and using their own funds to cover abortions provided using the broader definition. In all other states women receiving Medicaid services may receive an abortion only under the criteria set forth in the Hyde Amendment or when a physician documents the threat to the mother's life.

Since 1977, the Hyde Amendment has also been expanded to limit federal funds for abortion services in the Indian Health Service and for abortion services for federal employees and women serving in the military. It also prohibits abortion coverage from being required as part of any essential health care benefits package and does not allow federal premium or cost-sharing subsidies to be used to purchase abortion coverage. Further, if a woman who is receiving federal assistance purchases health insurance coverage in a plan that does cover abortion services beyond what the Hyde Amendment provides for, her federal subsidy funds must not be used to purchase abortion coverage and must be segregated from private premiums or state funds. In other words, federal law de facto limits the spectrum of reproductive health care services available to women.

More worrisome, the percentage of all mothers beginning prenatal care during the first trimester of pregnancy has continued to decline; pre-term birth rates have risen to 12.8 percent of all births, an increase of 25 percent since 1990. The low birth-weight infant rate rose to 8.3 percent in 2006, the highest level in four decades. Teenagers and poor women are both more likely to give birth to premature or low birth-weight babies, more likely to experience complications of pregnancy, and very much less likely to seek early prenatal care.

Among teen mothers, substantial variations are found in levels of educational achievement. However, becoming a mother while still a teenager is a very strong predictor of educational failure and future poverty for women, even with special high school programs aimed at keeping teen mothers in school.

The chief reason teen pregnancies often do not end in termination is that teens and women who become unexpectedly pregnant are often in denial and reluctant to admit the possibility of a pregnancy until it is too late to abort the fetus safely. Second is the religious factor, particularly among Hispanics, for whom unmarried pregnancy rates are highest. Most Hispanics are Catholic, a religion that expressly forbids abortion or practicing any form of contraception, making these women very unlikely to seek pregnancy termination. Other religions are also vocal in their "right to life" stance and vehement opposition to abortion.

Third, poor teens in particular appear reluctant to terminate a pregnancy, even when the means to do so are available. In her study of female gang members Gini Sykes says the girl gang members she interviewed "didn't really believe in abortion" and were reluctant to use contraception because it required too much forethought, and preplanned sex carried a negative connotation.[35] Many of the girl gang members had sex with their male counterparts in exchange for some form of street protection, which was valuable enough that the girls didn't ask the boys they were having sex with to use condoms, for fear of insulting them or encountering resistance that would lead to an argument and perhaps a break-up. In other words, the girls gave sex to the boys as a means of holding on to them, and to the relationship they represented, which is a notion women and girls have been grabbing onto for millennia.

In rural areas, where everyone knows everyone else, and has an opinion about them, having a group of protective friends can be very important, especially for a poor rural girl living in an abusive home and looking at a bleak future. In her eyes, getting pregnant is not the tragedy it is for a girl who has the economic means to hope for a bright future and a realistic ability to follow her dreams.

Adolescent pregnancy generally is an acute public health concern because of the associated risks for both mother and child. Add to these the extra health liabilities associated with poverty and the issue takes on much greater significance. While various types of teen-pregnancy prevention programs do exist, the jury is still out on the effectiveness of available sex education programs in schools and the effectiveness of access to birth control.

Some parents, believing sex education belongs in the home, vehemently oppose these programs. Some states do not allow sex education in public schools at all, and teens are still very prone to thinking pregnancy, like many other dangers, "won't happen to me," thus leading them to engage in all kinds of risky behaviors without fear of likely consequences. Further, teenagers are still learning about themselves and tend to question the limits of appropriate social behavior, so a "just say no" strategy for avoiding teen pregnancy is unlikely to be successful, particularly in rural areas.

Reproductive health is only one aspect of the spectrum of health care issues unique to women. Providing health care services to rich and poor women alike is much more intensely driven by cost-benefit decisions than moral concerns over how to control reproduction. The difference is that poor women, particularly in rural areas, are at the mercy of federal policies regulating available health care services. Non-poor women are better able to obtain private health insurance or pay for wanted or needed medical care themselves, thus significantly broadening their health care choices.

Poverty and Mental Health

Our largest mental health institutions are our jails. —Gene Farley, M.D.

While many argue that anyone who ends up in jail has mental health issues, the mental health picture becomes complicated when considering that, in rural areas, the most frequent reasons for an individual being jailed usually involves alcohol or drug use in addition to the primary offense—and both alcohol and drug use are significant mental health issues. Further, the poor tend to be jailed more often than the non-poor, who can put up bail on a signature bond.

The strong connection between poverty and mental health is not surprising. Day in and day out poor people live very stressful lives without much hope of relief, and sooner or later this takes a significant emotional toll. Anxiety and depression—and all the behavioral manifestations of these illnesses—haunt the poor, and self-medication of symptoms, most often with drugs and alcohol, is the usual result.

Rural physician Aaron Dunn expresses great concern about the mental health issues his patients face. "It's rare when I don't see a woman who isn't exhausted, depressed, smoking, and probably drinking too much," Dunn says. As a result, Dunn says he sees a lot of mood-altering drug and alcohol issues among those he treats, and his ability to make mental health treatment referrals is constrained by the lack of available services—and patients' ability to pay for it.

A complex set of factors conspires against obtaining mental health services in rural areas, and the hardest one to overcome is the cultural expectation that "you solve your own problems." No question rural people are very good at doing that, but the downside to this ability is that men in particular don't often ask for help, even when they desperately need it. "I don't mind asking somebody to help me out on the farm, but if I'm upset about something, I keep it to myself ... it's too embarrassing to talk about it," rural Iowa farmer Joe Hayes said.

Women are more likely to talk to their girlfriends, and are more frequent users of the mental health system generally, but not necessarily in rural areas. Dunn says women's stress usually revolves around some combination of childrearing responsibilities, caring for disabled and/or elderly relatives, employment problems complicated by the cost of child care and trying to manage on an inadequate income. "Either she needs a job and doesn't have one or has one (or two) but can barely manage to do either one at the same time she's looking after a sick parent who is more dependent on her than the kids are. She has trouble sleeping because of exhaustion and worry so she comes to me asking for something to help her out," Dunn explains, adding that given the circumstances of her life, it's no wonder she can't sleep, plus "she really could use some help sorting out some of this stuff, but there isn't much available to her." Dunn believes the new health care legislation will help with the mental health issue for those who have health insurance, but it won't do a thing for those who don't—because Medicaid doesn't cover outpatient mental health services. "You have to be sick enough to be admitted to a psychiatric unit or treatment facility before Medicaid will pay," Dunn explains.

According to the American Psychological Association (APA) there is a "critical need" for psychologists in rural areas.[36] The APA believes rural residents often have a greater need for the mental health services psychologists are trained to provide yet have much less access to care than their urban counterparts. There are approximately 39 psychologists per 100,000 residents in urban/suburban areas but only 16 psychologists per 100,000 residents in rural areas. Additionally, according to the APA[37]:

- State offices of Rural Health have identified suicide, stress, depression and anxiety disorders, and lack of access to mental and behavioral health as major rural health issues.
- By the late 1990s, rates of suicide were 54 percent higher in rural areas than in urban areas and suicide is the second leading cause of death in states with primarily rural populations.
- Rural areas have a higher proportion of people who are at risk for mental and behavioral health problems, especially older adults and the chronically ill.
- The National Health Interview Survey found that the prevalence of major depression was significantly higher among rural (6.11 percent) than among urban (5.16 percent) populations.

Further, rural residents are more likely than urban residents to report fair to poor health status and are more likely to have experienced a limitation of activity caused by chronic conditions.[38] According to the APA, rural residents have an equal or even greater likelihood of suffering from substance abuse problems as urban residents. And, due to the shortage of mental and behavioral health providers, primary care physicians who do not have the sufficient training and skills to deal with mental and behavioral health issues, provide as much as 70 percent of mental and behavioral health services in rural areas.[39]

Alcohol and Drug Use in Rural Areas

> *We should be embracing our tavern culture as a promoter of family values.—* Editorial in *Milwaukee Journal-Sentinel*

> *This bill will not solve all of our state's problems with alcohol, but it certainly will help reduce some of the problems.... Drinking at a young age can shape a person's drinking patterns for a lifetime.—*Wisconsin state sen. Judy Robson

> *The sad fact is that money is tight in every area of government.... But that should not be a reason for those who set budgets to turn their backs on the heroin problem and refuse to help fight it because of costs.—*J. Patrick Reilly, Dodgeville Chronicle

In the rural Midwest the local tavern is where people find out what's going on, play pinball machines, chew the fat—and drink. The rule of thumb when defining most rural Wisconsin towns is that there are at least as many bars as churches; however the reality often is that there are more bars. Parents start bringing their children to the local tavern while they are still in baby seats, and in Wisconsin, a child of any age can consume alcohol anywhere, under their parent's supervision.

"Alcohol use is a huge problem in rural areas," says Jeanie Lewis. "Adults drink too much and the kids get the idea it's OK—and it leads to all kinds of trouble—violence, accidents, men beating their wives and kids, and bad behavior generally.... It's really awful."

Excessive alcohol and drug use is a mental health, public health or criminal issue, and sometimes is all three. Regardless of how the problem is classified, excessive alcohol use can quickly graduate from a mental health addiction problem to a costly public health issue to a crime involving jail time or prison. Yet any effort to curtail or control alcohol consumption is met with an intense response, particularly in rural areas where a "tavern culture" defines the social life of the community.

Youth 4-H leader Debra Ivey, who heads a county-wide coalition on adolescent alcohol and drug use in Iowa County, Wisconsin, believes allowing young people to drink, even under parental supervision, is a serious mistake that sets them up to become alcohol abusers in young adulthood. "The negative effects of early alcohol consumption on adolescent and pre-adolescent brain development are very conclusive," Ivey says, adding that the importance of curtailing teen alcohol use cannot be understated.[40]

That this is a problem is evident from answers to the 2007 Southwest Wisconsin Youth Survey of 5,700 7th–12th graders, which indicates that 34 percent of males and 23 percent of females began drinking at age 12 or younger, and 49 percent of teens who consume alcohol say they started before age 14.

Nearly half of all teens who drink do it most often at parties. Sixteen percent of teens who use alcohol, including 30 percent of 7th graders, do so at home with their parents' permission. Thirty-three percent of 7th graders (about age 12) who drink say they most often drink at home or at their friends' homes without parental permission, Ivey explains.

Data gathered in 2005 from 1,264 7th–12th students indicate that 33 percent had consumed alcohol in the 30 days prior to the survey. By grade level, 45 percent of 11th graders and 65 percent of 12th graders had consumed alcohol within 30 days of taking the survey. Later data indicate alcohol consumption among teens is dropping off slightly, but no one believes this is because they are underage and alcohol consumption is illegal. There is general agreement among alcohol experts that these are very alarming statistics, particularly when considering that habitual alcohol use hijacks an adolescent brain and permanently damages it.

According to the Pacific Institute for Research and Evaluation, over 300,000 teens drink in Wisconsin each year, accounting for 18 percent of all alcohol consumed statewide and $433 million in alcohol sales. Among the teen drinkers 28 percent began drinking before age 13, 54 percent drink regularly, and 34 percent binge drink, meaning consuming five or more drinks in succession.[41] These are staggering statistics.

However, not all teens drink alcohol. Abstaining seems to be most closely associated with parental values around the issue, but not entirely. "Fifty-three percent of those who say they haven't tried alcohol also say their parents think it is wrong for teens to drink," said Ivey, adding that 18 percent of teens who don't know what their parents think about teen drinking don't drink and 16 percent of teens who believe their parents think it's OK for teens to drink don't consume alcohol. Data also indicate that about 53 percent of teens who say drinking is against their values eventually succumb to peer pressure to drink.

According to Ivey the social and dollar costs of adolescent drinking in Wisconsin, which ranks 29th among the 50 states, are a staggering $1.4 billion. This translates into $2,109 per teenager per year. "Early alcohol consumption is associated with later addiction and other drug abuses," Ivey says. She also believes the need for intense mental health intervention to discover why a teen (or anyone) drinks or uses drugs excessively is an absolute necessity, because the problem spirals out of control so quickly.

Unfortunately, in rural areas professional treatment options are sparse, most rural motor vehicle accidents involving teens and young people also involve alcohol, and not all states consider drunkenness a crime. Also unfortunately, it is hard to imagine any social situation in a rural area, even the weekly Friday night fish fry in the local church basement, that doesn't involve serving alcohol.

Missouri is a state particularly hard hit by drug problems. According to a member of the rural Franklin County sheriff's department the biggest culprit is methamphetamine. "It's the first drug in the history of the United States we can make, distribute, sell, and take, all here in the Midwest. You can't grow a coca plantation or an opium plantation here to get your heroin or cocaine, and marijuana takes four or five months to grow a good plant. With methamphetamine, you can go out and for a couple hundred dollars, you can make your drugs that day."[42] Further complicating the picture is that recipes for methamphetamine abound, and unregulated on-line pharmacies will sell narcotic drugs without a prescription.

Nationwide data from multiple sources indicate that alcohol and illicit drug use in rural areas is much higher among those having an income of less than $10,000 and who are unemployed; among that population, heroin use is also increasing. Heroin availability also appears to be increasing dramatically in rural areas.[43] According to Carsey Institute data, anyone who has Internet access and a credit card can obtain nearly any illegal substance they seek, regardless of their age.[44]

Suicide

> *Any time you see a younger person listed in the obituaries who didn't die in a car wreck, chances are good it was suicide.* —Mary Gotham

Suicide is the second leading cause of death in states with primarily rural populations, and adolescent males in rural areas, particularly those from poor families, have higher suicide rates than their urban counterparts. Because of the stigma attached to having a family member, particularly a son or daughter, commit suicide, official death records of adolescent suicide are believed to be underreported in rural areas and may be three times higher than the actual number of suicides. Suicide rates of young adults are approximately 1.5 times the rates for the overall U.S. population.[45]

Mary Gotham has had a lot of suicide in her family and says it "really messes people up." "The mental health needs for suicide survivors are through the roof, but insurance coverage to pay for it is pretty poor and a lot of people are afraid of counseling."

According to Marshfield, Wisconsin Clinic data:

- One in five adolescents seriously considers suicide.
- One in twelve adolescents attempts suicide.
- Suicide is the third leading cause of death for all adolescents.
- Recent increases in suicides have been attributed to the widespread availability of firearms.[46]

Risk factors associated with suicides in rural areas include undiagnosed, unrecognized, or untreated mood disorders/mental illness; access to lethal means of carrying out the act; family violence; acquaintance or a friend who committed suicide; social isolation and community disorganization. In addition to limiting access to lethal means of self harm, Gotham believes reducing the stigma surrounding mental health problems is very important to the future of rural communities, "right up there with providing opportunities for gainful employment, education, and community involvement."

Free Medical Care

> *We see some very sad cases and some very sick people with nowhere else to go. Many people are employed but they don't have health insurance.* —Jane Wisler, Free Medical Clinic volunteer

Free medical clinics have been true lifesavers for the poor, but they don't really come free, and are very limited in the kinds of health care they can offer, and patients have to get to the clinic at a time when it is open, which is usually for two or three hours one or two evenings a week, on a first come–first served basis. Most free clinics carry the burden of needing to fundraise to stay afloat, are staffed by volunteer medical personnel with day jobs, and are only able to see a limited number of patients. Because of malpractice insurance issues most free clinics do not provide emergency care, obstetric services, or immunizations, or perform minor surgical procedures. And they depend upon a cadre of non-medical volunteers to connect patients with the services they need.

By partnering with many local human services agencies Dr. Aaron Dunn established a free medical clinic in Iowa County, Wisconsin, in 2005. Dunn was driven by his frustration over seeing so many uninsured patients in his private practice who were ill and had no place to turn and by a true desire to work with this unmet need. "I had too many patients telling me they had to choose between paying for food and paying for medication," Dunn said, adding that this was the driving force behind getting the clinic moving forward.

Most often, the clinic assists with chronic disease management (diabetes, high blood pressure, chronic allergies and obesity-related problems), ongoing depression, anxiety and alcohol abuse, and acute illnesses such as colds and sore throats. "Some nights, the doctors prescribe lots of inhalers, antibiotics or Tamiflu—sometimes we remove growths and send them out for what we hope is a benign diagnosis. But whatever comes our way, every single clinic night, patients in our little neck of the woods know that there is somewhere they can go," explains Molly Zuehlke, Free Clinic manager and also a registered nurse.

Prescription Assistance Programs (PAP) are an invaluable part of the operations of free clinics because they connect patients to drug company programs that provide free or low-cost medication to qualifying individuals and can save a patient as much as $6,000 in drugs needed to treat just one illness. According to free clinic volunteer Jan Cooper the PAP program has saved the clinic over $650,000 since it opened.[47] The 90 clinic volunteers give approximately 4,800 hours each year, serving over 2,300 patients and providing approximately $1 million in free health care, explains clinic volunteer Jayne Wisler.[48]

Meanwhile, the Poor Get Sicker and the Sick Get Poorer

> *[I've] heard stories about heartbroken parents pleading with the doctors: "What chance does my child have if I can only afford half of the prescribed treatments? Or two thirds? I've sold everything. I've mortgaged as much as possible." No parent should suffer that torment. Not in this country. Not in the richest country in the world.*—Senator Edward Kennedy (D-MA)

The big questions surrounding the complex relationship between being poor and becoming ill are three: The first is to wonder how sick poverty actually makes those who are poor. While no one is entirely immune to illness, we know certain chronic health problems such as hypertension, diabetes, and obesity occur much more frequently among the poor; and being poor puts women at greater risk for mental health problems and increases the likelihood of dying from certain cancers and problems related to childbearing. We also know that being poor presents a unique set of issues that make taking care of oneself, both emotionally and physically, nearly impossible, so any efforts at preventative health care practices are, for all practical purposes, out of the question. And we know that the list of poverty-induced illnesses is much longer than these concerns imply. Thus it appears that the short answer to the question of how sick poverty makes people is that it dramatically increases the probability of becoming very sick indeed.

Second is to wonder how the poor decide between buying medicine and buying food, paying the heating bill or paying the doctor bill, seeing the doctor or doctoring themselves as best they can? These answers vary widely by individual circumstances, but it isn't hard to imagine how difficult daily life is when these are the choices one has to worry over week after week, month after month, with no end in sight.

Third, it is extremely difficult for people who are ill to work at all, much less to perform well, and the rural poor, who often work at part-time jobs with no benefits and no sick leave, risk losing their job if they call in sick. One wonders how the poor who suffer significant health problems can be expected to hold a job and support themselves when they can't access medical treatment or supportive care for their illnesses.

Finally, and perhaps most important of all, one wonders what kind of treatment decisions health care providers make when working in an atmosphere of profit-motive medicine. How do doctors and nurses resolve the dilemma of providing the best possible care for their patients and still turn a profit? Do they view this issue as a moral dilemma or a business plan decision?

For those who see practicing medicine as a "calling" and are concerned that everyone receives the best possible care because it is the morally right thing to do, how do the existing rules get bent to see that this happens? Alternatively, for those who see providing medical care as a business just like any other business, and are bottom-line driven, it's fair to wonder how they sleep at night knowing that human beings desperately in need of medical care they can't afford go wanting.

The vitriol and emotional debate surrounding America's health care legislation exposes a level of greed a nation as wealthy as America is should be profoundly ashamed of. Affordable health care access and availability should be basic human rights and not a political football tossed between warring, power-hungry senators and representatives of opposing political parties living in an eastern city far from, and out of touch with, most of rural America.

But America is a free-enterprise, profit-motive economy and that philosophy drives everything, including health care. It shouldn't be this way, but it is. Health care should be far above politics, but it isn't. All but the wealthiest Americans receive health care based not upon best practices, but upon what their health insurance will cover and whether they can afford the co-pay. This leads to the conclusion that the real issue fueling the health care access and coverage debate is the lucrative opportunity providing health care services presents in an environment of unrestrained profit-motive capitalism—and there's no profit in providing health care to the poor who can't pay for it.

When a politician says, "The American people can't afford this [national health care] legislation, what he really means is that the policy risks cutting into health insurance industry profits. No one talks about the simple facts of being sick and unable to work or being unable to work and therefore being without health insurance, and getting sicker as a result.

Ultimately the "Great Healer" every sick American encounters most often is the profit-driven health insurance company and the "Great Decider" is the public policy surrounding American health care, which operates in a nation that does not believe everyone is entitled to basic health care or that it is government's responsibility to see that this happens. Not all Americans believe it is society's responsibility to care for each other's basic needs equally and favor concentrating power and wealth within a small segment of society that derives its wealth through economic exploitation, meaning that the poor work for the benefit of the rich, and their job doesn't necessarily include benefits such as health insurance. A surprising number of Americans are willing to accept this inequality, and never is it more apparent than when considering the plight of the rural poor when they get sick.

8

One-Cop Towns

Rural Crime and Punishment

> *You look at these scattered houses, and you are impressed by their beauty. I look at them, and the only thought which comes to me is a feeling of their isolation and of the impunity with which crime may be committed there.*—Sherlock Holmes, in "The Adventure of the Copper Beeches"

"It seems we're importing a lot of big city problems now ... all you have to do is read the crime report section of any local paper to understand there's a lot more than cow tipping[1] going on," says J. Patrick Reilly, editor and publisher of the Dodgeville Chronicle. He is likely correct in his assessment that crime in rural areas is changing. Nevertheless, the crime sheet of most small town newspapers is populated with reports of motor vehicle violations, domestic violence incidents, vandalism and other nuisance crimes, and illegal possession of alcohol. A robbery, drug bust or murder is front page news.

Reilly thinks the reasons for the boring crime blotter are several:

- In rural areas local residents exert considerable informal social control over each other, so minor crime is often dealt with informally.
- Rural people have a general reluctance to air personal problems, thus much criminal behavior in rural areas often goes unreported.
- The local enforcement officer is most likely someone the offender went to high school with, goes bowling with, is related to, or whose wife is his wife's best friend and the two couples barbeque together on summer Sunday afternoons, so reporting something like a drunk and disorderly or domestic violence incident can, all too easily, pit friends and relatives against each other.
- In rural areas, where the tax base is small and resources committed to law enforcement are sparse, there is a tendency for citizens not to bother reporting crimes because they know law enforcement is understaffed and slow to respond. Additionally, when a crime does occur, local police officers often must wait a long time for back-up before closing in on the situation. Consequently, rural residents tend to personally take care of problems urban residents would turn to law enforcement for assistance with.

"It's true that it used to be when someone was caught driving drunk the officer would just take the person home to sleep it off and that would be the end of it," says rural Wisconsin Circuit Court judge Willard Davis. "Now the law says that for every accident investigation there has to be a citation issued, every time someone is caught driving drunk they have to be arrested, and for every bar fight or domestic incident an arrest for disorderly conduct must occur. Police and sheriff's officers who are doing their job right don't have any choice, no matter who is involved," Davis says.

Shoot First, Ask Questions Later: Gun Violence

The vast majority of gun owners don't kill, but people who do kill, tend to kill with guns, and often with illegal guns.—Attorney Alan Dershowitz

In rural areas guns are something a farmer or rancher needs to protect himself and his livestock out on the open range, to eliminate nuisance animals, and to hunt for food. Consequently, nearly everyone owns at least one gun, and nearly all are legally registered firearms. This means guns are widely and readily accessible to almost everyone living in a rural area.

Rural residents, who favor liberal gun ownership laws, are quick to point out that automatic weapons have been illegal for years and that if someone is going to use a gun to engage in criminal activity they aren't going to obey the laws governing gun use regardless of what those laws are. Thus, they view the raging gun debate as a remote discussion about an issue that is irrelevant to their lives because they don't believe guns are a problem.

Data show that rural Americans—roughly one-sixth of the population—are more than twice as likely as those living in large cities to have a gun inside the home and are six times more likely to be hunters. Rural residents are also most likely to say the best way to reduce gun violence is to better enforce current gun laws rather than pass new, more restrictive ones, an argument echoed by the National Rifle Association and other gun rights groups.[2]

Another often cited issue among rural residents, is that law enforcement can't respond quickly to a home invasion or other threat, so they need a gun to protect themselves. Individuals living in rural areas, where guns are more accepted as a part of life, and used for recreation, sports and dealing with problems with wild animals, feel there is nothing wrong with owning one. And while, to a soldier, a gun is a weapon, to most rural residents, it's just another tool in their necessarily vast array of equipment needed to live and work where they do.

"My law enforcement colleagues who live and work in the rural areas definitely have a different sense of what gun ownership means," Judge Davis says, "and, relative to urban law enforcement, an entirely different level of perception about what constitutes gun violence."

Dealing Desperation: Rural Poverty and Crime

When a man is denied the right to live the life he believes in, he has no choice but to become an outlaw.—Nelson Mandela

No one living in desperate poverty is living the life he or she wants to live. When that person also lives in a relatively more isolated area where job choices are few, school achievement is lower, and simple needs, like reading glasses, go unmet, hopelessness and desperation all too easily set in.

Imagine a life where drinking water is contaminated by e-coli or nitrates from fertilizer runoff,[3] you don't have enough money to purchase a cell phone plan and can't afford a house phone, your house or trailer lacks electricity unless the bill is paid, and a computer is out of the question because you can't get an Internet hookup, even if you could afford one. Perpetual deprivation is what the day-by-day life of someone living in desperate poverty feels like, and helps explain why some poor are especially vulnerable to seeking illegal means for generating income.

While high rates of poverty have long been associated with high crime rates, and although poverty is a continual, and common, problem in most rural areas, it is difficult to discern whether more poor than non-poor find themselves in trouble with the law. Nevertheless, Judge Davis thinks this is the case. "I can't give you hard data on this, but my impression is that poverty is a very common problem among those I see in my courtroom. Last week I signed off on five divorce decrees and all five petitioned for a waiver of fees and court costs.[4] This means, among other things, that the state is footing the bill for a lot of divorces, restraining orders, and other family problems—and these applications are not unusual. And if you add in those who are arrested for other things and come into my court requesting I appoint a lawyer for them because they can't afford one themselves, then there's no question that lot of the people who come before the court are indigent."

Davis wouldn't speculate on whether this reflects the fact that poor people who do commit crimes are more often caught or whether a greater proportion of poor people in rural areas commit crimes. The 2012 criminal statistics for his court, which serves a 768 square mile county with a population of 23,599 and a 7.6 percent unemployment rate, indicated a total of 604 criminal cases (felony, misdemeanor and criminal traffic offenses); 4,494 forfeiture cases, mostly uncontested traffic offenses; 793 civil cases, including divorce, paternity and other family matters; 113 probate cases; and 46 juvenile cases, most of which pertained to delinquency. Davis says the delinquency cases are dropping off thanks to the good work of the local social services agency. "Unless it is a heinous crime, a juvenile is first referred to counseling and social services and only makes it into my court room when he or she has completely exhausted the patience and resources of the local social service personnel and they don't have any options left.... None of these kids come from solid homes, and most of them, and their parents, are known to social services and to law enforcement for quite a while before they end up appearing before me."

What Rural Crime Really Looks Like

> *We usually recover stolen property when one of these idiots beats his wife or girlfriend. She's so pissed that she rats on him and his buddies.*—Rural Kansas deputy sheriff

"We have personally experienced several burglaries at our farm, as have many of our neighbors," says Jerry Hambley of rural Kansas. Living in the country "means you and your neighbors will have to defend and protect your own.... Criminals know the local authorities can't patrol an entire county. They could rob you 50 times over before a patrol car reached you."[5]

Hambley also claims the county sheriff's department is overwhelmed and being forced to work with limited resources makes it impossible to investigate crimes against property. "If they do catch the criminals red-handed, the justice system simply slaps them on the wrist and returns them to the community—a crime in and of itself. The county attorney blames it on lack of funds to actually house prisoners in the county jail."

Unquestionably rural crime and policing are both distinctly different from urban areas in ways that affect law enforcement practices and public policy, yet little research has been done on either. According to the National Institute of Justice (NIJ), even though rural crime rates have been lower than urban rates, patterns of rural crime indicate an exporting of urban problems to rural areas, and when this occurs, the rural environment affects these crimes.[6] The NIJ also indicates that:

- Urban drug trafficking is viewed as the driving force behind the spread of drug use and development of gangs in rural areas.
- Person crimes (homicide, rape, and assault) in rural areas are more likely to occur among acquaintances than is true in urban areas.
- Crimes unique to rural areas include agricultural crimes (e.g., theft of crops, timber, or livestock) and wildlife crimes (e.g., poaching).
- Rural law enforcement works with lower budgets, less staff, less equipment, and fewer written policies to govern their operations. Despite these problems, rural police appear to be more efficient than urban police and are more respected by the public.
- Traits of the rural culture affect law enforcement and include informal social control among rural citizens, a mistrust of government, and a reluctance to share internal problems, which may result in failures to report crime out of the belief that it is a "private matter."

Some argue that, with modern communication and transportation differences, both rural and urban crime rates are shrinking, and indeed, the rank order of property crime offenses is roughly similar for both urban and rural areas, meaning that larceny is the most common crime and motor vehicle theft is the least common crime in both rural and urban areas.[7] That gap is greatest for homicides and robbery, both of which occur much more frequently in urban areas.

Emerging Problems in Rural Crime

> *Drugs are, in my view, a cottage industry, at least around here. People who otherwise wouldn't break the law will commit crimes to support a drug habit. Alcohol's easier to get your hands on so people tend not to steal to support an alcohol habit—but the effects of either one are basically the same.*—Attorney Stephen Chiquoine

Although there is not yet hard evidence to support the notion, it does seem that either drug-related crimes are increasing in rural areas or more attention is being paid to drug problems. In recent months Reilly's newspaper has had an illegal drugs-related story on the front page nearly every week. But drugs aren't the only law enforcement problem facing rural areas. Others include:

Gangs: Typically, rural areas have been considered immune to gang problems, a notion that has been increasingly challenged because increased drug trafficking is seen as the driving force behind rural gang formation. This has been enabled by an improved interstate highway system that allows individuals to cover a lot of miles relatively quickly and anonymously. Judge Davis believes youth gangs are not common in rural areas, but he acknowledges that motorcycle gangs do travel rural roads and historically most have a history of criminal activity in rural settings. "Bikers are notoriously difficult to learn much about, so we don't know a lot about what they are up to unless they happen to get caught," Davis says.

Substance abuse: Substance abuse has two dimensions: alcohol and drug use by rural citizens and criminal drug trafficking in rural areas. Alcohol is among the most popular of mind-altering substances, and, according to the U.S. Department of Justice, is of particular concern in rural areas, where OWIs (operating while intoxicated) are more common.

According to Reilly, alcohol is involved in most crimes against persons and nearly all motor vehicle accidents, which mostly occur on two-lane, rural roads, and Judge Davis, who has been in his position nearly 20 years, concurs. "I'm hard put to recall any domestic violence incident that got as far as my court room that didn't involve alcohol," he says, "and you know what the OWI statistics for this county are—it isn't a good situation."[8]

"Previous research has shown that rural adolescents are more likely to use alcohol than those in urban areas," say John Gale and David Hartley, lead researchers on a study exploring alcohol use in rural areas.[9] Using national data, Gale and Hartley conclude that, after controlling for a broad range of key risk and protective factors, "it is clear that an unexplained rural effect persists with rural adolescents exhibiting higher alcohol use than their urban counterparts ... and our findings suggest that rural adolescents who start drinking at an earlier age are more likely to engage in problem drinking behavior as they get older." This research also suggests that the more rural the area, the greater likelihood underage drinking will occur, which is partially explained by the rural tavern culture existing in small towns. "When the local bar is the center of social life, parents bring their children along when they stop in for a beer and to visit with friends, so children grow up in an environment of frequent alcohol consumption," Davis explains, adding that some states, like Wisconsin, allow children to begin consuming alcohol under their parents' supervision at a very young age, which he feels is "a very bad idea."

Most law enforcement professionals believe the drug problem in rural areas is growing rapidly and dramatically. In recent years the drug of choice in the Midwestern states has been locally manufactured methamphetamine.[10] Indiana and Missouri lead the region in the number of "meth lab busts" while Minnesota has had the fewest.[11] One reason for the popularity of the drug is that it is quick and easy to manufacture from common household ingredients, and the results are satisfying to the user.

Reilly agrees that drugs are impacting rural communities in ways not seen previously, and he decided to look into the problem further. What he learned surprised him enough that he began writing about it in a series of articles that appeared in his newspaper, which serves a community of 6,000, 55 miles from the nearest urban center. His articles paint a portrait of family fracture, abuse and alcoholism that a teenage boy could not cope with, and he turned first to alcohol, then to prescription drugs he could buy on the street, and finally to heroin.[12]

When Reilly interviewed the mother, she indicated that both law enforcement assistance and medical intervention was weak, and she felt she was on her own in trying to solve the problem. She also believes that the rural drug addiction problem is tied to big city drug suppliers inserting themselves into rural areas and creating a market, coupled with rural law enforcement being unable to deal with it.

"Addicts are being asked by law enforcement to serve as narcs,"[13] she says. "They are asked to set up drug buys and are paid for doing it. My son was asked to become a narc but decided against it because it would put us all at risk," she said. "We would have feared for our lives." She indicated she knew about a person who had become a narc and the suppliers in Chicago issued a hit on him. "His body was found in a field with a bullet in his head," she said.

There are several striking things about Reilly's story. One is that it was front page news in a small-town rural newspaper. Another is the sense of helplessness and isolation the boy's mother expresses. Third is the level of family dysfunction and chaos present in the young man's life at the time he began using drugs, and for a long time afterwards—an issue that seemed to entirely escape his mother's notice.

More importantly, if one did not know the articles were written about an experience in a rural area, there would be no way to tell where the individuals live. In other words, drug problems in rural areas are not characteristically different from drug problems in urban areas—they just occur less frequently. "We're not like the cities where drugs are everywhere," Chiquoine says, "but they're definitely here ... and not that hard to find."

Prosecuting drug offenses are the decision of individual county district attorneys, and vary widely. "In some counties, possession of an ounce of pot[14] will be prosecuted; other counties have a first offender drug program that allows for plea bargains. Personally, I think prosecution resources should focus more on multiple offense drunk driving charges than on being caught with a little pot that was probably growing wild in the guy's backyard," Chiquoine says.

According to DOJ researchers Ralph Weisheit, David Falcone and Edward Wells, little is known about the specific issue of drug trafficking and production in rural areas.[15] They indicate that some reports suggest that "rural areas may serve as production sites for methamphetamine, designer drugs, crack cocaine, and marijuana," while other observers argue that the problem is exacerbated by an improved highway system, the large number of isolated air strips serving corporate farms, and crop dusters serving rural farmlands.

In a compelling account of his love affair with recreational heroin use, Nathan Comp describes how he and his girlfriend accessed the drugs, what they did to keep from dying when one or the other accidentally overdosed, and how it all ended in a dead-end motel in rural North Dakota.[16] "Our [heroin] use was infrequent because it was difficult to find, not to mention very expensive. In time, we met an actual trafficker who cut preferred-customer deals and it was on...." Eventually, Comp's girlfriend died from an overdose he failed to intercept, because he had gotten high himself and had fallen asleep. Comp expresses surprise at this outcome because, typical of addicts, they never think the unthinkable will happen to them.

Comp expresses great sorrow over the loss of "the best friend I ever had," but says nothing about the drug use itself, other than to observe that it wasn't a difficult habit to maintain, particularly in Dickson, North Dakota. The motel he managed was frequented by addicts, drug dealers, and prostitutes lured to the area by the North Dakota oil boom. "Boredom and cabin fever set in," he explained. "Then the cold came and we receded further inward.... We became even more reckless, this time without any pretense of being responsible junkies."

Comp's descent followed 13 heroin-free years, when he began crushing painkillers for no particular reason other the high they gave him. He took a job transfer to rural New Mexico, America's opiate capital, and things went downhill from there. He switched back to heroin because it gave him a bigger buzz at half the cost. "It was an old times sake kind of thing," he says.

In reality, easy access to drugs, poor law enforcement of drug laws and boredom form a perfect storm at enables drug use in rural areas. In theory, with enough resources two of these variables are fixable; boredom is a much more difficult issue for rural communities to deal with.

Vice and organized crime: Gambling, prostitution, pornography and other crimes involving activities society considers immoral are less obvious features of the rural landscape. Small communities located near interstates or other major highways often have problems with prostitution rings established to serve the trucking industry. Areas with a history of moonshine production can use some of the same routes to transport drugs, stolen auto parts and other illegal merchandise, commonly home grown marijuana. There is not much question that these activities exist in rural areas; what is not known is how similar these operations may be to, or whether they are affiliated with, organized crime.

Violent crime: Further complicating the crime picture in bucolic rural areas is that sexual assault and rape most often occur among acquaintances, and when things cool off, the victim is likely to decide not to file a complaint because the offender is her brother's best friend, her girlfriend's brother, or someone else she knows well and sees often. As a result, she decides that "We got a little drunk and things went too far..." and then lets it go.

However, the monthly crime reports in small town rural newspapers almost always include some reference to domestic violence or assault, and there is no question that women living in rural areas are more vulnerable to domestic violence, for several reasons. One is that farmhouses are isolated and no one will overhear a spousal argument that gets out of hand and call authorities; another is it's highly likely that there are guns in the home; third is that it takes law enforcement a long time to respond to a call in a rural area, and most officers are keenly aware of the danger involved in responding to a domestic disturbance and are not eager to interject themselves into a very emotionally volatile situation without backup, particularly in states where the law requires that in cases of domestic violence someone must be arrested.

Complicating matters further is that safe shelters for domestic violence victims are generally in short supply in rural areas, a prevailing belief in the privacy of family life, and the notion that a man has authority over his wife, so if he has "to beat her into submission, it's because she deserves it." Consequently, most data indicate that the highest rates of domestic violence occur in the least populated areas.[17]

Occasionally a truly heinous crime occurs in a rural area. "Don't kid yourself—we have some pretty bad stuff happening in rural areas ... it just doesn't happen as often, because there aren't as many people to do it," Reilly says. However, despite the rural gun culture, neither of the two worst crimes occurring in rural Wisconsin in recent memory involved firearms. In the first case, a 30-year-old man convinced his brother to help him set fire to his house, located a few miles outside a small town, with the intent of killing his pregnant wife and children. He was partially successful in that three of the four children died, and his wife was critically burned, causing her to miscarry. Armin Wand III, who was seen carrying one of the children back into the burning house, told law enforcement agents he wanted to collect the life insurance policies on his wife and children because he was "tired of his family living from paycheck to paycheck and listening to his wife complain about wanting more money." He added that his wife was contemplating divorce and he wanted a fresh start. "This was one of the worst cases I've seen in my law enforcement career," said local sheriff Scott Pedley.

The brothers pleaded guilty and Armin Wand received several consecutive life sentences. Wand's wife Sharon was burned over 86 percent of her body and will never regain full use of her arms or legs. Her lungs were so damaged from the fire that she will always need oxygen. She told the court she could never forgive her husband for what he did. "If your goal was to hurt me, you have succeeded. Not because of the terrible physical pain I have had to endure, but because you have done the worst thing you could do to a mother, take her children from her."

The pre-sentence investigation determined that Wand was a psychopath who never showed remorse for killing his children. He was described as "calculating, selfish and unhappy with his life" and that he spent great time and effort planning to kill his family for money. The report also cited Wand's low IQ and "rough upbringing" with an alcoholic, abusive father. The court felt that Wand's low IQ did not affect his ability to reason or understand that his actions would cause grave harm to his children.

In a bizarre twist to the case, nearly a year after Armin Wand's sentencing, his wife returned to court to plead for her husband's release, saying that she was coerced into saying what she did and that her husband wasn't really responsible for what had occurred. Most viewed this sudden change as the behavior of a confused, severely abused woman who feared the consequences of testifying against her husband, even though he was serving a life sentence without parole, and that she had little grasp of the realities of normal family relationships.

The back story of this crime speaks forcefully to the desperation of a poor family living in an isolated rural area, without access to the needed resources to successfully manage their lives. It also illustrates the consequences of generational abuse, child maltreatment, and multiple social policy failures. "I sincerely hope I never see anything like this again," Pedley said.

Unfortunately, a few months later, Sheriff Pedley faced another grisly murder scene. This time a middle-aged man, his wife, and his brother, all upstanding, highly respected members of their community, were beaten to death one Sunday morning upon returning home from a vacation trip. The perpetrator, Jaren Kuester, was a stranger to the area who had been released from a mental health facility in Milwaukee, northeast of the county where the murders occurred, 48 hours previously. He made his way more than 120 miles into a remote rural area, where he broke into a home while the owners were away. He surprised them upon their return and somehow managed to beat all three to death, in a crime where the victims had done nothing other than to be in the wrong place at the wrong time.

Kuester was found mentally competent to stand trial and pleaded guilty to the crimes. "That case supports the common belief that most truly violent crime in rural areas is committed by outsiders, which is one reason outsiders are viewed very suspiciously in small towns," Chiquoine explained.

The Kuester case raises other issues regarding crime in rural areas. One is the acute stress incarcerating violent criminals' places on smaller rural facilities, which are often short-staffed and not well equipped to manage dangerous offenders. That this crime also reflects failures in mental health laws goes without saying, except to note that, as Pedley and other rural county sheriffs have observed, their jails are not equipped to function as mental health facilities, yet over 70 percent of their inmates have significant mental health issues in need of immediate attention.[18]

Non-violent crime: "Robberies aren't common in rural areas, because everybody knows everybody else, so it's hard to get away without being identified," Chiquoine says. As a result the ones that do occur are usually committed by area outsiders or teenagers from another town. "The strangest one in a long time was when someone broke into Harris Lumber and stole Homer Harris' nine by ten by six foot, ten ton safe right out of his office.... They sawed all around the wall it was in, got a fork lift from the lumberyard and lifted it into a flatbed truck parked in the yard and took off. It probably took most of the night, but the yard is located a few miles out of town and doesn't have an alarm system, because Homer never saw any need for one, and nobody driving by noticed any unusual activity. They never caught whoever did it and funny thing is, the safe was there when Homer's dad bought the building over a hundred years ago, and everybody knew he never kept any money in it," Chiquoine laughed.

Because of the lack of anonymity, vandalism is generally rare in a small town. Property crimes such as school vandalism are usually dealt with by the school administration and rarely involve law enforcement.

However, the severe economic recession has led to more of what Chiquoine calls "crimes of opportunity," mostly in the form of embezzlement. Church secretaries, treasurers of organizations, and public officials in his area have all embezzled money. "The treasurer of a local hockey club managed to embezzle $175,000 over a period of years, and the treasurer for a local volunteer fire department in a nearby town did the same thing ... and both were prosecuted. But if the people had no prior criminal record they usually got probation, a fine, and an agreement to make restitution," he said.

Chiquoine says the most bizarre embezzlement case in recent years occurred in a nearby village where the municipal clerk was embezzling village funds, not for himself, but to be used as a "revolving loan fund" to assist village residents, who were his friends and neighbors, and had come up against hard times. "He didn't keep a cent for himself, but it was still stealing, and still wrong. He got probation and a fine, and I imagine the community took up a collection to help pay it," Chiquoine chuckled.

Hate crimes: Hate crimes in rural areas usually arise from some combination of anti–Semitism, racism, fundamentalist Christianity and a deep suspicion of government.[19] Sometimes these beliefs lead directly to violence, as when members fight paying taxes or farm foreclosures, commit robbery to fund their activities, or weave together violence and religion by thinking they must be heavily armed for self protection because Armageddon is near.

The most famous proponents of rural hate crimes is the Posse Comitatus,[20] a loosely organized, far right social movement that opposes the federal government and steadfastly refuses to recognize any government authority higher than the county sheriff. Many Posse members practice survivalism and have played an active role in the formation of the armed citizens' militias in the 1990s.

Members of the Posse Comitatus frequently refuse to pay taxes, to obtain driver's licenses or otherwise to comply with regulatory authorities. They have unusual legal documents drawn up and attempt to record them, declaring independence from the United States, or claiming to file "common law" liens against perceived enemies like Internal Revenue Service employees or judges. They are often involved in various tax protests and have invoked arguments popularized by tax protesters.

In 1983, former Posse member (and accused parole violator) Gordon Kahl killed two federal marshals who had come to arrest him in North Dakota and became a fugitive. Another shootout ensued on June 3, 1983, in which Kahl and Lawrence County, Arkansas, sheriff Gene Matthews were killed. Other members of the group have been convicted of crimes ranging from tax evasion and counterfeiting to threatening the lives of IRS agents and judges, and of various violent encounters with authorities. Some Posse members embrace the anti–Semitic and white supremacist beliefs of Christian Identity. Others believe the federal government is illegitimate and in the hands of "ZOG," an alleged Jewish conspiracy.

Some rural hate groups base their beliefs on distortions of existing rural values and emphasize religion, patriotism, and independence from government tyranny. While they are believed to have a high potential to commit violence, rural hate group numbers are small and, unlike urban skinhead groups, are composed of "ordinary" people who shun public attention for themselves or their cause.[21]

Agricultural and wildlife crimes: Agricultural crimes include theft of livestock, crops and supplies, and single thefts of these sorts can be extremely costly and have very poor recovery rates. Gale and Hartley indicate that one study of agricultural theft reports that 80 percent of Iowa farmers indicated being victims of theft during a three-year period.[22] Additionally, embezzlement at an Iowa grain elevator produced a loss of $10,000 over the same period. According to other researchers "anecdotal evidence is that organized crime is active in agricultural crimes in several states."[23]

Wildlife crimes, particularly poaching[24] has become a major concern for conservation law enforcement. Wildlife shipments entering and leaving the United States are known to have a value in excess of one billion dollars. The estimated replacement costs of illegally harvested fish and wildlife in Illinois exceeded $45 million more than ten years ago, and the cost of poaching deer exceeded $96 million.

Sometimes rural residents poach merely for food; others do it to obtain a wildlife trophy, and for some poaching is an engaging cat and mouse game between the poacher and the local game warden. If the game warden and the laws he or she is supposed to enforce are believed to represent outside interference in the life of rural residents, then poaching reinforces mistrust of outsiders and of government and increases the "them versus us" mentality poachers often possess.

Calling the Cops

> *There's not much point in calling the cops because by the time they get here the crisis is over ... or we've taken care of it ourselves.* —Rural Wisconsin resident

Rural areas are governed as much by informal social control as by formal law enforcement efforts. Because rural locales have a tendency toward low levels of mobility, and low population density, local law enforcement officers are usually well acquainted with the criminal offenders in their communities. If, for example, a crime victim can identify the perpetrator, the local sheriff is likely to know where to find this person and to already know quite a bit about him or her, about the family, and about their social and economic circumstances—and will react to the situation in that context.

Another level of informal social control is not calling law enforcement at all, particularly in instances of minor crimes like petty theft or shoplifting. Criminal justice officials often complain that they "can't get people to tell me anything ... and if I hear about it later, and ask why they didn't call me, they tell me they took care of it." However, if a local merchant does call the police when he catches a teenager shoplifting, rather than handling the situation personally, on the spot, the merchant faces the possibility that the youngster's parents will be very upset, not because their teen committed a crime, but because the merchant involved law enforcement rather than calling them "to work it out" informally. And if the merchant presses charges, he risks a negative reaction from the wider community, particularly if the youngster involved is a star athlete or the parents are prominent in the community.

Law enforcement itself is suspicious of big government law enforcement operations, particularly in situations when they are called upon to cooperate with federal or state police agencies. According to Gale and Hartley, "rural sheriffs believe that if federal government has the funds to run special operations in rural areas, they should just give the funds to local law enforcement officials" because they know much more about who's doing what and can more efficiently and easily break up things like marijuana growing operations, which are not unusual in many rural areas."[25] This viewpoint ignores the undeniable fact that if local law enforcement knows about illegal activity and hasn't done anything about it, it is not an effective law enforcement agency.

"I know they are dealing drugs in the house across the street from me, but every time I call the police they blow me off.... It's like they're so afraid of the drug dealers they won't confront them," a woman who was a lifetime resident of a small rural town told me. "I can't remember that the police around here have ever fired a gun—they just won't get that involved."

Law enforcement styles also vary according to department size, with smaller agencies more focused on crime prevention and providing non-crime services (e.g., safety checks, elderly assistance) and larger ones being more concerned with enforcing criminal laws and controlling crime by making arrests. Rural communities have smaller policing agencies, and less complex community structures, making policing of these communities much easier, which may act as a natural deterrent to local crime. However, this also places rural police departments in the position of being called upon to provide a variety of services because other social service agencies in their counties are either entirely non-existent or too remote to easily access, particularly in a crisis situation.

We Don't Have a Policy for That—Day-by-Day Police Operations

> *The biggest county board fight in years around here was when the sheriff requested a new jail. I guess people thought they might get arrested more often if there was a place to put them, because they turned out in droves at the public hearings.* —J. Patrick Reilly, *Dodgeville Chronicle*

Frequently the number one item on any county budget is law enforcement, but that doesn't mean there is a lot of money to commit to preserving public safety. The less formal environment of rural life, together with the small size of many rural law enforcement agencies, makes complex bureaucratic written procedures less necessary for day-by-day operations, and, in reality, most issues that come through the sheriff or police department doors can be handled with a little common sense and responsiveness to the unique traits of their local community, but sometimes mistakes happen.

Recently in Judge Davis's county seat community of 6,000, local law enforcement, together with a regional drug task force, attempted a drug bust in a main street apartment building. They broke down the door of the wrong apartment, frightened an elderly couple so badly they ended up being hospitalized, and the individuals they were intending to arrest escaped—and were never caught. Local residents were unforgiving, because they believed the local police knew who lived in the apartments and "should've gotten it right." The local police chief said the city would pay to replace the door and acknowledged they didn't have "well thought out policies" to deal with an arrest effort involving other agencies. The locals felt that their law enforcement agency should "plan better and not make such a stupid mistake."

Most small rural law enforcement efforts suffer from lack of sufficient resources and being thinly stretched across a vast geographic area. In poor rural counties the degree and extent of poverty directly impacts its tax base, which in turn affects the amount of money the county is able to generate to pay for county law enforcement services. It is not difficult to imagine that an adequately staffed, fully resourced rural law enforcement agency is an extreme rarity. But one thing that almost all rural sheriffs' departments must deal with is the fixed costs of jail operations.

While urban jails tend to suffer from overcrowding problems, rural jails are more likely to operate under capacity. In some rural areas, sheriff departments increase their revenue stream by renting beds to house jail inmates from other jurisdictions or for the federal government. These jails are often old, poorly staffed, and unable to segregate inmates by age or provide jail services. Supervision is lacking and inmates from other than the local area are unknown to local law enforcement and find themselves isolated from quick, efficient legal representation or family contact.

Sheriffs in rural areas generally have fewer support services available to them and, as a result, they are not able to quickly or efficiently process inmates. Limited probation services may result in fewer alternatives to jail for misdemeanor offenses. And in rural areas that rely on part-time judges, the inevitable result is less than timely dispositions in bail hearings, preliminary hearings, trials and other legal proceedings requiring a judge to preside over them.

Sometimes the bottom line is that local municipalities want to have a police presence to deter strangers from spending too much time there and will ask their only law enforcement officer, who is most likely part time and jobs-shares with other small communities, to spend most of his/her time trying to catch speeders on the local roads. This identifies a police presence in the community and generates revenue in a situation where the reality is that not much happens in the town or village that actually requires police assistance.

Nevertheless, police can, and do, check on the elderly and homebound, particularly in winter, help rescue a treed cat or find a lost dog, talk to the local children about obeying the law, and referee arguments between town neighbors, so, for most small town residents, it feels good just to know they're there.

9

Go to School or Go to Work?

Is Formal Education the Answer?

> *It's pretty hard to convince a kid to stay in high school when he doesn't really like it and is already earning 10–12 bucks an hour at a job he does like.*—Pete Ryan, rural school district board

"Keeping kids in school long enough to finish high school is one of the major challenges facing rural school districts," explains Pete Ryan, who served on a rural Wisconsin school district board for 20 years. His district serves about 1,000 students and includes two elementary schools, one middle school, and one high school having 445 enrollees. Ryan estimates that 70 percent of the students in the district are enrolled in the free or reduced cost lunch program for low-income families. The district employs 120 teachers and has a $7 million annual operating budget, with slightly over half of its funding coming from property tax assessments levied by the locally elected school board.

Ryan believes most families value education and see it as their child's "ticket out of town," but many, particularly those in low-income and poverty situations, don't push their teenagers hard enough to succeed academically in high school, so the kids don't move forward with their education. "Maybe families say they really want their kids to leave and get good jobs, but in reality, they don't want them to go anywhere."

Janice Fitzgerald, a former rural school district administrator in remote north-central Wisconsin agrees. "We had the achievers—kids we knew would leave the area, and probably never come back; other kids weren't great students but stuck with it and would pursue technical college degrees, and the ones who barely made it through high school, or dropped out altogether, and never intend to leave … they come from poor families and will probably remain poor all their lives."

Follow the Money

> *Only a liberal senator from Massachusetts would say that a 49 percent increase in funding for education is not enough.*—President George W. Bush

Conventional wisdom suggests that more money spent on education will result in lower poverty rates because education is commonly viewed as the road out of poverty.

Frequently the conversation ends there, without giving further consideration to where the money should be directed and how it should be spent. If the dollars are not earmarked specifically for programs to serve economically disadvantaged students, and if these programs are not carefully designed to meet these students where they are academically and raise them up from there, then all the money in the world won't give poor students what they need to move forward.

Table One outlines the per-pupil spending and rural poverty rates for the 12 Midwestern states. These data indicate that the Midwest average expenditures on education closely mirrors the nationwide average that includes both the poorest and least poor states. And although counterintuitive, the data also suggest that there is no correlation between educational spending and poverty rates, which means the educational dollars are finding their way to the places where they are needed most to do the labor-intensive work of helping poor students learn and keeping them in school.

Table One: Midwestern States 2010 Per-Pupil Funding Amounts, Sources and National Ranking for Elementary and Secondary Schools[1]

State	Total Education dollars* (rank)	Federal Source (rank)	State Source (rank)	Local Source (rank)	Total Funding (rank)	Instruction Per-pupil cost (rank)	Rural Poverty Rate
IL	$13,124 (16)	$1,816 (11)	$4,145 (40)	$7,162 (11)	$11,634 (16)	6,920 (20)	14.5%
IN	13,374 (17)	1,440 (35)	7,156 (9)	4,778 (25)	9,611 (31)	5,594 (34)	14.2
IA	11,264 (31)	1,483 (32)	4,515 (37)	5,267 (17)	9,763 (27)	6,046 (27)	12.5
KS	11,566 (26)	1,429 (36)	6,069 (16)	4,068 (34)	9,715 (28)	6,016 (28)	14.9
MI	12,081 (24)	1,564 (27)	6,362 (15)	4,154 (33)	10,664 (23)	6,206 (25)	17.0
MN	12,757 (21)	1,554 (28)	7,459 (7)	3,744 (36)	10,685 (22)	7,082 (17)	12.4
MO	10,596 (38)	1,594 (23)	3,869 (47)	5,132 (20)	9,634 (29)	5,836 (30)	18.8
NE	12,353 (22)	1,579 (25)	4,018 (43)	6,757 (12)	10,734 (21)	7,085 (16)	12.5
ND	13,273 (18)	2,926 (1)	5,817 (20)	4,529 (28)	10,991 (20)	6,604 (21)	12.9
OH	13,531 (16)	1,384 (38)	5,982 (17)	6,165 (19)	11,030 (14)	6,171 (26)	16.1
SD	10,437 (41)	2,028 (6)	3,226 (49)	5,183 (19)	8,858 (40)	5,336 (36)	12.2
WI	12,775 (20)	1,290 (42)	5,725 (22)	5,760 (16)	11,364 (18)	6,931 (19)	13.1
Midwest average	12,261	1,674	5,362	5,225	10,390	6,319	14.25
U.S. average	12,305	1,535	5,352	5,419	10,615	6,478	17.7

*Includes expenditures for adult education programs, community educational services, and other non-elementary/secondary education programs.

Looking at the Midwestern states, Missouri has the highest rural poverty rate, and its educational spending is 38th, while Michigan has a poverty rate nearly as high as Missouri's, and its total educational spending, at 24th nationwide, is considerably higher. South Dakota has the lowest rural poverty rate, and its total education spending, at 41st, is considerably lower than Michigan's and Missouri's.

Ohio spends the most on education, ranking 16th nationwide, and its rural poverty rate is 16.1 percent, third highest among the Midwestern states. Nebraska ranks highest in per pupil instructional spending, at 16th nationwide. Nebraska's rural poverty rate is among the lower, at 12.5 percent. South Dakota spends the least on per-pupil instruction, ranking 36th nationwide, yet the state has a 12.2 percent rural poverty rate.

To put these findings in perspective, Washington, D.C., ranks first in the nation in overall spending for primary and secondary education and has had a consistently high 19.5 percent poverty rate for many years. Utah ranks 51st in overall primary and secondary education spending yet has a poverty rate slightly lower than the national average.

The most likely explanation for educational spending failing to impact rural poverty rates is that successful students from poor homes in rural areas leave to go where the jobs are and rarely return to their communities. As a result, money spent on rural education does not directly impact the rural poverty rate; instead it contributes to an exodus of successful students. "Good jobs are what help rural areas come out of poverty, not quality education," a rural Wisconsin school district administrator observed. "Quality education not lifting people out of poverty is true from the standpoint that this population of people never leave the area and relocate where adequate vocational opportunities exist," he said.

Funding sources are another important, albeit complex, variable in the total picture of educational funding. In many states school funding is interwoven with property tax assessments, and many states cap annual property tax increases, meaning schools are limited in how much they can assess tax payers to pay for education.

In affluent, middle and upper middle class suburban areas, houses are nicer and lots are larger, so property taxes, the chief local funding source for education, are typically higher than in rural areas, thereby establishing a higher baseline from which to assess taxes and generating more money. Some states provide less state aid to school districts with higher property values, even though net incomes in these districts are low.

In rural areas, property taxes, which are levied by local county boards and include assessments for schools and other public services, vary according to land use, and agricultural land is taxed at a much lower rate than residential or business property. In a largely rural, primarily agricultural county, the amount of tax money generated, which must be divided among public services, schools, law enforcement, and county government, can be relatively small even when the amount of taxable land is large. Minnesota ranks 36th nationwide and lowest among the Midwestern states in the amount of local dollars generated for educational spending, while Illinois, at 11th, ranks highest.

When schools need more money than property taxes can generate, their only option is to go to referendum, asking voters to agree to higher taxes so schools will have more money. School districts typically go to referendum for purposes of repairing and building buildings, closing or consolidating schools as a cost-saving measure, and for additional operating dollars. In rural areas where money is tight, referenda often fail, leaving schools with no alternative other than making draconian cuts to staff and services. "In our school district, in the last ten years, we've had to cut 88 employees, reduce employee benefits, eliminate 10 bus routes, and deferred desperately needed maintenance, sometimes adding up to a million dollars in just one year, so we can make budget," says rural Wisconsin school board president Mike Bolding.[2]

Another school funding source is state aid, which is tied to student enrollment. Rural schools typically have smaller enrollments, thus receive fewer state dollars overall. These schools also pay their teachers less; their teachers are more likely to be hired from a local hiring pool, thus may have fewer qualifications and less experience than those in more affluent schools; and rural teachers are often expected to do more than one job.

It's not unusual for the middle school principal to also be the high school athletic director; the district administrator to be the district finance director and go-to person for technology issues; or for the math teacher to also coach basketball and teach Spanish I. When one position is eliminated, one salary might be saved but several jobs are vacated. As a result, rural schools have fewer overall resources, yet must work equally as hard as urban and suburban schools to meet the national No Child Left Behind[3] educational achievement expectations, absorb much higher transportation costs than urban schools, and work within a bare bones educational infrastructure.

Another important issue pertaining to per-pupil expenditures is the difference between total per-pupil educational costs, which include teacher salaries and administrative costs, and per-pupil instructional costs, which are the dollars that go directly into resources needed to teach students, and include things like computers, laboratory equipment, text books, library books, art supplies, and on-line instructional programs.

The gap between total per-pupil educational dollars invested in education and total per-pupil instructional costs is a good indicator of teacher salaries, paid benefits, and administrative costs. This gap is particularly wide in Indiana, Missouri and Ohio, three states with higher than Midwest average rural poverty.[4]

In Indiana, whose rural poverty rate is close to the Midwestern average, the difference between total educational costs and total per-pupil costs is $4,017. Indiana ranks 37th nationally in teacher salaries and 19th in paid teacher benefits.

Missouri, the Midwestern state having the highest poverty rate, which is 1.1 percent higher than the national rural poverty rate, shows a difference of nearly $3,800 per student. The state ranks 27th in teacher salaries and 36th in teacher benefits.

Ohio, whose rural poverty rate is third highest among the Midwestern states, has a difference of $4,859 between per-pupil instructional costs and total per-pupil educational spending. Ohio ranks 21st in teacher salaries and 24th in paid benefits.

Overall, these numbers suggest there is no correlation between teacher salaries, per-pupil instructional spending, and rural poverty rates among the Midwestern states. In other words, the amount of money invested in pupil instruction and/or in teacher salaries has no discernible positive effect on rural (or urban) poverty rates because it is across-the-board spending and not targeted toward the greatest need.

Fitzgerald suggests another reason for this non-effect is that small rural school budgets can be too easily decimated by the cost of meeting the educational requirements of special needs students. "Low birth-weight babies are a huge problem in rural areas, partly because of the high number of teenage mothers, but also because of a lack of access to prenatal care," she explains. "When these kids start school they nearly always have special needs the school district is legally obligated to provide for, and this includes hiring teacher aides, providing adaptive educational equipment, transportation, and personal assistants. Those costs add up very fast, and it all comes out of the general instruction funds, which have to be shared by everybody. Small districts don't have handicap equipped classrooms, or special education classes, so each child's needs have to be met on an individual level," she says.

But meeting the special educational needs of one group of children clearly is not the whole story. Other variables come into play when trying to determine why dollars spent on education don't equate with lower rural poverty rates, particularly when the rural poverty rates have remained fairly steady or risen in recent years, and dollars spent on education has steadily increased. However, to date these have not been clearly identified.

In reality, having children who attend public school is an added expense for poor families. Even with income-based fee reductions that include free or reduced-cost lunch, parents must purchase school supplies, pay activity fees and meet other incidental costs that come with attending school.

Su Scott, whose family income varies between 25 percent below and 133 percent above the poverty line, has three children attending public school. "It's very hard to say no to the kids when they want to participate in sports and other activities, but it costs us several hundred dollars for athletic equipment and band uniforms, instrument rental, gym clothes and dance costumes," she says. "And that doesn't include the gas money to travel for their games ... it all adds up fast ... and none of this helps them get better grades." She adds that keeping her kids supplied with the electronics and clothes they want and think they need is another school expense. She and her husband both have degrees from the local technical college and want their children to do well in school, but the kids have no plans to go on with their education after finishing high school.

Who's in Charge?

> *The word "public" in public school refers to the fact that it is the citizens themselves who control the public schools. In most states, they do this in part by electing a school board of—depending on the size and configuration of the district—three, five or seven members who must be residents of the school district.*
> —National Association of School Boards

Locally elected school boards are the educational policy–setting bodies around issues of discipline (including suspensions), curriculum, sports, staffing and extra-curricular activities, extra-curricular participation fees, and even controversial issues such as allowing prayer in the local public schools. The school board establishes a vision for the community's schools within its district that reflects a consensus of the board and adheres to common community-held values.

Additionally, the school board is responsible for adopting a balanced annual budget and issuing interim financial reports, adopting the school calendar, negotiating contracts with employee unions, approving curriculum materials, school maintenance, construction and making decisions about school closings. Commonly, school boards must address questions such as: What philosophy of education do we want our local schools to have? What should our students know and be able to do when they graduate? How can our schools best educate students who come from diverse backgrounds? This last question is vitally important in small rural school districts faced with meeting the needs of economically disadvantaged and academically challenged students on a limited budget.

Local public school boards are the smallest units of government a citizen can be elected to; nevertheless, in rural communities school board positions are considered a very important form of public service—sometimes. "I've had some great school boards some years, especially when somebody new comes into town and runs for the board. If they win, new blood is infused into the group, which is very good. Other years positions go vacant," says James Burton, superintendent of a small Wisconsin school district in a community of 1,000.

"Most of the time the school board is made up of local folks who graduated from our high school and never left the community. Right now I have a couple members who have been getting re-elected to the school board off and on for over 30 years. They tend to run for the board when one of their kids or grandkids is enrolled in school and go off when they don't have anyone in school. Recently a young mother who moved into the area because her husband inherited the family's home farm was elected in an uncontested race."

A rural reality is that in small communities where everyone is known to everyone else, school boards don't always function in the best interests of the school district. It can be very difficult to fire, or even discipline, a poor teacher when she is a neighbor, a friend, a friend's friend or distantly related to one or more school board members, and in a small town, this includes nearly everyone. It can be even more difficult to suspend a star athlete for failing to adhere to the athletic code of conduct for the same reason, with the added layer being that the team is small and doesn't have a lot of other talent to fall back on.

"These are difficult issues, no question about it, but the worst ones are when the sons and daughters of the local community movers and shakers get caught cheating and their parents think we should look the other way," Burton says.

School board member Ryan says the worst cheating scandal he recalls is when a prominent local business owner's daughter got caught cheating in her junior year of high school and the National Honor Society advisor refused to induct her. "Her parents never questioned the fact she cheated; they just thought it should be overlooked, and brought the issue directly to the school board. The board backed the honor society advisor, but it wasn't unanimous. If I recall correctly, it was only by one vote. What I never understood is that the parents went to the local newspaper with the story."

Another school governance issue is that rarely do poor families in rural areas have representation or advocates on a local school board and, as a result, they have no voice in school policy decisions directly affecting them. Burton, Ryan and Fitzgerald all agree that, for the most part, when parents of high-achieving, high-academic-potential students are on the school board, the focus of the board will be toward promoting and supporting activities aimed at enriching the highest-achieving, highest-potential students—leaving poor students, who are in the minority, behind. "Often economically disadvantaged parents aren't articulate and are very uncomfortable appearing before the school board to argue an issue, so they don't show up to advocate for their kids," Burton explained.

Generally speaking, community residents are willing to serve on local school boards because they can be powerful positions in small communities. But school board meetings are always reported in the local newspaper and no school board decision goes unnoticed. Consequently many potential candidates decide the hassles and time commitment aren't worth it. As a result, often school board elections go uncontested, and seats are left vacant. In the 2014 school board elections in a rural Wisconsin county of 22,000 having seven school districts serving 4,000 students, 12 positions were up for election; five had no candidates, three had no challenger, and only four were contested.

Homeschooling—The Cheap Alternative

> *Homeschooling and public schooling are as opposite as two sides of a coin. In a homeschooling environment, the teacher need not be certified, but the child MUST learn. In a public school environment, the teacher MUST be certified, but the child need NOT learn.* —Gene Royer

The homeschooling movement originally arose from conservative religious groups' objections to the contents of public school curriculums. Today parents home school their children for a variety of reasons, that can include religious preference, expenses associated with attending public schools, a personal desire to teach one's own children, convenience, or having a child who has had difficulty adjusting to the public school environment. Some parents prefer homeschooling as an alternative means for educating children because they retain total control over the child's educational experience.

In most states homeschooling is not carefully regulated and Royer, a vocal homeschooling advocate, is wrong about the necessity for homeschooled children to learn, because most states don't have a systematic means for assessing whether learning occurs in the homeschool environment. "We don't regulate home schooling very well at all. We really need to do a better job with it," Fitzgerald says.

Whether homeschooling is less expensive than sending children to public school is debatable. On the face of it, homeschooled children don't pay activity fees, don't find themselves having to compete with other children in terms of clothing, electronics, sports, and other activities, and are not vulnerable to bullying as a consequence of not always having what other children have or being somehow "different" because of their socio-economic status. However, homeschooling a child requires a parent to be home to do it, and this can mean giving up opportunities to be employed and generate an income.

"We have eight kids, and it's cheaper for me to home school them than to send them to school and try to get a job—all my salary would go to paying for the kids' school stuff," says Autume Jones. She and her husband are raising their family on $37,000 per year, which, for a family that size, is $10,000 below the poverty line. Jones feels she is "doing a pretty good job" teaching her children and, at the same time, is protecting them from the "unkindnesses" that comes from being poor. She relies heavily on the resources available through the public library and manages to pick up used text books and other materials. But there is no way to know whether her children are learning at grade level, or learning at all, because there are no testing requirements they must meet. So the question of whether this mode of education, which is cheaper for this family in the short run, is disadvantageous for these children and limiting their futures is unanswerable.

Other Educational Options

> *We try very hard to make the local schools work for our kids, because the reality is, they don't have any other choices.* —Pat Ryan

School choice, whereby public school children can elect to attend a school outside their district, or receive a school voucher to attend a private school, is not a common practice in rural areas. Practically speaking, most rural public school districts only have one grade, middle and high school, and the next school district can be many miles away. Most rural parents don't have either the time or the gas money needed to transport their children to a school beyond the one the local school bus delivers them to daily.

Some rural communities have a private, church-affiliated school. Most often these are Catholic schools, which give admission preference to Catholic families and charge tuition. And some states have on-line public education opportunities available to students in upper grades. While these are technically tuition-free, there are book and supply costs, including access to a personal computer and Internet—and not all rural areas have broadband systems large enough to enable Internet access.

Unfortunately, rural schools often don't work very well for poor kids, who need educational assistance the most, yet are least likely to receive it. "It's just human nature for teachers to throw their greatest efforts at kids they know are likely to succeed," Fitzgerald says. "Poor kids probably aren't going any further in school, so they don't get as much attention as the kid who's headed for the university ... and the star athletes who are candidates for college athletic scholarships really get attention. It's not right, but it happens."

Another reality is that rural schools don't have the resources to hire a lot of teachers or spend a lot of money on supplemental teaching aids, so classes are large, and no one student is likely to receive a lot of individual attention. The self-starters, advantaged by a lot of parental support to succeed, quickly rise to the top, and it's all too easy for the others to be left behind to fend for themselves.

A Community Without a School Isn't Really a Community

> *If we lose this school, we might as well all pack up and leave, because we won't have a community any more.* —Parent speaking at a rural school funding meeting

The profound impact a local school has on a small rural community is something everyone is aware of, but rarely talk about. Besides being a place fairly close to home where their child can get an education, having a high school football or basketball team brings the entire community together on Friday nights through the fall and winter, and everyone looks forward to the school carnival in the spring. Bake sales and other fundraisers draw mothers together socially, and school sports teams provide coaching opportunities for dads. None of these would occur without the local school, which is an important informal social networking site for nearly all families in the community— if they can afford to participate. "I'm not sure why it is, but we don't see the parents of poor kids at school social events very often," Fitzgerald says. "Maybe they don't feel as welcome, don't know the other parents, or just feel like outsiders."

Local schools are often the biggest local employer, and they provide good jobs with decent retirement and health insurance benefits, particularly in states where teachers are unionized.[5] As an economic entity, schools also purchase goods and services from local businesses. Fueling the local school buses is likely the largest account the local gas station has. Milk and non-commodity food is often purchased in bulk through the local grocer. And the local hardware store probably supplies most of the tools and equipment for the school's maintenance staff. Despite these benefits, not all families are 100 percent behind the school and the extracurricular activities it provides.

"Farm kids are needed at home after school to help out, so they can't stay for football practice, drama club or debate classes," Ryan explains, "and this cuts deep into their school experience ... until pretty soon school isn't much fun for them.... The other thing is that participating in sports is expensive. Some kids can't afford the fees, and their parents don't have the time, or gas money, to travel for their games, so they're socially excluded as a family and as students."

A difficult truth facing rural education is that rural schools have also contributed to the decline of rural communities in several ways: One is that by focusing on the best and brightest students, who are also the easiest to teach, these schools are, albeit indirectly, creating an educational vortex that encourages outward mobility of the best and brightest who, if they did not leave, would mature into future community leaders.[6] As a result those who are left behind to lead by default, because there is no one else to step up, are not always well prepared for this role. When searching for leadership, often rural communities must skim off the bottom.

Second, students who exit the community and do not return after receiving additional education take with them an economic potential that the community needs and can't compensate for losing. Chances are a small rural community will never recover what it loses when the brightest students leave.

Third, rural school districts usually cannot generate sufficient local resources to adequately supplement the state school finance programs the way more affluent localities can, forcing difficult school budget and enrollment decisions that have forced rural schools to consolidate. Rural schools are pushed into turning their backs on their important role in sustaining the life of their communities.

"The problem is that the school is a major employer in a small town, and it's also the one institution that nearly every person in town has an interest in—either their own children or grandchildren are currently enrolled, and they probably attended the school themselves, so there's a lot of emotion tied up in what is, in reality, a financial and business decision," says Fitzgerald. Ryan agrees that school consolidation is a "very emotional" issue for a community, plus taking away the community school is decimating a major source of social connections and activity for everybody. "Even people who don't have kids or grand kids playing sports show up at the games because, let's face it, it's fun watching young athletes compete.... At least four pages of every issue of the local newspaper are devoted to school sports."

Core Standards and No Child Left Behind

> These reforms express my deep belief in our public schools and their mission to build the mind and character of every child, from every background, in every part of America. —President George W. Bush

Three days after taking office in January 2001 George W. Bush announced the No Child Left Behind (NCLB) initiative—a framework for bipartisan education reform that he described as "the cornerstone of my administration." President Bush emphasized his deep belief in our public schools, but an even greater concern that "too many of our neediest children are being left behind," despite the nearly $200 billion in federal spending since the passage of the Elementary and Secondary Education Act of 1965 (ESEA). The new law reflects a remarkable political consensus—first articulated in the President's No Child Left Behind framework—on how to improve the performance of America's elementary and secondary schools while at the same time ensuring that no child is trapped in a failing school.[7]

"The [NCLB] legislation is devastating to rural school districts," says Burton. "This is an unfunded mandate,[8] and we don't have the money to meet the requirements, but if we don't meet them we end up on a watch list and parents really don't like the idea that their child's school is underperforming, and on top of that, their tax dollars are paying for it."

The NCLB Act, which reauthorizes the ESEA, incorporates the principles and strategies aimed at accountability for states, school districts, and individual schools; greater choice for parents and students, particularly those attending low-performing schools; more flexibility for states and local educational agencies in the use of federal education dollars; and a stronger emphasis on reading, especially for children in lower grades.

The NCLB Act requires states to implement statewide accountability systems covering all public schools and students based on established state standards in reading and mathematics, annual testing for all students in grades three through eight, and annual statewide progress objectives ensuring that all groups of students reach subject matter proficiency levels within 12 years. Assessment results and state progress objectives must be broken out by poverty, race, ethnicity, disability, and limited English proficiency to ensure that no group is left behind. School districts and schools that fail to make adequate yearly progress (AYP) toward statewide proficiency goals will, over time, be subject to corrective action and restructuring measures aimed at getting them back on course toward meeting state standards. Schools that meet or exceed AYP objectives or close achievement gaps will be eligible for Academic Achievement Awards.

Although the NCLB legislation significantly increases the choices available to the parents of students attending Title I schools that fail to meet state standards, the reality is that, in rural areas, this is meaningless. The local school is the only one available for many miles, and most parents and children don't want to spend excessive amounts of time traveling to and from a school in a neighboring district, particularly when their friends are in the home school. And requiring districts to fund transportation costs for students who leave the district for another one adds a significant financial burden onto schools that don't have enough money to begin with. Nevertheless, according to the law, schools that fail to make AYP for five years run the risk of being reconstituted under a restructuring plan, which is guaranteed to hit rural schools hardest.

Another provision of the NCLB legislation pertains to teacher qualifications, again a difficult challenge for rural schools. Schools are required to demonstrate annual progress in ensuring that all teachers teaching in core academic subjects are "highly qualified," meaning they have educational degrees in the subject matter they teach, and are not teaching subjects for which they have no formal training. In other words, a high school math teacher must have a college degree in mathematics and teachers having English degrees are not teaching classes in the natural or social sciences.

Burton says finding qualified teachers willing to come to rural areas is an "enormous" challenge. "New graduates and young teachers want to go someplace where there's a social life—they don't want to be stuck out in the boonies 50 miles from the nearest Starbucks."

Ryan echoes this observation. "Unless a young teacher has family in the area to hold her here, she's looking for another job before the ink is dry on her hiring contract." He adds that, in his view, it's not true that "a good teacher can teach anything."

"Parents were pressuring us for more foreign language options, so we had the French teacher teaching Spanish I and it didn't work well at all. She sat in the classroom with an iPhone looking up words and looking for the answers to student questions, and her pronunciation was apparently very poor." Ryan steadfastly believes most rural schools are "really good schools" but they don't necessarily have all the bells and whistles urban and suburban schools enjoy, so they aren't as much fun for teachers to teach in. "You have to have a deep, deep commitment to education to teach in a rural school," he says.

In addition to working toward meeting the NCLB standards, many states have also adopted common core "should know" curriculum standards (CCCS) in mathematics and the language arts in grades K-12. Proponents claim this represents a move toward better overall education and elimination of wide variations in the quality of education nationwide, as well as providing a consistent, clear understanding of what students are expected to learn, as set forth, for example, in the 2014 Common Core State Standards Initiative.[9]

"Every one of our students deserves the opportunity to graduate from high school with the knowledge and skills necessary for college and career success," says Boston Public Schools superintendent Carol Johnson, who chairs the Great City Schools Council Panel on Core Curriculum State Standards,[10] which pushed this idea forward nationally, without much thought for its effect on rural schools. "These national standards help raise the bar for schools, educators and students alike, moving us closer to our ultimate goal of closing achievement gaps and putting all of our children on the path to a bright future," she adds. This sounds solid and doable, particularly for urban schools; the fly in the ointment for rural schools is finding enough teachers trained to implement the standards and figuring out how they are going to pay for it.

Critics view the CCCS idea as too vague and lacking well-developed curriculum guidelines to assist teachers in implementing the standards. Opposition has also been fueled by a drop in student assessment scores in some states that have moved forward with CCCS implementation which, not surprisingly, caused an uproar among both parents and students and cast serious doubt on whether they are such a good idea after all. And they force teachers to "teach to the test," which many feel "takes all the fun" and creativity out of teaching.

Nebraska is the only Midwestern state that has not adopted CCCS. And, not everyone has bought into the CCCS idea in states where they have been adopted, partly because the idea was originally conceived and promoted by the National Governors Association, thus flying in the face of all-important local control over what is taught in local public schools, as well as being seen by many as a step closer to government taking control of education.

Successful implementation of CCCS is a state responsibility, and most states are not so naïve as to expect rural schools to be able to meet the core curriculum requirements without assistance. Thus, unlike NCLB legislation, most states that committed to implementing core curriculum standards have put at least a few dollars into the effort. It won't be enough to cover the costs in rural schools, but rural schools, like rural people themselves, are skilled at making things work and are not likely to be left entirely in the dust regarding this educational initiative.

Virtual Schools

> *I'm not sure about on-line classes; we don't really get to know the students and there are risks associated with that. I once recommended a student for advanced study in a human services discipline, and when I finally met him face to face I realized I'd made a terrible mistake.*—Online technical college course instructor

Virtual schools come in all sizes, including post-secondary formats, and vary in cost from nothing to a hefty per-course fee, even for students still enrolled in publicly funded middle or high schools.[11] Some view virtual schools as the school choice answer for students who are unhappy with the educational prospects their local school district offers and as a valuable post-secondary education option to those who cannot receive an advanced education any other way; others believe they rob students of the all-important social experiences that come with middle and high school and lack sufficient oversight to guarantee a respectable level of quality control.

In most states that have virtual public schools, they are used as a supplemental online course provider that partners with school districts to offer online courses to middle and high school students. Generally, school district participation is optional, and there is a cost to the districts involved, making this option beyond the reach of poorer rural school districts.

There are some definite advantages to virtual school options, including an expanded curriculum, and more educational options for students. The chief reasons students elect to participate in virtual school learning include:

- Accessing course not offered locally
- Course or work schedule conflicts
- Home-schooled, homebound or temporarily living outside the home district
- Recovering credit from a failed or incomplete course
- Grade acceleration/enrichment
- Having been expelled and wanting to continue with school

Students choosing to participate in online courses are advised to carefully examine their personal skills and aptitudes for taking a class online. To succeed in a virtual school, students must possess certain attributes:

- Self-motivation: Students must be able to direct their own learning environment, fulfill course requirements, and achieve individual academic success.
- Skills as an independent learner: The online environment enables students to learn at their own pace—traditional, extended, or accelerated—relieving the stress of feeling rushed or pressured and providing enjoyment in the learning process.
- Computer literacy: Although it is not necessary to have advanced computer skills, students should possess a working knowledge of e-mail, the Internet, and basic keyboarding and word processing skills.
- Good time-management skills: Students must be able to organize and plan their own best "time to learn." There is no one best time for everyone, but the key to learning is to commit the time to learn.
- Effective written communication skills: Students must use e-mail and discussion boards to communicate with their peers as well as the instructors. The ability to write clearly in order to communicate ideas and assignments is very important to student success as well as a means to inform instructors of any concerns or problems.
- Personal commitment: Since there are no bells that begin and end classes, students must have a strong desire to learn and achieve knowledge and skills via online courses.

Making a commitment to learn in this manner is a very personal decision and requires a strong commitment to participate in order to achieve academic success.

Obviously, virtual schools are not the "wave of the future" that guarantees an education for poor children, particularly those in rural areas. The virtual education opportunities offered through public school districts have course enrollment fees and students must own a computer. It is also necessary to have ongoing Internet access, which is not available in all rural areas. And most rural school districts cannot afford to supply each student with a personal computer. Thus a student living in a poor family, even if he/she could scrape up the money for the course fee, would have to use the school or public library computer to do the required assignments, and these are only available during certain hours and for limited amounts of time.

Post-Secondary Virtual Education Options

Online learning is the future of American education. Precisely because it's so transforming, it's threatening to the established institutions. —Terry Moe

Virtual schools as a post-secondary education option are slightly different from what the public schools offer. Most are for-profit educational endeavors, are accredited by some educational accreditation agency, and offer various educational options to non-traditional students. Financial aid in the form of student loans and grants is available, but per-credit fees can be substantial, and sometimes there are residency requirements that must be met before a degree is awarded.

Using Capella University, a for-profit higher education initiative, as an example of on-line college education costs, and assuming a 125 credit minimum requirement to receive a bachelor's degree, the total tuition cost is between $38,125 and $45,000.[12] This figure excludes the cost of books, other supplies, and program residency requirements, which entail self-funded travel plus room and board costs for students outside the greater Minneapolis area where Capella is based. While the overall cost is considerably less than attending a traditional college or university, it is still substantial, and nearly out of reach for someone who comes from an impoverished background, most likely would be working full time while attending this school, and have great difficulty funding the residency requirements and other associated costs.

Charter Schools

> *By the way, school choice was only open to rich people up until No Child Left Behind. It's hard for a lot of parents to be able to afford to go to any other kind of school but their neighborhood school. And now, under this system, if your public school is failing, you'll have the option of transferring to another public school or charter school. And it's—I view that as liberation; I view that as empowerment.* —President George W. Bush

Charter schools are schools of choice whereby parents and students are able to choose to enroll in a school that may offer a unique learning environment and alternative teaching and learning methodologies. Teachers and administrators have more authority to make decisions than occurs in most traditional public schools. Charter schools are free from many of the regulations that apply to traditional public schools, tend to be small (median enrollment is 242 students compared to 539 in traditional public schools) and serve different communities with a wide variety of curriculum and instructional practices.[13]

Charters are granted for a particular period of time, usually for 3–5 years, and are renewed after the end of the term by the granting entity. The charter itself is a performance contract that provides details about that school's mission, program, goals, target student population, methods of learning assessment, and ways to measure success—i.e., a business plan. These schools are under constant pressure to perform well, as they are accountable to their sponsor, usually a state or local school board, for good academic results. The charter school administration must adhere to their charter contract; however, in reality these schools enjoy greater autonomy in return for accountability. Instead of being asked to comply with various rules and regulations, they are measured on the yardstick of academic results and adherence to their charter.

In order for a charter school to work, the proper state legislation must be in place, there must be available people who want to run the charter school, and the state's authorizing entity (usually a board) must be functioning. To open a charter school, the administrators must first submit a charter school proposal to their state's charter authorizing entity, which varies from state to state depending on the state's charter law. Generally, four types of entities authorize charter schools: the local school board, state universities, community colleges, and the state board of education.

In most states, the spirit of the legislation governing charter schools intends to:

- Increase opportunities for learning and provide access to quality education for people

- Create choices for parents and students within the public school system
- Provide a system of accountability for results in public education
- Encourage innovative teaching practices
- Create new professional opportunities for teachers
- Encourage community and parent involvement in public education
- Leverage improved public education

Charter schools have shown promising, but mixed, results over the years. Though more data is needed, overall these schools appear to be faring well. On the one hand there are success stories whereby some charter schools receive renewals of their charters because they met the goals of their charter. On the other hand, there are schools whose charters have been revoked due to lack of proper financial management or lack of achievement.

Charter schools often serve the special educational needs of severely impoverished children much better than conventional public school environments but are very rarely available as a school choice option in rural areas. However, this may be changing because Goodwill Industries, which serves the poor through retail second hand stores and focuses on "eliminating barriers to opportunity and helping people reach their full potential through learning and the power of work," has entered into the world of charter schools.[14]

The Goodwill charter school model was first implemented in central Indiana and opened with a view toward providing adults who failed to complete high school with an opportunity to earn a high school diploma, rather than obtain a general educational development (GED) certificate, and prepare them for further education and career preparation. Students are provided with learning coaches who are responsible for keeping them engaged in the learning process.

"The relationship that coaches create with each student is a critical factor in student success, as that relationship will provide security, confidence and encouragement for students to continue when the work becomes difficult and life barriers become difficult to manage," the charter school application states. "Coaches will work with students to identify potential barriers to students' continued education, whether through short-term barriers such as housing and childcare or long-term challenges, including student self-efficacy and self-confidence."

Termed the Excel Center, each Goodwill charter school serves several hundred students, often partnering with local community or technical colleges to seamlessly move students beyond a high school diploma on to career specific training. "An Excel Center helps some of the more disadvantaged members of the local community become skilled and productive members of the workforce," the universal Goodwill charter school application states.

Excel Center schools have flexible hours to accommodate working adults, pay for bus passes for students who can't afford transportation otherwise, and provide free, on-site child care. Nearly 70 percent of the student population in the Indiana Excel Center schools qualify for free and reduced-price lunch.

The Indiana Excel Center schools have been operating since 2010, and student performance data do not paint a picture of overwhelming success. Thirty-seven percent of students passed the English 10 end-of-course assessment; 45 percent passed the Algebra I end-of-course assessment; and the graduation rate was 15.2 percent. Nevertheless, these schools are providing educational opportunities for individuals who would not be receiving them otherwise and the concept appears to be catching on.

"Since the opening of the Excel Center in 2010, many organizations and community leaders across Indiana have asked whether it would be possible to open an Excel Center in their local community," the charter school application states. "The Excel Center will allow more students to have stable, convenient access to an educational model designed around the unique needs of adults who have dropped out of school." And because there are Goodwill stores in most rural areas, this educational and training opportunity is reaching deeper than other educational initiatives into areas where it is needed.

Technical and Community Colleges

> *Anyone who doubts that Wisconsin's technical colleges are the proven solution should ask themselves, "If not the technical colleges, then whom?" There is simply no other organization with the expertise, resources, programs, employer relationships, and demonstrated success.* —Duane R. Ford

In many ways technical and community colleges are the educational savior of rural areas because they are much more affordable and have much less rigorous admission standards than four-year post-secondary schools and focus exclusively on job skill training. According to Wisconsin's Department of Workforce Development (DWD) there are 32,000–45,000 jobs currently (2013) available in Wisconsin.[15] The majority of these require the mid-level skills and credentials provided by technical colleges. DWD also indicates employers report difficulties finding properly skilled workers. According to the technical colleges budget proposal to the Wisconsin legislature, Wisconsin has a skills gap.

"Furthermore, the problem may only get worse ... the technical colleges estimate a need over the next two years for at least 39,000 more skilled workers than they have the capacity to train," according to the DWD.

Unquestionably the Wisconsin Technical College System (WTCS), like most technical and community colleges, has a proven track record of success. The WTCS schools offer more than 450 degree, diploma, and apprenticeship programs aimed at preparing new workers. Each program has an employer advisory committee to ensure graduates obtain the skills and credentials employers need. The colleges also are the major provider of responsive, flexible, onsite, customized training for workers currently employed by Wisconsin's businesses and industries. The Wisconsin model is a universal one used by most technical and community colleges nationwide.

WTCS serves 370,000 students per year. Its annual number of graduates, also known as "new workers," has increased 54 percent during the past decade and nearly 90 percent of the graduates work in Wisconsin. Median starting salary for WTCS associate degree graduates is $36,000 and five-year studies document inflation busting wage growth. Among employers who hired 2010 graduates, 93 percent were satisfied or very satisfied with their new hires. WTCS estimates Wisconsin taxpayers realize a $12.20 return, in added taxable income and avoided social costs, on every $1 spent on the WTCS.[16]

However, WTCS's ability to address Wisconsin's skills gap is limited by three issues. There are "pipeline issues" that result in under-enrolled programs. "Capacity issues" exist in programs filled with students, yet the number is still insufficient to meet employers' needs. "Flexibility issues" exist when technical colleges lack the financial or physical resources or when non-value-adding federal or state policies hamper their ability to respond to employers' needs.

Regardless, it's very difficult to envision a rural world that does not include widespread access to technical or community college training for those who are unable, because of financial or achievement problems, to obtain post-secondary education that will prepare them to enter the workforce. In rural areas the curriculums always include a focus on agricultural, mechanical, health care and secretarial skills, in addition to information technology, various leadership and professional development workshops, in-service and continuing education credit opportunities, and enrichment classes, among others.

However, a particular strength of technical college courses is that they are taught by instructors who have a breadth of knowledge and direct experience working in the subject-matter area. A definite weakness of technical college education is that often the instructors do not have a background in teaching methodology or extensive experience working with students in a learning-centered environment, and thus may not be able to work with those for whom learning is particularly difficult.

Technical and community colleges are able to offer various forms of financial aid, and their tuition structure is considerably less costly than that of a traditional four-year college or university. The cost factor alone puts this option within reach of a great many low-income individuals. Nevertheless, the issue of taking out student loans and incurring debt to pay for a college or technical degree looms large and is surrounded by questions of just how good an investment education is when "on-the-job" training can be just as effective and whether the return on the loan dollar will ever be realized.

"I understand people's concern for students graduating with significant debt; my son will be one of them," says Duane Ford, president of Southwest Wisconsin Technical College (SWTC). Ford believes the problem may not be as bad as people think. "In 2012–13, only 65 percent of the students in SWTC's financial aid eligible programs took out a federal student loan. That year, the average amount borrowed per student was $3,303. SWTC offers one- and two-year programs, so a typical graduating student might owe less than $7,000."[17]

By comparison, the University of Wisconsin System, which offers both baccalaureate and graduate degrees, reports that only 72 percent of its undergraduate (bachelor degree) students currently take out federal student loans. "Those who borrowed and graduated in 2012 owed an average of $28,002," Ford says.

Ford is not an advocate of free higher education. "All citizens, regardless of their personal financial situations, deserve the opportunity to obtain an education they can use to support and better themselves and their families, but I believe students should contribute a fair share [toward attaining an education]. Perhaps the challenge is to find the right balance between public funding and what students pay either out-of-pocket or through debt."

Ford advises students to "Buy the education you can reasonably afford. If you have to borrow, find the best interest rate options. Know that good employers care more about the skills, work ethic, and value you bring to their business than about how much you paid for an education or the logo on your diploma."

Education, Poverty and the Working Poor in Rural Areas: The Big Picture

> *Public education is the key civil rights issue of the 21st century. Our nation's knowledge-based economy demands that we provide young people from all backgrounds and circumstances with the education and skills necessary to become knowledge workers. If we don't, we run the risk of creating an even larger gap between the middle class and the poor. This gap threatens our democracy, our society and the economic future of America.* —Eli Broad

Unquestionably, the most severe challenge facing rural schools is persistent poverty. A large percent of rural residents live on a marginal income—some years below poverty and other years above poverty. This is an enormously stressful fact of life for many rural families. Yet it is not uncommon for rural school administrators to openly claim that the reason students fail is because of the families they come from. "School failure is always a family issue," Burton says. "Kids who come from good families always do better in school."

Unquestionably, poverty reduces children's opportunity to learn, both in the family and at school, but Burton's statement unfairly, and all too readily, places blame for school failure on parents, too easily forgives schools that fail to educate students, and ignores the basic philosophy of every good teacher, which is that there isn't a child alive who can't learn. The problem with teaching poor children is that often it is harder, much more labor intensive, and time consuming, but that doesn't mean it's impossible.

Research from the University of New Hampshire's Carsey Institute (CI) verifies that people living in chronically poor rural areas have among the lowest education attainment levels from generation to generation, underscoring that a lack of educational opportunities for these students has persisted for decades.[18] "There was a time, even a generation ago, when a strong back and good work ethic could mean a decent job and good life in rural America. Unfortunately, this is no longer the case. In today's increasingly competitive and unstable economy, rural Americans need increasingly higher levels of education or specialized technical skills to obtain even low-paying jobs. Thus, although education has for generations been a key predictor of economic success, it is even more important today simply for basic survival," explains Jessica Ulrich, a CI research assistant.

According to Ulrich, the research found that people living in chronically poor communities[19] had significantly lower education levels, compared with those living in amenity-rich (high levels of population growth), amenity-transition (modest to low population growth and relatively high employment and education levels), and declining communities (stagnant economic conditions and population). In Ulrich's report, 14 percent of those in chronically poor communities report not completing high school, while only 6 percent in amenity-transition, 4 percent in declining, and 2 percent in amenity-rich communities report the same. A higher percentage of respondents from chronically poor regions said high school was their highest level of education, and fewer report completing or attending college than other rural residents.

When looking at generational trends in education, nearly one-half (43 percent) of fathers from chronically poor rural areas had less than a high school education compared with only 19 percent of fathers from amenity-rich areas. Almost one-third (30 percent) of the fathers from chronically poor places completed only the eighth grade or less. Similarly, 21 percent of the mothers from chronically poor places completed only eighth grade or less.

"Growing up in households with parents with low education levels and in communities with inadequate educational opportunities makes it difficult for those growing up in chronically poor rural areas to achieve a high level of education themselves," Ulrich says.

Other key findings include:

- Educational achievement varies significantly by type of place in rural America. In chronically poor rural areas, 45 percent of residents have completed only high school or less, compared with 22 to 33 percent in amenity-rich, amenity-transition, and declining resource-dependent rural areas.
- Parents of respondents in amenity-rich and amenity-transition rural communities have higher levels of education than parents of respondents in declining and chronically poor communities.
- Although people from all types of rural communities generally have more education than their parents, those in chronically poor rural areas still have relatively low education levels—a disadvantage that persists across generations.
- Concern about school quality is highest in chronically poor rural places where education levels are lowest; however, respondents from declining resource-dependent places were less concerned about school quality than respondents from amenity-rich and amenity-transition rural communities.

"These findings highlight the importance in investing in the educational systems of chronically poor rural areas where generations of underinvestment have contributed to persistent poverty," Ulrich said.

Rural School Violence and Drugs

> *Rural America can no longer be characterized as a safe haven from crime and violence, but information on rural violence and rural school violence is limited.*—Gwen Schroth and Mary Susan Fishbaugh

The widespread availability of guns in rural areas brings the question of school violence into sharp focus and calls into question the notion that, because they are small, and teachers know students and their families well, violence is less likely in rural schools. In reality, exposure to violence does occur in rural schools at about the same rate as in urban and suburban schools. However, Schroth and Fishbaugh identify a good point in the discussion, namely that what is known about rural school violence is very limited.[20] This is due in large part to the way guns are woven into common, everyday rural life.

In a comprehensive study of rural school violence, researchers "found no evidence to support the common assumption that rural youth are protected from exposure to violence. Of the 15 measures of violent activities, none showed a significantly lower prevalence among rural teens when compared to suburban and urban teens. In fact, rural teens were more likely than urban or suburban teens to have carried a weapon within the last 30 days."[21] These results suggest that rural teens are equally or more likely than suburban and urban teens to be exposed to violent activities," the report states.

Researchers have also found that rural teens are at significantly greater risk of using drugs than both suburban and urban teens.[22] Measures of drug use show a significantly higher prevalence rate among rural teens: chewing tobacco (11.5 percent), chewing tobacco at school (7.6 percent), smoking cigarettes at school (14.8 percent), using crack/cocaine (5.9 percent), and using steroids (7.4 percent). Only one measure showed a significantly higher prevalence rate among urban teens (smoking marijuana at school at 6.8 percent). Other drug use measures showed no differences by residence.

"Of important note is the prevalence of crystal meth use among rural teens. The proportion of rural teens who reported ever using crystal meth (15.5 percent) was almost double the proportion of urban (8.8 percent) and suburban teens (9.5 percent). Crystal meth was the 4th most commonly used drug among rural teens after alcohol, cigarettes, and marijuana, making it more popular among rural teens than chewing tobacco," the study reports.

Among rural teens, only one measure of drug use differed by race: rural white teens were more likely to report chewing tobacco. This pattern was strikingly different from the racial differences found among urban teens.

Exposures to violence and drug use vary by gender among rural teens. Among rural teens, females are more likely than males to be coerced into sex or engage in suicide behaviors, while males are more likely than females to use weapons, be threatened at school, or engage in fighting behaviors. Male teens are also more likely than female teens to chew tobacco and smoke marijuana, both on and off school grounds.

With regard to school services, not surprisingly, rural schools offer somewhat fewer teen violence services and were less likely than urban schools to offer peer counseling and self-help services. Mental health-trained staff working in rural schools are often spread across several schools, thus available for fewer hours, have fewer hiring requirements, and receive training for fewer teen violence services than their counterparts in urban schools.

While rural and urban schools were equally likely to have a guidance counselor, a psychologist, and a social worker on staff, all three of these professionals were available for significantly fewer hours per week in rural schools. And during budget crunches, these are the positions most likely for rural schools to cut. "Parents can assume many of these duties," Burton told his rural school board as he explained why he wanted to cut these three positions from his school budget.

Mental health staff from rural schools were less likely than their counterparts in urban schools to receive training for certain teen violence services. Specifically, mental health care coordinators were less likely to receive training in suicide prevention, family counseling, peer counseling, and self-help, while health education coordinators in rural schools were less likely to receive training in tobacco use prevention.

One of the most important findings of this research pertains to the school environment. Overall, rural schools report fewer policies and security practices that prevent violence and drug use than do urban schools. "Rural schools were less likely than urban schools to report using several administrative policies to prevent student violence, prohibiting gang paraphernalia, student education on suicide prevention, violence prevention, tobacco use prevention, and having a council for school health."

Rural schools were more likely than urban schools to monitor school hallways and to arm their security staff, but less likely to have a closed campus, prohibit book bags, require school uniforms, or use surveillance cameras, uniformed police, undercover police, and security guards.

Rural schools are just as likely as urban schools to provide mental health services that address violence and drug use activities. However, in rural schools, prevention staff receives less training, have lower hiring requirements, and are available for fewer hours each week.

The Glory Days: High School Sports

> *I've heard people say high school is about getting an education and getting into a good college to succeed in life. It's that too, but to me, high school is about making memories and good times that will last forever.* —Pat Reilly

In 1964 all 400 Wisconsin high schools competed in the same division, in all sports, regardless of enrollment. For small rural schools, most years the talent pool to draw from was pretty thin. Then came two magical years the small town of Dodgeville is still talking about.

In 1963 the Dodgeville basketball team upset the state tournament favorite Eau Claire, then went on to lose the state championship game. In 1964 Dodgeville beat rural Merrill, then Waukesha, a large suburban Milwaukee high school, and finally defeated the tournament favorite, Milwaukee North, an even larger inner city school. Milwaukee North's basketball team was comprised of kids who had been shooting hoops since they could walk, and they were soundly defeated, 59–45, by a bunch of farm kids from some small town nobody ever heard of.

"We did it in fine Hoosiers fashion, the small school prevailing over the bigger, favored school," Pat Reilly, a member of the storied 1964 Dodgeville High School basketball team recounts. Reilly remembers it like it was yesterday, and so do his teammates. "What made it so special was we were one of the last eight teams in the state and size did not matter. We faced schools with enrollments much larger than the entire population [2,900] of our community. But in 1963 and 1964 the team made back-to-back state tournament appearances, finishing second in 1963 and then winning the gold ball in 1964."

Reilly contends it wasn't so much about winning or losing as it was about playing as a team, and for a great coach. "We were lucky to play for Weenie Wilson—a coach well ahead of his time, and for quite a while he was the only coach in the football, basketball and baseball halls of fame," Reilly says. Those who remember that game, which is just about everybody in Wisconsin over age 60 who ever followed high school sports, make the same observation—that Dodgeville was much smaller and much slower than Milwaukee North, but they were very disciplined and knew how to play as a team, and that made all the difference. They won the championship game they weren't supposed to win by 14 points, which suggests it wasn't even much of a contest.

"We didn't need movies made about our team those two years, because we lived it. I lived during that special time and every so often when I feel less happy than I should I think about those years and I am instantly cheered up. I don't think so much about the games as I do how the community came together to live through it with us. To use the term "magical years" would be selling those years way too short," Reilly, who has remained in Dodgeville his entire life, recalls 50 years later. "They were the best days of my life."

This story says everything there is to say about high school sports in small rural communities. For some kids, it's the very best time of their life, and if the team is a winning one, the entire community gets behind them, and remembers them always—and they never, ever forget that feeling that they "were somebody important." It's not the same in bigger schools, where the athletic talent pool to draw from is much larger and this year's star athlete becomes last year's news six months later when he/she is replaced by someone just as good, or even better.

In small, rural schools the talent pool in every sport can be pretty shallow, and when a really good athlete comes along, he or she is never forgotten. For rural kids who don't have as many opportunities to achieve as students from bigger schools, playing high school sports may be their one shot at glory. Even if they don't win a state championship they'll always remember the three-point basket they sank that won the game, the 75-yard touchdown run that had everybody in town on their feet, or the grand slam home run out of the park.

"Sports can be the great equalizer in high school life like no other, because no matter whether you're rich or poor, if you're good, you're good, and that's what matters," Reilly says.

Those Who Make It and Those Who Don't

I don't know whether education is the whole answer or not, but you gotta start somewhere ... and nobody's come up with a better idea. —Pat Ryan

While both conventional wisdom and political rhetoric strongly suggest that education is the most direct pathway out of poverty, many questions surrounding the relationship between poverty and education remain unanswered. Chief among these is whether money spent on education as a means for getting people off the welfare rolls is a good use of taxpayer dollars, particularly in rural areas where individuals seem to be able to pick up useful employment skills in more informal ways.

When throwing educational dollars at the poverty problem isn't working, which is what the relationship between dollars spent on education and concurrent poverty rates suggest, it's time to look deeper, bearing in mind that certain truths govern any exploration of poverty's causes and consequences:

- Children, who are the individuals educational dollars are spent on, are poor because their parents are poor.
- Parents are poor for many reasons, and in rural areas where mobility among the poor is significantly curtailed, poor parents are very likely products of the same schools their children are attending. The children may have the same teachers their parents had, and these teachers remember the parents as low-achieving students and don't expect their children to be much better.
- Inequalities in educational experiences among students in the same school exist and can be very significant. Children from non-poor families can afford to participate in sports, extra-curricular activities and educational enrichment opportunities that are financially out of reach for many poor children.

- Teachers everywhere are more likely to make a greater effort with students they perceive as having greater potential to succeed. This excludes many poor students who come from family backgrounds that do not necessarily value educational achievement. Students who do not exhibit the qualities indicating a high probability of success are easily overlooked because they aren't as satisfying to teach and are not the students who will go on to the higher educational pursuits that make their home-town high school look good.
- Poor children are often apart from mainstream school activities, making their overall school experience less satisfying and rewarding. They are social outsiders whose peers perceive them as "different." This makes them more vulnerable to bullying and other negative social experiences.
- Poor children, particularly in rural areas, frequently come from families who do not necessarily expect their children to be high achievers and do not support their child's academic efforts. These parents know they can't send their children to college and have a great deal invested in keeping them close to home where they can "help" the family stay afloat. These students are the "stayers" Fitzgerald refers to—the ones who don't want to leave the comfortable familiarity of the community where they were born and raised.
- There are many fewer jobs in rural areas, and the ones that are there are often manufacturing jobs that don't necessarily require the kinds of skills public school education provides. Most skill requirements for jobs in rural areas can be met by on-the-job training or by taking a few courses at the local technical college, which have more relaxed academic entrance requirements than four-year post-secondary educational institutions.

There is, perhaps, no greater 21st-century social catch–22 than the one facing rural education. Rural schools that do an outstanding job of educating all their students, preparing them well for the future and enabling them to go on to earn further educational degrees are robbing the local rural community of its future leaders and future economic potential—a loss that can never be regained. Rural schools that do less well run the risk of indirectly holding their students back, sentencing them to lives in rural communities where there are far fewer economic opportunities and the community overall cannot enjoy the advantages that come with a well-educated, creative and visionary leadership. This is not a problem in larger school districts where the population is much larger and choices and opportunities, for everyone, are much greater.

There is no good answer to this dilemma, because no school administrator and no school board in any rural school district anywhere can envision doing anything other than pursuing success for those who are likely to succeed and investing many fewer of their already sparse resources on the poor students who aren't likely to go nearly as far. School district administrators and school boards may or may not be aware that they are, by their singular focus on promoting success, hollowing out the middle of their community, but either way, they don't see any alternative, because there isn't one.

10

Conclusion

The Invisible Poor

> *That the poor are invisible is one of the most important things about them. They are not simply neglected and forgotten as in the old rhetoric of reform; what is much worse, they are not seen.* —Michael Harrington

Rural America is the Other America—the place everybody knows is there but nobody wants to think too much about. And, when nobody thinks much about someplace, it's easy for it to become invisible. After all, who really knew, in 1964 when Lyndon Johnson declared war on poverty, that rural Appalachia was so poor it uniformly lacked electricity and indoor plumbing?

More to the point, who cared? The answer is nobody cared, until Robert Kennedy saw it with his own eyes, told his brother, President John Kennedy, about it, thus beginning a broad-based political initiative Kennedy's successor determined was worth continuing.

The present work takes up the discussion on rural poverty half a century later. Most of Appalachia now in fact has electricity and indoor plumbing, many other rural areas have diversified, agriculture has exploded into a very widespread corporate endeavor, and the current American political environment is heavily populated with policy makers who weren't even born when poverty officially became part of the national conversation.

In attempting to move the discussion about the rural poor forward, it became obvious that the difficulties the rural poor face haven't improved, and the injustices operating in the rural economy have gotten worse. While the rural poor have options the urban poor, who get all the press, do not have, the rural poor remain invisible, which adds insult to the hidden injuries they suffer.

This book has attempted to expose those hidden injuries and provide a story of ultimate survival, despite all the odds, within an economic system that famously works best for the giants of corporate agriculture and barely works at all for the largely invisible rural poor.

Scarcity in the Land of Plenty—Have We Lost the War on Poverty?

> *Today, the ranks of the poor are again swelling.... These and other statistics have led careless observers to conclude that the war on poverty failed. No, it has achieved many good results. Society has failed. It tired of the war too soon, gave it inadequate resources and did not open up new fronts as required ... and we cannot afford not to resume the war.* —Hyman Bookbinder

Exactly 50 years have passed since Lyndon Johnson, envisioning a Great Society, told the nation he was declaring a war on poverty. Because the poverty rate has only fallen four points, from 19 percent to 15 percent, since that war began, many believe we lost it. Others see it differently, arguing that if the nation hadn't confronted poverty in 1964, things would be a lot worse today. Either way, embarrassingly high rates of poverty have remained a remarkably consistent feature of an American society where many enjoy an embarrassment of riches. However, that's only part of the story.

Progress in the war on poverty has been disappointingly slow, and in rural areas, has been like being stuck behind a manure spreader traveling down a narrow, winding dirt road—it moves very slowly, kicks up a lot of dust, and smells bad—and it's impossible to ever see far enough ahead to get around it, so it takes a long time to go a short distance. When the rural poor depend upon government to help them out, they come up against a public policy machine moving even slower than a manure spreader. What little progress that does occur is frequently underfunded and breaks down often, because it's hard to get anybody to be concerned about what's going on in a place they've never been to and aren't interested in going. But the problems don't end there.

Rural areas are too far away to be seen by policy makers on a day-by-day basis and don't represent big voting blocks. Representatives of more densely populated urban areas far outnumber their rural counterparts and are so far removed from the struggles of rural life that rural poverty rarely, if ever, crosses their minds. "Politicians think we're just dumb farmers out here," a friend told me. "We might not be the brightest guys in the world, but we sure as hell know the difference between chicken shit and chicken salad, and I wouldn't bet the same could be said of most of them."

My farmer friend is right when considering that most of the poverty legislation today focuses on urban poverty, because that's the poverty most people can't avoid seeing, and the current rhetoric accusing low wages of being the culprit in keeping people in poverty is relatively meaningless in rural areas. Wages don't matter as much to rural poor because so many are self employed; where the wage issue does reach them is as an effect of a sluggish labor market that no longer offers good jobs, with decent wages, to workers seeking off-farm employment to augment farm income. And nearly all farmers must find some way to supplement their farm earnings because, in this era of having to compete in a marketplace controlled by big corporate farming, the family farm can't support the family. For those who don't farm and try to earn a living some other way, the wage issue is relevant only if they can find a job, and jobs are scarce in rural places.

In simplest terms, what is occurring now is that the national politics surrounding rural poverty have been woven into the broader problem of rising income inequality, which brings wildly abundant growth to a small, elite 1 percent and leaves everyone else behind, coughing in the dust. The social programs that began with the New Deal, particularly Social Security and Medicare, have helped the poor, but these programs haven't closed the income gap or balanced the scales of economic justice for anyone, and particularly not for the rural poor.

The rural economy, like the wider national economy, rises and falls on the principles of free-enterprise, profit-motive capitalism, and it is difficult to reconcile these with the basic tenants of economic justice. Further, in the rural Midwest, profit-motive driven corporate invasion has guaranteed there won't be any economic justice anywhere in sight. Wisconsin state senator Kathleen Vinehout, speaking to a proposal to eliminate a 640-acre cap on foreign ownership of Wisconsin farmland, and objecting to the purchase of 9,600 acres of farmland by foreign interests, puts it this way: "I am concerned that land prices will spike, costs will increase, and new farmers will be priced out of farming ... and my constituents are very worried about foreign corporations purchasing such large tracts of land. They tell me that we had better think twice about foreign ownership of our food supply."[1]

The Economic Justice Alternative

> *The New Deal was going to redistribute the national income according to ideals of social and economic justice.*—Garet Garrett

Garet Garrett spoke these words in criticism of the New Deal, and of the ideals of social and economic justice, because he didn't believe free enterprise, profit-motive capitalism and economic justice could co-exist. Many people agree with him, particularly those who see economics as a competitive game of winners and losers. People who don't like win-win solutions and don't believe all ships, even ones in need of repair, rise with the tide, don't like the concept of economic justice because they believe that, in order for everyone to gain, the rich will lose. In other words, the wealthy have no interest in balancing the scales of economic justice because they are already tipped in their favor.

The economic justice alternative encompasses the individual person as well as the larger social order and encompasses the moral principles and ethical standards that guide in designing our economic institutions. These institutions determine how each person earns a living, enters into contracts, exchanges goods and services with others and otherwise produces an independent, marketable product for his or her economic sustenance.

Mainstream economics overwhelmingly argues that ethical standards are essentially relative, that they differ from one person to the next, and therefore are entirely outside the limits of legitimate inquiry. Not everyone agrees. "Our view is that there are certain objective ethical standards to be applied in economic affairs, and that proximately those standards come from ethics," says research economist Edward O'Boyle, adding that, ultimately "ethical standards originate in the human experience."[2]

According to O'Boyle, justice, as applied to economics, is "the virtue or good habit of rendering to another that that is owed." The term is broken down to include participatory, distributive and social justice. Participatory justice describes how one engages in the economic process in order to make a living. It requires equal opportunity in gaining access to private property and productive assets as well as equal opportunity to engage in productive work. Participation does not guarantee equal results, but it does require that social institutions guarantee every person the equal human right to make a productive contribution to the economy, both through one's labor (as a worker) and through one's productive capital (as an owner). Accordingly, this principle rejects monopolies, special privileges, and other exclusionary social barriers to economic self-reliance.

Distributive justice defines the "output rights" of an economic system matched to each person's labor and capital inputs. Through the distribution features of private property within a free and open marketplace, distributive justice becomes automatically linked to participative justice, and income becomes linked to productive contributions.

The principle of distributive justice involves the sanctity of property and contracts. It turns to the free and open marketplace, not government, as the most objective and democratic means for determining the just price, the just wage, and the just profit. The principles of distributive justice are based upon the notion of each according to his contribution and break apart when all persons are not given equal opportunity to acquire and enjoy the fruits of income-producing property. Distributive justice demands that individuals who work equally hard should share equally in the results of their labor.

Social justice is the ability for individuals to realize their potential in the society where they live and ensures that individuals both fulfill their societal roles and receive what is owed to them by the larger society. The term generally refers to a set of interacting institutions that will enable citizens to lead fulfilling lives and be active contributors to their community.[3] The goal of social justice is generally identical to that set forth in human development—to realize one's fullest possible potential.

The principles of economic justice do not operate within either the context of the wider American economy or the rural, agriculturally based economy. Corporate agriculture is tethered to the principles of maximum profit and has little interest in economic justice or concern for the farmers they are squeezing out every year. There is no economic justice for farmers who must work 70–80 hours per week in order to participate in capitalism's free market, yet are not rewarded in any way commensurate with their efforts. Worse, most of the government subsidies intended to support agriculture go to corporate farming enterprises.

The notion that if one works hard enough he or she will succeed is simply not true either for farmers or for most rural small businesses. Rural America is the backbone and heartland of the nation, where the food on our tables and tables around the world comes from. The people who grow this food and the small business owners who support agriculture are both victims of an unfair economic system that doesn't work for them.

As a result the rural poor continue to be swallowed up by larger economic interests that impoverish them in two ways. First is by working twice as hard as 40-hour wage workers for less than their fair share of the rewards for their labor. Second is that the capitalist-based economy is cleverly designed to work best for large corporate interests whose economies of scale result in lower production costs and higher output, thus guaranteeing their success is the competitive marketplace. Small independent farmers can't compete successfully in this economic environment.

Farming's Hard, But We Make Do—The Heartbeat of America

> *For all the labor, it came clear that most people [in rural areas] had led satisfying lives.... "We didn't have so much to choose from, and so learned to make the best of what we had.... We were happier then—we were truly happy people," was something I heard again and again.*—Sherry Thomas

Despite the struggles and hardships of being a farmer and living in a rural area, I've never come across anyone who wants to live some other way, someplace else—which speaks volumes about life on the land and reveals certain truths about rural life. First is that land is everything in rural Midwestern America. It is a livelihood, a place of emotional grounding, a source of spiritual nourishment and the ticket to freedom from the constraints of city life. Land is the quiet place in nature that restores a soul to wholeness, saves it from the chaos of daily life, brings solace in times of grief and reveals meaning in times of empty loneliness. The land sustains life in ways nothing else can do.

Second, there's a reason why the Midwest is affectionately termed America's heartland—with its hundreds of thousands of acres of rich farm land, it is the place where the heart truly finds a home. It doesn't matter if the land is flat and the desolate scenery it provides lacks grand majesty—it's still land, and land is everything.

"When I had to sell off that parcel of land over there, part of me went right along with it. It was worse than somebody in the family dying. It was like cutting off my arm. I still think about the days when my dad planted it, I planted it, and my son followed after me ... and all I lost when I was forced to sell because the county wanted it for an airport we sure as hell didn't need," a Wisconsin farmer told me, pointing across the highway onto a ridge where a bulldozer was moving mounds of dirt he still considered his own.

Third, most who live off the land can't live any other way, and don't even want to try. Their land is a deeply treasured member of their family and it's extremely difficult to move away, leaving a beloved family member behind. Rural folks have a covenant with their land. They are committed to being good stewards of it and to passing it on to the next generation. This responsibility is not a job, it's a calling. In this way, land sustains rural life, bringing it full circle generation over generation.

Fourth, rural life works as well as it does because of rural women, and wouldn't work at all without them. Beginning with the pioneers who set out across unknown territory in search of a new life, frontier women knew how to build and sustain community, how to work 18-hour days, how to feed and clothe their families and the needy, how to minister to others when their health fails, and how to organize social movements. Rural life is the birthplace of suffrage, temperance, abolition, and religious movements more sympathetic to women's rights than mainstream churches. Rural women today have inherited this legacy and keep it alive. They nurture that within themselves that arises from living in concert with nature and use this ability for the benefit of all.

According to New York Times columnist Charles Blow, "Poverty is a diabolical predicament that not only makes scarce one's physical comforts, but drains away one's spiritual strength. It damages hopes and dreams, and having deficits among those things is when the soul begins to die."[4] He's correct, as far as he goes; however, the statement reflects an urban view of poverty and is not something anyone living in a rural area would be likely to say, because rural people, beginning with the pioneers who advanced the western frontier, figured out how to make their own dreams, and they've never let them go. Rural people, even though poor, won't let their soul die, because most believe they have too much to live for, and that, despite her unpredictable moodiness, Mother Nature commands their respect.

In a world where the more things change, the more they stay the same, rural people are bearers of incredible intuitive ability to take care of themselves and each other. They know money for social assistance programs rarely stretches deep enough to reach them, so they don't depend upon the government to provide for them. They figure things out for themselves because, beginning with the early days on the frontier, rural life has always been a life lived in poverty—but a hopeful, optimistic one nevertheless. In the beginning farmers were alone, with not much more than their resilience and optimism to sustain them. Farmers today are still alone, still resilient and still tirelessly optimistic, even though corporate agriculture has created the dust bowl of the 21st century, and this time there isn't a President Roosevelt, a New Deal, or even a Congress functional enough to step up to the problems facing the rural poor and help them out.

Despite the frustrations of rural life, farmers and rural people today still have to save themselves, just like they have always had to do—and they willingly, optimistically step up to the challenge.

"Sometimes I feel like a jackass in a hailstorm—I just have to stand here and take it," a struggling farmer told me. "But what the hell—it'll stop hailing sooner or later."

Appendix One

Methodology and Interview Schedules

Data and other information for this book came from several sources, including prior research for articles I wrote while employed at a rural newspaper, conversations with local officials, interviews with individuals who work with the rural poor or interact with them on a regular basis, and interviews with poor individuals and families who were clients of a local Habitat for Humanity organization, which assists the poor to obtain housing.

It was surprisingly difficult to find rural poor people willing to talk about their circumstances. Many did not think of themselves as poor and claimed ignorance about "what being poor" means. Finding out at least some of what I wanted to know often took engaging them in a less direct way, together with many reassurances not to "use my real name." None agreed to being tape recorded, and although they understood what the information was being used for, many were not comfortable with my taking notes while we talked. In those cases I wrote up our conversations promptly after they had ended.

Interviews occurred in person, by telephone, through email, and with the assistance of an intern working with a low-income housing assistance program. Individuals who did not want their actual names used were assigned pseudonyms; the names of individuals who did allow their actual names to be used in this book are included in the bibliography.

The following permission forms and interview questions were used for this study.

Permission form.1

Name: Interviewee ID #_____

I agree to be interviewed by Dr. Paula Dáil for the upcoming book *Rural Midwestern Poverty* being published by McFarland Publishing Company. Interview topics may include, but will not necessarily be limited to, material conditions of poverty (unmet needs in health care and education); limited resource problems; the specifics of economic deprivation (housing, food scarcity, clothing, standard of living); social concerns (inequality, lack of income security, family issues, crime); and the emotional aspects of poverty.

I understand that I will not receive any compensation for this interview from Dr. Dáil or McFarland Publishing Company.

_____ I agree to allowing my actual name and location to be used
_____ I prefer anonymity. In this case, I will be assigned a pseudonym and my location will not be specifically identified.

Signed:

Date:

Permission form.2—introduction for telephone interviews

ID #

DATE:

You are being asked to participate in an anonymous survey that involves several open-ended questions about your current living situation. Topics include the material conditions of poverty (unmet needs in health care and education); limited resource problems; the specifics of economic deprivation (housing, food scarcity, clothing, standard of living); social concerns (inequality, lack of income security, family issues, crime); and the emotional aspects of poverty.

Your name will not appear on the questionnaire and no one will know who participated.

We are working with a professor who is writing a book about the struggles of low-income rural families and, as part of the book project, will be helping us put the information together. She may use some parts of your answers in the book, but will have no access to other information about you, including your name.

We want you to feel very comfortable about honestly answering the questions, so if you have any questions while we're going through the questionnaire, please ask them. Participants will not be financially rewarded for their participation.

Questionnaire

This is an anonymous, confidential survey about obtaining a home through Habitat for Humanity. Your name will not appear anywhere on the questionnaire and no one will know, or even be able to guess, who participated in the survey. We will compile everyone's answer into general statements about each question, and want you to feel very comfortable about answering the questions honestly. Most importantly, there are no right or wrong answers—we just want to hear your thoughts about your new lifestyle as a home owner.

We are working with Professor Paula Dáil, who is writing a book on rural poverty. Some of the information you provide may be used in that book. However, you will never be personally identified. If you have any questions as we go along, please don't hesitate to ask.

This first part is general background information.

ID#:_____

Age:

Gender:

Educational level:

Years in the area:

Ever married (how many times):

Current relationship status:

Current household size: #Adults: #Kids

Current monthly income:

Current income sources

Current social program participation

Employment history

For HFH Clients:

Next we'll talk about your housing opportunity:

In what ways has living in a home changed you (less free time, more responsibility, added stress…)?

Going in, did you feel prepared (financially, emotionally, socially) for homeownership?

What do you like best about owning your own home?

What don't you like about owning your home?

How has owning a home changed relationships that are important to you (less time w/the kids, some of my friends are jealous, now have a place for family and friends to come…)?

What sorts of things did you try to purchase when you moved into your new home (furniture, TV…)?

What were your thoughts about the responsibilities that come with owning a home before you owned one?

Knowing what you know now, would you partner with the organization or find some other way to get housing?

Next are some questions about finances:

Do you feel that most months you have enough money to meet your basic needs?

Living on a limited budget is like being on a diet—you always feel a little hungry and deprived. With this in mind, what needs that are important to you go unmet b/c you don't have enough money (new clothes, food, etc…)?

How do you decide which bills to pay in the months when you're stretched really thin?

How often do you worry about falling behind financially?

Do you have a rainy day savings account you regularly deposit money into? How much?

How much money per month do you feel would be enough for you to do what you want to do without worry?

What are the most upsetting things about not always having enough money (can't afford entertainment, no new clothes, can't afford stuff I want to do around the house…)?

What would you do differently if you had enough money (quit 2nd job, get new car...)?

Do you have long-term personal/financial goals (no debt ... pay off mortgage...)?

What do you worry about when you think about money (losing job, incurring medical bills, low wages ... don't worry)?

How often do you borrow money from family members or friends?

Life Stressors:

Who do you rely upon for emotional support?

On average, how much alcohol do adults in the house drink per day?

Has anyone ever expressed concerns about alcohol use among members of your household?

Has any immediate family member ever been in treatment for alcohol or drug use?

Does anyone in the household have a gambling problem?

Does any household member have any ongoing medical or mental health issues? How much do these affect your daily life?

Has anyone in your household ever been involved in an episode of family violence or abuse? *(If yes, ask if this is ongoing; If yes, offer the phone number for domestic violence services)*

What else do you feel it's important for me to know?

Do you have any questions?

Open-ended Interview Schedule:

1. Demographics (age, gender, education, years living in rural area; income sources).
2. Who are the people you feel most dependent upon?
3. In what ways do you feel isolated from the mainstream?
4. What things do you lack that you would have if you had more money?
5. What things can't you do that you would like to do if you had more money?
6. What basic needs of yours go unmet b/c of lack of money?
7. How would you characterize your standard of living overall?
8. In what ways do you feel "insecure"?
9. What family issues dominate your life? Would these be different if you had more money?
10. What are the most upsetting things about not having enough money?
11. What is your relationship w/the wider community?
12. What would you do differently if you had enough money?
13. In general, how do you feel about your life? Would you trade it for a different life?
14. What concerns about the future do you have?
15. What else do you want me to know?

Appendix Two

Agricultural Traits of Midwestern Farm States[1]

Illinois

Located midway between the Continental Divide and the Atlantic Ocean, and about 500 miles from the Gulf of Mexico, Illinois has excellent soil and a well-distributed average annual precipitation of 32–48 inches. Taken together, these conditions favor a highly productive agricultural economy.

About 1.5 million workers are employed in the food and fiber (wool) industry, making Illinois one of the top agricultural states in terms of dependence upon agriculture. In addition to farming, the state is among the leaders in agricultural-related industries such as soybean processing, meat packing, dairy manufacturing, feed milling, vegetable processing, machinery manufacturing, foreign food exports and service industries.

Additionally, Illinois produces 43,000 bushels of apples and 7,580,000 tons of peaches each year.

While home to fewer than 4 percent of the nation's farms, Illinois produces about 14 percent of the U.S. soybean crop, 16 percent of the corn, 7 percent of the hogs and accounts for 6 percent of the total U.S. agricultural exports. Illinois ranks second among states in corn and soybean production, third in summer potato production, eighth in grain sorghum, ninth in snap bean processing and peach production, and 12th in oat and apple production.

Sixty-two percent of Illinois farmers work on less than 180 acres of land, which is approximately half the size of the average Illinois farm. Fifty-five percent of Illinois farmers report earning less than $25,000 per year in farm income, which falls below 125 percent of poverty for a four person household. Five Illinois counties report poverty rate at or above 20 percent, while 35 counties have poverty rates between 13 and 19.9 percent.

Indiana

Located east and adjacent to Illinois, Indiana enjoys a similar agricultural environment. In addition to corn, its principal crop, the state also produces tobacco, various vegetables, potatoes, peppermint, spearmint and sweet potatoes in marketable numbers, and has nearly four thousand acres of orchard land. Nationally, the state ranks third in egg-producing chickens, fourth in soybeans, fifth in hogs and pigs, corn for grain, oilseeds, dry beans and dry peas, seventh in turkey production, and tenth in total value of agricultural products sold.

Seventy-four percent of Indiana farmers work off of less than 180 acres, which is 74 percent of the average size Indiana farm. Sixty-five percent of all farmers report less than $25,000 total farm income, which is less than 125 percent of poverty for a family of four. One Indiana county reports a poverty rate at or above 20 percent, while 21 counties have poverty rates between 13 and 19.9 percent.

Iowa

With miles of fertile farm and pasture land Iowa is a highly productive farm state, ranking third in the nation in total value of agricultural products sold, and in both crop and livestock values. The state is first among all states in amount of revenue generated from hogs and pigs, corn for grain, soybeans, and egg-producing chickens, second in oilseeds, dry beans and dry peas, fourth in cattle and calves, seventh in grain oats and eighth in silage corn production. The state produces small amounts of vegetables, potatoes, fruit, Christmas trees, sheep and goats.

Fifty-five percent of Iowa farmers work off of less than 180 acres, which is just over half the acreage of the average Iowa farm. Forty-six percent of all farmers report less than $25,000 total farm income, which is less than 125 percent of poverty for a family of four. Iowa is tied with Nebraska in having the second lowest rural poverty rate (12.5 percent) among the Midwestern states. One Iowa county reports a poverty rate at or above 20 percent, while 16 counties have poverty rates between 13 and 19.9 percent.

Kansas

Kansas has been referred to as the buckle on the Bible belt because it is home to a number of radical fringe religious movements. Not surprisingly, Kansas, as a highly productive farm state, ranks number one in wheat production and also in grain sorghum. The state ranks second in cattle and calf inventory and value and ninth in hog and pig inventory. Kansas ranks fourth in total livestock value and fifth in total value of all agricultural products. The state ranks seventh in corn for grain, oilseed, dry beans and peas, and seventh in the amount of forage land.

Forty-eight percent of Kansas farmers work off of less than 180 acres, which is approximately one quarter the acreage of the average Kansas farm. Sixty-one percent of all Kansas farmers report less than $25,000 total farm income, which is less than 125 percent of poverty for a family of four. One Kansas county reports a poverty rate at or above 20 percent, while 30 counties have poverty rates between 13 and 19.9 percent.

Michigan

In 2010–11, Michigan's top commodities, in terms of cash receipts, were milk, corn, soybeans, floriculture, cattle and calves, hogs, sugar beets, wheat, eggs and potatoes. The state also produced substantial amounts of blueberries, apples, pickle cucumbers, tart cherries and other vegetables, and sold honey and fresh water trout fished from Lake Michigan. Nationally, Michigan ranked 19th in total cash receipts.

Seventy-nine percent of Michigan farmers work off of less than 180 acres, which is also the acreage of the average Michigan farm. Seventy-two percent of Michigan farmers report less than $25,000 total farm income, which is less than 125 percent of poverty for a family of four. Michigan's rural poverty rate (17 percent) places the state third poorest among the 12 Midwestern states. Two Michigan counties report a poverty rate at or above 20 percent, while 43 counties have poverty rates between 13 and 19.9 percent.

Minnesota

Minnesota's top crop item is sugar beets used for sugar, placing the state number one in this agricultural item. The state also leads the nation in turkey production. The state ranks third in hog, pig and soybean production, fourth in corn for grain, oilseeds, dry beans and peas, fifth in Christmas trees cut, and sixth in milk and other dairy product value. The state ranks seventh in total market value of all agricultural products sold, fourth in crop value, and eighth in livestock value.

Fifty-seven percent of Minnesota farmers work off of less than 180 acres, which is slightly over half the acreage of the average Minnesota farm. Fifty-seven percent of Minnesota farmers also report less than $25,000 total farm income, which is less than 125 percent of poverty for a family of four. Minnesota's rural poverty rate (12.4 percent) ranks the state as the least poor among the 12 Midwestern states. No Minnesota counties report a poverty rate at or above 20 percent but 9 counties have poverty rates between 13 and 19.9 percent.

Missouri

Missouri leads the Midwestern states in the number of female farmers (12,754) and ranks second among all fifty states in the amount of forage land, fourth in turkey inventory, fifth in soybean production, sixth in cattle and calves inventory, seventh in hog and pig inventory and sales value, eighth in cotton and cottonseed value, ninth in poultry, egg, cattle and calf production, corn for grain, and amount of cotton produced. The state ranks 12th in total value of agricultural products sold and 13th in market value of both crops and livestock.

Missouri also produces small amounts of cut Christmas trees, fruits, vegetables, nursery and greenhouse stock, sheep, goats, horses, ponies, mules, burros and donkeys. The state is 12th in tobacco production.

Sixty-four percent of Missouri farmers work off of less than 180 acres, which is 67 percent of the acreage of the average Missouri farm. Seventy-three percent of Missouri farmers report less than $25,000 total farm income, which is less than 125 percent of poverty for a family of four. Missouri's rural poverty rate (18.8 percent) places the state as the poorest among the 12 Midwestern states. Twenty-three Missouri counties report a poverty rate at or above 20 percent and 62 counties have poverty rates between 13 and 19.9 percent.

Nebraska

As a lucrative agricultural state, nationally Nebraska ranks fourth in total value of agricultural products and fifth in both crop and livestock value. The state is third in cattle and calf inventory, corn for grain, other grains, oilseeds and dry beans and peas, fourth in grain sorghum, sixth in hog and pig production, seventh in soybean crops, eighth in forage land, and ninth in wheat production. The state also produces small amounts of fruits, vegetables, nursery stock and sod, sheep, goats, horses, ponies, mules, burros and donkeys.

Forty percent of Nebraska farmers work off of less than 180 acres, which is 19 percent of the acreage of the average Nebraska farm. Forty percent of Nebraska farmers report less than $25,000 total farm income, which is less than 125 percent of poverty for a family of four. Nebraska's rural poverty rate (12.5 percent) ties Iowa as having the second lowest poverty rate among the 12 Midwestern states. One Nebraska county reports a poverty rate at or above 20 percent and 18 counties have poverty rates between 13 and 19.9 percent.

North Dakota

North Dakota is first in the nation in barley production and second in both wheat production value and number of bee colonies. The state ranks sixth in oilseed, dry beans and peas, and ninth in soybeans and amount of forage land. North Dakota ranks 18th in terms of total value of agriculture products, ninth in crop value and 35th in total livestock value among the 50 states. The state also produces cut Christmas trees, small amounts of fruits, vegetables, and more substantial amounts of sheep, goats, poultry, milk and other dairy products, horses, ponies, mules, burros and donkeys and other animal products.

Twenty-seven percent of North Dakota farmers work off of less than 180 acres, which is a mere 15 percent of the acreage of the average North Dakota farm. Forty-eight percent of North Dakota farmers report less than $25,000 total farm income, which is less than 125 percent of poverty for a family of four. North Dakota's rural poverty rate (12.9 percent) places the state third lowest among the 12 Midwestern states. However, Sioux County is among the top five poorest counties in the entire nation. Three North Dakota counties report a poverty rate at or above 20 percent and 10 counties have poverty rates between 13 and 19.9 percent.

Ohio

Although not known as a dairy state, Ohio leads the nation in Swiss cheese production and ranks fourth and fifth in sour cream, low-fat cottage cheese, cheese curd and creamed cottage cheese production. Ohio is second in chicken inventory, egg production, and number of calves slaughtered. The state ranks ninth in pounds of chicken sold, hog and pig inventory and pork production. The state also produces honey and maple syrup.

Regarding crop production, Ohio ranks eighth in corn for grain and tobacco and sixth in soybeans. The state did not report its national rankings in total agricultural product value or for either crop or livestock market values.

Fifty-six percent of Ohio farmers work off of less than 180 acres, which is the approximate acreage of the average Ohio farm. Sixty-eight percent of Ohio farmers report less than $25,000 total farm income, which is less than 125 percent of poverty for a family of four. Seven Ohio counties report a poverty rate at or above 20 percent and 27 counties have poverty rates between 13 and 19.9 percent.

South Dakota

Lemmon, South Dakota, is the geographic center of the North American continent, about 1,500 miles in each direction from the Atlantic and Pacific Oceans, the Gulf of Mexico and the Arctic Archipelago. The state is number one in the nation in pheasant inventory and ranks second in sunflower seed production and third in forage land acreage. The state is fifth in sheep, goats and related products value, sixth in corn and wheat for grain, eighth in cattle and calves inventory and soybean production, and ninth in oilseeds, dry beans and peas. South Dakota ranks 17th in total value of agricultural products, 14th in crop value, and 19th in livestock market value. The state produces very small amounts of cut Christmas trees, fruits, vegetables, somewhat more poultry and egg products. Both North and South Dakota are believed to possess great potential to produce wind energy.

Thirty-four percent of South Dakota farmers work off of less than 180 acres, which represents 14 percent of the acreage of the average South Dakota farm. Forty-three percent of South Dakota farmers report less than $25,000 total farm income, which is less than 125 percent of poverty for a family of four. South Dakota's rural poverty rate (17.2 percent) places the state third poorest among the Midwestern states. Four of the poorest counties in the nation are in South Dakota, which is also home to the impoverished Pine Ridge Indian Reservation. Twelve South Dakota counties report a poverty rate at or above 20 percent and 17 counties have poverty rates between 13 and 19.9 percent. Four of the five poorest counties in the nation are in South Dakota.

Wisconsin

Although known as the Dairy State, nationally Wisconsin ranks second, behind California, in milk production and production of other dairy products. The state leads in corn for silage, is fourth in harvested vegetable production, sixth in cut Christmas trees, seventh in forage land, potato and sweet potato production and tenth in corn for grain and turkey inventory. Wisconsin ranks ninth in overall total value of agricultural products sold, eighteenth in crop value, and seventh in value of all livestock and poultry products marketed. Farmers in the state also raise goats, sheep, hogs and pigs, as well as produce a few horses, ponies, mules, burros and donkeys.

Sixty-nine percent of Wisconsin farmers work off of less than 180 acres, which is 14 acres less than the size of the average Wisconsin farm. Sixty-five percent of Wisconsin farmers report less than $25,000 total farm income, which is less than 125 percent of poverty for a family of four. One Wisconsin county reports a poverty rate at or above 20 percent and six counties have poverty rates between 13 and 19.9 percent.

Appendix Three

Medicaid Eligibility Groups and Services

The existing federal Medicaid health care system mandates care for certain impoverished population groups, and states are required to include certain categories of individuals in their Medicaid programs but may broaden their eligibility requirements to include others.[1] At the federal level, the key Medicaid eligibility groups are:

Categorically Needy

Categorically needy Medicaid recipients include:

- Families who meet state Temporary Assistance to Needy Families eligibility requirements.
- Pregnant women and children under age six whose family income is at or below 133 percent of the FPL.
- Children ages six to nineteen with family income up to 100 percent of the FPL.
- Caretakers of children under age eighteen (nineteen if still in high school).
- Supplemental Security Income (SSI) recipients.
- Individuals and couples who live in medical institutions and who have a monthly income up to 300 percent of the SSI income standard.

Medically Needy

Individuals categorized as medically needy exceed the income guidelines for receiving regular Medicaid and must assume part of the cost of their health care. Thirty-five states offer a medically needy health care program, which must include pregnant women through a sixty-day postpartum period, children under age eighteen, certain categories of newborns for one year, and blind persons. States may also, at their discretion, provide Medicaid to:

- Full-time students under age 21.
- Child caretaker relatives.

- Persons over age 65.
- Blind and disabled, according to SSI or state-established standards.
- Persons enrolled in health maintenance organizations who would be otherwise eligible for Medicaid.

Special Eligibility Groups

Certain individuals who do not fall into either of the above categories may also receive Medicaid. These include:

- Medicare beneficiaries—Medicaid pays Medicare premiums, deductibles and co-insurance for individuals whose income is at or below 100 percent of the FPL and whose resources are at or below twice the SSI standard, or have an income less than 135 percent of the FPL.
- Qualified working disabled individuals having incomes below 200 percent of the FPL and resources that are no more than twice the allowed SSI standard. Medicaid can pay Medicare Part A (medical services) premiums for certain disabled individuals who lose Medicare coverage because of employment.
- Working disabled people between ages 16 and 65 who have incomes and resources greater than allowed under SSI can receive expanded Medicaid coverage, increasing their access to employment, training, and job placement. States can also, at their discretion, expand Medicaid eligibility for this population even further to include individuals whose medical conditions improve, but may require such individuals to share in the cost of their medical care.
- Two categories of specific medical conditions: women with breast or cervical cancer and otherwise uninsured tuberculosis (TB) patients. Women with breast or cervical cancer receive all plan services for a limited period of time. TB patients only receive services directly related to the treatment of this illness. Eleven states and the District of Columbia (DC) include TB patients in their Medicaid eligibility; all states and DC provide Medicaid services to women having a breast or cervical cancer diagnosis.

1115 Medical Waivers

Section 1115 of the Medicaid law allows for waivers, or exceptions, to stated eligibility standards. Thirty-one states expand Medicaid eligibility through a waiver program. However, the expanded eligibility is often only available to those enrolled in managed care. Alaska and Wyoming are the only states that do not include managed care in their Medicaid program.

Mandatory Medicaid Services

The categorically needy are entitled to the following medical services, unless waived under section 1115 of the Medicaid law. These entitlements do not apply to the State Children's Health Insurance Program (SCHIP):

- Inpatient and outpatient hospital (excluding mental health) services.
- Laboratory and Xrays.
- Certified pediatric and family nurse practitioners.
- Nursing facility services for those over age 21.
- Early and periodic screening, diagnosis and treatment for children under age 21.
- Family planning services and supplies.
- Physician services.
- Dental, medical and surgical services.
- Home health care services, including part-time nursing care, home health aides, and medical supplies and home use devices.
- Nurse midwife and pregnancy-related services for up to 60 days postpartum.

States vary widely in the Medicaid services they provide. Many states provide only minimal, not comprehensive health care services to the poor, and individual state governors and legislatures have discretion in deciding whether, or how much, of the federal Medicaid match they are willing to accept because these dollars force states to provide additional medical services. Table A outlines available Medicaid services and the number of states who provide them.

Table A: Medicaid Services by State

Service, in addition to physician-provided care	Number of states providing some form of service
Chiropractic	27
Podiatry	44
Optometry	49
Psychologist	34
Nurse anesthetist	31
Private duty nursing	27
Dental	44
Physical therapy	43
Occupational therapy	40
Speech, hearing and language disorder therapy	40
Prescribed drugs	51*
Dentures	35
Prosthetic devices	49
Eyeglasses	43
Diagnostic services	33
Screening services	33
Preventive services	36
Mental health rehab and stabilization	46
Other rehab services	33
Inpatient hospital/nursing facility > age 65	43
Intermediate care for mentally retarded	51*
Inpatient psychiatric services <age 21	46
Personal care services	36
Targeted case management	48
Primary care case management	25
Hospice care	48
Respiratory care for ventilator dependent	16
PACE (inclusive elderly care)	22
Institutional religious (non-medical) health care	12

Transportation services	49
Emergency hospital services for non–Medicare patients	35
Nursing facility care < age 21	50
Critical access hospital care	25
Home Health Therapies	
Physical	49
Speech and language	48
Occupational	49
Audiology	44

*includes District of Columbia

One area where Medicaid fails is in providing medical care to single adults, both male and female, without dependent children. States have the option of either including or excluding these individuals. The only health care option available to individuals living in states that exclude single adults from their Medicaid programs is the emergency room, where costs are absorbed through the hospital's charity care funds.

A Midwestern State Example: Wisconsin Medicaid

Historically Wisconsin's BadgerCare Health Care Plan has been one of the best Medicaid programs in the country and is included because it provides a good example of how health care access should work for families earning up to 185 percent of the FPL. BadgerCare Plus reaches beyond the minimal federally mandated health care services and has been expanded to include single adults.[2] Having a 10.4 percent poverty rate (range: 5.4 percent—21.2 percent)[3] Wisconsin has had a 58 percent match agreement with the federal Medicaid program. Enrolling in a particular BadgerCare Medicaid Plan depends on income, assets, and type of care needed, and the program has provided a good example of how Medicaid can work. Unfortunately, this health care plan is on the political chopping block and facing severe cuts. Table B describes the basic BadgerCare Program and associated patient costs as they presently exist.

Table B: Benchmark BadgerCare Plus Medical Plan and Associated Co-pays[4]

Service	Co-Pay
Chiropractic	$15 per visit.
Dental	Coverage limited to $750 per year; co-pay 50 percent of allowed amount plus $200 per year. Limited coverage of preventive, diagnostic, simple restorative, periodontics, extractions for both pregnant women and children.
Disposable medical supplies	$.50 for syringes and diabetic pens.
Prescription drugs	$5 for generic drugs only. Brand drugs are available at a discount through the Badger Rx Gold Plan. If brand drugs are required, enrollment in Badger Rx Gold is automatic.
Durable medical equipment	$5 each item, limited to $2,500 of paid amount in an enroll-

	ment year. Co-pays not applied to rental items but count toward $2,500 cap.
Emergency room	$60 per visit for non-emergencies. Co-pay not applied if hospital admission results.
Family planning services	$0.
Health care screenings for children	$0.
Home care services (home health, private duty nursing and personal care)	$15 per visit, limited to 60 visits per enrollment year.
Hospice care	$2 per day, limited to 360 days lifetime.
Hospital (including mental health and substance abuse)	Inpatient: $100 per stay; $50 for mental health/substance abuse; outpatient: $15 per visit. Inpatient stays in general acute hospital for substance abuse are limited to $6,300 per year; inpatient stay for mental health and/or substance abuse limited to $7,000 per year. Other annual limits include: • Outpatient services—$1,800 • Transitional services—$2,700 • Alcohol/drug services—$7,000
Nursing home	10 percent of allowed amount limited to 30 days per enrollment year.
Physicians visits, including laboratory and radiology	$15 per visit; no co-pay for emergency services, preventive care, anesthesia or clozapine management.
Podiatry	$15 per visit.
Prescription smoking cessation services	$5 each generic drug prescription.
Speech, physical, occupational, cardiac rehabilitation therapies	$15 per visit up to 20 visits per type per enrollment year; also covers up to 36 cardiac rehabilitation visits provided by a physical therapist that do not count toward the 20 physical therapy visits. No monthly or annual co-payment limits.
Transportation (emergency/ambulance)	$50 per trip.
Vision	$15 per visit for 1 exam per 24 months.

Co-payments are not required for:

- Children under age 19 with family income up to 100 percent of FPL, enrolled through express enrollment, institutionalized or enrolled in a BadgerCare Plus extension.
- Children under age six with family incomes between 100 percent and 150 percent of FPL, except for newborns whose mother were enrolled on the newborn birth date.
- Children age one through five who are tribal members with family incomes between 185 percent and 300 percent of FPL.
- Pregnant women, except those under age 19 with family income above 300 percent of FPL, enrolled through express enrollment, or enrolled in BadgerCare Plus Prenatal Services.

Wisconsin's ForwardHealth Medicaid plans include the following programs:

- Elderly, Blind or Disabled Medicaid is a program for people who are age 65 or older, blind, or disabled and have a family income at or below the monthly program limit, and are U.S. citizens or legal immigrants.
- Community Waivers help elderly, blind or disabled people live in their own homes or in the community, rather than a state institution or a nursing home.
- Family Care is a long-term care program for groups who are elderly, or have physical or developmental disabilities.
- Medicaid Purchase Plans provide health care for people with disabilities who work.
- Medicaid Deductible Plans help with high medical bills when an individual's income is over the Medicaid program income limits.
- Medicare Savings Plans can help some people pay their Medicare Part A and B premiums, coinsurance and deductibles.
- Tuberculosis (TB) Related Services help people who need treatment for tuberculosis.
- Emergency Services Plan only covers medical services needed for the treatment of an emergency medical condition for documented and undocumented non-citizens.
- Well Woman Medicaid Plan helps women who have been diagnosed with and are in need of treatment for breast and cervical cancer and includes a presumptive eligibility clause that allows for immediate care during the application-processing period.

Those who are not elderly, blind or disabled, and need health care coverage may be able to enroll in a BadgerCare Plus Plan, including the Family Planning Waiver and the BadgerCare Plus Prenatal Plan. Anticipating about $1.2 billion in federal economic recovery stimulus money, in mid–2009 BadgerCare Plus was expanded to include single persons having a monthly income level up to $1,805 and married couples without children having a total monthly income up to $2,428.33. Both figures are 200 percent of the FPL.

BadgerCare Plus requires co-pays ranging from $.50 to $3, limited to $30 per provider per year, for some services accessed by those whose income falls below 100 percent of the FPL. In cases of hospitalization, co-pays equal $3 per day up to a $75 maximum, and no more than $300 in co-pays per year. Prescription drug costs are up to $5 per drug, not to exceed $20 per month. Co-pays are slightly higher for those whose income falls between 100 percent and 200 percent of poverty. Regardless, if one falls sick and doesn't have enough money to live on to begin with, a co-pay is still a cost they can't afford to assume.

Chapter Notes

Preface

1. John Steinbeck, *The Grapes of Wrath* (New York: Viking Press, 1939).
2. Ibid., 120–21.
3. Although the majority of farmers are male, my use of "his" and "he" refers to both female and male farmers.
4. Martha T. Moore, "In Midwest, Prairie Populists a Fading Species," *USA Today*, June 3, 2013.
5. For a full discussion, see "Hustling Backwards: 21st Century Poverty as It Affects Women," in *Women and Poverty in 21st Century America*, by Paula vW. Dáil (Jefferson, NC: McFarland, 2012).
6. By comparison, California and Texas have 53 and 36 congressional representatives respectively.

Introduction

1. The Midwest is defined to include the states of Ohio, Indiana, North Dakota, Illinois, Wisconsin, Minnesota, Nebraska, Michigan, Kansas, Iowa, Missouri and South Dakota.
2. The Mississippi and its tributaries drain almost all the plains between the Appalachian Mountains and the Rocky Mountains. Its drainage basin is the third largest in the world, exceeded in size only by the watersheds, and encompasses 1.2 million square miles. The Mississippi River and its tributaries are vital sources of water for the Midwest, as well as an important means of transportation carrying the food grown on the Great Plains to market.
3. As of 2014, the federal minimum wage was $7.25 per hour.
4. Agricultural land, which comprises most of rural counties, is taxed at a different rate than other land parcels (commercial and residential), which reduces overall tax revenue, particularly in counties that are mostly zoned agriculture. Not all rural counties (or states) generate revenue through property taxes, which rise and fall according to land values. Other sources of county revenue can include sales tax, income tax, motor vehicle taxes and surcharges, licenses and permits, fines and forfeitures, miscellaneous food taxes, recreation and sin taxes (tobacco and alcohol).
5. In 2013 Sauk County, Wisconsin, had a total population of 61,976, an 11 percent poverty rate, a 14 percent food insecurity rate and an 8 percent unemployment rate. The county covers 848 square miles, is located about 50 miles from the state capital and has a primarily agriculturally based economy.
6. This calculation assumes a typical household as consisting of three people, divides the county's population by three, divides the number of households into the property valuation of the county and rounds up to the next $100,000.
7. Loring P. Jones, "Distinct Features of Midwestern Rural Poverty: Implications for Social Workers," Paper presented at the National Institute on Social Work in Rural Areas (Beaufort, NC, July 1981).
8. *Capital Times* (Madison, WI), June 5–11, 2013.
9. U.S. Department of the Interior, Indian Affairs, http://www.bia.gov.

Chapter 1

1. The economy food plan is the cost of consuming the minimum number of calories needed to maintain a healthy diet containing a balanced mix of breads, cereals, rice, pasta, fruits, vegetables, dairy items, and proteins.
2. Leslie A. Whitener and David A. McGranahan, "Rural America: Opportunities and Challenges," *Amber Waves* 1, no. 1 (February 2003): 14–21.
3. White House, http://www.whitehouse.gov.
4. Ibid.
5. Ibid.
6. Bruce Weber, Leif Jensen, Kathleen Miller, Jane Mosley, and Monica Fisher, "A Critical Review of Rural Poverty Literature: Is There Truly a Rural Effect?" *International Regional Science Review* 28, no. 4 (October 2005): 381–414.
7. Poverty rates of 20 percent or more in each decennial census between 1960 and 2000.
8. Janet M. Fitchen, *Poverty in Rural America: A Case Study* (Boulder, CO: Westview Press, 1981).

9. Margaret K. Nelson and Joan Smith, *Working Hard and Making Do: Surviving in Small Town America* (Berkeley: University of California Press, 1999).

10. Good jobs are defined as being more stable, well paying, having benefits, including health insurance, and flexibility, while bad jobs lack these qualities.

11. Stein Ringen, "Direct and Indirect Measures of Poverty," *Journal of Social Policy* 17, no. 3 (July 1988): 351–65.

12. Filip Spagnoli, "Measuring Poverty (4): The Problem of Definition," http://www.filipspagnoli.wordpress.com

13. Bruce Meyer and James Sullivan, "Identifying the Disadvantaged: Official Poverty, Consumption Poverty, and the New Supplemental Poverty Measure," *Journal of Economic Perspectives* 26, no. 3 (Summer 2012): 111–36.

14. "Report: U.S. Poverty Risk Rising," *Wisconsin State Journal*, July 29, 2013.

15. *WOW: Wider Opportunities for Women*, Economic Security Institute, http://www.wowonline.org.

16. Robert Chambers, *Rural Development: Putting the Last First* (London: Routledge, 1983).

17. World Bank, http://www.worldbank.org.

18. Paul Spicker, "Definitions of Poverty: Twelve Clusters of Meaning," in *Poverty: An International Glossary*, eds. Paul Spicker, Sonia Álvarez Leguizamón, and David Gordon, 229–43 (London: Zed Books, 2007).

19. M. MacDonald, "Evaluating Alternative Approaches to Measuring Basic Needs: Final Report," University of Wisconsin–Madison Institute for Research on Poverty, 1984.

20. U.S. Department of Health & Human Services, http://www.hhs.gov.

21. U.S. Census Bureau, http://www.census.gov.

22. Programs administered through the U.S. Department of Health and Human Services include Community Services Block Grants, Head Start, Low-income Home Energy Assistance Program (LIHEAP), Community Food and Nutrition Program, Parts of Medicaid, Hill-Burton Uncompensated Services Program, AIDS Drug Assistance Program, Children's Health Insurance Program, Medicare Prescription Drug Coverage (subsidized portion only), Community Health Centers, Migrant Health Centers, Family Planning Services, Student Loans (health professions and disadvantaged students), Health Careers Opportunity Program; Scholarships for Health Profession Students from Disadvantaged Backgrounds, Job Opportunities for Low Income Individuals; and Assets for Independence Demonstration Program. Programs administered through the U.S. Department of Agriculture include Supplemental Nutrition Assistance Program (formerly Food Stamps); Special Supplemental Nutrition Program for Women, Infants and Children (WIC); National Free and Reduced School Lunch and Breakfast Programs; Child and Adult Care Food Program; Expanded Food and Nutrition Education Program. Programs administered through the U.S. Department of Energy include Weatherization Assistance for Low Income Persons. The U.S. Department of Labor administers the Job Corps, National Farmworker Jobs Program, Senior Community Service Employment Program and Workforce Investment Act Youth Activities. The U.S. Department of the Treasury oversees the Low-income Taxpayers Clinic; the Corporation for National and Community Service administers the Foster Grandparent and Senior Companion Programs. The Legal Service Corporation provides Legal Services to the Poor.

23. "Defining Poverty Measure by Measure," *Economist*, March 21, 2013.

24. The NAS poverty threshold, below which a family is considered poor, is established on the basis of expenditures necessary for a family to have (clothing, food, shelter, and utilities) and is determined based upon key expenditures from a population that is not poor but falls somewhere below the national median income level. This results in a poverty threshold representing approximately the 33rd percentile of what families can expect to spend on food, clothing, shelter and utilities plus slightly more for necessary personal and household supplies. The threshold differs by family type and is affected by where a family lives, whether it receives in-kind assistance, pays taxes, or has non-discretionary expenses.

25. Laura Wheaton and Jamyang Tashi, "Measuring Poverty," *Fact Sheet #2* (Washington, D.C.: Urban Institute, February 2010).

26. U.S. Census Bureau Current Population Survey, 2009 Annual Social and Economic Supplement, October 19, 2009.

27. U.S. Census Bureau; U.S. Department of Health & Human Services.

28. Wheaton and Tashi.

29. U.S. Census Bureau.

30. Weber et al.

31. U.S. Department of Agriculture, http://www.usda.gov.

32. Per capita income is a measure of average income based upon total population and commonly used in demographic reports. It is a deceiving measure to use when exploring poverty because the average is artificially inflated by high income individuals, and there are always more of these individuals than individuals living below the poverty line.

33. U.S. Department of Agriculture, Economic Research Service, http://www.ers.usda.gov.

34. National Center for Children in Poverty, http://www.nccp.org.

Chapter 2

1. For a complete discussion of this concept, see Michael T. Lubbrage, "Manifest Destiny: The Philosophy That Created a Nation," *American History: From Revolution to Reconstruction and Beyond*, http://www.let.rug.nl/usa/essays/1801–1900/manifest-destiny/manifest-destiny—the-philosophy-that-created-a-nation.php.

2. Stephen R. Demkin, Lecture Notes, HIS 110–83, Delaware County Community College, 1996.

3. Alan Brinkley, *American History: A Survey*, Volume I, 9th ed. (New York: McGraw-Hill, 1995).

4. Ibid.

5. Rudolph C. Rÿser, *A Publication of the Center for World Indigenous Studies*, cited in Lubbrage.

6. For further insights into the Louisiana Purchase, see Thomas Fleming's *The Louisiana Purchase* (Hoboken, NJ: John Wiley & Sons, 2003).

7. The land purchase included all of present-day Arkansas, Missouri, Iowa, Oklahoma, Kansas, and Nebraska; parts of Minnesota that were west of the Mississippi River; most of North Dakota; most of South Dakota; northeastern New Mexico; northern

Texas; the portions of Montana, Wyoming, and Colorado east of the Continental Divide; Louisiana west of the Mississippi River, including the city of New Orleans; and small portions of land that would eventually become part of the Canadian provinces of Alberta and Saskatchewan.

8. The British Corn Laws, in force between 1689 and 1846, were designed to protect English landholders by encouraging the export and limiting the import of corn when prices fell below a fixed point. They were eventually abolished in 1846—a significant political and economic triumph indicative of the rising political power of the English middle class.

9. Preemption is a doctrine based on the Supremacy Clause of the U.S. Constitution that holds that certain matters are of such a national, as opposed to local, character that federal laws preempt or take precedence over state laws. As such, a state may not pass a law inconsistent with the federal law.

10. Lee Ann Potter and Wynell Schamel, "The Homestead Act of 1862," *Social Education* 61, no. 6 (October 1997): 356–64.

11. Marlene Springer and Haskell Springer, eds., *Plains Woman: The Diary of Martha Farnsworth, 1882–1922* (Bloomington: Indiana University Press, 1986): 63–64.

12. Joanna L. Stratton, *Pioneer Women: Voices from the Kansas Frontier* (New York: Simon & Schuster, 1981): 81.

13. For a full discussion of this, see Deborah Fink, *Agrarian Women: Wives and Mothers in Rural Nebraska, 1880–1940* (Chapel Hill: University of North Carolina Press, 1992).

14. Willa Cather, *My Antonia* (Boston: Houghton Mifflin, 1949).

15. Willa Cather, *O Pioneers!* (Mineola, NY: Dover Books, 1993).

16. Stephen Ambrose, *Nothing Like It in the World* (New York: Simon & Schuster, 2000).

17. National History Day, U.S. National Archives and Records Administration, and USA Freedom Corps, *Our Documents*, http://www.ourdocuments.gov.

18. Ibid.

19. Thomas A. Bland, *How to Grow Rich*, cited by Benjamin Heber Johnson in "Red Populism, Agrarian Radicalism and the Debate over the Dawes Act," in *The Countryside in the Age of the Modern State*, eds. Catherine McNicol Stock and Robert D. Johnston (Ithaca, NY: Cornell University Press, 2001).

20. Ibid., p. 26.

21. Thomas A. Bland, *The Council of Fire*, cited in Benjamin Heber Johnson, "Red Populism, Agrarian Radicalism and the Debate over the Dawes Act," in *The Countryside in the Age of the Modern State*, eds. Catherine McNicol Stock and Robert D. Johnston, 28 (Ithaca, NY: Cornell University Press, 2001).

22. The Morrill Act committed the federal government to grant each state 30,000 acres of public land issued in the form of "land scrip" certificates for each of its representatives and senators in Congress. Although many states squandered the revenue from this endowment, which grew to an allocation of over 100 million acres, the Morrill land grants laid the foundation for a national system of higher education. In some cases, the land sales financed existing institutions; in others, new schools were chartered by the states. Major universities such as Nebraska, Washington State, Clemson, and Cornell were chartered as land-grant schools and have brought higher education within the reach of millions of students. In 1890 the Morrill Act legislation was extended to include Confederate states that had previously seceded from the Union.

23. National History Day, U.S. National Archives and Records Administration, and USA Freedom Corps.

24. Frederick Jackson Turner, *The Frontier in American History* (New York: Henry Holt, 1920).

25. Richard Slotkin, "Nostalgia and Progress: Theodore Roosevelt's Myth of the Frontier," *American Quarterly* 33, no. 5 (Winter 1981): 608–37.

26. An alluvial plain is a largely flat landform created by sediment deposits occurring over a long period of time by one or more rivers coming from highland regions, from which rich alluvial soil forms.

27. Dryland farming is a technique for non-irrigated cultivation of dryland common in the Great Plains. Winter wheat is the typical crop although skilled dryland farmers sometimes grow corn, beans or even watermelons. Successful dry land farming is possible with as little as nine inches (230 mm) of precipitation a year; higher rainfall increases the variety of crops. The choice of crop is influenced by the timing of the predominant rainfall in relation to the seasons. For example, winter wheat is more suited to regions with higher winter rainfall while areas with summer wet seasons may be more suited to summer growing crops such as sorghum, sunflowers or cotton. Success as a dryland farmer requires careful husbandry of the moisture available for the crop and aggressive management of expenses to minimize losses in poor years. Dryland farming is uniquely dependent on natural rainfall, which can leave the ground vulnerable to dust storms, particularly if poor farming techniques are used or if the storms strike at a particularly vulnerable time. The fact that a fallow period must be included in the crop rotation means that fields cannot always be protected by a cover crop, which might otherwise offer protection against erosion.

28. U.S. Department of the Interior, Bureau of Land Management, http://www.blm.gov/wo/st/en.html.

29. "Granger Movement," *Encyclopedia Britannica*, http://www.britannica.com/EBchecked/topic/241647/Granger-movement.

30. The Greenback Party (known successively as the Independent Party, the National Independent Party, the Greenback Party, and the Greenback Labor Party) was an American political party with an anti-monopoly ideology that was active between 1874 and 1889. The party's name referred to the non-gold-backed paper money, commonly known as "greenbacks," issued by the North during and shortly after the Civil War. The party opposed the deflationary lowering of prices paid to producers entailed by a return to a bullion-based monetary system, the policy favored by the dominant Republican Party. Continued use of unbacked currency, it was believed, would better foster business and assist farmers by raising prices and making debts easier to pay. Initially an agrarian organization associated with the policies of the Grange, the Greenback Party took the name Greenback Labor Party and attempted to forge a farmer-labor alliance, adding industrial reforms to its agenda, such as support of the eight-hour day and opposition to the use of state or private force to suppress union

strikes. The organization faded into oblivion in the second half of the 1880s, with its basic program reborn shortly under the aegis of the People's Party, commonly known as the Populists.

31. Theodore Roosevelt Association, http://www.theodoreroosevelt.org.

32. Roosevelt's reclamation projects included Milk River (Montana), March 14, 1903; Newlands (Nevada), March 14, 1903; North Platte (Nebraska and Wyoming), March 14, 1903; Salt River (Arizona), March 14, 1903; Uncompahgre (Colorado), March 14, 1903; Belle Fourche (South Dakota), May 10, 1904; Lower Yellowstone (Montana and N. Dakota), May 10, 1904; Minidoka (Idaho), April 23, 1904; Shoshone (Wyoming), February 10, 1904; Yuma (Arizona and California), May 10, 1904; Boise (Idaho and Oregon), March 27, 1905; Huntley (Montana), April 18, 1905; Klamath (California and Oregon), May 15, 1905; Rio Grande (New Mexico), December 2, 1905; Carlsbad (New Mexico), December 2, 1905; Okanogan (Washington), December 2, 1905; Strawberry Valley (Utah), December 15, 1905; Sun River (Montana), February 26, 1906; Umatilla (Oregon), December 4, 1905; Yakima (Washington), December 12, 1905; Orland (California), October 5, 1907; and the Blackfeet, Flathead and Fort Peck Indian reservations.

33. Wessels Living History Farm, http://www.livinghistoryfarm.org.

34. Ibid.

35. John Steinbeck, *The Grapes of Wrath* (New York: Viking Press, 1939).

36. For a full discussion of New Deal conservation programs, see Neil M. Maher, *Nature's New Deal* (New York: Oxford University Press, 2008).

37. "The Civilian Conservation Corps," *American Experience*, PBS, http://www.pbs.org/wgbh/americanexperience/features/photo-gallery/ccc/.

38. Only 37 days elapsed between FDR's inauguration on March 4, 1933, and the induction of the first CCC enrollee.

39. "The Civilian Conservation Corps."

40. Independence Hall Association, http://www.ushistory.org.

41. Ibid.

Chapter 3

1. Official definitions of the term *rural* vary widely and are determined by land use, economic development, or local government administrative boundaries. Most commonly, *rural* refers to a defined non-metropolitan area having no population centers with 50,000 or more people. Another definition of *rural* is an area comprised of open country and settlements with fewer than 2,500 residents. Areas designated as rural can have population densities as high as 999 per square mile or as low as less than one person per square mile. Presently, 21st-century rural America includes 2,305 counties and lays claim to 80 percent of the nation's total land mass.

2. U.S. Census Bureau.

3. Ibid.

4. U.S. Department of Agriculture, Farm Service Agency, http://www.fsa.usda.gov.

5. U.S. Department of Agriculture.

6. Farm women and children play key roles in farming success because, from a young age, children help with daily chores, while farm wives keep the books and often hold down the all-important second, off the farm job that supplements the farm income.

7. For a full discussion of the 1980s farm crisis, see Chapter 2.

8. Cynthia Nickerson, Mitchell Morehart, Todd Kuethe, Jayson Beckman, Jennifer Ifft, and Ryan Williams, *Trends in U.S. Farmland Values and Ownership* (Washington, D.C.: USDA, Economic Research Service, 2012).

9. Ibid.

10. USDA Census of Agriculture, http://agcensus.usda.gov.

11. Ibid.

12. For a full discussion, see Paula vW Dáil, *Women and Poverty in 21st Century America*.

13. This discussion assumes farmers, who are self-employed, paid into Social Security during their active farming years; if they did not, they will not receive this income.

14. Social Security retirement benefits are a wage-based system. During an individual's working years he/she pays a 6.2 percent payroll tax, matched by an equal employer contribution, which is then paid back in monthly installments when retirement age is reached. Self-employed individuals, which include most farmers and small business people in rural areas, must pay the entire 12.4 percent payroll tax. In rural, agriculture-dependent economies, annual income levels can vary widely and during low-income years considerably less is paid into the Social Security retirement system, making less money available at retirement. Those who earned more during their working years receive more back, through a series of monthly installments that last as long as the individual lives and then pass on to the surviving spouse, if there is one, up to a 2012 maximum payment of $2,513 at full retirement age. The Social Security payment system is adjusted so that lower-income workers will receive a higher percentage of their former wages than higher-income workers receive. After reaching full retirement age there is no limit on the amount of additional income an individual can earn without having his/her Social Security benefits reduced. Social Security benefits are subject to annual cost-of-living increases based on the CPI (Consumer Price Index for Urban Wage Earners and Clerical Workers). These adjustments are based on the price of goods purchased by approximately 32 percent of U.S. workers and averages between 3 and 4 percent each year.

15. Dáil, *Women and Poverty in 21st Century America*.

16. Ibid.

17. U.S. Census Bureau. These figures are for illustrating a calculation and do not discriminate between rural and urban residents receiving Social Security.

18. U.S. Department of Agriculture. Nationwide, the 2010 average cropland value was $2,100 per acre, with New Jersey having the highest cropland value per acre and North Dakota having the lowest.

19. Phillip Kunkel, Jeffrey Peterson, and Jessica Mitchell, *Farm Leases* (Minneapolis and St. Paul: University of Minnesota Extension Service, 2009).

20. Kathryn Marie Dudley, *Debt and Dispossession: Farm Loss in America's Heartland* (Chicago: University of Chicago Press, 2000).

21. A land contract is a legal agreement between a seller and buyer of real estate in which the seller provides financing to purchase the property. Until the loan is paid off the seller retains legal title to the prop-

erty, while permitting the buyer to take possession of it. When the terms of the loan have been met, the seller transfers legal title of the property to the buyer.

22. Some Midwestern tribes, such as the Ho Chunk, have become very successful in the gaming industry and, as a result, have been able to pay registered tribal members significant annual allowances, but this is an exception to the general economic plight of American Indians nationwide.

23. Statistics summarized by Dante McAuliffe, "Native Americans and Extreme Poverty (Pine Ridge Reservation)," *Soapboxer Magazine,* April 14, 2013, http://www.thinkaboutit-knowaboutit.com/2013/04/native-americans-and-extreme-poverty.html.

24. Sequestration refers to automatic spending cuts instituted by Congress. Under sequestration, an amount of money equal to the difference between the cap set in the Budget Resolution and the amount actually appropriated is "sequestered" by the Treasury and not handed over to the agencies to which Congress originally appropriated it. Under sequestration not all programs were treated equally; some, such as Social Security, were entirely exempt, placing non-exempt programs in the difficult position of being forced to make up for the exempted programs by accepting massive budget cuts, virtually paralyzing their ability to meet their program responsibilities or carry out their program activities.

25. "Jesuit Highlights Consequences of Budget Cuts for Native Americans," August 19, 2013, *Jesuits,* http://www.jesuit.org/news-detail?TN=NEWS-20130818010425.

26. U.S. Department of Agriculture, Census of Agriculture, http://www.agcensus.usda.gov.

27. Ibid.
28. Ibid.
29. Ibid.
30. Ibid.

31. Rural Poverty Research Institute, http://www.rupri.org.

32. Ibid.

Chapter 4

1. Aaron Smith, "Cash-strapped Farmers Feed Candy to Cows," CNN, October 10, 2012, http://money.cnn.com/2012/10/10/news/economy/farmers-cows-candy-feed/.

2. An operating farm is any establishment from which $1,000 or more agricultural products were sold or normally would be sold during the year.

3. U.S. Department of Agriculture.

4. "Rust Belt," *Dictionary of American History* (Detroit: Gale Group, 2003), http://www.encyclopedia.com/topic/Rust_Belt.aspx.

5. U.S. Census Bureau.

6. NAFTA presumes that the United States, Canada and Mexico each have unique natural advantages that allow production of certain goods or services more cost-efficiently than others are able to provide it. By eliminating tariff barriers, NAFTA allows all three member countries to focus their productive efforts on their natural advantages. For example, the United States produces high-quality consumer goods at low cost, while Mexico produces certain foods and crops at low cost. Eliminating tariff barriers between the two nations allows Mexicans to purchase cheap consumer goods from the U.S. while allowing U.S. food distributors to purchase cheap Mexican crops. However, shifting the industrial focus in each country causes job losses for both, particularly during the transition from domestic purchase to imported goods. The industry in the importing country loses business, causing significant job losses. In some cases, entire industries can weaken to the point of disappearing entirely as the result of free trade agreements such as NAFTA.

7. According to the Census Bureau, the average wage for a manufacturing job ranges from $14.85 per hour for someone with less than a high school education to just over $20 per hour for a high school graduate.

8. Medicaid is the government subsidized indigent health care program.

9. *America's Farmers,* http://www.americasfarmers.com, 2012.

10. U.S. Environmental Protection Agency, http://www.epa.gov/.

11. Lester Brown, "Iowa Eclipses Canada in Grain Production, Challenges China in Soybean Production, *Treehugger,* July 28, 2011, http://www.treehugger.com/corporate-responsibility/iowa-eclipses-canada-in-grain-production-challenges-china-in-soybean-production.html.

12. Ibid.

13. U.S. Department of Agriculture, National Agricultural Statistics Service, http://www.nass.usda.gov/.

14. "Crop Values: 2011 Summary," U.S. Department of Agriculture, National Agricultural Statistics Service, February 2012, http://www.nass.usda.gov/Publications/Todays_Reports/reports/cpvl0212.pdf.

15. U.S. Drought Monitor, http://www.droughtmonitor.unl.edu.

16. Silage is fermented, high-moisture fodder that can be fed to cud-chewing animals such as cattle and sheep or used as a biofuel feedstock for anaerobic digesters.

17. The amount of land dedicated to corn silage production varies based on growing conditions. In years that produce weather conditions that do not favor high corn grain yields, corn crops can be "salvaged" by harvesting the entire plant as silage.

18. National Corn Growers Association, http://www.ncga.com/home.

19. U.S. Environmental Protection Agency.

20. United Soybean Board, http://unitedsoybean.org/.

21. National Hay Association, http://www.nationalhay.org/.

22. U.S. Environmental Protection Agency, National Agricultural Statistics Service.

23. Ibid.

24. "Crop Values: 2011 Summary."

25. U.S. Department of Agriculture.

26. U.S. Department of Agriculture, National Agricultural Statistics Service.

27. U.S. Department of Agriculture.

28. Ninety percent of cow herds have less than 100 cows (avg. 44 head).

29. U.S. Meat Export Federation, http://www.usmef.org.

30. The hundredweight or centum weight (cwt) is a unit of mass defined in terms of the 16 oz. pound (lb.). The short hundredweight is defined as 100 lbs. and is customarily used in the U.S. weights and measures system.

31. Overview of United States Dairy Industry, U.S. Department of Agriculture, National Agricultural Statistics Service, September 2010, http://www.nass.usda.gov/.

32. Ibid.

33. Ibid.

34. According to the USDA, the milk-feed ratio is an indicator of the quantity of 16 percent protein mixed dairy feed equal in value to one pound of whole milk and is an indicator of the quantity of 16 percent mixed dairy feed that can be purchased with a pound of milk (http://usda01.library.cornell.edu/usda/current/USDairyIndus-09-22-2010.pdf).

35. Farrow-to-finish hog operations typically practice some form of confinement whereby pigs are bred and raised to their slaughter weight, usually 225–300 pounds.

36. As the name implies, a forward sale production contract is a contract between a buyer and a seller whereby the seller agrees to purchase, at a future date, a specified number of hogs from the seller for an agreed-upon, predetermined price.

37. Nigel Key and William McBride, *The Changing Economics of U.S. Hog Production* (Washington, D.C.: USDA Economic Research Service [ERS], 2007).

38. Ibid.

39. Ibid.

40. Ibid.

41. Ibid.

42. John D. Lawrence and Shane Ellis, *Monthly Returns from Finishing Feeder and Weaned Pigs*, Iowa State University, July 2007, http://www.econ.iastate.edu/estimated-returns/files/ERassumptions/FE07a.pdf.

43. Ibid.

44. The price of Midwest No. 2 over-the-road diesel is estimated from an historic price database maintained by the U.S. Department of Energy.

45. Breeding hogs removed from the group.

46. USDA, ERS using data from USDA's 1992 Farm Costs and Returns Survey and 1998 and 2004 Agricultural Resource Management Surveys, http://www.ers.usda.gov.

47. Key and McBride.

48. "Estimated Livestock Returns: Summary of Estimated Returns," Iowa State University, University Extension, http://www.econ.iastate.edu/estimated-returns/summary.html.

49. Ibid.

50. According to Iowa State University agricultural economists, annual return estimates assume that producers market an equal number of animals every month. While this assumption may be realistic for many hog producers, cattle feeders tend to sell only one or two groups per year. Further, with the health advantages of all-in, all-out feeder pig finishing, producers may, wisely, want to consider timing sales to achieve more profitable marketing because the difference in average monthly returns suggests that there may be more profitable months to buy, feed, and sell cattle or hogs. Annual return estimates also help determine which months feeder pig producers should choose to retain ownership of the pigs all the way to slaughter rather than selling as younger pigs (http://www2.econ.iastate.edu/faculty/lawrence/lawrence_website/estreturns.htm).

51. Osha Gray Davidson, "In the Wake of Huge-Hog Lots, What Is Replacing the Heartland's Family Farms?" *Des Moines Register*, January 5, 1997.

52. U.S. Department of Agriculture.

53. Ibid.

54. Ibid.

55. U.S. Environmental Protection Agency.

56. Food and Agriculture Organization of the United Nations, http://www.fao.org.

57. Chicago Mercantile Exchange (formerly Chicago Board of Trade), http://www.cmegroup.com/.

58. Alden C. Manchester and Don P. Blayney, *Milk Pricing in the United States* (Washington, D.C.: U.S. Department of Agriculture, Economic Research Service, Market and Trade Economics Division, 2001).

59. Milk can be preserved by dehydrating it into dried milk; otherwise, it is a high-spoilage commodity that must be refrigerated and consumed fresh and, unlike meat and grain products, cannot be canned or frozen. Pasteurized fresh milk has a shelf life of about ten days.

60. Edward V. Jesse and Robert A. Cropp, *Basic Milk Pricing for Dairy Farmers* (Madison: University of Wisconsin Cooperative Extension, 2004).

61. The Producer Price Differential (PPD) varies geographically, and tends to move higher in the Upper Midwest where cheese production is strong and drop lower in the Northeast where fluid milk production is greater.

62. Jesse and Cropp.

63. Futures are contracts that state that producers promise to pay growers now for a specific crop to be grown and delivered at a later date.

64. Chicago Mercantile Exchange.

65. U.S. Department of Agriculture, National Agricultural Statistics Service.

66. Rachel Carson, *The Silent Spring* (New York: Houghton Mifflin, 1962).

67. Ibid.

68. Jan E. Zejda, Helen H. McDuffie, and James A. Dosman, ", Canada. Epidemiology of Health and Safety Risks in Agriculture and Related Industries: Practical Applications for Rural Physicians," *Western Journal of Medicine* 158, no. 1 (January 1993): 56–63.

69. U.S. Department of Energy, http://www.doe.gov.

70. David Cobia, ed., *Cooperatives in Agriculture* (Englewood Cliffs, NJ: Prentice-Hall, 1989).

71. Farmers Cooperative Society, http://www.farmerscoopsociety.com.

72. In Wisconsin and other states where public schools are funded through property tax levies, public schools, by law, must go to referendum to fund school building expansion or update equipment when the costs exceed a pre-determined amount. This places the final decision about school maintenance and operations in the hands of local taxpayers.

73. *America's Farmers*.

Chapter 5

1. Joel Solkoff, *The Politics of Food* (San Francisco: Sierra Club Books, 1985).

2. The federal funds rate is the interest rate at which depository institutions actively trade balances held at the Federal Reserve (called federal funds) with each other, usually overnight and without having to provide collateral. Institutions having surplus balances in their accounts lend those balances to institutions in need of larger balances. The interest rate

that the borrowing bank pays to the lending bank to borrow the funds is negotiated between the two banks, and the weighted average of this rate across all such transactions is the federal funds effective rate. The rate had averaged 11.2 percent in 1979, and suddenly rose to a peak of 20 percent in June 1981. As a result the prime lending rate rose to 21.5 percent.

3. Dudley, 35–36.

4. For a full discussion of the 1980s farm crisis, see Chapter 2.

5. Dudley, 35.

6. Agricultural land values are determined in part by the land's own ability to produce a profitable crop. When crop prices fall, land values follow soon after, because the land, while remaining exactly the same as it always was, is no longer able to generate as much income for the farmer, thus its value to the farmer falls.

7. "Campaign Notes: Reagan's Farm Policy Assailed by Democrats," Reuters News Service, April 28, 1984.

8. http://www.farmbillfacts.org.

9. Congressional Budget Office, http://www.cbo.gov.

10. Ron Kind press release, "Rep. Ron Kind Slams Farm Bill's Lack of Meaningful Reform," January 29, 2014, http://kind.house.gov/latest-news/rep-ron-kind-slams-farm-bills-lack-of-meaningful-reform/.

11. Pat Schneider, "Q&A: Jonathan Bader Says Congress, Legislature Should Create Jobs, Not Skimp on Food Stamps," *Capital Times*, June 2, 2013.

12. Deficiency payments are paid to farmers or producers by the government for all or part of the difference between the government-guaranteed price and the market price of a commodity.

13. Target prices were eliminated in the 1996 farm bill (P.L. 104–127), but restored again in the 2002 farm bill (P.L. 101–171, Sec. 1104).

14. Ibid.

15. Direct payment subsidies are limited to $40,000 per person or $80,000 per couple, which enables the farmer receiving a subsidy to borrow $40,000 or $80,000 less in operating money each year.

16. In recent times corn has been the top subsidy payment crop, primarily as a direct result of the Energy Policy Act of 2005, which mandated that billions of gallons of ethanol be blended into vehicle fuel each year, thus guaranteeing demand for corn. U.S. corn ethanol subsidies are between $5.5 billion and $7.3 billion per year, and through 2011 corn producers also benefitted from a federal subsidy of 51 cents per gallon, additional state subsidies, and federal crop subsidies that can bring the total to 85 cents per gallon or more. However, the federal ethanol subsidy expired December 31, 2011.

17. Environmental Working Group, http://www.ewg.org.

18. Ibid.

19. Veronique de Rugy, "Veronique de Rugy on Why Farm Subsidies Must Die," March 13, 2012, http://reason.com/blog/2013/03/12/veronique-de-rugy-on-why-farm-subsidies.

20. Brian M. Riedl, "How Farm Subsidies Harm Taxpayers, Consumers and Farmers, Too," Heritage Foundation, June 20, 2007, http://www.heritage.org/research/reports/2007/06/how-farm-subsidies-harm-taxpayers-consumers-and-farmers-too.

21. Ibid.

22. Ibid.
23. Ibid.
24. Ibid.
25. Environmental Working Group.
26. Suburbs of Madison, Wisconsin, the state capital.
27. Riedl.
28. Ibid.

29. When the 1996 farm bill increased the marketing loan rate of soybeans from $4.92 to $5.26 per bushel (which meant larger subsidies), farmers responded by planting an additional 8 million acres of soybeans, which contributed to the 33 percent decline in soybean prices over the next two years. Instead of alleviating low soybean prices, the new subsidies accelerated their fall at considerable taxpayer expense.

30. Riedl.

31. Fruits, vegetables, livestock, and poultry, which comprise two-thirds of all farm production, are generally not subsidized at all.

32. Riedl.

33. American Farm Bureau Federation, www.fb.org.

34. Kind.

35. Carson.

36. Helmut F. van Emden and David B. Peakall, *Beyond Silent Spring: Integrated Pest Management and Chemical Safety* (London: Chapman & Hall on behalf of the United Nations Environment Programme, 1996).

37. Ibid., 3.

38. Ibid., 5.

39. Pierre Desrochers and Hiroko Shimizu, *The Locavore's Dilemma: In Praise of the 10,000-Mile Diet* (New York: PublicAffairs Books, 2012).

40. For a full discussion, see Michael Wines, "Wells Dry, Fertile Plains Turn to Dust," *New York Times*, May 19, 2013, http://www.nytimes.com/2013/05/20/us/high-plains-aquifer-dwindles-hurting-farmers.html?pagewanted=all&_r=0.

Chapter 6

1. A reference to the Green Bay Packers, Wisconsin's professional football team.

2. Barron County is a rural county encompassing 890 square miles. It has a population of 49,883, a 9.3 percent unemployment rate, a 14 percent poverty rate and 15 percent food insecurity rate.

3. Richard Critchfield, *Trees, Why Do You Wait?* (Washington, D.C.: Island Press, 1991).

4. Kathleen Norris, *Dakota: A Spiritual Geography*. (New York: Ticknor & Fields, 1993).

5. Ibid.

6. Linda Tirado, "Why I Make Terrible Decisions, or, Poverty Thoughts," *Killermartinis*, http://killermartinis.kinja.com/why-i-make-terrible-decisions-or-poverty-thoughts-1450123558.

7. Habitat for Humanity, http://www.habitat.org.

Chapter 7

1. Wisconsin and many other Midwestern states have laws forbidding the over the counter sale of many common cough remedies because most contain an ingredient useful in making methamphetamine—a highly dangerous illegal drug.

2. South Carolina Rural Health Research Center, 2005, http://www.rhr.sph.sc.edu
3. Paula Dáil, "Rural Health Care Delivery Challenges Are Many and Varied," *Dodgeville Chronicle*, May 6, 2006.
4. Congressional Budget Office.
5. Ibid.
6. Medically indigent individuals are those whose income is too high to receive government-funded health care and too low to afford the cost of purchasing health care insurance.
7. Betsy McCaughey, *Beating ObamaCare: Your Handbook for the New Health Care Law* (Washington, D.C.: Regnery Publishing, 2013).
8. Sabrina Tavarnise and Robert Gebeloff, "Millions of Poor Left Uncovered by Health Law," *New York Times*, October 2, 2013, http://www.nytimes.com/2013/10/03/health/millions-of-poor-are-left-uncovered-by-health-law.html?pagewanted=all.
9. Red states are Republican-controlled states. Seventy-five percent of Midwestern states are red; the exceptions are Illinois, Minnesota and Missouri.
10. Citizen Action of Wisconsin, http://www.citizenactionwi.org.
11. Carmen DeNavas-Walt, Bernadette D. Proctor, and Jessica Smith, *Income, Poverty and Health Insurance Coverage in the United States: 2008* (Washington, D.C.: U.S. Census Bureau, 2008).
12. U.S. Department of Health and Human Services, Centers for Medicare and Medicaid Services, http://www.cms.gov.
13. Wisconsin Department of Health Services 2009 federal Medicaid guidelines set the poverty level for a family of four at $1,837.50 per month. For each additional person add (or subtract) $311.67 per month.
14. University of Wisconsin–Madison, Institute for Research on Poverty, 2007, http://www.irp.wisc.edu.
15. Center for Studying Health System Change, 2009, http://www.hschange.com.
16. Urban Institute, Health Policy Center, 2009, http://www.urban.org/center/hpc.
17. Wisconsin Department of Health Services Report on Health and Physical Activity, 2009.
18. Larry D. Gamm, Linnae D. Hutchison, Betty J. Dabney, and Alicia M. Dorsey, eds., *Rural Health People 2010: A Companion Document to Healthy People 2010*, Vol. 1 (College Station: Texas A&M University System Health Science Center, School of Rural Public Health, Southwest Rural Health Research Center, 2003), http://srph.tamhsc.edu/centers/rhp2010/Volume1.pdf.
19. "Eye on Health" report, Rural Wisconsin Health Cooperative, 2010, http://www.rwhc.com/News/EyeonHealthNewsletter.aspx.
20. Rand Corporation, http://www.rand.org.
21. American Farm Bureau Federation, http://www.fb.org.
22. Press Release, U.S. Department of Health and Human Services, Washington, D.C., February 4, 2010.
23. U.S. Centers for Disease Control and Prevention, National Institute for Occupational Safety and Health (NIOSH), http://www.cdc.gov/niosh.
24. "Farm Safety," U.S. Department of Labor Program Highlight Fact Sheet No. OSHA 91–39."
25. Bureau of Labor Statistics, http://www.bls.gov/cpol.
26. National Safety Council, http://www.nsc.org.
27. U.S. Centers for Disease Control and Prevention, National Institute for Occupational Safety and Health (NIOSH).
28. Dáil, "Rural Health Care Delivery Challenges Are Many and Varied."
29. National Campaign to Prevent Teen and Unplanned Pregnancy, http://www.thenationalcampaign.org.
30. *U.S. Teen Pregnancy Statistics: Overall Trends by Race and Ethnicity and State-by-State Information* (New York: Alan Guttmacher Institute, 2004). Updated 2007 by Peter Chen, MD, Department of Obstetrics and Gynecology, University of Pennsylvania Medical Center, Philadelphia, PA.
31. K. E. Fottergill, "Probing the Reasons Underlying Adolescent Pregnancy: A Qualitative Study," Paper presented at the 133rd Annual Meeting of the American Public Health Association, Philadelphia, PA, December 2005.
32. Joyce A. Martin, Brady E. Hamilton, Paul D. Sutton, Stephanie J. Ventura, Fay Menacker, Sharon Kirmeyer, and T. J. Mathews, "Births: Final Data for 2006," *National Vital Statistics Reports* 57, no. 7 (January 2009).
33. For a full discussion of this issue, see Paula Dáil, *Women and Poverty in 21st Century America*.
34. "Facts on Induced Abortion in the United States," *Fact Sheet*, July 2008, Guttmacher Institute, http://www.guttmacher.org.
35. Gini Sikes, *8 Ball Chicks* (New York: Anchor Books, 1998).
36. American Psychological Association, http://www.apa.org.
37. South Carolina Rural Health Research Center.
38. Ibid.
39. Rural Assistance Center, http://www.raconline.org.
40. Paula Dáil, "IWATCH Tackles the Underage Drinking Issue," *Dodgeville Chronicle*, 2007.
41. Pacific Institute for Research and Evaluation, http://www.pire.org.
42. Karen Van Gundy, *Substance Abuse in Rural and Small Town America* (Durham: Carsey Institute, University of New Hampshire, 2006), http://www.carseyinstitute.unh.edu/sites/carseyinstitute.unh.edu/files/publications/Report_SubstanceAbuse.pdf.
43. "County Drug Task Force Meets to Discuss Growing Heroin Problem," *Dodgeville Chronicle*, March 27, 2014.
44. Ibid.
45. Marshfield Clinic, http://www.marshfieldclinic.org.
46. Ibid.
47. Ibid.
48. Shirley Barnes, "A Day in the Life of the Free Clinic," *Voice of the River Valley*, April 2013, http://voiceoftherivervalley.com/wp-content/uploads/2013/03/201304-voice-print-proof.pdf.

Chapter 8

1. Cow tipping is a common prank in rural areas that occurs because cows have precarious balance and three or four persons can push one over onto its side. The cow is unable to right itself, and if not discovered quickly, often dies.
2. Chuck Raasch, "In Gun Debate, It's Urban vs. Rural," *USA Today*, February 27, 2013.

3. E-coli is a bacteria commonly found in drinking water contaminated by fecal material and causes severe diarrhea that can be fatal in young children and older adults; nitrate contamination is the result of excessive use of farm chemicals that seep into the groundwater and contaminate wells.

4. The fee waiver application requires the applicant to swear under oath to poverty status and provide extensive financial and household information.

5. Jerry Hambley, "Crime in Rural America on the Rise," *Lemon's Corner,* February 2, 2012, http://www.lemonscorner.com/crime/.

6. Ralph A. Weisheit, David N. Falcone, and L. Edward Wells, *Rural Crime and Rural Policing* (Washington, D.C.: U.S. Department of Justice, Office of Justice Programs, National Institute of Justice, 1994).

7. Ibid.

8. In this rural county, in 2005 there were 67 drunk driving arrests per 10,000 people, a rate significantly higher than occurred in the state's largest urban area during the same time period.

9. John A. Gale and David Hartley, "Adolescent Alcohol Use in Rural Areas: What Are the Issues?" Maine Rural Health Research Center, June 2012.

10. Substance Abuse and Mental Health Services Administration, http://www.SAMHSA.gov.

11. Ibid.

12. J. Patrick Reilly, "Heroin Turns Lives into Hell," *Dodgeville Chronicle,* August 15, 2013.

13. "Narc" is a slang term for a person who is not a member of law enforcement but turns individuals into the police for doing or dealing drugs.

14. "Pot" is another name for marijuana.

15. Weisheit, Falcone, and Wells.

16. Nathan J. Comp, "The Heroin Blues: A Story about Love, Addiction and Loss," *Capital Times,* February 26, 2014.

17. Gale and Hartley.

18. "Killing of Wiota Farmers Points to Holes in Mental Health System, Critics Say," *Wisconsin State Journal,* January 26, 2014.

19. Gale and Hartley.

20. Daniel Levitas, *The Terrorist Next Door: The Militia Movement and the Radical Right* (New York: Thomas Dunne Books, 2002).

21. Gale and Hartley.

22. Ibid.

23. Charles R. Swanson and Leonard Territo, "Agricultural Crime: Its Extent, Prevention, and Control," *FBI Law Enforcement Bulletin* 49, no. 5 (May 1980): 8–12.

24. Illegal hunting, capturing or killing of wild animals, particularly on posted land where hunting is not permitted.

25. Gale and Hartley.

Chapter 9

1. U.S. Census Bureau 2010 Annual Survey of Local Government Finances: Public Education Finances Report, http://www.census.gov.

2. "Outlook Bleak for Rural Schools," *The State Journal,* March 10, 2014.

3. The No Child Left Behind (NCLB) Act of 2001 and the revised Elementary and Secondary Education Act offered a potent blend of new requirements, incentives and resources, as well as posing significant challenges for states. The law set deadlines for states to expand the scope and frequency of student testing, revamp their accountability systems and guarantee that every teacher is qualified in their subject area. NCLB required states to make demonstrable annual progress in raising the percentage of students proficient in reading and math, and in narrowing the test-score gap between advantaged and disadvantaged students. After 10 years, NCLB has successfully re-focused attention on the need for states and the nation to close the achievement gap that plagues our education system. However, over the years, significant flaws in the law have come to light and there is widespread outcry for a new and improved NCLB. As a result, the federal government is offering flexibility from the law's provisions to states in exchange for innovative efforts to close achievement gaps, promote rigorous accountability, and ensure that all students are on track to graduate college and be career-ready. As of August 2012, 33 states have been granted waivers (http://www.ecs.org/html/issue.asp?issueID=195).

4. U.S. Census Bureau 2010 Annual Survey of Local Government Finances: Public Education Finances Report, http://www.census.gov.

5. In recent years Wisconsin governor Scott Walker "broke" the state teacher's union by stripping away its collective bargaining rights and removing the provision that allows union dues to be collected through a payroll deduction. As a result, Wisconsin teachers now receive a salary increase that is tied to the cost of living index and cannot bargain for health care insurance costs, terms of leave, or other common benefits. Union membership is now optional, but without the ability to collectively bargain, most unions are ineffectual.

6. For a full discussion, see Patrick J. Carr and Maria J. Kefalas, *Hollowing Out the Middle: The Rural Brain Drain and What It Means for America* (Boston: Beacon Press, 2009).

7. U.S. Department of Education, http://www.ed.gov.

8. Unfunded mandates are requirements that must be met but have no money available to assist schools in achieving the requirements.

9. http://www.corestandards.org.

10. Council of the Great City Schools, http://www.cgcs.org.

11. For a good example of a virtual school framework, go to http://www.wisconsinvirtualschools.org.

12. Capella University, http://www.capella.edu.

13. http://www.uscharterschools.org.

14. Goodwill Industries International, Inc., http:www.goodwill.org.

15. State of Wisconsin, Department of Workforce Development, http://www.dwd.wi.gov.

16. Wisconsin's Technical Colleges, http://www.witechcolleges.org.

17. Southwest Tech, http://www.swtc.edu.

18. University of New Hampshire, Carsey Institute, http://www.carseyinstitute.unh.edu.

19. Chronically poor communities typically suffer from persistent poverty, chronic high unemployment, and long-term failure to adequately invest in, and support, their educational systems, infrastructure, and civic institutions.

20. Gwen Schroth and Mary Susan Fishbaugh, "Increasing Caring and Reducing Violence in Rural Schools," ERIC Publication #439869, March 2000.

21. Michael D. Mink, Charity G. Moore, Andrew O. Johnson, Janice C. Probst, and Amy Brook Martin,

Violence and Rural Teens: Teen Violence, Drug Use and School-based Prevention Services in Rural America (Columbia: South Carolina Rural Health Research Center, March 2005).

22. Ibid.

Chapter 10

1. "Senators Call for Public Hearing into Grant County Farmland Sale and Budget Provision to Allow Foreign Ownership of State's Farmland," State Senator Kathleen Vinehout, http://legis.wisconsin.gov/senate/vinehout/PressReleases/Pages/Senators-Call-for-Public-Hearing-into-Grant-County-Farmland-Sale-and-Budget-Provision-to-Allow-Foreign-Ownership-of-State.aspx.

2. Edward J. O'Boyle, "Principles of Economic Justice: Marketplace and Workplace Applications," *Forum for Social Economics* 34, nos. 1–2 (Fall 2004 and Spring 2005): 43–60.

3. The relevant institutions usually include education, health care, social security, and labor rights. Broader social systems and policies around public services, progressive taxation and regulation of the economic marketplace with a view toward ensuring fair distribution of wealth, equality of opportunity, and no gross inequality in outcomes are also central organizing principles of social justice.

4. Charles M. Blow, "Giving Thanks," *New York Times*, November 27, 2013.

Appendix Two

1. U.S. Department of Agriculture, National Agricultural Statistics Service.

Appendix Three

1. Center for Medicaid and CHIP Services, http://www.medicaid.gov.

2. In October 2009 Wisconsin suspended access to BadgerCare Plus because the total number of applications exceeded the number of places available. The state created a waiting list and individuals opting to pay the $60 application fee were placed on this list. In the meantime, they could receive core medical care services if their income fell at or below 200 percent of poverty, are between ages 19 and 64, and do not have dependent children.

3. Health Policy Research Center, Urban Institute, Washington, D.C., 2009, http://www.urban.org/center/hpc.

4. Wisconsin Department of Health and Human Services, BadgerCare Plus 2009 Covered Services and Co-payment Schedule.

Bibliography

Ambrose, Stephen. *Nothing Like It in the World.* New York: Simon & Schuster, 2000.

Apps, Jerry. Interview, January 12, 2013.

Bland, Thomas A. *How to Grow Rich* (1881). Cited in Benjamin Heber Johnson. "Red Populism, Agrarian Radicalism and the Debate over the Dawes Act." In *The Countryside in the Age of the Modern State,* edited by Catherine McNicol Stock and Robert D. Johnston. Ithaca, NY: Cornell University Press, 2001.

Brinkley, Alan. *American History: A Survey.* Vol. I. 9th ed. New York: McGraw-Hill, 1995.

Brown, Miriam, ed. *Sustaining Heart in the Heartland: Exploring Rural Spirituality.* New York: Paulist Press, 2005.

Carson, Rachel. *The Silent Spring.* New York: Houghton Mifflin, 1962.

Cather, Willa. *My Antonia.* Boston: Houghton Mifflin, 1949.

Cather, Willa. *O Pioneers!* Mineola, NY: Dover Books, 1993.

Chiquoine, Stephen. Interview, August 8, 2013.

Cobia, David, ed. *Cooperatives in Agriculture.* Englewood Cliffs, NJ: Prentice-Hall, 1989.

Dáil, Paula vW. *Women and Poverty in 21st Century America.* Jefferson, NC: McFarland, 2012.

Davidson, Osha Gray. *Broken Heartland: The Rise of America's Rural Ghetto.* Iowa City: University of Iowa Press. 1996.

Dudley, Kathryn Marie. *Debt and Dispossession: Farm Loss in America's Heartland.* Chicago: University of Chicago Press, 2000.

Dunn, Aaron. Interview; Presentation to Iowa County Health Care Coalition, August 26, 2013.

Fink, Deborah. *Agrarian Women: Wives and Mothers in Rural Nebraska, 1880–1940.* Chapel Hill: University of North Carolina Press, 1992.

Fitchen, Janet M. *Poverty in Rural America: A Case Study.* Boulder, CO: Westview Press, 1981.

Fleming, Thomas. *The Louisiana Purchase.* Hoboken, NJ: John Wiley & Sons, 2003.

Herzog, John. Interview, August 25, 2013.

Ivey, Debra. Presentation on Findings from Iowa County Youth Survey. Dodgeville, WI. February 17, 2014.

Jones, Loring P. "Distinct Features of Midwestern Rural Poverty: Implications for Social Workers." Paper Presented at the National Institute on Social Work in Rural Areas. Beaufort, SC, July 1981.

Kingsolver, Barbara. *Animal, Vegetable, Miracle.* New York: HarperCollins, 2007.

Larson-Sell, Douglas. Presentation at Free Congregation of Sauk County, August 17, 2013.

Lewis, Jeanie. Interview, March 12, 2013.

Maher, Neil M. *Nature's New Deal.* New York: Oxford University Press, 2008.

Marchetta, Melina. *Jellicoe Road.* New York: HarperTeen, 2008.

May, Katharyn. "Rural Health Care." Presentation, Dodgeville, WI, September 16, 2005.

Meyer, Bruce, and James Sullivan. "Identifying the Disadvantaged: Official Poverty, Consumption Poverty, and the New Supplemental Poverty Measure," *Journal of Economic Perspectives* 26, no. 3 (Summer 2012): 111–36.

Nelson, Margaret K., and Joan Smith. *Working Hard and Making Do: Surviving in Small Town America.* Berkeley: University of California Press, 1999.

O'Boyle, Edward J. "Principles of Economic Justice: Marketplace and Workplace Applications." *Forum for Social Economics* 34, nos. 1–2 (Fall 2004 and Spring 2005): 43–60.

Orzchowski, Wally. Interview, December 12, 2013.

Potter, Lee Ann, and Wynell Schamel. "The Homestead Act of 1862." *Social Education* 61, no. 6 (October 1997): 356–64.

Reilly, J. Patrick. Interview, September 12, 2012.

Ringen, Stein. "Direct and Indirect Measures of Poverty." *Journal of Social Policy* 17, no. 3 (July 1988): 351–65.

Singer, Peter. "Animal Liberation: A Personal View." In *Writings on an Ethical Life*. London: Fourth Estate, 2001.

Slotkin, Richard. "Nostalgia and Progress: Theodore Roosevelt's Myth of the Frontier." *American Quarterly* 33, no. 5 (Winter 1981): 608–37.

Solkoff, Joel. *The Politics of Food*. San Francisco: Sierra Club Books, 1985.

Spicker, Paul. "Definitions of Poverty: Twelve Clusters of Meaning." In *Poverty: An International Glossary*, 2nd ed., edited by Paul Spicker, Sonia Álvarez Leguizamón, and David Gordon, 229–43. London: Zed Books, 2007.

Springer, Marlene, and Haskell Springer, eds. *Plains Woman: The Diary of Martha Farnsworth, 1882–1922*. Bloomington: Indiana University Press, 1986.

Steinbeck, John. *The Grapes of Wrath*. New York: Viking Press, 1939.

Stratton, Joanna L. *Pioneer Women: Voices from the Kansas Frontier*. New York: Simon & Schuster, 1981.

Taylor, Steven J., and Robert Bogdan. *Introduction to Qualitative Research Methods: The Search for Meaning*. New York: John Wiley & Sons, 1984.

Thieman, Alice. Interviews, September 2012 and February 2013.

Van Emden, Helmut F., and David B. Peakall. *Beyond Silent Spring: Integrated Pest Management and Chemical Safety*. London: Chapman & Hall on behalf of the United Nations Environment Programme, 1996.

Index

Affordable Care Act 24, 168–69, 171; *see also* ObamaCare
agribusiness 6, 110, 119–20, 126, 139, 145, 148–49
agricultural waste management 119
Agriculture and Consumer Protection Act (1973) 140
Alabama 110
American Chemical Society 150
American Farm Bureau 149; *see also* Farm Bureau
American Farmland Trust 139
American Indian 23, 25–26, 60, 83, 97, 134, 175; *see also* Native American
anti-trust laws 76
APM *see* National Academy of Sciences Alternative Poverty Measure
Appalachia 22–23, 228
Apps, Jerry 43, 89, 112, 157
Arkansas 78, 116, 202

Babcock, Bruce 146
Bader, Jonathan 140
BadgerCare 179, 248–50, 260
Barron County, WI 156
Beckman, Jayson 91
beef 4, 80, 112, 119–20, 146, 148, 161
beef cattle 12, 101, 110–11, 121
Berry, Wendell 119
Beveridge, Sen. Albert 60
BIA *see* Bureau of Indian Affairs
biological farming 150
Black Elk, Charlotte 68
Bland, Thomas 70
Bowles, Chester 58

Bowman, Robert C 166
Boyer, Robert 175
Brady, David 54
Buchanan, Pres. William 62
Bureau of Indian Affairs (BIA) 25, 69
Bureau of Reclamation 77
Burr, Dale 20
Bush, Pres. George W. 206, 214, 218
Butz, Sec. Earl 6, 7, 72, 126, 135, 139, 149–50

California 2, 23, 26, 66, 79, 83, 98, 113, 128, 154
capitalism, profit-motive 6, 95, 191, 230–31
Carsey Institute 189, 222
Carson, Rachel 126, 150
Carter, Pres. Jimmy 136–37
cash lease 92
Cather, Willa 65
CBO *see* Congressional Budget Office
CCC *see* Civilian Conservation Corps
charter schools 218–19
child-care assistance 219
Children's Health Insurance Program (CHIP) 173, 179, 246, 252
CHIP *see* Children's Health Insurance Program
Chiquoine, Stephen 21, 96
Civilian Conservation Corps (CCC) 80, 82, 84
Clapp, Norman 85
Cleveland, Pres. Grover 69
colleges: community 218, 220; technical 219, 220–21

Colorado 1, 67, 77, 79, 111, 116, 152
Commodity Credit Corporation 122, 124, 140
common core curriculum standards 215
Community Services Block Grants 262
Congressional Budget Office (CBO) 139
Corn Belt 87
crime: agricultural 196, 203; assault 196, 199; hate 201; non-violent 210; organized 199, 202; violent 199, 210 (*see also* violence); wildlife 196, 202
Critchfield, Richard 159
Crocker, Charles 66
crop inventory 102
crop share lease 92
crop values 107, 109
Cropp, Bob 122–23
Custer, Gen. George Armstrong 67

Dáil, Paula 235–36
dairy cattle 90, 110, 112
Dairy Price Support Program 123–24
Davidson, Osha Gray 117
Dawes Act 68–70, 253, 261
Dershowitz, Alan 194
de Rugy, Veronique 144
Dodd, Sen. Christopher 106
Dodge, Gen Grenville 65
Doyle, Gov. James 87, 178–79
Drought Relief Service (DRS) 80
DRS *see* Drought Relief Service

263

Dunn, Aaron 170, 174, 186, 190
Dust Bowl 1, 3, 77, 78, 81–82, 85, 105, 233

Edsall, Thomas 44
Eisenhower, Pres. Dwight 98
Elementary and Secondary Education Act (1965) 214, 259
Emergency Banking Act 80
Emergency Conservation Work Act 82
Emergency Farm Mortgage Act 88
energy assistance 252
Environmental Protection Agency (EPA) 114, 120
EPA *see* Environment Protection Agency
Erie Canal 66–67

Falcone, David 198
farm accidents 127, 163, 179–80
Farm Act 122; *see also* Farm Bill
Farm Bill 9–10, 135, 139–41, 144, 149, 257; *see also* Farm Act
Farm Bureau *see* American Farm Bureau
farm crisis 3, 11, 137–38, 254
farmer cooperatives 129
farming: organic 126, 151; wind 119, 127
Farnsworth, Martha 63
Federal Land Policy and Management Act 73
federal poverty line (FPL) 52, 90, 172
Federal Social Security Disability Insurance (SSDI) 45
Federal Surplus Relief Corporation (FSRC) 80
Fishbaugh, Mary Sue 223
Fitchen, Janet 46
Five Civilized Tribes 69
Fixed rate loans 90
food insecurity 55–56; 251, 257
Food Stamp Act (1972) 140
food stamp program 24, 139, 176; *see also* Supplemental Nutrition Assistance Program
Ford, Duane 221
Ford, Pres. Gerald 135–36
FPL *see* Federal Poverty Line
Franken, Sen. Al 173
Franklin, Benjamin 133–34
Franklin County, Mo 188
Frazier Lemke Farm Bankruptcy Act 80
free enterprise 6, 95, 148, 191, 230

free soil policy 63
Frontier Thesis 72
FSRC *see* Federal Surplus Relief Corporation

Gale, John A. 197
Gates, Gen. Horatio 61
General Allotment Act 69
General Land Office 63
generational land transfers 94
Ghost Dance Movement 69
Grain Belt 10, 87, 98, 106, 108
Grange Movement 74–75
Great Depression 11, 79, 80, 84–85, 135–36, 140
Great Lakes 67, 86, 98
Great Plains 3, 14, 46, 65, 71–72, 74, 77–79, 81–82, 84, 86, 98, 104, 108, 152, 251, 253
Greeley, Horace 60
Greenback Party 75, 253
Gunderson, Keith 159–60

Habitat for Humanity 164
Harkin, Sen. Tom 6
Harrington, Michael 228
Hartley, David 197, 202–3
health care, women's reproductive 183
herbicides 126, 141, 150
Heritage Foundation 145
Herzog, Rev. John 20–21, 158
High Plains Aquifer 152
Hill-Burton Legislation 179, 252
Hoetz, Peter 167
Hoisington, S.N. 64
home schooling 211, 214, 216
Homestead Act 60, 62, 65, 68, 71–72
homesteader(s) 61, 64, 66, 71, 73, 77, 109
Hyde Amendment 184

IBP *see* Iowa Beef Processors
Ickes, Sec. Harold 80
ICRA *see* Indian Civil Rights Act
Ifft, Jennifer 91
Illinois 29–30, 67, 75, 86–87, 105–7, 112–14, 116, 118, 124, 135, 143, 178, 202, 208, 239, 251, 258
immigrant workers 26, 62–63, 66, 250; *see also* migrant farm workers; migrant workers
Indian Civil Rights Act (ICRA) 97
Indiana 31, 49, 67, 86–7, 104–7, 112, 114, 116, 134, 143, 147, 171, 197, 208, 219–20, 240, 251

Indiana Excel Center 219–20
inland waterways 67
integrated pest management 150
Iowa 3, 6, 10, 14, 17, 20, 29, 32, 75, 79, 86–87, 93, 98, 103–4, 106–7, 110–12, 114, 171, 119, 126, 130–31, 137, 140, 142–43, 146, 154–55, 162, 186, 188, 190, 202, 240, 251–52
Iowa Beef Processors (IBP) 110, 119
Ivey, Debra 187

Jefferson, Pres. Thomas 61
Jesse, Ed 122–23
Johnson, Pres. Lyndon 71, 228–29
justice: distributive 231; economic 230–31; participatory 230; social 231, 260

Kahl, Gordon 202
Kansas 10, 33, 63–64, 75–76, 78–79, 86, 91, 106–8, 111–12, 116, 126, 138, 143, 152, 162, 178, 195, 202, 240–41, 251, 252
Keilor, Garrison 87
Kennedy, Sen. Edward 22, 190
Kennedy, Pres. John 120, 228
Kennedy, Robert 228
Kuester, Jared 200
Kuethe, Todd 158
Kuhlmann, Annette 158

land conservation 77
land contract 94–95, 254
Land Reclamation Service 77
land use policy 61
land-use politics 73
Lawrence County, AR 202
LIBOR Indexed Variable Rate 89–90
Lincoln, Pres. Abraham 62
livestock inventory 100–1
Livingston, Robert 61
loan: farm operating 89–90; fixed rate 90; variable rate 90
Lone Tree, IA 20
Louisiana Purchase 60

Mandela, Nelson 194
Manifest Destiny 59–60, 66, 70, 96, 194
market: grain 3, 120, 124; livestock 101, 115, 120, 165, 243
May, Katharyn 168, 181
McAuliff, Dante 95
McCaughey, Betsy 170
Medicaid 24, 47, 49, 106, 162, 164, 169–71, 173–79, 184, 186, 245–50, 252, 255

Index

Medicare 157, 169, 171–73, 176–77, 179, 181, 230, 246, 248, 252
Meyer, Bruce 147–8
Michael, Robert 52
Michigan 29, 34, 67, 86–87, 105, 107, 112–3, 116, 126, 142, 147, 207, 241, 251
Midwest farm crisis 3, 11, 137–38
Midwestern values 86–8
migrant farm workers 23, 138; *see also* immigrant workers; migrant workers
migrant workers 70; *see also* immigrant workers; migrant farm workers
Milk Price Support Program 123
milk pricing 121–22
milk production 104, 112–13, 116, 126, 142, 144, 147, 207, 241, 243, 251, 256
Mining Act, 1872 74
Minnesota 35, 75, 86–87, 103, 106–7, 112–13, 115–16, 118, 136–37, 144, 197, 208, 241, 251–52, 258
Mississippi River 14, 60–61, 63, 67, 83, 154, 173, 251–53
Missouri 10, 14, 29, 36, 49, 79, 86–87, 103, 106–8, 112, 114, 116, 118, 126, 142, 144, 171, 188, 197, 207–8, 241–42, 251–52, 258
Monroe, Pres. James 61
Morehart, Mitchell 91
Morrill, Sen. Justin 71
Morrill Act 71, 253

NACAC *see* National Agricultural Compliance Assistance Center
NAFTA *see* North American Free Trade Agreement
National Academy of Sciences Alternative Poverty Measure (APM) 54–56, 180
National Agricultural Compliance Assistance Center (NACAC) 120
National Association of School Boards 209
National Farmers Alliance 75
National Indian Defense Association 70
National Institute for Occupational Safety and Health (NIOSH) 180–81
NCLB *see* No Child Left Behind
Nebraska 10, 29, 37, 65, 77, 79, 86–87, 103–4, 106–8, 111–12, 116, 126, 142, 144, 152, 171, 207, 216, 240, 242, 251–54
Nevada 77–78, 254
New Deal 79–82, 84–85, 136–37, 141, 230, 233
New Mexico 68, 70, 78–79, 152, 199, 252, 254
Newlands, Rep. Francis G. 77
Newlands Reclamation Act 77
Nez Perce 68
Nickerson, Cynthia 91
NIOSH *see* National Institute for Occupational Safety and Health
Nixon, Pres. Richard 135–36
No Child Left Behind (NCLB) 214–16, 259
Norris, Kathleen 159
North American Free Trade Agreement (NAFTA) 105, 255
North Carolina 114, 116
North Dakota 38, 86, 98, 107, 112–3, 144, 158, 170, 183, 198, 202, 251–52, 254

ObamaCare 169–72, 174; *see also* Affordable Care Act
O'Boyle, Edward 230
Ohio 29, 39, 67, 83, 86–87, 105–7, 112, 114, 116, 118, 126, 144, 147, 171, 178, 207–8, 243, 251
Ohio River 67
Oklahoma 68, 70, 76, 78–79, 108, 116, 152, 252
Oklahoma Territory 76
Oregon Territory 61, 254
Orzechowski, Wally 162–65
O'Sullivan, John 59

Pacific Institute for Research and Evaluation 188
Pacific Railroad 65–66
PAP *see* Prescription Assistance Program
Paul, Rep. Ron 212
Pennsylvania 116
People's Party 76, 254; *see also* Populist Party
pesticides 120, 126–27, 141, 147, 150, 181
Petri, Rep. Tom 146
Pine Ridge Indian Reservation 95–96, 243
Populist Party *see* People's Party
pork 5, 80, 110–11, 114, 121, 140, 243
Posse Comitatus 201
poultry 101, 110, 117–18, 140, 146, 148, 241, 243–44, 257
poverty: clusters of meaning 44; defining 4, 44–45, 47–48, 51; diseases of 167–68, 173; mental health issues 9, 163, 170, 176, 185–89, 190, 200–1, 224–25, 238, 247, 249; war on 228–29
prairie populism 6
preemption 62, 253
Prescription Assistance Program (PAP) 190

Railroad Act 65
railway rate laws, 1903, 1906 76
REA *see* Rural Electrification Administration
Reagan, Pres. Ronald 138
Red Cloud, Chief 97
Reilly, J. Patrick 11, 114, 131, 187, 193, 196–99, 203, 225–26
Riedel, Brian 145–48
Ringen, Stein 42
Robson, Sen. Judy 187
Roosevelt, Pres. Franklin D. 79–84, 136–37, 233
Roosevelt, Pres. Theodore 60, 72, 76, 77
Roosevelt's Tree Army 82
Royer, Gene, 211
Rural Development Act (1972) 140
rural elderly 18–21, 48, 52, 55, 92–94, 97, 156, 169, 172, 177, 186, 203–4, 247, 250
Rural Electrification Administration (REA) 85
Rural Environmental Conservation Program 140
rural values 202; *see also* Midwestern values
Rust Belt 87, 98, 105
Ryan, Rep. Paul 169

Salazar, Rep. John 86
Sand Creek Massacre 67
Sauk County, WI 18, 251
school sports 15, 113, 213–4, 225–26
Schroth, Gwen 223
Sebelius, Sec. Kathleen 169
Shannon County, SD 96
Sherman, Gen. William Tecumseh 67
Sioux Wars 67
Sitting Bull, Chief 67–68, 70
Smith-Lever Act 71–72
Social Security Retirement (SS) 92–93, 139, 172, 230, 254–55, 260
Soil Conservation Service 80, 83
Soil Erosion Service 80

Solkoff, Joel 135
South Carolina 75, 116
South Dakota 10, 29, 40, 49, 78, 86, 96, 98, 103, 106–7, 111–12, 116, 126, 144, 152, 159, 170–71, 178, 207, 243, 251–52, 254
Southwest Wisconsin Community Action Program 162
Southwest Wisconsin Youth Survey 187
Spagnoli, Filip 47
Spicker, Paul 51
SS *see* Social Security Retirement
SSDI *see* Federal Social Security Disability Insurance
Steinbeck, John 1, 3, 78
Stock Raising Homestead Act 73
subsidies: direct payment 141, 257; farm 141, 144–49
substance abuse 163, 187, 188, 197, 249
suicide 3, 96, 176, 186, 189, 224
Sullivan, James 47
Supplemental Nutrition Assistance Program 2, 25, 54, 140; *see also* Food Stamp Program

Taylor Grazing Act 80
teen pregnancy 181–82, 185
Tennessee 77, 85, 116
Terado, Linda 160–61, 163
Texas 26, 78–9, 81, 108, 111, 116, 152, 251, 253
Thatcher, Mary Kay 149
Todd County, SD 170

Transcontinental Railroad 65–66
tribal governance 97
Turner, Frederick Jackson 72
Tyson Foods 111

Union Pacific Railroad 65–66
United Nations Environmental Programme 119, 150
United Nations Food and Agriculture Organization 120
U.S. Department of Agriculture (USDA) 45, 55, 90–91, 111–12, 115, 120, 124, 134, 139, 144–45, 148, 256; Farm Service Agency 90
U.S. Department of Justice (DOJ) 197
Utah 116, 207

Vilsack, Sec. Tom 17, 26, 89, 104, 109
Vinehout, Sen. Kathleen 230
violence: domestic 193, 197, 199, 238; rural school 223
virtual education options 217; *see also* virtual schools
virtual schools 216–17; *see also* virtual education options
Volcker, Paul 136

Walker, Gov. Scott 171, 179, 259
Wallace, Sec. Henry 135
Wand, Armand 200
WDWD *see* Wisconsin Department of Workforce Development

Weisheit, Ralph 198
Wells, Edward 198
White House Council of Economic Advisors 45
Williams, Ryan 91
Winthrop, Rep. Robert 59
Wisconsin 18, 19, 24, 29, 41, 43, 49, 52, 75, 86–87, 89, 92, 106–7, 112–13, 116, 122, 133, 141, 147, 154–56, 170–71, 173–75, 178, 183, 187–90, 194, 197, 199, 205, 207–8, 210–11, 220–21, 225, 230, 232, 243–44, 248, 250, 251, 256–57, 259, 260
Wisconsin Community Action Programs 140, 162
Wisconsin Department of Health Services 175
Wisconsin Department of Workforce Development (WDWD) 220
Wisconsin Technical College System (WTCS) 220
Works Progress Administration (WPA) 80–81
World Bank 44, 49–50
World War II 84–85
Wounded Knee, Battle of 69
WPA *see* Works Progress Administration
WTCS *see* Wisconsin Technical College System

Yunus, Mohammad 23

Ziebach County, SD 170

www.ingramcontent.com/pod-product-compliance
Ingram Content Group UK Ltd.
Pitfield, Milton Keynes, MK11 3LW, UK
UKHW050538150426
5217IPUK00026B/1990